The Ella Fitzgerald
Companion

**Recent Titles in
Companions to Celebrated Musicians**

The Barbra Streisand Companion: A Guide to Her Vocal Style
and Repertoire
Linda Pohly

The Ella Fitzgerald Companion

NORMAN DAVID

Foreword by Tad Hershorn

Companions to Celebrated Musicians
Michael Meckna, Series Adviser

Westport, Connecticut
London

Library of Congress Cataloging-in-Publication Data

The Ella Fitzgerald companion / Norman David ; foreword by Tad Hershorn.
    p. cm. — (Companions to celebrated musicians)
    Includes bibliographical references and index.
    Discography: p.
    ISBN 0–313–31645–7 (alk. paper)
    1. Fitzgerald, Ella—Criticism and interpretation. 2. Singers—United States—
Biography. I. David, Norman. II. Series.
ML420.F52E44 2004
782.42164'092—dc22   2003057976

British Library Cataloguing in Publication Data is available.

Library of Congress Catalog Card Number: 2003057976
ISBN: 0–313–31645–7

First published in 2004

Praeger Publishers, 88 Post Road West, Westport, CT 06881
An imprint of Greenwood Publishing Group, Inc.
www.praeger.com

Printed in the United States of America

The paper used in this book complies with the
Permanent Paper Standard issued by the National
Information Standards Organization (Z39.48–1984).

10　9　8　7　6　5　4　3　2　1

For Mom and Philip

Contents

Foreword: "Somewhere There's Music" by Tad Hershorn   xiii

Preface   xvii

Acknowledgments   xix

Regarding the Music Examples   xxiii

1   The Ella Mystique   1

2   Overview   7

3   The Influential Singers   17
    Louis Armstrong   18
    Bessie Smith   30
    Ethel Waters   32
    Mildred Bailey   35
    Connee Boswell   37
    Billie Holiday   57
    Leo Watson   59

4   The Chick Webb Years   69

5   The Bebop Influence   81

6   Norman Granz   91

7   The Arrangers   99
    Recordings for Decca, 1942–1954   100
      Sy Oliver   102

Verve and Pablo: The *Song Books* and More   106
    Buddy Bregman   108
    Duke Ellington   116
    Paul Weston   122
    Nelson Riddle   124
    Billy May   138
Other Recordings for Verve   142
    Frank DeVol   142
    Marty Paich   144
    Bill Doggett   148
Two Years at Capitol   150
One for Prestige, Two for Reprise   153

8   Benny, Duke, and Count   155
    Benny Goodman and the Swing Era   155
    Duke Ellington   158
    Count Basie   167

9   The Principal Accompanists   181
    Hank Jones   183
    Oscar Peterson   184
    Ellis Larkins   192
    Paul Smith   202
    Lou Levy   210
    Tommy Flanagan   222
    Jimmy Rowles   231
    Joe Pass   233

Appendix 1: Complete Interviews   241
    Virginia Wicks   241
    Tommy Flanagan   246
    Phil Schaap   252

Appendix 2: A Selection of Ella's Honors and Awards   261

Notes   265

Ella Fitzgerald—CD Discography   275

Ella Fitzgerald—Selected VHS/DVD Videography   311

Bibliography   313

Index   321

Photo essay follows page 154.

Foreword: "Somewhere There's Music"

Tad Hershorn

Guitarist Herb Ellis was the first to arrive in the cavernous mezzanine of the Hotel Empire across from Lincoln Center where a rehearsal was to begin within the hour in the early afternoon of February 11, 1990. The setting looked more like a construction site than a rehearsal hall as it was undergoing renovation at the time. Ellis, who achieved international fame in 1953 as part of the Oscar Peterson Trio and the Jazz at the Philharmonic concert tours, joined a few dozen musicians who figured prominently in the life and career of Ella Fitzgerald.

To a question about why Fitzgerald had endured for the unmatched 56 years they were preparing to celebrate the next night, most of them at the top, Ellis said, "Ella has the ability to cross over between popular music and jazz and really bring audiences with her. She is the world's greatest singer by leaps and bounds. She has a great sound to begin with, her time is perfect, and she can hear. She couldn't tell you what the chords were, but she could hum the chord to you. That's something if you think about it."

For all her fame, Fitzgerald's circumspection and quiet, private nature over the course of her career placed her in a small circle among musical superstars who managed to avoid living their private lives in the too-public arena. One measure of Fitzgerald's focus on her craft can be inferred from comparing the length and basic premise of front-page *New York Times* obituaries of Fitzgerald in 1996 and Frank Sinatra, who died two years later, both written by Stephen Holden. Fitzgerald was *the* singer and merited the full page the newspaper devoted to chronicling the musical highlights of her momentous career. On the other hand, Holden needed two pages to weigh Sinatra's life, in which his music was only a part of what made him both a cultural icon and one of the century's most influential singers.

All of this is to say that Fitzgerald purposely obscured her life outside music, making for rough sledding for her biographers and students of her life. Writers Stuart Nicholson, James Haskins, and Geoffrey Mark Fidelman were all reduced at one point or another in their books to telling stories of concerts, recordings, and awards when they found it all but impossible to penetrate Fitzgerald's inner world. She gave few interviews about her personal life, a relatively lonely existence absent a satisfying long-term romantic interest, although there were some notable exceptions. The details of her hardscrabble childhood, in which she was placed in a reformatory for girls, did not fully emerge until shortly before her death. It is remarkable that word she had had both legs amputated below the knee as a result of diabetes in 1993 did not make the news for several months. The same elusive quality holds true for the Ella Fitzgerald Collection donated to the Smithsonian Institution after her death. It is a rich but relatively small collection, given the breadth of her achievements. There is no use searching for letters, diaries, or other personal items that might permit us to look into the woman who delighted us with her extraordinary talent for decades. They are not there.

Ella Fitzgerald, in short, preferred to be remembered for her music. This volume by Norman David joins other recent works, most recently J. Wilfred Johnson's comprehensive *Ella Fitzgerald: An Annotated Discography,* in granting Fitzgerald's wish.[1] David's mandate was that he avoid another detailed biography in favor of her music, and to speak to at least two constituencies in his writing: musicians and the rest of us. Fitzgerald's grooming during her days with Chick Webb and the trial by fire that went along with Jazz at the Philharmonic beginning in 1949 made her the most seasoned and musical of singers. Thus her improvisational and musical genius and what Herb Ellis said was her ability to listen closely and respond to the moment—the very essence of jazz—demand that the analysis of her musicianship be accorded Fitzgerald as with any major jazz artist.

A jazz musician, educator, and fine writer, David has transcribed and analyzed examples of her work from across the eras and styles of her career. He traces her musical development in a series of insightful and incisive sketches of the most important influences on her singing, as well as accompanists and arrangers who worked for her in the post-Webb years. In addition to the transcriptions and analysis of the music, David communicates his enthusiasm for his subject for musicians and musicologists and the close listeners among her fans. This is especially important given that her peerless recordings were matched by the singer's routinely electric live performances that brought even longtime fans back for more. One example is David's description of Fitzgerald's performance of "Mack the Knife" during the famous 1960 Berlin concert: "Ella swings magnificently, despite the fact that, true to the uncertainty she expressed in her opening remarks, she starts having trouble with the lyrics seemingly as early as the second chorus. She, of course, does not miss a beat, manipulating her phrasing so she can fit in what words she can remember. . . . Ella even throws in an impersonation of a scatting Louis Armstrong for half a chorus before ending the take. She absolutely floors her Berlin fans, dazzling them with her spontaneity and inventiveness. This version of 'Mack the Knife' has attained legendary status in the world of recorded music."

However, Fitzgerald the star was a sum greater than that of her musical gifts, discipline, ability to connect with her audiences, and the somewhat innocent personality that allowed her to tap repeatedly into the pure emotion that kept her music fresh and beyond self-caricature over the decades. The legendary status that began to envelop her career by the late 1950s was the result of a handful of key junctures with history. As he has done in analyzing the music, David provides the background necessary for her listeners to appreciate the connective tissue of her professional life. Among the highlights are David's retelling of the Webb years, when Fitzgerald shot to fame with "A-Tisket, A-Tasket," and that, despite her demure, ugly duckling reputation, she had the steel to lead the band and keep it alive for three years after the death of the hunch-backed drummer in 1939. He offers further context in placing Fitzgerald's early development as a singer in a musical environment defined by Benny Goodman, Duke Ellington, and Count Basie, of whom the two latter would cross her path regularly through the decades. David follows suit in looking at the top-flight arrangers that Norman Granz put at her disposal for their groundbreaking projects.

As for the brilliant, indefatigable, and volatile Granz, David lays the groundwork to an understanding of one of the most complex and successful managerial relationships in the history of jazz. What began with her addition to the Jazz at the Philharmonic (JATP) lineup, when in Granz's words, his touring jazz concerts "became an important package," ended over four decades later with Fitzgerald as the preeminent singer in jazz, an arguable point among jazz critics, but not to the public at large. The storied impact Granz had on her career unfolded in two stages. The first, finalized in November 1953, came during JATP's tour of Japan when he asked her to allow him to manage her for one year with no commission or contract, freeing either to walk away from the arrangement. Immediately, he began booking Fitzgerald into some of the more prestigious and high-paying nightclubs, where black jazz artists and vocalists were not previously welcome, and routinely broke house records. Granz created

Verve Records as a pop label in December 1955 into which he would fold his previous labels when it became apparent that he had pulled off one of the greatest coups of his career in successfully pressuring Decca Records into releasing Fitzgerald a year ahead of schedule. She was in the studio during her first month as a Verve artist working on the *Cole Porter Song Book*, the first volume in the legendary series produced by Granz and made all the more memorable by her relatively straight reading of the songs. A wave of highly acclaimed Verve recordings, when combined with upscale exposure, broadened appeal and international touring, transformed her into the authoritative interpreter for the remainder of her career of the Great American Song Book.

For 20 years, until her final Carnegie Hall concert in 1991, I spent many splendid evenings hearing Fitzgerald perform with such figures as Count Basie, Benny Carter, Oscar Peterson, and Joe Pass as well as her top-drawer trios led by Tommy Flanagan, Jimmy Rowles, and Paul Smith. In the process, her road manager, the under-sung hero Pete Cavello, befriended me and enlightened me about his experiences with Fitzgerald and Granz since 1953. (It was his encouragement and generosity that allowed me to make some of the photographs Norman David reproduces in these pages.) The same can be said of Fitzgerald's longtime bassist, friend, and confidant, Keter Betts, who said she used to call him her "lawyer," for his inspiring, impeccable time and discretion.

Possibly the most special memory of all was the first time I heard her, at the Venetian Room of the Fairmont Hotel in Dallas. A high school classmate had recently lent me a copy of *Ella in Berlin* and I, nurtured in the art of jazz singing of Dinah Washington and Billie Holiday, just flipped. To experience the energy and, yes, the verve with which she engaged her music and audiences was to experience the same joy that had infused listeners since the Webb and JATP days. My mother, an entertainment writer for *The Dallas Morning News*, had a front table for the evening. Through the tall red velvet curtains outside the showroom, Fitzgerald greeted well-wishers, and as my turn came, she smiled broadly and said, "Aren't you a little young to be staying out this late?" We took in the second show as well. On the way out after the last set, I caught her eye again as she said "You're still here?" from across the room.

With the aid of Norman David's book, I will be "here" (and better informed) quite a bit longer, though not as long as will the music and spirit of Ella Fitzgerald.

The title of this foreword, "Somewhere There's Music," is lyrics from the song "How High the Moon," by Nancy Hamilton and Morgan Lewis.

Preface

Her imitators shred songs; she explodes and reassembles them.

—Time[1]

[Her] voice . . . remained eternally young . . . And the combination, the sweet naiveté of that sound coupled with the sophisticated and secure command of her art, was startling, and inimitable.

—Gene Lees[2]

In an article about Ella Fitzgerald for *Down Beat,* Leonard Feather wrote that "it has always been the singing itself that means the most to her, and because her modesty and musical honesty remain deeply ingrained, there was never any danger that Ella would go . . . the route taken by those who, hell-bent for financial gain, become artistic dropouts."[3] Ella was a consummate artist who sang at an unparalleled level of excellence. Countless musicians, writers, reviewers, historians, and fans continue to rave about her exquisite tonal quality, breathtaking range, impeccable pitch, precise diction, improvising prowess, superior ability to swing, and sheer joy in performing. "When Ella Fitzgerald was singing at her peak," said Gary Giddins, "nothing in life was more resplendent."[4]

The most touching aspect of Ella was her sincere humility, something she always retained, in spite of the fact that she was a huge musical star. No doubt, it could be terrifying to work with her if one was not up to the challenge; indeed, this remains common with respect to most gifted artists. Yet, in spite of her unparalleled musicality, she was always an overridingly gracious person.

In his superb biography of Ray Charles, Michael Lydon recounts that Charles often declared: "I never wanted to be famous, but I always wanted to be great."[5] The statement could just have easily been made by Ella Fitzgerald. She was, like Charles, completely obsessed with providing audiences with first-rate performances.

When Ella was experiencing severe medical difficulties near the end of her life, Lawrence Hall wrote in the *Newark Star-Ledger:* "Practically every hour of the day, somewhere on this dreary planet thousands upon thousands of people are listening to one of her many recordings . . . There is a timeless quality to her singing, and it is a voice for all seasons."[6] Hall was speaking with heartfelt love and admiration. Ella Fitzgerald had that effect on people. The greatest singer of the twentieth century was a beloved icon of both jazz and popular music during a career that spanned almost sixty years.

It is obviously impossible to write about Ella Fitzgerald without spewing streams of accolades. It should be noted that this is not a biography, although there is inevitably biographical information interspersed throughout the text. This is, in fact, a celebration of Ella's great accomplishments and, as such, also a concurrent look at the superb colleagues with whom she collaborated during her career.

I have transcribed portions of Ella's recorded performances from many albums and offer them as a further means of understanding her genius and of studying her methods. There exists a debate about the merits of transcriptions, questions about the actual value of trying to comprehend or assimilate the work of a musician through the practice and study of reproductions of that artist's output. Some will fully endorse transcribing, while others will argue that it is far more productive to feel and hear the music naturally, that a solid knowledge of theoretical and practical principles addressed with soul and resourcefulness is the way to go. I subscribe to a combination of both viewpoints. Therefore, it is my hope that you will enjoy the total package—the written information and discussions, as well as the printed music.

I loved Ella Fitzgerald's singing long before I undertook this project. She never sang badly. On her worse days she was stupendous. Now, after immersing myself in her music, living with her, for two and a half years, I am thoroughly astounded. If you want to feel good, if you need to gain a more positive perspective on life in general, if you just want to be outright entertained and escape for a minute, or an hour, listen to Ella. She was—is—unbelievable.

Acknowledgments

While I was interviewing the great and legendary pianist Tommy Flanagan, there were butterflies in my stomach. These were good butterflies, the ones that come from the exhilaration of an exciting moment in one's life. Although I had previously met or performed with many famous people during the course of my professional activities, I had experienced a similar reaction on only a few occasions. As Tommy and I talked and ate at our table in the busy restaurant on New York's upper east side, I was enraptured, oblivious of the constant din of activity around me that was so apparent when I reviewed the recordings of our conversation a few days later.

I had been listening to the music of Tommy Flanagan, on albums or live, for many years. This was the pianist who performed with John Coltrane on the groundbreaking recording of "Giant Steps," the seasoned veteran who had played on so many outstanding sessions, either as an in-demand sideman or as the leader of his own burning trios. Having also been the long-time, brilliant accompanist for Ella Fitzgerald, he was undoubtedly asked about her frequently, often with the same or similar questions. He didn't have to honor my request for an interview. Tommy Flanagan was an absolute gentleman, with an engaging sense of humor. He answered my questions forthrightly and treated me with respect, even though we had never met before the interview.

When we had finished our meal and the interview was over, I took a big breath and sheepishly offered Tommy printed copies of two tunes I had composed and dedicated to him. I have composed hundreds of pieces over the years, and I believe I possess a reasonable combination of humility and confidence, but I found myself hoping Tommy wouldn't mind me offering him the lead sheets. He took more than a few minutes to look them over and size them up, thanked me, and placed them in his briefcase. I don't know if he ever performed them, or even wanted to perform them, but I will never forget the joy I felt from his accepting the music.

Exiting the restaurant, Tommy and I shook hands out front and he was off. I felt tears coming to my eyes and continued to follow him walking away until he was out of sight. These tears of happiness and respect turned to tears of sadness and respect a little over a year later when I heard of Tommy's passing. I will always be thankful that I got to meet him. Such are the rewards that result from writing a book. While spending so much time with a musical subject, one meets, reads about, or listens to many other wonderful musicians, authors, historians, archivists, and fans—and memories are born that last long after the writing is done. Thank you, Tommy Flanagan. My sincerest appreciation also to Diana Flanagan, who did all the groundwork to set up my interview with her husband. She is a lovely and caring woman.

I also had the distinct pleasure of interviewing Virginia Wicks, Ella Fitzgerald's long-time publicist and friend, whose obvious love for her former client is touching. She provided both enlightening information and insights about Ella's musical activities and character. Although we talked on the phone, I was keenly aware of Ms. Wicks's warmth and sincerity.

I was very excited and grateful to meet Phil Schaap, the brilliant archivist, record producer, radio personality, historian, and writer. I was of course already cognizant of his impressive credentials, but my appreciation of why he is so respected and in-demand in the music world was significantly enhanced after only a few seconds of talking with him. His gigantic wealth of knowledge is simply amazing, his perspective matched by few others. He answered my questions thoughtfully and comprehensively, providing me with invaluable data and pointing me in the right direction on a number of topics.

Anyone who writes or reads about jazz and American popular music is aware of the importance and magnitude of the distinguished Institute of Jazz Studies at Rutgers University, Newark. I spent a lot of time at the Institute when I started working on this book and returned several times over the next couple of years. Often, I stayed long after finishing my day's activities there just to continue enjoying the atmosphere. It is a magical world, full of tremendous resources and surprises. Thank you to Dan Morgenstern and his staff for their consistently thoughtful assistance. In particular, I would like to mention Tad Hershorn, an outstanding archivist, writer, and photographer, with whom I conferred often. In addition to being highly knowledgeable and insightful on many music topics, he is one of the world's foremost authorities on the life and accomplishments of Norman Granz, Ella Fitzgerald's legendary manager and producer. Tad made himself available whenever I called or visited and his input was extremely valuable. I am delighted that he contributed a Foreword, as well as some of his excellent photographs, to my book—and that we have become friends.

I transcribed a lot of Ella's recordings for this book and I was confident in doing so. However, when I *really* wanted to make sure about the implied harmonies on some of the transcriptions, I asked Tom Lawton, a fantastic pianist and jazz educator in Philadelphia, and my good friend and long-time colleague.

Speaking of the transcriptions, doing them was only part of the equation. I also had to obtain the copyright permissions before they could be published—and that was an involved process. My sincere thanks for assistance in this regard to Rosemarie Gawelko at Warner Brothers Publications, Chrissy Swearingen at Hal Leonard Corporation, Flora Griggs at Williamson Music Group, Fred Ahlert of Fred Ahlert Music Group, Aida Garcia-Cole at Music Sales Corporation, and Larry Spier at Memory Lane Music Group.

When I first considered writing this book I consulted with Michael Meckna of Texas Christian University, the series adviser for the *Greenwood Companions to Celebrated Musicians*. An accomplished musicologist, educator, and writer, he is familiar with the logistics and challenges that an author confronts when faced with an impossible schedule of activities that appears to leave very little time to write. Although I had fully braced myself for the inevitable and terrifying time constraints that consistently lurk in the professional world, it was always gratifying to hear the encouraging words of a talented and experienced colleague. Thanks, Mike.

My gratitude also to the production team at Impressions Book and Journal Services, Inc., for their expertise and focus in ensuring that my book would look good and that my words would make sense.

Lastly, I want to acknowledge the wonderful people at Greenwood Publishing Group. In particular, I was in touch often with Eric Levy during the initial stages of my work. Supremely professional and affable, he made sure I never strayed too far off the path. Nicole Cournoyer managed the project and saw that all the pieces fell into place. Marcia Goldstein provided invaluable direction in helping me coordinate and troubleshoot the copyright permissions.

Regarding the Music
Examples

Although this book contains many notated examples of recorded performances, it is not necessary to have a formal knowledge of music theory to appreciate the examples. The commentaries accompanying the examples will contain both descriptive language and general musical analyses, information suitable for singers and instrumentalists of all levels, as well as non-musicians. Brief explanations of some basic terms are provided here as a further aid, and to establish a contextual understanding of how the terminology will be used.

In the popular music world, the first half of the twentieth century is considered the golden age of the songwriter. It was during these years that the miraculous and vast repertoire of the American popular song was created by the Gershwins, Cole Porter, Jerome Kern, Irving Berlin, Rodgers and Hart, Harold Arlen, Duke Ellington, and other outstanding composers and lyricists. Songs that continue to be universally recognized and heard in concerts and on recordings, and there are many, are generally designated in the music world as *standards*.

Pitch = *Tone*. Specific musical notes. For example: A, B, C, etc. / F-sharp, G-sharp, D-flat, E-flat, etc.

Chromaticism / *adj. Chromatic*. The use of pitches not present in the normal major or minor scales. Pitches that are midway between two tones that are a whole step apart. Example 1: A-sharp = B-flat. A-sharp is half the distance between A and B, ascending; B-flat is half the distance between B and A, descending. Example 2: D is half the distance between D-flat and E-flat, ascending or descending; G is half the distance between F-sharp and G-sharp, ascending or descending.

Glissando = Gliss. Running or sliding through consecutive notes to a target note.

Measure = Bar. The space between *barlines* in a musical composition. Determined by the particular time signature of a composition—e.g., in 4/4 time there are four beats per measure (bar).

Straight ahead. Denotes when music is to be considered or performed in an ordinary manner—in other words, the music, whatever style it is, should not be too jazzed up.

Tuplet. An irregular grouping of notes.

The structure of a musical composition is called its *form.* A *verse* is a section of music, often irregularly structured, that precedes the main body, or *chorus* of a song. A song may or may not have a verse, depending on the intended use of the music and/or the whims of the song's composer. The lyrics in the verse contain the preliminary message of the song, setting up the principal action in the chorus. When an instrumentalist plays a song, he or she often omits the verse. In fact, many players do not even know the verses of the songs they are performing. In general, singers are more apt than instrumentalists to be familiar with the verses. Ella Fitzgerald, who had a huge repertoire, usually included the verses of the songs that she was performing.

A great majority of jazz and popular standards have choruses that are 32 measures long. These choruses are divided into four *sections* of 8 measures and sequenced most often in what is known as AABA form. This means that three of the 8-measure sections, the A sections, contain music that is virtually identical or, at most, has minimal differences; the lyrics in these sections usually differ. The B section contains contrasting material and is called the *bridge* since it almost always leads back to an A section. Of course, there are other 32-measure forms, the most common being AABC, ABAC, and ABCD. There are also multitudes of songs with choruses longer or shorter than 32 measures; they may be divisible by 2, 4, or 8, or they may have odd numbers of measures.

When a song, or any musical work, is adapted or designed to be played by any number of instruments, singers, or combination thereof, the resulting work is called an *arrangement.* Musicians also use the term *chart* to denote an arrangement. The person doing the arranging is called an *arranger.* To *score* a piece of music is to determine the particular instruments, singers, or combination thereof, that will be used in an arrangement. Example: "He wrote a great arrangement of that song. He scored it for a studio orchestra of woodwinds, brass, percussion, and a full string section. He's an excellent arranger. What a chart!"

Regarding the pulse of music, the *downbeat* denotes the principal attack on the first beat in a measure, or it can denote the principal attack on any beat in a measure. Conversely, the *upbeat* denotes the second half of a beat, or the preparation for the following beat. When a note on an upbeat is tied over to the note on the following beat—that is, when it *anticipates* the following note—the resulting shift in the rhythmic pulse is called *syncopation*. Syncopation is fundamental to *swing*. Music that swings has an energized feeling, a sense of foot-tapping, forward motion; it is not square.

An *interval* is the distance between two notes, calculated by counting the inclusive number of steps between two notes. For example, C up to F is a fourth—C, D, E, F; or G-sharp down to B is a sixth—G-sharp, F-sharp, E, D-sharp, C-sharp, B. When intervals are widened or shortened—this is done in half-step increments—their qualities change. Depending on the harmonic context of a music example, there may be major or minor sixths, perfect or diminished fifths, or any number of other alterations. These qualifiers appear frequently in the discussions of the musical examples in this book. For those who do not understand the distinction between major and minor, etc., it should suffice to simply remember an obvious fact and its likely implication: the larger an interval, the greater the distance to travel between its notes, and the more technically demanding its execution may be for a singer or instrumentalist.

CHAPTER 1

The Ella Mystique

My experience with Ella was mostly in the studios, where she hit about everything she did in one take.

—Urbie Green[1]

There was a sense of inevitability surrounding an Ella Fitzgerald performance, an intuitive realization by the audience, even before she started singing, that she could only be amazing. She was a transcendent musical artist, her appeal spanning the spectrum of the listening public. In their book, *Singing Jazz,* Bruce Crowther and Mike Pinfold remark how Ella "achieved . . . a joyful symbiosis of those elements that can be appreciated and enjoyed by the non-jazz audience, and those elements of pop that are acceptable to jazz fans."[2] The authors were referring to Ella's recordings of the late 1950s and early 1960s, but their comment could have been applicable to recordings, or concerts, at any stage in her inimitable career. "Billie Holiday and Frank Sinatra lived out the dramas they sang about. Fitzgerald, viewing them from afar, understood and forgave all," remarked Stephen Holden in the *New York Times.* "[S]inging in a style that transcended race, ethnicity, class and age, she was a voice of profound reassurance. At the end of everything, there was always hope."[3]

Ella's superior musical acumen was essentially unattributable to anything other than her extraordinary ability to assimilate whatever she heard. "It was a natural thing with her," exclaimed her long-time accompanist, Tommy Flanagan. "She had a great ear. And her ideas—she could duplicate what she heard, which is amazing." Aside from her occasional references to early schooling, as well as predominantly unproductive piano lessons, she appears to have never studied music formally. If she did receive any instruction at any time, it was likely in passing from some of the musicians with whom she worked. She apparently read music well enough to examine charts, and she used cue cards on occasion to remember lyrics, but that was it.

What is perhaps more remarkable is the virtually total absence of evidence regarding any extra work or preparation Ella might have undertaken before singing. She was never known to practice, warm up, or do any special vocal exercises. Ella's publicist Virginia Wicks remembers:

I never heard her say: "I have to go in the other room and practice." I never heard her do that. Sometimes she would have a cold and she'd be concerned about how it would come out. But did she try it first? No. I don't remember anything—other people may have—but I don't recall anything like that. She would just go do it. She was an amazing lady. If anyone tells you something differently than what I'm saying, they possibly heard something I didn't hear. So I don't say she never did. The thought of Ella standing in a room and going up and down the scales is something I don't think that ever happened. Maybe in the very early part of her career, but I wouldn't say so. She might sing a song around the house as she walked around dusting or something, just to sing it and to feel it. But I don't think she practiced per se—sit in a room and practice. I can't imagine it.

Ella was in a constant state of readiness to perform. The *Home News* (New Brunswick, New Jersey) described the beginning of a rehearsal with the Garden State Symphonic Pops Orchestra: "Conductor: 'All right guys, listen to the trio. If I've got the wrong time, go with them.' Now pianist Paul Smith . . . strikes up an uptempo 'Just One of Those Things.' Ella emerges out of the backstage riggings of the State Theater, steps to the mike, hits the first note right on. It's 4 P.M. on the dot, rehearsal under way as scheduled."[4] Ella strove to take care of her musical endeavors efficiently and with a no-nonsense approach. This certainly did not preclude her exhibiting a charming sense of humor, nor was she incapable of laughing at herself. She was simply a consummate professional who expected the same in return. Producer Norman Granz was probably more familiar with Ella's working habits than anyone else. "When we did the [Cole] Porter [*Song Book*] album, we came to some verses that were difficult or really didn't work," he recalled. "Ella would get uptight and say, 'Why do I have to do this?' Translation: She had to spend time working on them. Usually Ella would go in and do her songs very fast. We never laid down tracks or anything like that. Everything was live with the band. We would do two takes, three at the most, because that's how she worked."[5]

Ella commanded a level of respect that few singers achieve. The instrumentalists who backed her, both in the recording studios and on stage, frequently took their lead from her. According to Virginia Wicks:

They'd say "Ella, Give me E-flat," or whatever, and . . . it was automatic. [She had] perfect pitch. . . . She had that kind of God-given perfect pitch. Very often pianos would be out of tune and Ella could not work with an out-of-tune piano. They'd have to immediately tune it on the spot because she knew the difference. . . . They usually were quite careful with Ella . . . but I very often saw them come in with the tuning fork . . . [and] go up and down the scale, and Ella would listen. And it was Ella that [was] perfect out of everybody, everything.

The musicians didn't know necessarily, certainly not in every case, what Ella was going to do in a live performance or . . . a recording. They didn't know exactly. Naturally, they had to discuss tempo and all of that, but they didn't know where she would suddenly scat. Nor did Ella . . . [She] would just stand there and sing and the musicians, very often, would be in awe because she had not rehearsed exactly what she was going to do there and it would just happen. It was never wrong. She never sang out of tune or out of tempo or anything. She might not like something she did, but I don't recall anybody saying "Now wait a minute, Ella, let's go with the other part, or whatever." I don't recall that.

She would have gone over the lyrics. She was always afraid she'd forget the lyrics—not always—but very often, particularly with some new tune, not a standard, but some new tune. So that troubled her. But in terms of interpretation, I think she surprised herself.

During his lengthy stay with Ella, pianist Tommy Flanagan developed an almost telepathic connection with the singer. He was aware that anything was possible at any time, even if they had supposedly worked out an arrangement in advance. "[W]e get together to find the key," he recounted in 1974. "She tells me how she feels the piece should be done . . . I then work up an orchestration . . . She will still do all kinds of things within that framework. Often, she'll add a new twist or improvisation, even when we're actually on the stage performing . . . but she always knows exactly what she is doing. What would be musically risky for some singers, she pulls off easily. She rarely sings a song exactly the same way she did it last."[6]

As formidable an entertainer as Ella was—always ready at the drop of a hat, with seemingly little or no preparation, to deliver a stunning performance—and as unpredictable as she could be during a performance—nudging an arrangement in unexpected directions, spontaneously altering lyrics, or surprising musicians and the audience in any number of ways—she remained steadfast in her reluctance to discuss any aspect of her technique or approach to singing. That she was a very private person who guarded the details of her life was well-known, but the wall she erected around herself also concealed the secrets of her creativity. Despite the fact that it is easiest to explain Ella's genius by ascribing it to a once-in-a-lifetime inborn talent, a gift that other singers could only covet, it would almost certainly have been fascinating for her to step back from time to time and talk about her musicality. In any event, millions of fans were rewarded by Ella's egoless nature in that her purity and graciousness served to enhance her performances. "She had little to say about the processes, methodologies, and nuances of her interpretations, why she did this and not that, etc.," said John McDonough in *Down Beat.* "People who aren't given to analysis of such things are often blessed with a natural immunity to that most fatal virus that can strike an intuitive artist—self-consciousness, leading to self-imitation."[7]

During the early years of her career, Ella often declared her preference for ballads, a sentiment not surprising for her or any top song stylist. However, after her time with Chick Webb, with whom she began her professional career in the mid 1930s, she began to be associated with the angular and frenetic sounds of bebop, due in large part to her obvious delight with the post-World War II music innovations and her appearances with Jazz at the Philharmonic. Her recorded output consisted mainly of jazz selections, as well as more of the types of lighter material she had frequently done with Webb. "Despite all of the things I've done, despite the different kinds of songs I sing, I still consider myself basically a ballad singer," she told *Ebony* in 1949. "I suppose it'll always be that way. I love ballads. Despite what they'll say, that will never change."[8] Consequently, from about the mid-1950s, when her star began to rise exponentially, Ella was very purposeful in picking the songs that she wanted to sing. Virginia Wicks recounts:

They didn't come to her and give her a song—and she didn't like it—but she'd sing it anyway because she'd get a payoff or something. Some of the artists did that—she didn't. It was very important to her what she sang. I don't think she ever recorded anything she didn't like. After Norman [Granz] really began to handle her, it was Ella's choice, more than what Nelson Riddle or somebody would decide to arrange. They would never arrange a tune or have a tune ready for her without her total approval. And it wasn't that she was high-handed. . . . If some composer would come to her, some well-known composer with a beautiful song, with a song she liked, that would be wonderful—some she liked better than others, but nobody forced her to do anything.

Ella developed an uncanny knack for piecing together varied and well-balanced programs, her sense of pace enabling her to touch all bases during a performance. "I prefer ballads because you tell a story more," she said in *Melody Maker.* "The fast ones, however, do help to break it up. But you must always make the melody clear."[9] Jim Hall, the outstanding guitarist, once exclaimed that "Ella was a stunning performer. She's very careful about the sequence of tunes and organizing a set of music. I learned a lot from her."[10]

Ella was also not hesitant to tackle songs outside of the jazz and standard repertoires. She had been brought up on an eclectic repertoire during her time with Chick Webb and she remained open-minded in subsequent years, especially during the middle period of her career. Any tune was fair game for her; her commitment to what she sang, regardless of genre, had no limitations. In choosing her material she was much like Sonny Rollins, the superb tenor saxophonist and an improviser of almost unmatched inventiveness. Rollins can take songs that would not generally be associated with the hip world of jazz—for instance, "I'm an Old Cowhand," "I've Grown Accustomed to Your Face," and "Toot, Toot, Tootsie"—and put his personal imprint on them so that they become perfectly logical selections. Ella was even more diverse than Rollins in her programming. Her mixed bag included numbers from commercial pop, rock, and other genres, in addition to her huge repertoire of standards and jazz tunes. "What I try to do in my act is to satisfy everybody," she said. "Country and Western or whatever—it's all music. We don't have the Cole Porters and the George Gershwins anymore, but we have the Bert Bacharachs, Stevie Wonder and people like Paul Williams. I dig his lyrics. I also dig Marvin Gaye."[11]

In his exhaustive Fitzgerald discography, J. Wilfred Johnson reports that the amazing singer recorded differing numbers of versions of a whopping 1,117 song titles:

> The list comprises more titles than have ever been recorded by another singer. For this there are several reasons: First, Ella had a longer recording career than any other singer, . . . almost fifty-six years. Second, her manager, Norman Granz, recorded, or had others record, a great many of her concert performances, not a few of which were released on records. Third, Ella liked to experiment, recording the material of the day . . . Also, in her years at Decca, she was assigned material according to her popularity. . . . There are 2,279 known recorded performances . . . and these may well be supplemented by half that many more undocumented in the vaults, although it is doubtful that few, if any, new titles will be discovered.[12]

Pianist Lou Levy accompanied Ella in the late 1950s and early 1960s. "We'd . . . do 40 tunes . . . the next night do 40 different tunes," he recalled. "She'd give you a list of numbers at the beginning of a concert and by the second tune you're already off the list. She'll turn around . . . and give you something different or, for example, if there's a kid in the audience she'll sing *Three Little Pigs* or nursery rhymes, *Jingle Bells* if it's Christmas time—you never knew. . . . But it was always in tune and it always swung."[13]

Tommy Flanagan, a jazz purist, was usually unfamiliar with the commercial tunes that Ella liked. "Well she usually picked [the songs] because a lot of the things she ended up doing I wouldn't think of. It was strictly up to her. We worked on how the arrangement would feel and how we would approach it, and how to get out of it. . . . We'd find the lead sheet and find out where the song is really going and what they really meant by writing the song." Only toward the end of Ella's career, when her health was consistently a concern, did she return almost exclusively to the standard repertoire.

Ella Fitzgerald is in the rarest category of top-rank artists who excel through seemingly nothing else but naturally self-generating ability. For almost sixty years, she was a marvel. Underlying everything, there was the wide-ranging voice—crystal clear, in tune, and articulate. Unmatched in her versatility, she could croon on tender ballads, swing intensely on medium-tempo selections, take one's breath away with unmatched scatting at any tempo, or raise the roof with powerhouse romps on up-tempo takes. If it is possible for a singer to evolve through osmosis, to assimilate the best of all she hears and develop it to exemplary levels of technical execution and creative expression, then Ella Fitzgerald is pictured on the poster for this concept.

CHAPTER 2

Overview

[I]t's possible to speculate that Ella sang, with such joyousness in her sound and style, in part because, by singing, she could tame the memories of her early hardships and keep them at bay. The attitude she took in her singing made her a whole person and enriched the rest of us.

—Leslie Gourse[1]

To many, she personifies American music.

—James Billington, Librarian of Congress[2]

Ella Fitzgerald was born in Newport News, Virginia, on April 25, 1917, to common-law parents, William Fitzgerald and Tempie (Temperance) Williams. Ella never retained any recollection of her father because William abandoned the household in late 1920 and Tempie subsequently took up with Joseph Da Silva, a Portuguese immigrant. Soon after, her mother and stepfather, in search of better living and working conditions, moved with their daughter to Yonkers, New York. "I know nothing of Newport News," said Ella. "My mother left there when she married my stepfather. I don't know about my father . . . My stepfather was Portuguese. I should have learned Portuguese."[3]

As had countless other underprivileged families from southern black communities, Ella's parents discovered that the promise of an improved life in the north was predominantly fiction. For the majority of the thousands of migrants who made the move the hardships simply continued in new locations. In any event, Joe and Tempie found work and they managed as well as could be expected. "My mother worked first as a caterer, then at a laundry," recalled Ella. "My old man dug ditches and tried to be a chauffeur at night. We didn't have much."[4]

In 1923 a baby girl, Frances, was born into the family. Ella maintained a very close relationship with her half sister until Frances passed away in the summer of 1966. Also in 1923, Ella, who was six, began attending school. She was a very good student and she enjoyed dancing and singing, especially dancing. Although she would suffer abuse at the hands of her stepfather in later years, it appears that initially he provided Ella with positive artistic reinforcement. Biographer Geoffrey Mark Fidelman recounts that "Joseph was undoubtedly a nurturing influence on her music and cultural awareness."[5]

For a time, Ella harbored aspirations of a career as a dancer. She and her friend Charles Gulliver often made their way uptown to dance halls, observing and practicing all the steps. In fact, the two youngsters became adept at the latest styles, landing occasional dance jobs at the local clubs.

Ella was also listening regularly to the popular music of the day, taking in the sounds and styles of her favorite singers. Her mother Tempie was a significant influence, playing records and singing around the house. Tempie also paid for piano lessons for Ella, who turned out to be a less than industrious student. "I had private piano lessons . . . but my mother soon realized I was playing the same lessons over and over," recalled Ella. "Five dollars was a lot of money in those days, so she stopped the lessons."[6] Ella probably succeeded in attaining an elementary knowledge of piano and music theory.

During this period, jazz was continuing its steady evolution into America's great art form and Ella was becoming familiar with the best musicians on the scene. The Swing Era was just around the corner and there was much to fill the listener's ears at the time. In addition, like most youngsters in the community, Ella sang regularly at church. As a result, the combination of listening and participating provided her with informal lessons and valuable inroads to musical interpretation and performance. Furthermore, she was blessed with a great ear and was able to duplicate and assimilate what she heard.

Not surprisingly, one of Ella's earliest and most overwhelming influences was Louis Armstrong, the unsurpassed master from New Orleans whose artistry would have an effect on all musicians who followed. Ella spent much time marveling at and absorbing all she could of Armstrong's groundbreaking treatment of melody and rhythm. Foremost among Ella's other favorite vocalists were the Boswell Sisters and especially Connee Boswell, the lead singer for the trio. The three sisters were recognized for unique arrangements that included novel rhythmic invention and manipulation of tempo. Completely won over by Connee Boswell's originality and talent, Ella, throughout her career, cited Boswell as her prime influence.

In early 1932 Ella's mother Tempie died suddenly of a heart attack. This was a turning point for Ella; the dynamic in her home changed abruptly. Her stepfather became increasingly belligerent and the abuse that he inflicted on her was bad enough that Tempie's sister Virginia took Ella to stay with her in Harlem. Ella, however, soon became disenchanted with her new circumstances. Her aunt often paid little or no attention to her and it was not a happy time for her. She became close to her cousin Georgiana, and her sister Frances moved in after their stepfather Joe passed away. However, Ella still remained uncomfortable with the situation and her behavior began to change. She left school, hit the streets, and did whatever she could to survive. She ran numbers and also served as a lookout for a brothel. The authorities eventually caught up with her and, designating her a truant, sent her to the New York State Training School for Girls in Hudson, near Albany, the state capital.

Ella spent about two years in Hudson, a period of her life which, until only recently, has remained a mystery. Throughout her life Ella steadfastly avoided talking about her early hardships. However, in 1996, shortly after the great singer's death, writer Nina Bernstein, who had undertaken determined research, revealed some of the tragic details of Ella's time at the reform school in a remarkably eye-opening *New York Times* article:

State investigators reported that black girls, then 88 of 460 residents, were segregated in the two most crowded and dilapidated of the reformatory's 17 "cottages," and were routinely beaten by male staff.

Like Miss Fitzgerald, most of the 12- to 16-year-old girls sent to the reform school by the family courts were guilty of nothing more serious than truancy or running away . . . they were typically victims of poverty, abuse and family disruption. . . .
"She hated the place," Mr. [Thomas] Tunney [the institution's last superintendent] said from his home in Saratoga Springs, where he retired some years after the institution closed in 1976. "She had been held in the basement of one of the cottages once and all but tortured."

A more generous image of Miss Fitzgerald's experience there was painted by E. M. O'Rourke, 87, who taught English at the school in the 1930's and remembers Miss Fitzgerald as a model student. "I can even visualize her handwriting—she was a perfectionist," she recalled. There was a fine music program at the school, she said, and a locally celebrated institution choir.

But Ella Fitzgerald was not in the choir: it was all white.

"We didn't know what we were looking at," Mrs. O'Rourke said. "We didn't know she would be the future Ella Fitzgerald."

She did sing in public at least once while she was at the reformatory, . . . at the A.M.E. Zion Church in Hudson . . . "That girl sang her heart out," recalled Mrs. [Beulah] Crank [reformatory house mother].[7]

Ella finally ran away from the reform school in late 1934. Knowing she had to stay clear of the authorities she returned to the streets. Ill-fed and

often unable to bathe, she danced on street corners for tips and slept wherever she could. Needless to say, she was not an attractive sight; her be-
draggled appearance reflected her harsh situation.

In spite of her troubles, Ella persisted, refusing to submit to her hardships. Her strong artistic inclinations remained a sustaining force, so much
so that she decided to try her luck in an amateur night at the famous
Apollo Theater. Just the previous year, the Lafayette Theater, another of
Harlem's well-known night spots, had started staging these highly popular contests, and most of the top venues in the area had followed suit
with similar events. Ella often claimed in later years that she and a couple
of her friends had drawn straws to see who would apply for the amateur
contest; evidently Ella picked the short straw. Whatever the case, Ella
attended the preliminary audition and was selected to participate in the
weekly main event.

The story of Ella Fitzgerald's night at the Apollo has been documented
often. A brief summary would go as follows: (1) the contest in which Ella
appeared took place on November 21, 1934; (2) she had initially intended
to enter as a dancer, but lost confidence and changed her mind at the last
minute when she discovered that she would be preceded by the Edwards
Sisters, two highly accomplished dancers; (3) she opted instead to sing
two songs she knew at that time, "Object of My Affection" and "Judy"—
she sang them in the style of Connee Boswell, her favorite singer and
biggest influence; (4) after a shaky start she wowed the audience and won
the contest.

In lieu of a cash prize the weekly winner of the Apollo contest was
supposed to receive a return engagement at the club. Ella was never given
the opportunity. It appears that her unattractive appearance worked
against her; the club did not want to present her as she looked. It turned
out, though, that her performance had caught the attention of a young
Benny Carter, the arranger and saxophonist who would go on to become
one of the jazz world's most respected musicians. Sitting in the audience
while his orchestra backed Ella on stage, Carter was knocked out by her
tremendous potential and immediately introduced himself. "When I first
saw Ella and first heard her, I must say I was amazed, 'cause right then,
you know, she was a singer," reminisced Carter. "And she was a singer
who was born to happen, and I knew she was going to happen."[8] A number of days later Carter brought Ella to sing for Fletcher Henderson, the
great bandleader and his former boss. Henderson was not interested, perhaps also in part because of Ella's ragged look.

Undaunted, Ella applied for the amateur event at the Harlem Opera
House and she was accepted to participate at the end of January 1935. She
won, and, once again, she knocked out the audience. Unlike the Apollo
management, those in charge at the Opera House followed through with
Ella's award and let her appear for another week beginning on Friday,

February 15, 1935. She did not disappoint, singing up a storm—but she was never paid. Biographer Stuart Nicholson suggests this may "have been because the autocratic [manager of the Opera House] Frank Schiffman insisted on suitable clothing and deducted the cost from her pay."[9]

Ella's big break came when fortuitous circumstances resulted in her becoming the girl vocalist with Chick Webb and his Orchestra in 1935. Webb, a diminutive, hunchbacked drummer, was a tremendous player and led what was for a time one of the preeminent and most exciting big bands of the Swing Era. Ella flourished, growing from a talented but inexperienced singer to one of the best and most popular vocalists on the scene. She and Webb were a dynamic pair that reigned high up on the list of the many singer/bandleader combinations of the time. When, in 1939, Webb's life was tragically cut short because of health problems, Ella continued working for another three years with the band, serving as its nominal leader, although others in the organization actually ran the show. (For a detailed discussion of Webb, including Ella's work with him, see Chapter 4.)

Ella recorded often with Webb's orchestra for Decca Records, before and after the drummer's death, and when the group disbanded in 1942, she continued her full schedule without missing a beat. Moe Gale, who had been managing Webb, continued to manage Ella for over a decade. She would also stay at Decca well into the 1950s. With Milt Gabler as her producer, she recorded with vocal groups like the Three Keys and the Ink Spots, as well as with ensembles that included Bill Doggett, Wild Bill Davis, Charlie Shavers, Buddy Rich, Illinois Jacquet, Hank Jones, Louis Jordan, Roy Haynes, and other top-rank instrumentalists. Furthermore, on many of her studio dates she worked with the day's best arrangers and musical directors. (For detailed information on Ella's Decca years, including the musicians and musical directors with whom she collaborated, see Chapter 7.) Also during this period, Ella made her first recordings with the great Louis Armstrong and she cut two albums with pianist Ellis Larkins that are among the finest in her recorded output. (For detailed discussions of Ella's work with Armstrong and Larkins, see their sections in Chapters 3 and 9 respectively.)

The 1940s also saw the emergence and development of the bebop movement. The economic hardships of post-World War II America, coupled with an unstable music industry, effectively put an end to the great Swing Era and its many big bands. A new crop of modern musicians were forming smaller ensembles and reinventing the harmonic and melodic models that had shaped jazz to that date. Although musicians, critics, and the listening audience had conflicting views on the controversial new sounds, the changes progressed steadily. By the end of the 1940s, the remaining flashes of the Big Band Era essentially fizzled out for good. There were of course a number of elite bandleaders—for example Benny Goodman,

Duke Ellington, and Count Basie—who survived relatively unscathed and who were able to subsist because of their lofty stature, and because the demise of the Swing Era did not necessarily mean the elimination of big bands altogether. However, the advent of bebop and the looming rock movement certainly meant that jazz and jazz-oriented popular music were no longer the musical styles of choice for the greater listening public. (For detailed discussions of Goodman, Ellington, and Basie, including Ella's work with them, see Chapter 8.)

Ella Fitzgerald embraced bebop. She even did some tours with Dizzy Gillespie, who, with a number of other innovators, was a prime architect of the modern sounds. True to form, she was able to innately understand the new musical language and she soon added its phraseology and harmonic implications to her vocal style. Henceforth, her programs and recordings would include bop-oriented selections. Because of her un-matched abilities, she was the only singer of popular standards and ballads who was able to perform in the bop idiom with the same technical proficiency as the top instrumentalists. Furthermore, she never lost her mainstream audiences. (For a detailed discussion of bebop, including Ella's work in the idiom, see Chapter 5.)

In early 1949, Ella performed for the first time on a Jazz at the Philharmonic (JATP) concert produced by Norman Granz. This was a major turning point for Ella, who by the mid-1950s would be working exclusively for Granz, a legendary impresario who was a tremendous champion of jazz in general, and of Ella in particular. With the exception of a couple of years in the late 1960s, Granz managed Ella for the duration of her career, producing her countless live concerts and an amazing array of albums for his Verve and Pablo labels. She achieved superstar status and became wealthy in the process. Most importantly, Ella was finally able to sing the cream of the standard repertoire on a consistent basis. Although she had tackled this material previously with reasonable success, her repertoire had included a far greater percentage of light and novelty material under Milt Gabler at Decca. (For a discussion of Norman Granz, including his association with Ella, see Chapter 6. Detailed examinations of the recordings that Ella made for Granz are included in Chapters 7, 8, and 9.)

The decline of the big bands did not necessarily destroy the livelihoods of all the vocalists who had been working during the Swing Era. In addition to Ella, many of her singing contemporaries maintained comfortable and, in some cases, highly successful careers. These singers, however, would be confronted with another movement in the 1950s, one of huge proportions that would completely alter the musical landscape. "Singers and singing groups enjoyed a new primacy in the ordering of economic priorities in the pop market," commented James T. Maher. "The big dance bands . . . lost all claim to the attention of the pop audience, a predominantly young consumer group that is notorious for its short attention span, and its insatiable hunger for the *new* (a word that has since given way to the word *now*, with its dreary implication of manipulated hysteria)."[10] Rock and roll was simmering and about to explode.

"Pop, C & W [Country and Western], and R & B [Rhythm and Blues] coexisted in the early 1950s as three separate and distinct markets, as if separated by tall brick walls," comment Joe Stuessy and Scott Lipscomb in their comprehensive study of rock and roll. "But in a short three-year span (roughly 1954 to 1956), individual bricks were removed until the 'walls came tumbling down.' What emerged from the ruins was a new giant on the musical scene."[11] Once rock and roll had established its firm foothold, the sophisticated, intellectual genres of music—classical and jazz—began to feel themselves being nudged to the sidelines. Established jazz stars like Gillespie, Max Roach, Sonny Rollins, Miles Davis, Art Blakey, Horace Silver, and a young John Coltrane, forged decent livings for themselves, but the number of successful jazz performers was miniscule in proportion to the myriad rock stars who were springing onto the scene. Through all this, Ella Fitzgerald and her most famous singing contemporaries—Frank Sinatra, Nat "King" Cole, Tony Bennett, Dinah Shore, etc.—carried on. Stuessy and Lipscomb summarize:

The pop sounds of Perry Como, Eddie Fisher, and Doris Day yielded to the rocking sounds of Elvis Presley, Little Richard, and Jerry Lee Lewis. An industry dominated by five major record companies [RCA, Columbia, Capitol, Mercury, Decca] was now populated with hundreds of successful, small independent companies. A well-ordered succession of predictable hit records, each sustaining its popularity for months at a time, was replaced by a dizzying sequence of artists, many of whom zoomed to popularity only to fade into obscurity within a few weeks.[12]

In spite of the changing dynamic in the musical environment, Ella Fitzgerald would in fact record some of her greatest albums once she started working with Norman Granz. For example, in the mid to late 1950s, she reunited with Louis Armstrong for three outstanding albums, and she recorded the *Cole Porter Song Book,* the first in a series of seminal releases, each featuring the music of a single songwriter or songwriting team. (See the sections on Armstrong and the *Song Books,* in Chapters 3 and 7, respectively.) There were other great albums, too. Ella was at the absolute height of her powers and she would stay at her peak through most of the 1960s (even though an Ella at any level of ability was always wonderful).

The 1960s are remembered as a time of extreme change and as one of the most turbulent periods in American history, a decade during which three tragic assassinations stunned the nation and the world. Assessing the social climate in America at the beginning of the 1960s, historian William L. O'Neill emphasized that politicians and other public figures were not focused on the issues that would actually dominate the decade.

They worried about the missile gap when it was the arms race itself that mattered. They warned the civil rights movement against asking too much too soon, though it was really a case of too little too late. They were preoccupied with affairs abroad while it was conditions at home that wanted attention. . . . The economy flourished; the cities decayed. Airports and highways were built; railroad passenger service collapsed. Science and technology solved old difficulties while creating new ones—pollution, congestion, and contamination followed each advance. Kennedy had promised new leadership and new departures, yet his ideas were commonplace.[13]

The 1960s were Vietnam, the Civil Rights movement, the drug culture, flower power, anti-conservatism—and the second wave of rock. Thousands of Americans lost their lives in an unpopular war that should never have been contested in the first place; the rift between blacks and whites was more pronounced than ever; pot and hallucinogenic drugs permeated all levels of society; young people fought harder than ever to make their voices heard—and the Beatles and numerous new rock groups once again set the music world on its ear.

The influx of the Beatles and other British groups excited musical audiences in America and incited yet another wave of changes in rock and roll. If the sounds of Elvis Presley and others had taken over in the previous decade, the new rock and its proponents cemented their overall dominance of the musical scene. There were of course still phenomenal performers in the jazz world who survived more than just adequately, but virtually no one was immune to the effects of the rock movement. Miles Davis, John Coltrane, and Ornette Coleman were successfully forging new and astounding directions in creative jazz, but there were many excellent musicians who would not maintain the same levels of success. Coltrane died in 1967, but Davis and Coleman, especially Davis, eventually embraced the rhythms and electronic sounds of rock.

Ella Fitzgerald finished her series of *Song Books* in the early 1960s, and among the other superb recordings she made for Verve through 1966 were albums with Duke Ellington, Count Basie, Nelson Riddle, and her various accompanying small groups. It is a testament to her considerable appeal and resolve that she never backed down from her dizzying schedule and that she remained one of the supreme stars of jazz and popular music. Ever the adventurer, she stayed with the times and began including the hits of the day in her programs. Although some musicians and critics took her to task for doing so, that did not stop her from singing tunes by the Beatles and other rock stars, as well as by some of the popular songwriters of the day. If she liked the music, that was all that counted.

In the late 1960s, Norman Granz took a break from producing records, and Ella went her own way for the next couple of years, recording for Capitol and other labels and continuing her usual packed schedule. It is often pointed out that these last years of the 1960s did not constitute a very dynamic period of Ella's career. This would be hard to dispute, especially when comparing her output at this time to her great achievements of the recent past. In any event, she stayed busy and some of the lesser albums she made, especially those for Capitol, are nonetheless interesting, if for no other reason than the fact that it is Ella singing.

Granz returned once again to guide Ella's affairs as the decade of the 1970s was unfolding. He founded Pablo Records and produced her on another series of miraculous albums through to the early 1990s. Her voice was no longer as razor sharp as it had been in her peak years, but her innate talent and years of experience allowed her still to be miraculous more often than not.

The general public as ever adored Ella. In a musical environment that had succumbed to the excesses of the rock world, she was still the queen, the best at what she did—and all other artists, rockers and otherwise, knew it. As had been the case throughout her career, accolades and tributes were plentiful. On December 2, 1979, she was a recipient of the prestigious Kennedy Center Honors Medal at the second annual gala event. When she received the Will Rogers Award from the Beverly Hills Chamber of Commerce and Civic Association in early 1980, *Variety* reported that she "brought the capacity black-tie audience to its feet when she furnished the lion's share of entertainment at her own tribute with a medley of her biggest hits."[14] Four years later, when Ella received the Los Angeles Urban League's annual Whitney Young Award, presented in recognition of an individual's contributions to racial and economic equality, *Variety* was on hand again and wrote that "Fitzgerald, who has produced more than 150 albums that have sold more than 40,000,000 copies, said she was 'humbled' by the accolade."[15] In June 1990, Ella, who had previously been recognized by academia on several occasions, was at Princeton University, and the *Newark Star-Ledger* reported that "[j]azz singer Ella Fitzgerald received a standing ovation when she received an honorary Doctor of Music degree."[16]

Sadly, Ella was not in good health for much of the last part of her career. Interspersed among all her travel and affairs were many instances of medical and physical problems. In fact, she had come close to a breakdown as early as 1965 when she had to stop performing in the middle of a concert. In 1971 she was hospitalized for eye problems and the difficulties with her vision would never leave her. She had open-heart surgery in September 1986 and, to top it all off, she had been a diabetic for many years.

When Ella Fitzgerald passed away on June 15, 1996, the entire world lost one of the supreme artists of all time. She was and remains unmatched. Listen to her recordings.

CHAPTER 3

The Influential Singers

> In its smoothness and flexibility, that voice is arguably the most perfect all-around pop-jazz vocal instrument of the last half century. Sarah Vaughan ... could sound more beautiful, and Holiday and ... McRae had much greater emotional depth. But none could equal the range of Fitzgerald's far-reaching musicality or match the dynamism, stamina and inner musical logic of her improvisation.
>
> —Stephen Holden[1]

During her formative years, and over the course of her miraculous professional career, Ella Fitzgerald appreciated and learned from other masters in the music profession. She was a supremely gifted artist who did not let fame and success override her innate graciousness or get in the way of her artistic development. "She was a great fan of talent and a great respecter of other people," said Virginia Wicks, Ella's long-time publicist and good friend. "There was never any jealously—ever, ever, ever—between herself and another singer. If she liked the singer's work, then she was like a fan. If that wasn't her cup of tea, she was just very polite or respectful of their fame. . . . She was very pure."

Throughout the twentieth century, many top-rank singers—among them Lee Wiley, Peggy Lee, Maxine Sullivan, Helen Humes, Anita O'Day, Dinah Washington, Bing Crosby, Cab Calloway, Martha Raye, Lena Horne, Billy Eckstine, Frank Sinatra, Tony Bennett, Mel Tormé, and Sarah Vaughan—were both entertaining and influential, setting challenging standards for interpreters of jazz and popular song. The following short list names those vocalists whose styles and career accomplishments were most central, either directly or indirectly, to Ella Fitzgerald's development:

Louis Armstrong/1901–1971
Bessie Smith/[1890–1900]–1937
Ethel Waters/1896–1977
Mildred Bailey/1907–1951
Connee Boswell/1907–1976
Billie Holiday/1915–1959
Leo Watson/1898–1950

Louis Armstrong and Connee Boswell were the primary models for Ella. Of the two, Ella continually reiterated throughout her career that Boswell—highly original and influential in her time, although less remembered in later years—had been by far her biggest influence. Armstrong, the monumental genius and the most important jazz figure in history, was renowned for his virtuosic and groundbreaking skills, both as a vocalist and a trumpeter. Interestingly, Boswell also had a strong instrumental background, having achieved considerable proficiency as a classical cellist. Her formal instrumental training likely contributed to her added prowess as an arranger with surprisingly innovative ideas.

As of the early 1930s, each of the singers on the aforementioned short list, regardless of age or style, was still actively performing. Therefore, there were many crosscurrents here in that some or all of these singers also influenced some or all of the others. Brief examinations of the lives and talents of these accomplished vocalists provide fascinating and illuminating perspectives on both the evolution of American popular singing and the unparalleled artistry of Ella Fitzgerald.

LOUIS ARMSTRONG

Louis Armstrong, the first great jazz soloist, was a stunningly original performer who would become the most renowned musician of the twentieth century. His untouchable improvisations, unprecedented treatment of rhythm, and intimidating technique were things of wonder. While, in later years, Charlie Parker and John Coltrane may have been the only musicians who came close to matching Armstrong's overriding impact on the evolution of jazz, he was the only master to wield such power both as an instrumentalist and a singer. His instrumental prowess is often the first thing to be cited, but his singing was equally astounding. The manner in which he reshaped melodies, coupled with his vocal gymnastics and a penchant for extemporaneous lyrics, reflected an instrumental approach to his singing that would establish new standards and sway generations of jazz and popular singers.

Of Ella Fitzgerald's two prime influences, Connee Boswell differed from Louis Armstrong in that she was a direct model for Ella, whereas a good deal of Armstrong came to Ella via his influence on the musicians with whom she worked—or to whom she listened, including Boswell. This is not to say that she did not consciously pick up things when listening to Armstrong, but Ella always spoke of Boswell as the singer she tried to emulate the most. Jazz historian and archivist Phil Schaap describes the Armstrong/Fitzgerald connection as follows:

I think that Ella is one of the second liners in this regard, that her Armstrong influence is profound but filtered through a preceding genius, or preceding artists, like Connee Boswell, like Chick Webb's band. Taft Jordan [trumpeter in Chick Webb's band] is Louis Armstrong, but she doesn't know that. She knows he's Taft Jordan. I would [also] say Louis Jordan . . . [who] thought Louis Armstrong was the greatest thing that ever happened. Armstrong was a tremendous vocal influence on him. A lot of people forget that Louis Jordan was a singer even in the Chick Webb period. I think that Armstrong is the most under-acknowledged Ella Fitzgerald influence.

Born in New Orleans on August 4, 1901, Louis Armstrong grew up in poverty, raised by both his mother and grandmother. While still a young boy he managed to gain his first musical experiences when he and a friend formed a vocal group in order to earn some loose change singing on the streets. However, typical of adolescents from the ghetto, he was prone to brushes with the law and, in his early teens, after some mischievous behavior, he was placed in a home for delinquent boys. During his year and a half in the home, he continued to sing and, more significantly, was given his first cornet. The young Armstrong received basic lessons and he practiced diligently, becoming the strongest player in the home. Eventually, he began to work local engagements, further developing his musical skills. His cornet (later trumpet) playing, as well as his initial successes with instrumental groups, would garner him a good reputation and better performance opportunities. He would go on to play with countless musicians, most notably in the famous band of Joe "King" Oliver.

For three years beginning in 1925, Armstrong, as a leader in Chicago, recorded 60 selections for the Okeh label with his most historically significant bands, the Hot Five and the Hot Seven. On the third of these sessions in early 1926, it was decided that he would sing on some of the tracks. One of Armstrong's biographers, James Lincoln Collier, surmises that it was Richard Myknee Jones who suggested that Armstrong sing. Jones was a black New Orleans pianist, "but his real importance to the history of jazz was as a talent scout and recording director for Okeh and other companies."[2] On a tune called "Heebie Geebies," Armstrong sang two choruses in succession and scatted on the second, making up syllables and adding unusual vocal effects to improvise the melody. This chorus remains legendary both for Armstrong's scatting and for the supposed incident behind it. It is often alleged that he scatted after the sheet with the words on it fell off his music stand. This would certainly be a nice take on the situation because it makes for charming speculation. However, jazz researchers have known for some time that it is highly unlikely that it happened, even though Armstrong never abandoned the story of the dropped lyrics. Armstrong's latest biographer, Laurence Bergreen, puts the event in perspective, pointing out that "the story made no sense—if Louis had lost his way, he would simply have made another take. In addition, he scats throughout the recorded version of 'Heebie Jeebies,' long before he reaches the point at which he supposedly dropped the music."[3] The legend would also have it that this was actually the beginning of scatting. In fact, Armstrong was not the first singer to scat; this was not even the first time he had scatted in a studio.[4] This was the first time, however, that a recording containing a scatted solo became a hit. Consequently, it is not surprising that the listening public thought this manner of vocalizing was Armstrong's invention. The recording featured him doing something that was unique to the audience—and an eye-opener to other singers who, as Laurence Bergreen concludes, "listened to Louis singing and scatting and decided this was what they would do when they grew up; they would sing jazz just like this new musical phenomenon."[5] In later years, Ella Fitzgerald would advance scatting to levels that, to this day, remain unparalleled with respect to their musicality and breathtaking technical execution.

Because of the widespread appeal of "Heebie Jeebies," Okeh management decided to step up its promotion of Armstrong. By the time the Hot Five and Hot Seven recordings had been completed, Armstrong was on the verge of major stardom. James Lincoln Collier states that "it was becoming clear to musicians, entertainment entrepreneurs, and Armstrong himself that he was a potential star who could attract substantial audiences, both black and white, and make a good deal of money for himself and others."[6] Armstrong had grown from a top-rank musician to the great and original master who would influence generations of musicians. The Hot Five and Hot Seven recordings transformed the art of jazz. Armstrong's unprecedented level of excellence had a profound effect on all serious instrumentalists and singers, both at the time and for generations to come. His incredible sense of rhythm, the tremendous swing that he generated at any tempo, his ability to re-shape melodies, and his unparalleled inventiveness as an improviser established new standards of performance and placed the soloist at the core of jazz.

As the decade of the 1930s approached, Armstrong was in the process of joining Bing Crosby as one of the two biggest male singing stars of the time. "By 1929," said Will Friedwald, "Armstrong had all the elements necessary to become a great singer. The next move in the evolution of jazz-influenced popular singing would then be a matter of integration. . . . Fortunately, . . . Bing Crosby happened to be 'working on the same thing.'"[7] Crosby, the most popular singing star of the swing era, successfully infused elements of jazz into American popular music. In this regard, it may be that Armstrong was subsequently influenced in the choice of some of his repertoire, moving away from strictly jazz compositions. Interestingly, Collier and others have suggested that Crosby's influence may also have been a factor when, in the last years of the 1920s and into 1930, Armstrong opted to sing in a smoother, mellower voice on some recordings. This may or may not be the case, but anyone who has listened to early recordings of Armstrong knows that he was capable of softer, gentler tones when he wanted them. In any event, it was Crosby, a major star, particularly for the white listening public, who got so much more from Armstrong. If Crosby had any impact on Armstrong, it would most likely have been with respect to stage presence and repertoire.

Whatever the case, Armstrong eventually stopped singing in the smoother manner and returned to his familiar gravel-toned voice. How he came upon his particular vocal quality is subject to speculation. He may have been born with it—or it may have resulted from a periodically heavy smoking habit over the years or from oversinging in his youth. James Lincoln Collier recounts that Armstrong actually underwent surgery on his vocal chords in 1936 to have some growths removed.[8] Obviously, nothing changed because Armstrong's famous voice remained with him.

For the next 35 years Armstrong kept up a nonstop schedule. He performed in concerts around the world, bringing joy to millions of fans, and he appeared in the movies and on television. In 1956 his single of "Mack the Knife" was a million-seller and in 1964 his recording of "Hello Dolly," a song from the musical of the same name, resulted in an unexpected megahit that helped introduce him to a vast new audience. In the late 1960s his health began to deteriorate seriously but he persisted as best he could. The great Louis Armstrong passed away in Queens, New York, on July 6, 1971.

Ella Fitzgerald and Louis Armstrong recorded a number of sides together for Decca in the mid-1940s and very early 1950s, most of which can be found on compilations from Decca and Classics. The two singers also recorded three long-playing albums together: *Ella & Louis* and *Ella and Louis Again*, each a collection of venerable standards, and *Porgy and Bess*, featuring selections from George Gershwin's opera. The music from the first two albums will be examined in this section. Verve has reissued all three albums, both as individual CDs and collectively in a compilation called *The Complete Ella Fitzgerald and Louis Armstrong*. The latter includes an additional two duets by Fitzgerald and Armstrong, "You Won't Be

Satisfied (Until You Break My Heart)" and "Undecided," backed by the trumpeter's group and recorded at a Hollywood Bowl concert the night before the *Ella & Louis* recording session. When examining the collaborations of these two seminal artists, the facets of Armstrong's art that were so influential quickly become apparent. In addition to the music studied in this section, additional examples of Armstrong's singing from these sessions, as well as one from recordings with his big band, can be found later in this chapter and in Chapter 9.

In picking the music for these recordings, Ella and her manager Norman Granz would draw up a list of possible selections that they would narrow down after they consulted with Armstrong in the studio. In the liner notes for *The Complete Ella Fitzgerald and Louis Armstrong,* Granz explained: "I would have a meeting at [Fitzgerald's] house, and I would bring . . . maybe fifty songs. And we would go over those songs, 'cause she knew every song. . . . I never put a gun to an artist's head and said, 'This is what you've got to do.'"[9] With regard to keys and arrangements, the decision-making process was also uncomplicated. "In certain cases, because Fitzgerald was far more flexible, with more range than Louis, we would defer to Louis," added Granz. "But it wasn't a big issue, . . . if it [was] not a duet but on the same song, Louis would take a chorus, and [when] Ella would take a chorus, we'd simply change keys [if necessary]."[10]

In an interview with *Playboy*, shortly after the three Fitzgerald/Armstrong sessions were completed, Granz talked about the two singers: "When she made the album with Armstrong she insisted that he select the tunes, and sang them in all his keys even if they were the wrong keys for her."[11] It is certainly no surprise that Ella, always professional and selfless, was more than happy to accommodate Armstrong. She felt a genuine love for the artist who had been such a huge model for her and countless other musicians. Ella's publicist, Virgina Wicks, who was in the studio for two of the singer's recordings with Armstrong, remembered that "they had a wonderful camaraderie during the recording sessions." The two superstars formed a miraculous team. Biographer Stuart Nicholson comments that "it was not so much that Ella and Louis could make a silk purse from a sow's ear as that they could make a silk purse out of *anything.*"[12]

Ella & Louis was recorded in Hollywood on August 16, 1956. The formidable accompanying quartet included pianist Oscar Peterson, guitarist Herb Ellis, bassist Ray Brown, and drummer Buddy Rich. All were capable of intense virtuosity, yet their playing throughout was the epitome of economy and taste, a clear indication of their equally impressive sensitivity and adaptability.

The music on *Ella & Louis* is superb, at times infectiously swinging, other times more laid back and understated. Armstrong was 55 when he made this session. His voice has its accustomed raspiness and his singing possesses a looseness and breadth of feeling that reflects his miraculous forty-plus years of touring and recording up to that time. He plays with the lyrics, occasionally substituting vocal sounds for the words, and his elastic rhythm is typically superb. Ella's brilliance stems from her always-impeccable flexibility and intonation, as well as her sense of rhythm and time, which is the equal of Armstrong's. The contrast in conception and vocal texture between the two singers is at once exhilarating and touching. The album has a marvelous feeling of spontaneity to it, reflecting Granz's aversion to over-preparation. Some songs were completed in one take, the musicians having briefly discussed the general details before tackling the material.

The session opens with "Can't We Be Friends," an easy swinger. After Peterson's intro, Fitzgerald and Armstrong take choruses in the same key. Armstrong follows with a trumpet solo for half a chorus, his lines as inventive as ever, his horn sound bright and well-defined. The two singers split the bridge and then close out the track in harmony.

"Isn't This a Lovely Day," a pretty ballad by Irving Berlin, is a wonderful track, both for the singing and for some of Armstrong's finest trumpet work on the album. Ella opens freely with the verse before everyone settles into a medium-tempo lilt for Armstrong's vocal chorus. Herb Ellis interjects lovely guitar fills behind Armstrong's vocal. On Ella's ensuing chorus, Armstrong provides the fills on trumpet and then takes a half-chorus solo in which his creative lines and trademark high-note playing are particularly brilliant. Fitzgerald and Armstrong finish the chorus together, first riffing off each other and then harmonizing the last eight measures.

Ella does most of the singing and Armstrong throws in a short solo on "Moonlight in Vermont," another engaging ballad. "They Can't Take That Away from Me" and "Under a Blanket of Blue" are two relaxed swing numbers. On the former, an ebullient Armstrong coaxes his colleagues: "Swing it boys!" and "Swing it Ella!"

Armstrong opens "Tenderly" on trumpet, playing the melody in slow 3/4 rhythm above Peterson's relaxed fills. At the end of the chorus, everyone surprisingly shifts into 4/4 medium-tempo swing, at the same time modulating from the opening key of E-flat up to B-flat for Ella's entrance. She takes a chorus, Armstrong follows suit, and the musicians then slow it down again and return to the key of E-flat. Armstrong plays another half-chorus freely in 3/4, this time with Ella providing vocal fills. In a mini-tribute to her friend, she does her best Armstrong impression and scats a lick to close the take (Example 3.1).

"A Foggy Day" swings with a relaxed feel. Armstrong states the verse to get everything going and he can't resist another "Swing it Ella!" midway through. Armstrong opens "Stars Fell on Alabama" with a brief trum-

Example 3.1: Ella impersonating Louis Armstrong *(Ella and Louis)*

Bom boo duh zum ba   do   boo   zam, Oh yes!

pet flourish. During Ella's chorus, Armstrong either provides vocal fills or uses his uncanny ability to create a perfectly harmonized line. He repeats the bridge, this time with Ella supplying the vocal fills, and the two take the chorus out.

Ella recorded Irving Berlin's "Cheek to Cheek" several times during her career. The version here with Armstrong is virtuosic, a highlight of the album. Both singers take hard-swinging choruses and enjoy a little interplay toward the end. For a more detailed discussion of this track, see the section on Connee Boswell in this chapter.

"The Nearness of You," composed by Hoagy Carmichael and Ned Washington in 1938, is taken at a relaxed tempo and given a streamlined performance: Fitzgerald chorus, Armstrong chorus, half-chorus trumpet, Fitzgerald back in at the bridge, and out. The first half of each singer's chorus is shown in Example 3.2. In their respective third measures, each uses a triplet figure on the words "that thrills," Fitzgerald descending and Armstrong ascending. The singers also treat "oh no" differently, all four times that the words occur—in measure 5 of her passage, Ella descends on eighth notes; in measures 12 and 13 she uses three sixteenth notes and an eighth note to stretch "oh" before dropping down to "no"; in his measures 5 and 6, Armstrong keeps the two words on the same pitch, a common practice of his; and in measures 12 and 13 of his passage he ascends on quarter notes. Armstrong repeats notes on motives three other times, on the words "It's not the pale moon," in the pick-up measure through measure 1, on "just the nearness" in measure 6, and on "It isn't your sweet" between measures 8 and 9. Note the five-against-four rhythm that Ella uses on the words "it's just the nearness of" in measure 6 before she lands on the word "you" on the downbeat in measure 7. In measure 6 of his passage, Armstrong implies the word "of" on the third note of a triplet with the barest thrown-off inflection in his voice. He has fun with the lyrics also, twice answering "no" with "yes," in measures 5 and 13.

The album's last selection is "April in Paris" by E. Y. Harburg and Vernon Duke, another tune that Ella recorded a number of times over the years. Taken as a medium-slow ballad she sings a chorus in her most introspective mood of the album; Armstrong follows in an equally heartfelt manner. He adds a third chorus on trumpet and Ella returns, taking it from the bridge to end the track and bring to a close a remarkable session.

Example 3.2: "The Nearness of You" *(Ella and Louis)*

The *Ella and Louis* album did very well, moving high up in the charts. Intent on following up this success, Norman Granz was able to get Fitzgerald and Armstrong back into the studios about a year later. They completed *Ella and Louis Again* in Hollywood on July 23 and 31, and August 13, 1957; and *Porgy and Bess* in Los Angeles on August 18, 19, and 28, and October 14, 1957.

Ella and Louis Again contains 19 tracks and was originally released as a double long-playing album. Oscar Peterson, Ray Brown, and Herb Ellis were joined this time by drummer Louis Bellson in the accompanying group. The quartet playing was once again formidable. Because of the expanded session, Norman Granz programmed 12 vocal duets and 7 solo tracks. Ella is the only singer on "Comes Love," "These Foolish Things," and "Ill Wind (You're Blowin' Me No Good)"; and Armstrong takes "Let's Do It," "Willow Weep for Me," "I Get a Kick Out of You," and "Makin' Whoopee" (the latter discussed in the section on Ellis Larkins in Chapter 9).

The first track on the album, "Don't Be That Way," is also the first duet. The fine Edgar Sampson composition was first performed as an instrumental by Chick Webb and his Orchestra in 1934. In later years, with lyrics added by Mitchell Parish, Benny Goodman would enjoy success with the piece. After Ella states the brief verse, she and the quartet settle into a relaxed groove and she sails through the first chorus. Peterson supplies the fills and Ellis's tasteful comping on the track brings to mind Count Basie's outstanding guitarist, Freddie Green. Armstrong follows with two choruses, and Ella adds vocal fills throughout the second.

The Gershwins' "They All Laughed" is a straight-ahead swinger with no added frills. Armstrong takes the verse freely, after which he and Ella romp through a chorus apiece. To close it out Ella comes in at the bridge again, Armstrong soon joins her in harmony, and they tag an ending. On Vernon Duke's "Autumn in New York," both singers croon lovely choruses, Armstrong follows with a half-chorus on trumpet, and Ella returns to sing it to the end as her partner punctuates with some gentle scatting.

Ella first sang "Stompin' at the Savoy" in 1938 when she was with Chick Webb. She subsequently performed and recorded it many times in the years to come. It was always a hot scat feature for her and the version here is no exception as she and Armstrong have a ball. That this particular take was included at all was the result of a fortuitous break because, as Norman Granz pointed out in the album's original liner notes, this was actually a rehearsal run-through for which the tapes were rolling. Ella swings easily on her first chorus and then gives way to Louis Bellson for a four-bar drum break that shifts everyone into double time. She scats the next chorus, throwing in a brief quote of "Irish Washerwoman" in the process. Armstrong jumps in spiritedly on trumpet, stepping aside only on the bridge to let Bellson pound out eight more measures. Interestingly, Armstrong lets two measures go by after his trumpet solo before he begins scatting another chorus. Consequently, this puts him at a different point in the chorus than the players in the quartet who had continued swinging on after his trumpet solo. Of course, despite the fact that this was a rehearsal take that could have been shelved, there is no real problem here.

As Armstrong scats, both Ella, who has joined in, and the band right the ship seamlessly with scarcely the hint of a hitch. The two singers proceed to wail magnificently through four more choruses, no holds barred, Armstrong shouting encouragingly "One more, Ella!" and throwing in references to Norman Granz, Lionel Hampton, and Atlantic City ("No, we won't talk about that"); and Ella cleverly quoting "Here Comes the Bride" and matching her sidekick lick for lick.

This take of "Stompin' at the Savoy" is enlightening, a magical moment in the annals of recorded jazz. Here is an example of Armstrong, the greatest jazz musician of his time, stumbling ever so slightly, yet without cause for alarm in the company of his brilliant colleagues. It reveals an authenticity to the music that very few, if any, recordings in the artistically mediocre, over-produced pop/rock culture of the late twentieth and early twenty-first centuries could ever hope to achieve. Armstrong was caught up in the excitement that he and the other performers were generating. His insignificant misstep did not necessitate a mad rush to the editing booth. This is the beauty and purity of jazz recordings, or any recordings of merit, before advanced technology and the digital revolution made it possible for instrumentalists or *supposed* singers to sound good on albums that are always "perfect." Listening to authentic recordings—for instance, hearing Miles Davis crack an occasional note, or a young John Coltrane struggle with the fiendish chord progression of Thelonious Monk's "Epistrophy"—is an enthralling experience. Likewise, hearing Fitzgerald and Armstrong create great music together, on sheer talent alone, is pure magic.

On "I Won't Dance," an appealing medium-tempo swinger, Fitzgerald and Armstrong divvy up the verse before taking energetic choruses. Oscar Peterson's four-bar intro paves the way for Armstrong to open "Gee, Baby, Ain't I Good to You" with two choruses on trumpet. He swings with a down-home, bluesy feeling and follows by singing a chorus in a like manner. Ella comes in with two choruses of her own, Armstrong backing her with trumpet riffs on the second. On the Gershwins' "Let's Call the Whole Thing Off," Ella opens with the verse before she and Armstrong swing a chorus each and trade riffs on a third run-through. Both singers burn on Irving Berlin's "I've Got My Love to Keep Me Warm." Eschewing an intro, Ella and Armstrong take off up-tempo from the opening downbeat and do not let up for three choruses. On the album's other Berlin number, "I'm Puttin' All My Eggs in One Basket," Fitzgerald and Armstrong swing with equal abandon at a more moderate tempo.

Jerome Kern composed the music and Dorthy Field the lyrics for "A Fine Romance." After the quartet's four-bar intro sets up this chestnut, Fitzgerald and Armstrong breeze through four choruses and take turns singing on each run-through. Oscar Peterson supplies a steady stream of inventive background licks throughout. On the fifth and final chorus the two singers team up to trade passages before harmonizing briefly to end the track (Example 3.3). Their relaxed repartee is indicative of their compatibility in the recording studio, and of the affection they have for one another—Ella addresses her friend as "Louie" in measure 13. In the first four measures, Armstrong uses his formidable sense of timing and space to break up the melody. Not even bothering to add the preposition "A," he waits until beat three in measure 1 to open with the words "fine romance." Two and one-half beats later he adds "my dear duchess" and then pauses another two beats before stating the words "Two old" to begin the next phrase on the second beat of measure 5. Between measures 9 and 12, Ella sings the lyrics "True love should have the thrills that a healthy crime has" with some very sophisticated off-the-beat phrasing. Both singers speak words for emphasis, Ella in measures 13 and 14 on "we don't have half the thrills" and Armstrong in measure 20 on "woman." Typical of their playfulness, Armstrong finishes a phrase with the word "yes" in measure 27 and Ella responds with a "no" as she takes over in the same measure.

"Love Is Here to Stay" is the last song that George Gershwin composed before his death in 1937. The tune is given a straight-ahead rendering, with no frills attached. The two singers take their choruses, Armstrong follows with another half-chorus solo, and Ella returns to take it out with her partner. "Learnin' the Blues" is taken at a relaxed medium-slow tempo. Fitzgerald and Armstrong croon with lots of feeling and Herb Ellis's soulful guitar fills are a highlight.

Ella and Louis Again was a second masterpiece for the two stars. Compared with their first album, which had more of a laid-back quality throughout the session, it tends to be looser at times, with more sheer doses of high energy—if nothing else, the fastest tempos on both albums were on *Ella and Louis Again*. In any event, while it certainly has several exquisitely gentle moments, its more all-out nature complements the charm and general introversion of its predecessor.

Less than a week after completing *Ella and Louis Again*, Norman Granz had his two superstars back in the studio to commence work on their third collaborative album. This time around, the decision was made to record some of the best numbers from the Gershwin opera *Porgy and Bess*, songs that Granz knew would be perfect vehicles for Fitzgerald and Armstrong. In addition, theirs would be the first jazz interpretation of the opera.

Russell Garcia was engaged as musical director for the production and his scoring called for a large studio orchestra from which the standard jazz sounds could be extracted when needed. Garcia was a good choice for the project. A top Los Angeles arranger and conductor, he was born in Oakland, California, on April 12, 1916, and grew up in the area, attend-

Example 3.3: "A Fine Romance" *(Ella and Louis Again)*

ing Oakland High School and later studying composition at San Francisco State University. He is known primarily for his writing, but he also played trumpet in a number of dance bands early in his career and later recorded albums under his own name in the mid-1950s. He has been the musical director for many jazz and popular artists, including Buddy DeFranco, Roy Eldridge, Oscar Peterson, Anita O'Day, and Stan Kenton. In addition, he has many credits in film and television.

In the original liner notes to the *Porgy and Bess* album, Norman Granz recapped his thinking behind the production:

> In deciding to record *Porgy & Bess,* I felt that our best approach, since we were not recording the entire opera . . . was to use only two voices: thus, I decided that Ella Fitzgerald should sing all the female parts and Louis Armstrong all the male; in fact, I extended my license even further by having Miss Fitzgerald sing "The Buzzard Song," which in the play was sung by a male. . . .
>
> I felt that [Fitzgerald's] combination of jazz feeling for the melody and popular feeling for the lyric filled the requirements precisely as the Gershwins might have intended for a folk opera like *Porgy & Bess.* . . .
>
> Though [Armstrong] may not give it the trained voice that other versions have, he gives it, I think, far more poignancy, tenderness, and feeling—and that, after all, is what a "folk" opera really should have.

Although Fitzgerald and Armstrong recorded *Porgy and Bess* in 1957, its release was delayed, intentionally or not, for almost two years. William Ruhlmann, in the liner notes to *The Complete Ella Fitzgerald and Louis Armstrong,* mentions that "movie producer Samuel Goldwyn, in May of [1957] had obtained the film rights to [*Porgy and Bess*]. . . . Granz denies that he intended any tie-in with the upcoming film. . . . It is also true, however, that their finished album was held back from release until April 1959, two months prior to the opening of the film, at which time it found itself competing against at least ten other newly released versions, several of them jazz renditions." Whatever the case, the Fitzgerald/Armstrong *Porgy and Bess* became the most successful of all the versions, ranking well on the charts and presenting a third triumph for the legendary duo.

BESSIE SMITH

Those familiar with Ella Fitzgerald's career know that she was never considered a full-blown exponent of the blues. She could and did sing blues selections on occasion, but she did not project the exposed sense of despair and gut-wrenching emotion of a typical blues singer. "Like other musicians of her generation, she considered the blues genre to be beneath her," said Stuart Nicholson. "Self-conscious to the point of being embarrassed by her humble origins, she strove to improve herself socially."[13]

Jazz scholars often comment on Ella Fitzgerald's seeming lack of emotional depth. However, to consider this as a delimiting factor in her artistry would be inappropriate. *New York Times* writer John Rockwell offered the following perspective: "She has her limits, areas into which she will not venture. But in her case it seems more accurate to perceive her limits as the clear, precisely focused definition of her artistic personality. For her to push still farther, into areas of confessional Romanticism in which she felt uneasy, would be to shatter her image without substituting anything valuable in its place."[14]

Sarah Vaughan, the exceptional vocalist and a contemporary of Fitzgerald's, offered perhaps the best commentary on how the blues might relate to some popular singers. "I can't sing a blues—just a right-out blues," explained Vaughan, "but I can put the blues in whatever I sing."[15] This remark would have been just as appropriate coming from Ella Fitzgerald. In this regard, Bessie Smith, often deemed the greatest of blues singers, and a foundational figure in the evolution of American popular singing, is a significant *link* to Ella Fitzgerald. Although not as directly influential on Ella as Louis Armstrong or Connee Boswell, Smith's impressive talent and her awareness of the developments in singing, especially those made by Armstrong, did not go unnoticed by Ella.

Smith was born sometime between 1890 and 1900 in Chattanooga, Tennessee. She sang in church and on the street during her childhood and toured extensively during her teen years. "Hers was a genuine talent that had developed under the tutelage of the likes of Ma Rainey, when she began as a singer-dancer on the tent-show circuit," commented writer Daphne Duval Harrison. "When 'discovered' by [singer/bandleader] Clarence Williams, . . . Smith was a seasoned performer with a drive for stardom."[16]

After achieving modest fame, Smith was signed by Columbia Records in 1923. She would become a big star, enjoying many successes and making an excellent living. The legendary impresario, John Hammond, produced her last recordings for the label. Hammond had been a big fan since his mid-teens. "I had her records by then," he said, "and I considered her the greatest blues singer I had ever heard. I still do."[17] Smith's records sold in the millions. Her huge talent and influence earned her the nickname Empress of the Blues. "She drained each phrase of its substance and bathed each tone with warmth, anger, or pathos," said Daphne Duval Harrison. "Through Bessie Smith, the blues were raised to an artform that was to be the hallmark for every woman blues singer who recorded during the 1920s."[18]

Smith, who led a raucous lifestyle, was a heavy drinker with an aggressive, challenging personality. "It was no doubt this easy access to her feelings that made her singing so moving," observed James Lincoln Collier. "She had a grave voice of overpowering weight, excellent intonation, and a superb grasp of the blue notes, which she bent and twisted as if she was tearing at her own heart."[19] Smith's total commitment to a song was almost seductive. The soulful power she generated would enrapture listeners. When the writer Sidney Finkelstein succinctly described blues singing, saying "it requires an artistry of its own . . . [that] depends upon inner human resources, a capacity for the dramatization and projection of a human personality," he could have been writing about Bessie Smith.[20]

Smith worked with many of the foremost musicians of the twenties and thirties, all of whom held her in the highest esteem. Among her finest achievements at Columbia were two recording sessions she did with Louis Armstrong in 1925. Referring to the second session, Gunther Schuller, the eminent composer and conductor, attributed the "harder, more biting quality" in her voice and "an appreciably greater sense of swing" to the influence of Armstrong. This is certainly not surprising, but Schuller goes on to say the recordings "suggest how indebted Ella Fitzgerald . . . is to Bessie for much of her style and vocal quality."[21] This latter statement must be considered in the proper perspective. Certainly, Ella heard the Smith recordings and must have been impressed by them. It is also important to reiterate that jazz and popular singers—like the aforementioned Sarah Vaughan (as well as Ella, and especially Billie Holiday)—often integrate blues elements into their interpretations. Bessie Smith was indeed integral to the evolution of American popular singing and that is why she was a vital *link* leading to Ella. Smith's impact on Ella was significant in that it reflected much of what she (Smith) had assimilated from Louis Armstrong's singing.

Smith was the only major singer who worked into the 1930s by sticking solely with the authentic blues tradition. Unfortunately, in spite of her tremendous talent, Smith would be beset with hard times after the stock market crash of 1929 and the subsequent decline of the recording industry. "When I decided to record Bessie Smith," said John Hammond, "I faced the realities of the record business at its lowest point. . . . Blues records, even by an artist of Bessie's stature, were at the bottom of any list of record sales."[22] The swing movement that had started steadily moving in would pass Smith by. Radio productions and live on-air performances increased significantly and, as historian Lewis A. Erenberg points out, "Smith proved too bawdy for radio's family audience."[23] She trudged on as best she could. Tragically, on September 26, 1937, she died shortly after being in an automobile crash near Memphis, Tennessee.

ETHEL WATERS

Ethel Waters was born in Chester, Pennsylvania, on October 31, 1896. She spent an impoverished childhood there and in nearby Philadelphia. The young Waters enjoyed singing, but loved to dance even more, and she would often fantasize about being an actress. From about the age of 10, she would dress up as best she could, trying to look as old as possible, and make her way into dance halls. Eventually, a friend of her grandmother's who ran a successful dance hall on South Street in Philadelphia agreed to let her in for free if she would teach some of the female patrons how to dance.

On her fifteenth birthday Waters won an amateur singing contest which led to her first professional singing and acting job in Baltimore. "I liked to sing, and getting paid for something I liked, well, that appealed to me," she reminisced. "I couldn't read a note of music, but I guess I was just born singing, because it was no trouble to me to learn any song if someone just played it over once or twice for me."[24] It is striking to note some of the parallels between Waters and Ella Fitzgerald. The difficult childhoods, early love of dancing, and good ears were common to both singers.

Regardless of a lack of any significant training, as well as the fact that she did not have a particularly strong voice or wide range, Waters did possess several attributes that she used to great advantage. She had, above all, excellent tone and wonderful expression. Waters's singing was also enhanced by her personality, sophistication, and command of whatever style she undertook. She could sing the blues and she could also swing. She recorded for the first time in 1921 and would go on to perform and record with many of the stars and bandleaders of the swing era. Music historian and author Henry Pleasants talks of Waters in relation to the early important blues singers:

She thought of Ma Rainey, Bessie Smith and other blues singers as shouters. In her eyes it was the absence of shouting and growling in her own treatment of the same or similar material that distinguished her from her singer sisters. . . . The contrast was noted, and favorably, in the press, including the black press. Certainly it contributed to her success with white audiences. More importantly for her growth as an artist, her independence of the clichés of blues singing left her better equipped than most of her contemporaries to work in other, more widely popular styles.[25]

Waters's influence on popular singing rivals that of Louis Armstrong.[26] She was also astute about Armstrong, sensing the influence that his music would generate. She even recorded, in 1928, a version of *West End Blues*, possibly Armstrong's greatest and most famous performance. Waters had become a huge star, definitely the most popular black woman entertainer of the time. Producer and writer Leonard Feather, who worked with Waters in the late 1940s, remembers her as a courageous nonconformist. "On her early records she was backed by such black giants as James P. Johnson and Fletcher Henderson," says Feather. "Then, at a time when the recording industry was almost totally segregated, she became the first black singer to be supported by all white bands, as early as 1929."[27]

Waters was a singing compendium, knowledgeable of the performers and traditions that preceded her, and intuitively perceptive of the compatibility that American popular song and jazz would enjoy during the swing years. Gary Giddins has called Waters "the mother of modern popular singing; the transitional figure who combined elements of white stars like Nora Bayes, Fannie Brice, and Sophie Tucker with black rhythms, repertoire, and instrumentation."[28]

In addition to her wonderful rhythmic feel and ability to manipulate melody, Waters's articulation was masterful. She was definitely a big influence on Ella Fitzgerald, more so on Billie Holiday. "And I think neither properly recognized [that influence]," opined Phil Schaap. "I think the storytelling need of a song's delivery is understood by Ethel Waters. Ella Fitzgerald delays grasping that at the same profound level that Billie Holiday did. But I think for diction, and for its relationship to where the notes are, and what you've got to do to make those two be married, I think Ethel Waters is a huge influence on Ella Fitzgerald."

Waters would also become a fine actress. Between 1927 and 1959 she appeared in over twelve Broadway productions, as well as nine films. Eventually, Waters's fame as an actress would overshadow her singing accomplishments. She was particular about the roles she accepted, as any good actress should be, and this contributed to her eventually being considered a troublesome coworker. Consequently, she found herself out of acting work in the last half of the 1940s. This was a tough period for Waters and she had difficulty making ends meet. She took singing engagements occasionally, but by this time Ella Fitzgerald was establishing herself as the preeminent hot female jazz singer. Waters understood the situation. "I wasn't too eager to work the clubs, anyway," she said. "Nobody in the world can beat Ella Fitzgerald as a riff singer. Away back in 1929 I'd done a lick on 'I Got Rhythm.' But if I returned to that kind of singing I realized audiences would think I was imitating Ella. My big dream, of course, was to get another play."[29] Waters would not land anything of substance again until 1950 when she starred in the Broadway production of *Member of the Wedding*. Gary Giddins summarized Waters's life, saying "she was a recording star in the '20s, a Broadway actress and personality in the '30s, a film star in the '40s, and the architect and victim of her own myth in the '50s."[30] Waters passed away on September 1, 1977.

In spite of the ups and downs of Waters's career, she remains a foundational figure in the evolution of American popular singing. After her death at the age of 80, *New York Times* columnist C. Gerald Fraser celebrated her life, saying "she was at the head of the long line of black entertainers who achieved recognition, fame, money and success in show business. She triumphed on sheer ability and versatility as a singer and actress."[31]

MILDRED BAILEY

Mildred Bailey (née Mildred Rinker) was born in Tekoa, Washington, in 1907. At an early age her family moved to Spokane, Washington, where she spent her youth. Bailey's mother, who was part Coeur d'Alene Indian, was highly influential in her daughter's introduction to music and early development as a singer. "I spent most of my spare time running through Indian songs and rites with my mother," said Bailey. "I don't know whether this music compares with jazz or the classics, but I do know that it offers a young singer a remarkable background and training . . . you have to sing a lot of notes to get by and you've got to cover an awful range."[32] Bailey was also inspired by the great black singers of the day—including Bessie Smith, Louis Armstrong, and Ethel Waters—as well as by Connee Boswell. Bailey would develop into a highly talented and versatile singer.

Still in her teens, Bailey moved to Los Angeles, where she proceeded to sing in many night spots. When her brother Alton Rinker showed up with his good friend Harry Lillis (who would later become a huge star as Bing Crosby), Bailey used her pull to get them their first vaudeville singing job. Paul Whiteman eventually heard the boys and hired them. In a reciprocal move, the young men hyped Bailey extensively to Whiteman, who promptly auditioned and hired her in late 1929. "Up to that time none of the weaker sex had sung regularly with a jazz band," said Bailey, "and Paul wanted hard [sic] to be first to offer that combination. . . . Paul liked my singing enough to hire me on the spot."[33] This was a significant move by Whiteman, setting an obviously groundbreaking precedent for women vocalists. Six years later, Ella Fitzgerald would get her big break when she was taken on as girl vocalist with Chick Webb and his Orchestra.

Throughout Bailey's four years with Whiteman, she sang with many of the day's top white musicians, including many who had played with the legendary cornetist Bix Beiderbecke. "As a featured vocalist with Paul Whiteman, . . . she became the first girl singer to front . . . a jazz orchestra," noted Henry Pleasants. "More significantly, she and Connee Boswell were the first white singers, male or female, to absorb and master the blues, or rather the early jazz idiom of the black singers of the 1920s."[34]

In 1932, Bailey, with some of the Whiteman band members, recorded a version of Hoagy Carmichael's "Rockin' Chair." It became a big hit, propelling Bailey to fame and leading to her lasting nickname, the Rockin' Chair Lady. This proved to be the highlight of her years with Whiteman. Most of the subsequent recordings she did with the full band would not achieve the quality or excitement of "Rockin' Chair." After leaving Whiteman, Bailey maintained a busy schedule. John Hammond began producing some of Bailey's work, teaming her with a number of leading black jazz musicians in small group sessions.

Through all her work with Whiteman and others, Bailey's voice had assumed the distinctive qualities that would serve her well for the rest of her career. "The early voice sounds uncomfortably dark and deep, influenced in equal portion by the classic blues singers and the white belters of the acoustic twenties," said Will Friedwald. "As she got better her voice grew lighter and lighter until it became delicate and paper-thin but nevertheless solid."[35] Bailey also had exceptional articulation and reliable time. She manipulated a song much the same way that an instrumentalist would, toying with melody and rhythm without losing the essence of the song.

In 1933, Bailey married the vibraharpist Red Norvo. For three years, beginning in 1936, Bailey and Norvo fronted a band, performing the arrangements of Eddie Sauter. This resulted in several beautifully orchestrated recordings that would be highly influential to singers and arrangers. Concurrently, Bailey was also performing in small group sessions. Unfortunately, the grind of all this work had its negative results. "The . . . years she spent with the Red Norvo band nearly finished her," noted Dave Dexter, Jr., in *Down Beat*. "One-nighters, poor bookings, small financial remuneration and the constant war to establish discipline in the band wore Mildred down until she came within an inch of collapsing mentally as well as physically. . . . But that kind of stuff couldn't last. . . . Finally Mildred realized it. When she did, Red and she went separate ways."[36]

The decade of the 1940s was not as productive for Bailey compared to the previous 10 years. However, she still enjoyed a number of successes, including her own radio show for CBS. The decade also saw her suffering from medical problems on several occasions and, in 1949, she finally retired to upstate New York. She would undertake a few more engagements, including an appearance on Bing Crosby's television show, until her death in Poughkeepsie, New York, on December 12, 1951.

Despite her considerable talent, Mildred Bailey never achieved the full-blown fame and fortune of other singers, including some on whom she would wield more than a little influence. She had one foot in the past and one in the future. "As it happened," said Will Friedwald, "she never outgrew the twenties approach to rhythm, and never fully absorbed the new rhythmic language of [Bing] Crosby and [Louis] Armstrong."[37] Bailey was, as Gary Giddins put it, "the key transitional figure between Ethel Waters and Bessie Smith and band singers like Billie Holiday and Ella Fitzgerald."[38]

Although she chose to go in a different direction, Ella definitely listened to Mildred Bailey and admired her talent. Bailey's importance to the development of American popular singing is undeniable. Her time fronting a large band laid the groundwork for women singers and it is in this regard that Ella Fitzgerald had a critical role model. In a tribute to Bailey,

Leonard Feather cited the small number of top female singers present at her funeral and "wondered how many of the absentees realized what the term 'Girl Singer—With Band' owes to Mildred, who virtually brought it into being."[39]

CONNEE BOSWELL

Connee Boswell was a seminal figure in the history of American popular singing. "Few singers have influenced the development of America's everyday songs more than Connee Boswell," said John Lucas in *Down Beat*. "Still fewer have left so deep an impression upon the interpretation of these songs."[40] Among the many great vocalists who acknowledged their debt to her were Bing Crosby and Frank Sinatra—and Ella Fitzgerald.

Connee Boswell, the second of three sisters, was born in Kansas City on December 3, 1907, and raised in New Orleans after her family moved there while she was still young. At the age of three she was afflicted with polio. Although it left her legs paralyzed, she had a strong spirit and would not let her handicap stop her from pursuing her interests and, in later years, from enjoying a wonderful professional career.

Boswell's was a musical household and the sisters learned how to play a number of instruments. Martha, the eldest, became a very good pianist; Connee was most accomplished on the cello, which she studied seriously; Vet played guitar and violin. Through their studies the young girls would become familiar with the music of some of the great classical composers.

The Boswell sisters also sang. This was not surprising since they were constantly exposed to singing from several sources. "There was a barbershop quartet . . . composed of the parents and an aunt and uncle," said John Lucas. "There were also three colored women, members of the household, who sang incessantly. . . . In the streets passed the daily parades. Across the street a phonograph ground out the latest Mamie Smith number."[41] Connee was also inspired by the renowned operatic tenor, Enrico Caruso. "Caruso probably influenced me more than anyone else," she said some years later. "Of course, I don't sound like him, but I used to sit and listen and be amazed by his breathing. Then I'd try and do what he was doing. I'd take a long breath and hit a lot of notes."[42]

The Boswell sisters eventually formed a trio, singing and playing locally as often as they could. They achieved a considerable amount of notice and, by the mid-1920s, made their first recordings. Their popularity was such that they began to do some touring and were heard occasionally on the radio. In 1931, they signed with Brunswick Records, a very prestigious label at the time. The first recordings propelled them to fame, their trio-singing and arrangements virtually unprecedented in originality and quality. Their rapport was phenomenal, their performances exciting and multifaceted. Within the framework of an arrangement, the sisters might scat or they might take turns singing the melody. Their harmonies were at times unexpected, yet completely arresting in their originality. The sisters often ad-libbed spontaneous ideas on the spot, even occasionally during recording sessions.

Concurrent with these early trio successes, Connee Boswell was developing into a major solo singing star, as well as an accomplished arranger. She recorded many tracks on her own in the early 1930s. When performing with her sisters, she sang the lead parts and wrote the bulk of the groundbreaking arrangements, supplying the trio with its real excitement and the newest ideas. Still, she was quick to credit her sisters. "Almost every write-up about [us] says that I made all the arrangements," remarked Boswell. "Wrong. I did make some of them and I used to work wee hours in the morning, but Martha and Vet were loaded with talent and contributed much. . . . The band background, intros, fill-ins, and special endings were usually planned out by me. Some parts were free as the breeze, while others were kept right in the saddle."[43]

Whatever the case, Connee Boswell was an exceptional performer, a unique voice for the times. Bing Crosby, a white performer with immense popularity, undoubtedly reached a larger audience and exerted his own tremendous amount of influence, but Boswell did not take a back seat with respect to originality and overall ability. Boswell and Crosby shared some of the same influences—like Louis Armstrong, Mildred Bailey, and Ethel Waters—and both played major roles in adapting the styles of their heroes to the realm of American popular song. Gunther Schuller assessed Connee Boswell's outstanding talent as follows:

She was . . . remarkable for her early—and, for a white singer, very daring—absorption of black singing styles, especially the blues-singing of Bessie Smith, into what previously and otherwise generally was a field populated by white crooners, vaudevillians, and barbershop quartets. Connee was certainly a pioneer among white singers in using jazz inflection and phrasing, a 'horn'-like approach to singing, a rhythmically spontaneous off-the-beat syncopated swing style, and even what we might call a black-influenced jazz diction. Equally unusual was the use in her arrangements of frequent tempo changes. . . . All of this was absolutely unheard of in the early 1930s.[44]

The Boswell Sisters continued to perform regularly during the first half of the 1930s. However, in 1936, by which time all had married, Martha and Vet decided to retire. Connee went on to have a brilliant solo career. She recorded extensively for Decca Records, appeared in many films, and performed with the biggest stars of the time, including Bing Crosby, with whom she sang duets on a number of occasions. John Lucas commented in *Down Beat* that "the tremendous ease with which she sings . . . is partially the cause and partially the result of her superb phrasing. . . . Every word she sings can be clearly heard and easily understood. . . . Her amazing versatility is the real indication of her ability. Like Bing [Crosby], Connee can put over any type of tune."[45]

In many interviews during her career, Ella Fitzgerald enthused about how she had been affected by Connee Boswell. "I tried to sing like her all the time because everything she did made sense musically," raved Ella. "When I was a girl I listened to all the singers, black and white, and I know that Connee Boswell was doing things that no one else was doing at the time. You don't have to take my word for it. Just check the recordings made at the time and hear for yourself."[46] Referring to Boswell's influence on Ella, Phil Schaap comments: "Articulation and the rhythm of a syllable and maintaining swing. That confluence of three thoughts is a real challenge to a jazz singer. Ella Fitzgerald synthesized Boswell's success in doing it and made it her own."

Boswell maintained a whirlwind schedule during the 1940s and 50s, appearing in movies and on Broadway, performing at major live venues, and eventually enjoying many successes on television. However, having always been a strong advocate for the handicapped, she decided to shift her focus as the 1950s were coming to an end. "She and [fellow singer] Eddie Cantor were among the original founders of the March of Dimes," reported Werner Bamberger in the *New York Times*, "and from 1960 on her appearances were limited to benefits for hospitals and other institutions active on behalf of the handicapped."[47]

Boswell continued to pare down her schedule. Sadly, her husband had passed away in early 1975. Her last performance, in which she sang with Benny Goodman and his orchestra, took place at Carnegie Hall in October of the same year. Soon after, Boswell was diagnosed with cancer and she died on October 11, 1976.

Although jazz scholars and aficionados are cognizant of Connee Boswell's stature, she still remains in the background of general jazz lore, remarkably little having been written about her. The average enthusiast mentions Ella, Billie Holiday, Frank Sinatra, or a few others, when considering the great singers and their contributions. The *New York Times* once reported that Boswell's recordings sold 75 million copies during her career.[48] Ironically, in spite of this widespread popularity, and of the huge influence that she wielded, it may be her very uniqueness and brilliance that brought about her role of unsung heroine. She was so good, affecting so many other top singers, that she has been obscured as a primary source. Consider John Lucas's prescient comments in a 1944 *Down Beat* article:

Connee's influence may be less readily apparent than some, but it has been more pervasive than most. . . . She has never been copied directly. Instead, her influence has been general. Most current singers testify, in one way or another, to the per-

suasion of Connee's pioneer work. Won over unconsciously, not like the followers
of Ella Fitzgerald or Billie Holiday, her converts may never recognize an original
source in Connee. This is largely because her singing depends on no pet tricks, on
no favorite licks, thus making it almost impossible to identify any single feature
of her style taken over by other vocalists.[49]

The twists and turns of jazz phraseology and arranging sprung fresh
from Connee Boswell's performances. If Louis Armstrong was the omnip-
otent father of jazz, leaving his mark on all who followed, then Connee
Boswell was the innovative singer who fused the blues nuances of Bessie
Smith's singing and the jazz vocabulary of the genius Armstrong to create
her own unique style. The other top singers of the time, female and male,
took notice.

With a nod to Louis Armstrong, and a few others, Connee Boswell's
distinctive singing, her way of melding the jazz idiom with popular music,
is clearly discernible in Ella Fitzgerald's early work. Furthermore, it is
really not a mystery that the way in which Connee Boswell was *presented*
during her career also remained embedded in the back of Ella's mind. The
creative touches in Boswell's arrangements, like the tempo changes and
modulations, etc., as well as the varying instrumentation that backed her
on her recording dates, are performance elements that would continually
pop up in Ella's work in subsequent years. Throughout the mid to late
1940s and later, notwithstanding the artistic control that Norman Granz
would have during Ella's greatest years from the 1950s to the 1970s, she
made recordings with all manner of instrumental backing and with multifaceted arrangements that reflected the spirit of Connee Boswell. Ella became the greatest singer of the twentieth century and it is both touching
and exciting to recognize the impact of her strongest models.

Ella's early breaks occurred in 1934 when she won the amateur contest
at the Apollo Theater and in 1935 when Chick Webb took her on as his
girl singer. It is interesting to listen to Connee Boswell's recordings from
these same two years. She was already well-known at the time and had
enjoyed considerable success with her sisters, but her star as a soloist was
really just beginning to skyrocket. The young Ella, on the other hand, was
in the process of making a name for herself, but she would quickly begin
ascending toward the upper reaches of the singing world.

On December 12, 1934, Boswell recorded "With Every Breath I Take,"
a song written by Leo Robin and Ralph Rainger for the film *Here Is My
Heart*. The instrumentation of the studio orchestra on the date is a dance
band (big band) augmented with strings, essentially the type of ensemble
that backed Ella in later years on several albums, including on a large
segment of her *Song Books*. The first half of Boswell's opening chorus is
shown in Example 3.4. Her phrasing is incredible as she literally reshapes

Example 3.4: "With Every Breath I Take"—Connee Boswell (12/13/1934)

the melody in every measure. Motives built around triplets abound in her phrasing. On the words "I think of you with every breath I take," in measures 1 and 2, she sings through two eighth-note triplets within the first four beats. In measure 3, she starts similarly, on another eighth-note triplet, but completes the motive on swinging eighth-notes. In measure 9, she swings through ascending eighth-notes before completing the motive on a triplet rhythm. In measure 11, she starts the motive by attacking the word "on" on the second half of beat one, continues through a combination of sixteenth-notes and quarter-notes, and then ends on a triplet rhythm. Note how, on the words "sigh of despair" in measure 5, and "name of a song" in measure 13, the contour of her lines is identical, but her rhythms vary. In the former instance she jumps up the distance of a minor seventh on a quarter-note triplet; in the latter she rests on a quarter-note before jumping up a minor seventh to an eighth-note triplet rhythm. Another device that Boswell uses is that of shifting words from less stressed beats to stressed beats. For example, on the words "I take" in measure 2, the natural melodic rhythm would suggest that the pronoun "I" be sung on the less stressed beat two, and the verb "fall" on the stressed beat three. Instead, Boswell waits until beat three to sing the words. She does the same thing on the words "for you" in measure 7, starting on the stressed first beat, and on the words "I take" in measure 10, starting on the stressed beat three. Louis Armstrong phrased this way often, and Ella also followed suit frequently in her singing. All in all, this half-chorus by Boswell, loaded with creative flourishes, is a definitive example of exquisitely sophisticated phrasing.

On August 26, 1935, Boswell recorded a version of "I Can't Give You Anything but Love" backed by a small combo called the Ramblers. Again, we have an example of advanced interpretation that could only have turned the heads of other singers. Boswell's first chorus is illustrated in Example 3.5. On the title lyrics, she starts naturally enough, directly on the downbeat of beat one in measure 1, but then hits the word "can't" on the second half of beat two, holds it over to the first note of an eighth-note triplet, and takes "give" and "you" on the remainder of the triplet. In measure 2 she waits until the second half of beat one to swing the word "anything," then holds until the second half of beat four to add "but love" on two quick sixteenth-notes. In measure 4 she starts a motive earlier than might be expected by attacking the word "'Cause" on the second half of beat three and stretching it into measure 5 before adding "that's the only thing," starting on beat two. She does something similar in measure 12 when she sings "your" on beat four and holds through to the second half of beat one in the next measure before adding "happiness" on an eighth-note triplet. Here again is another device that was a staple of Louis Armstrong's phrasing, that of attacking the first word of a motive much earlier than would be expected. In measure 16, Boswell finishes a phrase by singing "has pined for" on a quarter-note triplet and then pauses for a half-beat before continuing on the second half of beat one in measure 17 and swinging the words "Gee I'd love" to begin the next motive. In measure 22, she starts the word "doesn't" on the second note of a quarter-note triplet, holds over the barline, and delays until the second half of beat two to sing the word "sell." Between measures 29 and 31 she completes the chorus by singing the title lyrics on a combination of on-the-beat quarter-notes, sixteenth-notes, an eighth-note triplet, and swinging eighth-notes.

On her second chorus, Boswell doubles the tempo and modulates *down* a whole-step from the opening key of C to the key of B-flat (Example 3.6). The uncommon direction of the modulation and the tempo change are both excellent examples of the original ways that Boswell designed her arrangements. Her chorus is yet another gem of inventive phrasing. She starts by singing "I" and "can't" on quarter-notes placed on beats one and three. The original melody has four words—"I" and "can't," plus "give" and "you"—on four consecutive quarter-notes in the first measure, and the words "anything but" placed on four more quarter-notes in the second measure. To compensate, Boswell speeds up the phrasing in measure 2 by finishing the title lyrics on mostly eighth-notes, so as to fit everything in.

Example 3.5: "I Can't Give You Anything but Love"—Connee Boswell (8/26/1935)

(Ella Fitzgerald starts her second chorus of "Caravan" on the *Duke Ellington Song Book* with the word "night" on four quarter-notes that fall on beats one and three in the first two measures. See the section on Ellington in Chapter 7.) In measures 9 and 10, where the lyrics are normally on ascending chromatic motives, Boswell sings the words "Dream awhile" on a motive that drops down a fifth from F to B-flat and follows up by singing "scheme awhile" on a motive that remains on repeated Fs. From

Example 3.6: "I Can't Give You Anything but Love"—Connee Boswell (8/26/1935)

the end of measure 12 through measure 14, on the words "your happiness and I guess," she phrases exactly the way she did in her first chorus, a la Armstrong, attacking early on beat four in measure 12 and moving through an eighth-note triplet rhythm. Beginning the second half of this chorus, on the words "Gee I'd love to see you looking swell," Boswell shifts up in her range for added emphasis, starting on B-flat and moving down over the distance of a minor seventh to the C below. In measures 22 and 23, on the words "Woolworth doesn't sell," she alters the melodic rhythm nicely, placing "Woolworth" on consecutive on-the-beat quarter-notes and then swinging "doesn't sell" across the barline. Beginning the last 8 measures of the chorus, she once again jumps up and sings on repeated B-flats, this time descending only a fourth through the motive to the F below. For the rest of the passage she stays in this range and, with the exception of measure 28, spends most of the time back on B-flat notes.

Ella Fitzgerald sang "I Can't Give You Anything but Love" often during her career. See the section on pianist Paul Smith in Chapter 9 for her lovely version with him, and the section on Lou Levy, also in Chapter 9, for the version from her famous Rome concert in 1960.

In the 1950s, Boswell recorded exclusively in New York, putting out several excellent albums. On one of these sessions for Decca, *Connee: Connee Boswell with Orchestra Directed by Sy Oliver* (LP DL8356), she sings Hoagy Carmichael's all-time standard, "Star Dust." Interestingly, Ella Fitzgerald, accompanied by Ellis Larkins on piano, sang the same song on a 1954 Decca session entitled *Songs in a Mellow Mood*. (See the section on Ellis Larkins in Chapter 9.) The recordings provide a contrasting view of two artists at the peak of their skills—Boswell, the highly original and influential vocalist of her time, and Fitzgerald, the ardent disciple who would leave her mark as the voice of the twentieth century.

The opening eight measures of each take of "Star Dust" are shown in Example 3.7. On the recordings, both singers employ a significant amount of vibrato; Boswell's is a bit more pronounced. Each puts a lot of feeling into the plaintive lyrics, Ella at a slightly faster tempo. It is fascinating to focus on the middle of the passages, where the singers take the same approach in their phrasing of the song's angular lines. In measure 4, they sing the words "dreaming of a song" using virtually identical phrasing. Both sing the word "dreaming" on eighth-notes that anticipate beat two before descending through the rest of the measure. Boswell holds just long enough so that when she adds "of a song" she throws off two quick thirty-second notes to connect to the low F; Ella uses a regularly-spaced triplet on the same words. In measure 5, both singers use triplet-phrasing on the words "the melody," and in measure 6, both fit the word "reverie" on a descending eighth-note triplet and hold the last note over to the next beat.

In the late 1950s, after Ella's first successes with the *Song Books,* a series of recordings for Norman Granz and Verve that featured the music of some of the great songwriters and lyricists (see the section on the *Song Books* in Chapter 7), Connee Boswell recorded two of her own collections for Design Records, *The Golden Age of Irving Berlin* (DLP-101) and *The Rodgers and Hart Song Folio* (DLP-68). It is perhaps not surprising that Boswell chose the particular songwriters that she did since their works were represented in two of the first four collections that Ella completed, in 1956 and 1958 respectively. Both Boswell albums, arranged and con-

Example 3.7: "Star Dust"—Connee Boswell *(w/Sy Oliver);* **Ella** *(Songs in a Mellow Mood)*

ducted by Warren Vincent, were reissued by Pickwick in 1989 as a CD compilation entitled *An Evening with Connie* [*sic*] *Boswell* (PMTD 16008). Comparisons of the Boswell and Fitzgerald recordings are intriguing because we hear the two singers doing the same repertoire in identical settings. Although Ella was backed by larger ensembles, both singers were working with studio musicians and performing arrangements written specifically for the sessions. Above all, the goal on the respective albums was the same: presenting wonderful songs by outstanding songwriters.

In putting together these celebrations, the singers were left to their own devices within the framework of the arrangements. They could keep a vocal fairly straight ahead or opt for a more adventurous tack. For instance, on Rodgers and Hart's "I Could Write a Book," both Boswell and Fitzgerald present faithful renditions with minimal melodic embellishment. The versions swing, showing that less can often be more. The first half of each singer's opening chorus is shown in Example 3.8. We have here two examples of how a prodigiously talented artist can tell a story while displaying a cultivated sense of melody.

On "Where or When," Connee Boswell's opening chorus is a marvel of rhythmically sophisticated phrasing, a revealing example of why she affected so many singers (Example 3.9). She manipulates Richard Rodgers's melody with grace, always in control, whether swinging steadily or

Example 3.8: "I Could Write a Book"—Connee Boswell *(The Rodgers and Hart Song Folio)*; **Ella** *(The Rodgers and Hart Song Book)*

Connee Boswell

Example 3.9: "Where or When"—Connee Boswell (*The Rodgers and Hart Song Folio*)

playing with the feel by stretching the lyrics into intricate patterns. In particular, note the elasticity of her phrasing between measures 1 and 4, with tuplet figures across barlines on the words "seems we stood and talked like this"; between measures 21 and 22, where she sings "things that happen" on a quarter-note triplet; between measures 25 and 26, on another tricky tuplet; and between measures 29 and 31, where she embeds a quarter-note triplet and a tuplet among off-the-beat attacks. Boswell delivers her lines with ease, making everything sound so natural that the listener follows along comfortably. Above all, her rhythmic freedom, the manner in which she phrases both around and through the beat, reflect the inventive phrasing of Louis Armstrong, whose innovations moved everyone. As she nears the end of her first chorus, Boswell adds one more nice touch, swooping down a major ninth in measure 38 as she ponders who might "know where or when."

Ella Fitzgerald sings a reserved first chorus of "Where or When" that is masterful in its subtlety, an example of economical and tasteful phrasing (Example 3.10). She enters on beat two in measure 1, as did Boswell, and follows immediately with an octave jump, between the words "It" and "seems," down to low F-sharp. Beginning the second A section in measure 11—"The clothes you're wearing are"—she again delays her entrance, this time entering on the second half of beat two on "The," and then continuing through a quarter-note triplet on "wearing are." She adds a little more rhythmic flair to the melodic line—between measures 21 and 22, placing the words "that happen" on a sixteenth-eighth-sixteenth-note figure; and between measures 25 and 26, singing "to be happening" on syncopated rhythms across the barline—before she concludes the chorus. All in all, this is pure Fitzgerald, swinging and inventive while paying proper respect to the tune.

On her second chorus, Ella takes liberties in shaping the music, her singing more in line with Connee Boswell's interpretation. We see here that Ella, similar to a horn player, has used the approach of staying relatively true to the melody in the initial chorus before opening up as the take progresses. Of interest is Ella's phrasing as she leaves the bridge and starts the final A section of the chorus (Example 3.11). "And so it seems like we have met before," she sings, using a combination of intricate off-beat attacks; longer, held notes; and an embedded eighth-note triplet to end the passage.

Boswell and Fitzgerald both sing "Cheek to Cheek" on their Irving Berlin collections, one of the composer's most appealing melodies. When comparing the two versions, it is uncanny how alike the singers sound. More to the point, Ella, on her take, is the personification of Boswell. Despite having already raised the level of popular singing to unprecedented heights, Ella demonstrates that the spirit of Boswell is still with her. This may even be an example of how Ella tried to sound when she

Example 3.10: "Where or When"—Ella *(The Rodgers and Hart Song Book)*

Example 3.11: "Where or When"—Ella *(The Rodgers and Hart Song Book)*

And_ so it_ seems_   that we have____ met___ be-fore__

took part in her first amateur night at the Apollo Theater in Harlem over two decades earlier. On that fateful night, too intimidated to dance in the competition as she had originally intended, she changed her plans and sang songs in the style of Connee Boswell. It would follow then that some-one as influential as Boswell would continue to reside inside Ella's soul. Consequently, it is a nice surprise to get this unexpected glimpse into that soul.

The first A sections of both Boswell's and Fitzgerald's opening choruses are shown in Example 3.12. (The A sections in "Cheek to Cheek" are 16 measures long.) Both singers add their own twists to the melody although, between measures 5 and 7, they use identical phrasing. The most pro-nounced difference is the manner in which they each close the passage, Boswell singing "dancing cheek to cheek" between measures 14 and 15 and Ella stretching the same words through an extra measure.

About seventeen months prior to recording the *Irving Berlin Song Book*, Ella Fitzgerald had completed *Ella & Louis,* the first of three long-playing albums with Louis Armstrong (see the section on Louis Armstrong). For this amazing collaboration, Ella and Armstrong had included "Cheek to Cheek" among the selections. Here is another instance where we can ex-amine the interrelationship of these top artists from a number of perspec-tives. Connee Boswell was Ella's avowed champion, and Armstrong was a primary influence on both women. Although the Ella/Louis recordings predated Ella's Irving Berlin collection, as well as Boswell's, the albums were still contemporaneous, all having been recorded in the three-year span between 1956 to 1959. One interesting distinction is that the playing fields were different. The two Berlin song collections were unrelated ef-forts; the Fitzgerald and Armstrong session was a collaboration that pro-vided opportunities for the principals to feed off one another.

In Example 3.13, we look at the first A sections of Armstrong's and Fitzgerald's opening choruses on "Cheek to Cheek," as we did when ex-amining Boswell and Fitzgerald. Armstrong's singing is relaxed and un-affected, the lyrics spaced apart in the first four measures. He proclaims "Heaven" in measure 1 and allows us to digest that for three beats before he adds "I'm in heaven." He then pauses another three beats until his next entry—"And my heart beats . . . " One might be tempted to attribute the sparseness of his phrasing to physical shortcomings that he was beginning to experience at this stage in his life. Armstrong was 55 when this session

Example 3.12: *"Cheek to Cheek"*—Connee Boswell *(The Golden Age of Irving Berlin)*; Ella *(The Irving Berlin Song Book)*

was made. After the rigors of 40 years of touring and recording, he no longer had the supreme breath control he once possessed. From a purely technical standpoint, these limitations may very well have influenced some of his performance practice. However, the fact remains that Armstrong had always been a unique melodist, letting his unparalleled imagination guide him as he shaped lines. His inventiveness also included an

Example 3.13: "Cheek to Cheek" *(Ella & Louis)*

innate understanding of how to use space, or silence, to create a feeling of expectation or momentary tension. He used phrasing like this throughout his entire career.

In measure 10, Armstrong anticipates the pronoun "I" by a half-beat, something that Boswell did in her take (Example 3.12) and that Ella does on this recording. The practice of anticipating the beat (syncopation), a staple of the swing feel, is not surprising in and of itself. However, after his anticipation of "I" on the second half of beat three, Armstrong holds "I" into the next measure, sustaining the pronoun for two full beats. This prolongation is another way that Armstrong manipulates the cadence of the melody. Boswell and Fitzgerald also incorporated this effect of prolongation into their interpretations, an example being Boswell's anticipation and prolongation of the word "on" between measures 10 and 11 of "I Could Write a Book" (Example 3.8). In a reversal of procedure, Armstrong finishes the phrase by adding the word "seek" on the second half of beat one in measure 11. This deliberateness in completing the motive, of holding back so as to delay a turn of phrase past the expected moment of conclusion, was also a trademark of Armstrong's style that Connee Boswell, and subsequently Ella Fitzgerald, assimilated magnificently into their own singing. Note, for instance, Boswell's delayed entrance of the word "when" in measure 19 of "Where or When" (Example 3.9) and Ella's attack on the word "spend" in measure 2 of "Star Dust" (Example 3.7). Armstrong ends the passage with a device that he used often, singing lyrics on repeated pitches instead of over a melody's original contour. In this case, we hear "dancing cheek to cheek" on repeated A-flats.

Ella's singing on "Cheek to Cheek" is as relaxed and easy swinging as Armstrong's. On the opening lyrics—"Heaven, I'm in Heaven"—she stretches words, swings every syllable, and phrases across the barline. Note also, in measures 9 and 10, how she states the words "the happiness" on a quarter-note triplet that crosses the barline. Overall, she does fill up most of the horizontal space in her passage, but her vertical conception is much closer to Armstrong's. The singers weave their lines through almost identical ranges, the distance between the lowest and highest notes in the respective passages being an octave for Armstrong and a major ninth for Ella.

Irving Berlin's "Cheek to Cheek" has a form that does not follow a common pattern. The chorus, which is a whopping 72 measures long, contains three 16-measure A sections, and is analyzed as an AABBCA pattern. Example 3.14 shows section C from both Boswell's and Fitzgerald's chorus on their respective Berlin albums. Louis Armstrong's playfulness and rhythmic style loom again in a number of places.

Boswell starts by proclaiming "honey," a word not in the original lyrics. In measures 18 and 19 she sings "I want your arms" on repeated G-flats, rather than on the original melody; and she prolongs the words "the" and "will" leading into measures 21 and 23 respectively. She sits on the word "me" for five beats from the end of measure 23 through measure 24, and then drops out for one beat in measure 25 before adding "in heaven."

On the lyrics "arm about you" in measures 19 and 20, Ella swoops down a sixth to attack the latter two words on successive upbeats. Moving into the final A section, she stretches the word "to" into five quarter-note syl-

Example 3.14: "Cheek to Cheek"—Connee Boswell (*The Golden Age of Irving Berlin*)**; Ella** (*The Irving Berlin Song Book*)

lables, but crunches them into the space of four beats between measures 24 and 25—"to-o-o-o-o heaven."

Example 3.15 shows section C from both Armstrong's and Fitzgerald's chorus of "Cheek to Cheek" on the *Ella & Louis* album. Armstrong begins mischievously by proclaiming "Now Mama" before asking her to "dance with me." Both singers attack the word "will," in measure 22, on the second half of beat three, each holding until the next measure to add the words "carry me through"—Armstrong descends a major second and lands on "carry" on beat two in measure 23 before dropping a minor sixth to complete the motive; Ella also descends a major second, but lands on "carry" a half-beat earlier, holds on the same pitch while adding "me" and moving through a quarter-note triplet, and then drops a minor sixth to the word "through." Armstrong finishes the section by attacking the word "It's" on the second half of beat three in measure 24 and holding until the second half of beat one in measure 25 to add the word "heaven";

Example 3.15: "Cheek to Cheek" *(Ella and Louis)*

Ella starts in measure 24 and pulls the word "to" through two quarter-note triplets before finishing with "heaven" directly on beat three in the next measure.

Connee Boswell listened intently to Louis Armstrong, among others, and learned from him. Ella Fitzgerald followed the lead of Boswell and also learned a great deal from Armstrong. Both Boswell and Ella Fitzgerald sang with great joy, their mature ideas flowing seamlessly and naturally, always with a feeling of spontaneity. Neither singer needed to consciously calculate the rhythmic complexity of her lines. Interpretations at such an advanced level were the fruits of a fertile artistry that, in turn, was the product of years of hard work and unwavering dedication.

Connee Boswell is a foundational figure in the history of American popular singing. She set examples that were impossible to ignore for anyone serious about singing. Her articulation, dynamic control, focused intonation, and swinging interpretations established new standards of excellence for her profession. From the time in the early 1930s when she branched off from her sisters to pursue a solo career, many a vocalist altered his or her interpretive approach to conform more closely to the Boswell model. Ella Fitzgerald was an exceptional devotee. As is often the case, the student absorbed the lessons of the teacher, synthesized the information, and advanced to new and greater heights.

BILLIE HOLIDAY

Billie Holiday was born in Philadelphia on April 7, 1915, and spent her early years in Baltimore. During a difficult childhood she was a victim of poverty and child abuse. By the time she was 12, she was earning pocket money by doing general work for the Madame at a local whorehouse. Stuart Nicholson, in his comprehensive biography of Holiday, recounts that "she soon discovered that the principal attraction of working for the Madame was not so much the extra money as listening to the wind-up Victrola left in a downstairs room for the use of patrons."[50] Enthralled with the sounds of jazz, she resolved to become a famous singer.

Louis Armstrong was Holiday's prime influence. She spent countless hours listening to his records and studying the nuances of his trumpet playing and singing. She was moved, as were so many other musicians, by the constant improvisatory nature of Armstrong's performances. She did not copy him outright, but she did assimilate both his sense of rhythmic invention and his free treatment of melody into her singing.

Holiday also paid much attention to Ethel Waters and Bessie Smith. Waters's impeccable diction and storytelling ability made a great impact on Holiday. Bessie Smith's vocal control was inspirational for Billie. Holiday, like Smith, had limited range, but she was enthralled by how Smith could still be so powerfully in command when interpreting songs. Although her voice was not as strong as Smith's—it deepened somewhat in later years—Holiday herself would become masterful at varying dynamics, phrasing, and articulation in her singing.

After moving to New York with her mother in 1928, Holiday began singing around town, working with many different musicians. This served as her advanced education and she listened intently, working diligently to absorb the jazz language. She also began leading a lifestyle in which alcohol and marijuana played prominent and detrimental roles.

Holiday's singing was attracting attention and, in 1933, John Hammond signed her to a contract. He would produce her for the next six years, during which time she worked with many top-notch musicians, including Benny Goodman, Count Basie, Artie Shaw, Teddy Wilson, and Lester Young. Holiday and Young became close friends. "Each recognized the other's talent," said Luc Delannoy in his biography of Lester Young. "It was a simple meeting of two musicians who appreciated each other as soon as their paths crossed."[51] They would also eventually give each other their well-known nicknames: Lady Day and Pres.

Holiday's work with Artie Shaw was particularly significant in that she was a black vocalist working with one of the most popular white bands of the time. Unfortunately, no matter how musical and entertaining the Shaw/Holiday collaboration was, they could not overcome the oppressive attitudes of the time. "Although all mixed bands met resistance," commented historian Lewis A. Erenberg, "mixing race and sex challenged deeper taboos."[52] The widespread prejudice she endured certainly played a part in her eventually leaving Shaw.

In early 1938, Holiday participated in a remarkable event that took place at Harlem's famous Savoy Ballroom. In an exciting showdown, Count Basie's band, featuring Holiday, squared off against Chick Webb's band, whose singer was Ella Fitzgerald, already an emerging superstar. Holiday sang "My Man" and Ella opted for "Loch Lomond." It was a memorable evening and *Down Beat* reported that "the ballot taken showed Chick Webb's band well in the lead over Basie's and Ella Fitzgerald well out in front over Billie Holliday [sic] and James Rushing. . . . When Ella sang she had the whole crowd rocking with her."[53] The result was not surprising in light of the fact that Ella sang with unmitigated joy, her great ability to sing anything and make it swing a sure crowd-pleaser. Holiday was far more connected to her material, often choosing songs with dark messages. In any event, the Webb/Basie match-up showcased two superb singers in top form.

Jazz historian and archivist Phil Schaap enjoyed close friendships with several musicians who worked with Count Basie. Consequently, he has first-hand insights on the development of Ella Fitzgerald in relation to Billie Holiday and the Basie band:

I think that Ella learns about the rhythmic breakthrough of the 1930s through a variety of musical episodes, including as an under-acknowledged one, [drummer] Jo Jones. There is no acknowledgement of Jo Jones being an important musician in Ella Fitzgerald's career, but I'm telling you otherwise. Jo's rhythmic sensibility is part of a change in rhythmic elasticity in jazz in the 1930s, which is a very profound thing, and Ella grasps that and gets it from a number of people. One of them would be Billie Holiday. She sees how Billie Holiday has applied the rhythmic breakthrough of the 1930s to singing per se and jazz singing in a more specific way and she goes there. She learns a lot about relaxation at any speed. Jo Jones . . . told me Ella Fitzgerald seemed to like him. All the Basie-ites . . . mentioned the Jo Jones connection to Ella. . . . I got a lot of very important men in her life talking to me much later and giving me insights into the younger Ella Fitzgerald.

Throughout the 1940s, Holiday maintained a busy working and recording schedule. It was during this period that her singing prowess advanced to its greatest height. Anything she sang became hers; the depth of her feeling was unparalleled. Her intense expressiveness was in stark contrast to the often over-polished deliveries of many popular singers of the time.

Holiday had also begun using hard drugs. She would experience drug- and alcohol-related health and legal problems (including losing her New York cabaret card) for the rest of her career. Consequently, it was not sur- prising that although she had a varied repertoire, much of what she sang appeared to reflect the troubles she experienced. In any event, her singing was acclaimed widely, most importantly by the great musicians with whom she worked. She had a singular style and personality; an ability to convey the essence of what she sang without any unnecessary histrionics. She was always her own person.

In the early 1950s, Norman Granz started managing Holiday. Even though she no longer had her cabaret card, she could still work the larger venues in the New York area. She also toured Europe in early 1954. Sadly, though, Holiday's health continued to deteriorate steadily. The already narrow range of her voice diminished even more. Remarkably, despite her physical problems, she would somehow manage to summon her muse at performances, usually to the astonishment of those present who knew what she was going through.

Billie Holiday passed away on July 15, 1959. It is interesting to note how, although both she and Ella Fitzgerald suffered abusive childhoods and later faced similar oppressive issues during their careers, their lives played out so differently. "Each was the product of a broken home, each suffered years of poverty and each stared racism square in the face in the musical milieu of the 1930s, 1940s, and 1950s," summarized Stuart Nich- olson. "Yet Ella worked her way to Beverly Hills luxury and was still singing in the early 1990s, while Billie Holiday was never able to come to terms with her personal demons."[54]

LEO WATSON

Leo Watson was born in Kansas City in 1898. Although details of his early years are nonexistent, it is most probable that he had no formal training in music. On the other hand, he most likely listened to and was inspired by the blues and popular singers of his time. Leonard Feather, in an *Esquire* article entitled "The James Joyce of Jazz," summarized what little was known about Watson:

Everybody who has followed his career knows him mainly from the era when he loomed into view around 52nd Street [in New York City] with a vocal and instru- mental group called the Spirits of Rhythm. Leo played an instrument called a tiple, akin to a ukelele, but when he sang he would move his right arm up and down as though he were manipulating a trombone slide. It sounded like a surrealistic trombone, too, as this squat, dark, huge-mouthed figure let loose his riot of sound.[55]

Watson was performing his unique style of scatting, a rambling, incessantly energetic mixture of words and utterances. In the liner notes to Volume 3 of *Anthology of Scat Singing*, an excellent series released by Média 7, Philippe Beaudoin dubs Watson "the best of all singers when it came to adapting the sounds of brass instruments to the exercise of scat, whether wa-wa, growl, tonguing, tremolo or flutter-tonguing."[56] Additionally, Watson often cleverly quoted phrases from other songs in his scatting, fitting them into the flow of his improvisations. These were the aspects of his singing, the vocal sounds and the quoting, that most influenced Ella Fitzgerald.

Watson's talents were not unnoticed by other leading musicians of the time. In the late 1930s he toured with Gene Krupa's band for a few months and did some recordings with Artie Shaw. Subsequently, he worked in a number of clubs around New York, drawing attention to his wild, unpredictable behavior. Eventually finding his way to the west coast of the United States in 1940, he continued to perform occasionally, never abandoning his zany behavior. Perhaps not surprisingly, these unpredictable antics could also vex people and he got into trouble on a few occasions.

In early 1945, Leonard Feather, on a business trip to Los Angeles, tracked down Watson and arranged a recording session for him. "Leo . . . sang some of the most fantastic riffs in the world," enthused Leonard Feather. "Back in New York, I played the records to some of the greatest musicians in jazz. They listened not only with amusement, but with profound respect for this man's fabulous talent."[57] Feather was also able to get Watson into the studio again the following year for a date with trombonist Vic Dickenson. In the liner notes for an album on which the session with Dickenson was re-issued almost thirty years later, Feather lamented that "Leo Watson is one of those all too common representatives of the artist who passes through our scene and vanishes almost unrecognized. . . . [He] was one of those rare men in whom the gift of humor was superbly blended with a nonpareil improvisational talent. That he was recorded so little, and that his career and life were so brief, must be numbered among the real tragedies of jazz history."[58]

When Leo Watson died in San Pedro, California, on May 2, 1950, *Down Beat* said that he was "credited with having been the original 'scatman.'"[59] *Metronome* reported that "the music world lost one of its most colorful and broadly gifted members."[60] Watson has become a predominantly forgotten artist, except to die-hard jazz aficionados and researchers, but his importance to the evolution of jazz singing is significant. Without a doubt, he influenced many bop-oriented singers. Ella Fitzgerald, in particular, was attracted to his spontaneity and sense of humor, as well as the spirit of his uninhibited personality. She incorporated into her own singing his use of vocal sounds, his penchant for impromptu lyrics, and his free-wheeling delivery.

Leo Watson was not recorded extensively during his career, but at least a good amount of the studio work he did complete has been reissued on CD. On his first recording with The Spirits of Rhythm in late 1933, he did a take of "I Got Rhythm." Written by the Gershwins for the 1930 musical *Girl Crazy*, Watson's version may well have been the first to include scatting. It was not, however, the first pure jazz recording of the number, Louis Armstrong having previously cut it with his big band in November 1931. On that session, Armstrong did not sing, but opted instead for an arrangement in which he first introduced the band members as they took brief solos and then blew his own hot chorus.

After the Gershwins composed "I Got Rhythm," the song took on a life of its own, becoming one of the standards of standards and absolutely required knowledge for any musician seeking to be considered a legitimate improvising artist. For detailed background information on the song, see the section on Nelson Riddle in Chapter 7.

Leo Watson (and Louis Armstrong) recorded "I Got Rhythm" when it was still very young, so his version is based on the harmonies of the swing era and not the more complex chords that the beboppers would use in later years. Taking the tune at a brisk tempo, he swings through an opening chorus and guitarist Teddy Bunn follows with a solo. Watson then returns to scat a second chorus (Example 3.16) revealing some of his stylistic trademarks that would so captivate other singers over the ensuing years. Between measures 1 and 6 he starts by riffing a short motive three times. Typical of how an instrumentalist might play these same licks, his phrasing includes ghost notes, pitches that are suggested within the flow of the passage rather than attacked directly. From the end of measure 8 through measure 12, he continues his riffing with two longer motives in succession. He also adds a blues tinge to his licks by using the pitches of D-flat, A-flat, and G-flat; respectively the lowered third, seventh, and thirteenth in the home key of B-flat. Between measures 17 and 20 he adheres to the original contours of the melody but changes the rhythm to quarter-note triplets. He also humorously alters his vocal timbre, constricting the muscles in his throat to produce an affected, almost babyish sound—"ya ga ga/ga ga ga." From measure 25 through measure 28, he belts out a staccato pattern that is rhythmically precise and clearly articulated. Watson was entranced by drums and his rat-a-tat-tat delivery in this passage is clearly percussive in nature.

Watson's impressive display of scatting is followed by another guitar solo. On the last chorus the musicians sing in harmony and trade fours with the guitar for half a chorus, Watson takes the bridge alone, and the

Example 3.16: "I Got Rhythm"—Leo Watson (1933)

track closes with everyone harmonizing again. This was quite a debut recording for Watson with The Spirits of Rhythm. His sophisticated rhythm, instrumental approach, vocal sounds, and humor would not go unnoticed by other singers.

Ella Fitzgerald's only recorded version of "I Got Rhythm" is the one on her *George and Ira Gershwin Song Book* album, released by Verve in 1957, 24 years after Watson's recording. Ella's opening chorus on that track is discussed in the section on Nelson Riddle in Chapter 7. The first half of her scatted second chorus is shown here in Example 3.17. Although musical director Nelson Riddle backs her with an arrangement built on the more involved bebop chord progression for "I Got Rhythm," Ella's scatting reveals elements that clearly suggest Leo Watson's tendencies. For example, in measures 7, 8, 9, 11, and 14, she produces ghost notes among her scat syllables that, throughout the whole example, reflect Watson's vocabulary—he utters "da da duh de da da duh da"; she scats "da da da ba do da." Ella starts the chorus with simple riffs, her lines clean, her harmonic implications clear. In measures 5 and 6, she sings a lick comprised of four mini-motives using the half-step interval between B and C. In measure 8 she adds the blues flavor to the last motive of the passage, singing a B-flat, the flatted seventh in the home key of C, before resolving it down a half-step to A, the thirteenth. At the top of the second eight

Example 3.17: "I Got Rhythm"—Ella *(The George and Ira Gershwin Songbook)*

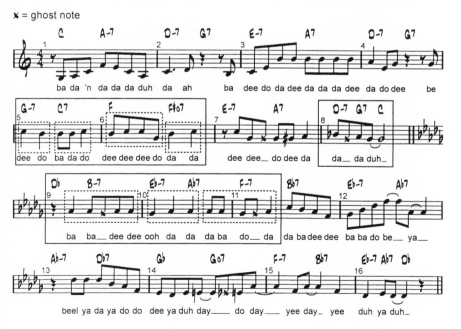

measures, the chart modulates up a half-step to the key of D-flat. In measures 9 through 11, Ella leads off again with a lick built on smaller components, in this instance, short motives using the step between A-flat and G-flat. This latter passage sounds like a slower rendition of Watson's drum impression—perhaps Ella's scatting represents a tom-tom, whereas Watson's represents a snare drum.

On his recording of "Ja-da" from a recording session on August 22, 1939, Watson is backed by a septet, although the Masters of Jazz CD, *Anthology of Scat Singing,* lists the ensemble as Leo Watson and his Orchestra. The cover for the original sheet music of "Ja-da" has a photo of three servicemen on it, including the composer Bob Carleton, and an inscription that reads: "The sale of this song will be for the benefit of the Navy Relief Fund. The Society that guards the home of the men who guard the seas." Ella Fitzgerald never recorded this novelty number, but Watson's remarkable version further illustrates the aspects of his singing that influenced her.

Omitting the verse, and after an eight-bar intro, the musicians swing through the 16-bar chorus eight times. In the opening chorus (Example 3.18), Watson, in measures 3 and 4, 7 and 8, and 15 and 16, runs the lyrics "Ja-da Ja-da jing jing jing" on repeated pitches, rather than on the predominantly step-wise contour of the original melody. This is something that Louis Armstrong often did in modifying melodies as he sang.

Example 3.18: "Ja-da"—Leo Watson (8/22/1939)

Obviously, Watson noticed, as did Ella Fitzgerald and any number of other singers. This is more closely illustrated in Example 3.19.

On the second chorus, Watson begins throwing in the occasional scatted phrase among the lyrics. On the next run-through the band plays mostly melody while he scats background licks. Next comes reed-man Paul Ricci's chorus on clarinet, an unexpected gem of a solo by a historically obscure but talented player who happened to be on the scene in the heyday of Benny Goodman, Artie Shaw, and a few other first-rate clarinetists.

Watson takes over again at the fifth chorus, shown in Example 3.20. His mature scatting here is something to behold. In measures 3, 6, and 7 he executes descending glissandos of a fourth, a minor third, and a major second respectively. The glissandos was a prime tool in the vocal arsenals of Ella Fitzgerald and other scatters. On the last half-beat of measure 7, Watson hits a B-natural and holds it through to the next measure in which the harmony is a C dominant-seven chord. As a result there is a split second of dissonance before he resolves the phrase to the expected B-flat by way of consecutive approach tones. Here, as he often did, he incorporates a harmonic twist in his scatting that jazz instrumentalists regularly used and that the upcoming generation of beboppers would expand upon exponentially. In measures 9 and 10, Watson quotes "Jingle Bells," displaying both his ability to draw from unexpected sources and his humor in doing so. Interestingly, he creates momentary dissonance again, as the last three A-naturals in measure 9 are not part of the A-flat diminished

Example 3.19: "Ja-da"—Leo Watson (8/22/1939)

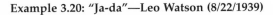

Example 3.20: "Ja-da"—Leo Watson (8/22/1939)

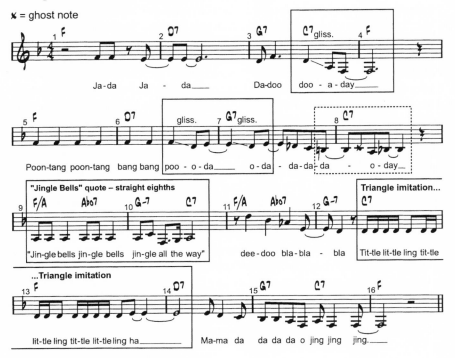

harmony. For a final display of virtuosity, from the second half of measure 12 through measure 13, Watson does one of his instrumental impressions, again related to the percussion family, by simulating a triangle on rapid sixteenth-note figures while he utters "tittle little ling" three times. Apparently satisfied, he exclaims "ha" before moving on to end the chorus. In a mere 16 measures he has produced a variety of delights that is a testament to his prodigious talent.

Watson's enthusiasm is boundless and he soars on, scatting another inventive chorus during which he utters "Well all right, do you dig, do you dig?" On the ensuing seventh chorus he lays out to allow for trumpet and guitar solos. With everyone completely buzzing now, Watson jumps in to scat yet one more chorus and a burning version of "Ja-da" comes to a close.

The aforementioned recording date pairing Leo Watson with the Vic Dickenson Quintet took place on September 7, 1946. Leonard Feather, who was obviously delighted with the results, remarked that "Watson and Dickenson, whether alone or trading fours, make for some of the most delightful, humor-tinged chemistry imaginable."[61]

One of the tracks, titled "Tight and Gay," is credited as being composed by Feather. In reality, it is simply an opportunity for the musicians to blow over the chords of Cole Porter's "Night and Day." Whatever the case, the chemistry among the musicians that Feather mentions is certainly evident. Without laying down a melody, Watson enters scatting in top form, the opening of his chorus shown in Example 3.21. In addition to his obvious inventive phrasing, we get an indication of his better-than-average range. He starts on his highest note in the passage, a B in the middle of the staff in the first measure, and eventually makes his way to a low E-flat in measure 15. There are also several instances in this example that illustrate Watson's logic in designing passages. For instance, he pops a syncopated two-note figure, spanning a fourth between the last half-beat of measure 2 and the second half of beat one in measure 3. He inserts this idea again between measures 6 and 7 and in measure 8. Although the figure spans a minor third on the two latter occurrences the similarity and interrelationship of all three as a unit is evident. For added effect, Watson articulates grace notes in the third instance. There are two other excellent examples in this passage of Watson's strength at developing motives. First, although not quite identical in rhythm, he repeats motives on similar pitches in measures 5 and 6. Later, in typical bop fashion, he states a motive in measures 9 and 10, and then transposes it down to accommodate the changing harmony in measures 11 and 12.

Example 3.21: "Tight and Gay" ["Night and Day"]—Leo Watson (9/7/1946)

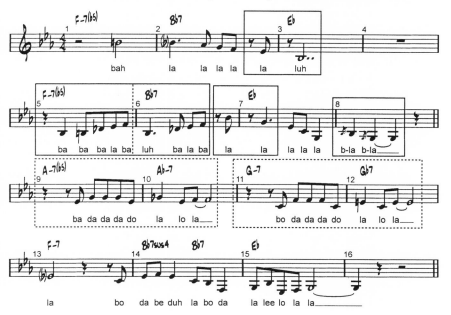

Following Watson's chorus, Vic Dickenson and guitarist Arv Garrison take strong solos. A second scatted chorus by Watson, on top of Dickenson's compatible trombone fills, ends yet another striking performance by the unique singer. A truly original vocalist with a zany personality that matched his wild singing, Leo Watson resides in the background of jazz lore. Fortunately, his singing has survived, not only on a few recordings that are still available, but also in the souls of many singers, past and present.

Watson's influence is clearly evident in Ella Fitzgerald's work. It was obviously an influence that was only a part of the equation in her development, but it was an especially significant part with respect to her scatting. Ella had creative and technical powers matched by few, if any, other singers. These powers included the uncanny ability to assimilate the best and most useful of what she heard in other musicians. The elements she got from Leo Watson would fully supplement and enrich the additional innovative ideas and musical vocabulary that she would acquire through her association with Dizzy Gillespie and other beboppers in the years ahead.

CHAPTER 4

The Chick Webb Years

His breaks and solos flowed; they exploded, like small arms fire and cannons going off.

—Burt Korall[1]

Chick Webb was born in Baltimore on February 10, 1909. Raised in impoverished circumstances by his mother and grandfather, he dropped out of school around the age of nine so he could work selling newspapers to help support the family. While still very young, he acquired a passionate desire to play the drums, a result of observing musicians in parading bands. Writer Burt Korall, in his book *Drummin' Men*, recounts that the youngster "played on pots and pans, garbage cans, marble stoops, and iron porch railings ... long before he earned enough money by selling newspapers ... to buy a secondhand set of drums."[2]

Webb's dedication was striking in light of the fact that, during his youth, he had suffered a severe back injury that would henceforth prevent him from growing properly. As a result, he became hunchbacked, with pain and physical problems that tormented him for the rest of his life. Nonetheless, he persisted with his intense practice regimen—his family also hoped that his drumming might help him gain back some strength—and by his early teens he was landing jobs with different jazz groups.

Webb moved to New York City in 1924 and immediately became active in the musical activities of the city. He participated in jam sessions, grabbed any performance opportunities that came his way, and gradually gained a reputation as an accomplished, up-and-coming drummer. In fact, it was none other than Duke Ellington, who was often approached by club owners seeking musicians, and who fully recognized Webb's impressive ability, that recommended the drummer for his first engagement as a bandleader in early 1926 at the Black Bottom Club, a newly opened Manhattan night spot.

Unsure at first, Webb relented and dove zealously into his duties. His total commitment, coupled with an undaunted spirit, paid off. He was an exceptional drummer, leading an ensemble that steadily matured into an accomplished jazz orchestra, with which he would achieve considerable success. Burt Korall explains that "Webb slowly put the pieces together as the 1920s became the 1930s. The band played the Cotton Club uptown, and the Strand Roof, Roseland, and later the Casino de Paris downtown. The drummer and his men toured with the show 'Hot Chocolates'; they performed in theaters and made records with Louis Armstrong. And they began making records on their own."[3]

Webb strove to improve the sound and identity of his band. In order to take maximum advantage of his core of strong players, he realized that it was necessary to upgrade the quality of music that he presented. He began engaging some of the top composers and arrangers on the scene to contribute to the band's repertoire. Among these writers were Benny Carter, Don Redman, George Bassman, and, perhaps most importantly, the very talented Edgar Sampson, a saxophonist in Webb's ensemble. Sampson would later write for Benny Goodman, contributing significantly to the successes of Goodman's band.

Webb's careful organization of repertoire and band personnel was inspired, but the widespread fame that he so desired eluded him. Undaunted, he pressed on, relentless in his desire to excel and always giving of himself completely whenever his band played. In this regard, the dominant factors underlying the diminutive drummer's growing professional stature were, in fact, his superior talent and his ability to inspire strong performances. He infused intense swing and feeling into the band's playing. Webb awed his drumming colleagues, as well as the listening public, through his masterful execution, sense of time, inventive musical ideas, unbridled energy, confidence, and matchless showmanship. "Chick's hi-hat work and his general approach to powering a big band set standards that were copied by a multitude of drummers right through the Swing Era," said Mel Tormé. "[H]is records have become a correspondence course for hundreds of drummers."[4] John P. Noonan suggested in *Down Beat* that Webb's dynamic control was central to his inspiring drum performances: "He is a past-master of the art of shading on drums. His playing drops to 'nothing' and up to a frenzied roar, as the arrangement demands."[5] One of the most succinct assessments of the drummer's playing was provided by writer Gary Giddins when he commented that Webb "may well have been the first jazz drummer to convey complicated emotions, at least on record."[6]

Among Webb's performances were his appearances at Harlem's famous Savoy Ballroom where his band reigned as champion of the legendary battles of the bands that were staged there. "Chick . . . knew how to take charge of his band," recalled writer George T. Simon. "He was a very sharp, aware little man, kind and generous but surprisingly rough and tough with people who tried to cross him. For Webb had been around a long time . . . [specifically] around the Savoy Ballroom . . . since 1928, when the management had seen his band cut down those of Fletcher Henderson and King Oliver and had offered him the house-band job."[7]

One of Webb's biggest breaks occurred in the latter half of 1929 when Moe Gale, head of Consolidated Radio Artists, signed the drummer. Now Webb could look to Gale, a major player in the management field, to guide him in his business affairs. The drummer was able to commit the bulk of his energies to leading engagements at prime venues in downtown Manhattan, as well as in Harlem, where he continued to square off in the big-band battles.

The landmark event for Webb occurred early in 1935 when his vocalist Charles Linton persuaded him and a representative of Moe Gale's agency to listen to a promising young singer, Ella Fitzgerald, who was just shy of her eighteenth birthday at the time. Gale had been looking for a girl vocalist to perform with the band and Linton had found Ella through the help of a friend. After considerable hedging—Webb didn't like her physical appearance at all—it was agreed that she would audition with the band during a two-week run at the Savoy Ballroom. Things went well and she impressed everyone on hand, leaving no doubts about her vocal prowess. Webb, still hesitant about using her on a regular basis, finally acquiesced at the insistence of other musicians who heard her and recognized that she was something special.

This recounting of how Ella came to sing with Chick Webb is drawn from research by Stuart Nicholson.[8] For years, the story had been that Webb agreed to hire Ella after hearing her sing with his band at Yale University. Nicholson, who had undertaken meticulous research and conducted myriad interviews for his biography of Fitzgerald, essentially lays the apocryphal event to rest. Ella, however, always stuck to the Yale version:

The guitar player with Chick Webb told Chick Webb about me and he said he didn't want no girl singer. So he took me to Yale with the band and he said, "If they like her, okay." And at that time I had won about four or five amateur contests so I sang the three numbers that I knew—"Object of My Affection," "Judy," and "Believe It Beloved." And at Yale, it was a prom—they liked me, so I got the job with the late Chick Webb.[9]

It would seem that Ella should be the best authority on what really happened, but she simply may have preferred to stick with the more glamorous account of appearing at the prestigious university. Like the great Louis Armstrong, who always maintained that he started scatting because he dropped the sheet of lyrics while recording "Heebie Jeebies," she knew a good story when she heard one.

From the outset, Ella fit in remarkably well with Webb's band, her talent impressive for someone so young. "Fitzgerald had an added advantage in dealing with musicians: she was clearly one of them," said Will Friedwald. "Long before she was out of her teens, her perfect time and command of the beat made her no less of a joy for the Webb sidemen to play with than for the Savoy audiences to dance to."[10] This was noteworthy in light of the Savoy's importance as a showcase venue for Webb. Years later, Duke Ellington would offer his perspective on Webb's performances at the famous locale: "You can dance with a lot of things besides your feet. . . . Chick Webb was a dance-drummer who painted pictures of dances with his drums. . . . The reason why Chick Webb had such control, such command of his audiences at the Savoy Ballroom, was because he was always in communication with the dancers and felt it the way they did. And this is probably the biggest reason why he could cut all the other bands that went in there."[11]

Adding Ella Fitzgerald to the mix provided a huge lift for Webb and his career, giving him the opportunity to finally make himself known outside the important, but relatively small, jazz establishment. He knew his singer was special, an incredible talent completely compatible with his band and music, and the star that would spearhead expanded fame for them. Before long, Ella would be included on almost every number that Webb performed, live and on record. Webb was intent on taking advantage of the situation to the fullest extent. Because he was already working on radio broadcasts, which was the best way to be heard and to enlarge one's fan base, Webb began loading his repertoire almost exclusively with the popular songs and lighter fare of the day. While the raw energy and excitement that the band could generate were still heard on occasion, predominantly in live performances, Webb now saw to it that the band featured mostly selections and arrangements that would attract a more extensive listening base. "In commercializing his band for the broadest possible appeal," noted Stuart Nicholson, "Webb was focusing on white America, the constituency that could provide the biggest paychecks."[12]

With Ella as an attraction, Webb's radio performances and live engagements increased considerably. The two stars rose to the summit of popularity and acceptance. *Down Beat* reported in March 1937 that "Chick Webb and his orchestra, featured on the NBC sustaining program, Good Time Society, receive an average of 5,000 fan letters a week."[13] Three months later, after Webb had topped Benny Goodman in one of the most astounding and remembered band battles to take place at the Savoy Ballroom,

Down Beat raved again: "When Ella Fitzgerald made her bow as the 'Queen of the Swing Singers', the thousands of people linked arms and swayed back and forth in rhythm with the music. . . . Chick Webb may wear his success as a fitting crown for Harlem's true 'King of Swing.'"[14] Gene Krupa, the brilliant drummer who propelled Benny Goodman's orchestra, and who graciously admitted defeat at the hands of Webb, never hesitated for the rest of his career to acknowledge Webb's overwhelming mastery and influence.

Unfortunately, just as things were going so well for Webb, his health began to deteriorate seriously in early 1939. Afflicted with fluid in his spine, as well as with kidney trouble, his musical activities also began to suffer. The courageous drummer, who had never let his ailments stop him from pursuing a busy and ambitious schedule, was finally forced to stop in his tracks. On June 16, 1939, he could hold on no longer. The music world lost a vibrant and innovative artist who passed away tragically at the height of his success. At his funeral in Baltimore, huge throngs of people would mourn the beloved and brave little man who for a time had been the greatest big-band drummer around.

Webb's passing was a sad affair, but the harsh realities of the music business precluded any lengthy period of mourning. Ella Fitzgerald and the band were soon back to work. Moe Gale wanted to continue benefitting from the singer's fame and decided to establish her as the de facto head of the band under the billing of Ella Fitzgerald and her Famous Orchestra. The day-to-day affairs would actually be run by Taft Jordan for the rest of the year, then by Teddy McRae from the beginning of 1940. From the outset of the new venture, problems beset the musicians, the most notable being the reluctance of the cost-cutting Gale to provide adequate financial arrangements for them. In addition, performances continued featuring Ella singing predominantly undistinguished lighter fare.

The group, however, plowed on with its full schedule of live engagements and recordings for the better part of the next two years. During this period, in late 1941, Dizzy Gillespie, who had just stopped working with Cab Calloway, joined Ella and the band for a brief time. "I played a couple of weeks with them in a place called Lavarge's in Boston, and then came back to New York," recalled Gillespie.[15] All through this period, the band's internal strife continued to take its toll. These lingering problems, coupled with both the looming war and an imminent musicians' union ban on recording, finally produced insurmountable obstacles. Ella Fitzgerald and her Famous Orchestra ceased operations at the end of July 1942.

It had been a memorable run during which Chick Webb and Ella Fitzgerald established themselves as headliners. Ella had matured from a highly talented young singer into a seasoned professional. Although it is true that the quality of material she performed did not progress significantly, the point is often unjustly overstated. No doubt, in the course of

her association with Chick Webb's band, her overall recorded output was
not comparable to the best jazz that was coming out of the big band era.
However, Ella's singing was exemplary and Webb's band was an accomplished and exciting unit. There are certainly more than a few fantastic
moments in the Webb/Fitzgerald discography.

From the outset of her work with Webb, Ella Fitzgerald exhibited vocal
clarity, as well as crisp diction and articulation, which were always on the
mark. Her intonation was sure and her range already considerable. She
benefited immensely from her experiences with Webb: further honing her
skills, establishing her credentials, and showcasing her formidable and
groundbreaking talent to an ever-expanding audience.

It is often pointed out that the girlish quality of Ella's voice that listeners
heard during her years with Webb—she had just turned 18 when she took
part in her first recordings—remained with her thereafter. Henry Pleasants puts it succinctly: "Ella has never entirely discarded either the girl or
the sound."[16] Interestingly, because Norman Granz claimed at the time
that Ella was born in 1920, Pleasants incorrectly states that she was 14
when she started with Webb. In any event, much has been made of her
lasting young-girl personality, almost to the point of overstating what is
now obvious to anyone who is familiar with her work. Still, it is certainly
difficult to avoid acknowledging this side of Ella because, in addition to
the fact that there was indeed a natural youthfulness to her voice, she was
also sincerely unpretentious and she continued to exude an obvious joy
and purity of heart whenever she sang for the rest of her career.

Ella fit in so well with Webb that she never disrupted his principal
mission of fronting a top-rank dance band. It was because of her quick
rise to popularity and her overriding importance to the band's success
that many of Webb's most impressive instrumental numbers were never
recorded. His band was comprised of excellent musicians who played
well-crafted arrangements at a high standard of execution. However, fully
aware of Ella's impact, it did not behoove anyone to alter what had become a winning formula. It was this formula that limited Ella's opportunities to sing music of a more sophisticated nature—but she was young
and energetic, and equally fantastic with the lighter fare. Her material
improved appreciably over time, but Webb stuck mostly to his routine,
filling programs with popular tunes and novelties, or songs that were
taken at faster-than-normal tempos to accommodate the jitterbuggers.

Almost all of Chick Webb's recordings, from his earliest dates through
the years with Ella Fitzgerald, have been reissued on CD. The most comprehensive collection, containing almost the complete discography on a
series of chronogically ordered compact discs, has been released on the
Classics label.

Ella recorded over 120 selections during her association with Webb—with Chick Webb and his Orchestra, with Ella Fitzgerald and her Savoy Eight (a smaller unit with Webb and sidemen drawn from the orchestra), and as the de facto leader of Ella Fitzgerald and her Famous Orchestra (after Webb's death). An excellent representation of this body of work, 85 selections, can be heard on the Decca set entitled *Ella Fitzgerald: The Early Years*. Released in two parts—each part is a double-CD collection—the set provides a fascinating overview of Ella's early development.[17]

On each of the first few selections that Ella recorded with Webb, she sang only after the band launched the arrangement with the opening chorus. This was typical of how band singers, up to this time, were considered auxiliary components within the whole performance, or as Geoffrey Mark Fidelman describes it, "ornaments to the festive musical package of their band."[18] The situation began changing for Ella rather quickly because of her impressive ability, as well as the fact that she was obviously a crowd pleaser. In relatively short order, she was being written more prominently into the arrangements. A good example would be "Sing Me a Swing Song (and Let Me Dance)," composed in 1936 by Hoagy Carmichael to lyrics by Stanley Adams, and recorded by Ella on June 2 that year, slightly less than 12 months after she started with Webb. In the arrangement, she follows the band's eight-bar intro by singing the verse and the opening chorus. After some brief ensemble riffing that includes a mind-boggling two-bar drum fill by Webb, she is back trading fours with the band for the first half of a second chorus before closing out the take. On this track, Ella's singing is the principal feature of the arrangement. Although the routine of her entering only after a chorus or other blowing passages by the ensemble would remain common for the rest of her association with the band, here was an indication that this format would be altered from time to time. This was a sure sign of Ella's rising stature; whatever she sang fit seamlessly into Webb's overall presentation.

The early recordings also present clear indications of Louis Armstrong's influence on Ella. For instance, the sweetness in her voice and her loose but ingenious phrasing on "Shine;" her altering of the melody on "Darktown Strutters' Ball" by repeating pitches in several instances, rather than sticking to the original contours of the lines; are a definite nod in Armstrong's direction. Additionally, examples of Ella's first forays into scat singing are heard on the Webb recordings. She scats on "Mr. Paganini," "Organ Grinder's Swing," "Just a Simple Melody," "Deedle-De-Dum," and even throws in a few brief licks on the minor-tinged "Bei Mir Bist du Schoen," a song that a number of singers, as well as Benny Goodman, would further popularize. Ella can also be heard digging into the blues on "Gulf Coast Blues" and crooning lovely renditions of ballads like "Stairway to the Stars" and "I Got It Bad (and That Ain't Good)."

To this day, the impressive interpretive skills that the young and rela-

tively inexperienced Ella exhibited during her Chick Webb years remain
a marvel. Excellent examples of her inventiveness are heard on the two
songs by Vincent Youmans that she recorded in a December 1937 session.
On the first, "I Want to Be Happy," with lyrics by Irving Caesar, Ella sings
a wonderful chorus in which she clearly illustrates her mature sense of
rhythm in virtually every measure (Example 4.1). Starting off the first A
section, she manipulates the opening phrase on the title lyrics by attacking
the pronoun "I" on the second half of beat one in measure 1, sitting directly on the beat for the lyrics "want to be," and syncopating the two

Example 4.1: "I Want to Be Happy" (Ella with Chick Webb)

syllables of "happy" in measure 2. Note how differently she handles this same motive at the beginning of both the second and third A sections. In measure 9, she begins by attacking the word "Life's," again on the second half of beat one, then sustaining it to the beginning of a quarter-note triplet on beat three, reversing the motive's direction on the word "really" by descending through the remainder of the triplet, and finishing with the words "worth living" by attacking on the second half of beat one in measure 10. In measure 25, she starts with the pronoun "I" on a middle C, once again on the second half of beat one, and continues with the lyrics "want to be" on the same pitch, and on the beat, before syncopating the two syllables of "happy" in measure 26. On the lyrics "till I make you happy" in measures 5 and 6, every word is sung off the beat. In measures 17 through 20, Ella sings the lyrics "When skies are gray and you say you are blue" in a phrase that combines both syncopation and straight time. She stretches the word "smiling" through ascending quarter notes between measures 22 and 23, and she ends the chorus with an unexpected octave leap between the words "you" and "happy," instead of between the syllables of "happy," as originally composed by Youmans.

"Hallelujah!," with lyrics by Leo Robin and Clifford Grey, was the second Youmans song that Ella and Webb recorded in the late-1937 session. Ella's chorus is full of nice touches, but the last eight measures are particularly noteworthy (Example 4.2). Between measures 25 and 27, she twice runs the title word "Hallelujah" through engaging eighth-note patterns that sound as if they might have been borrowed directly from a classical etude. From the second half of measure 28 into measure 29, she reverses the original motive by descending through the words "Helps to shoo." In closing the phrase, she attacks the word "clouds" on the second half of beat two in measure 30 and delays stating the word "away" until the downbeat of measure 31, instead of placing the first syllable on beat four of measure 30 as in the original.

Ella uses ingenious phrasing in these eight bars and it is intriguing to see her interpretation alongside the melody as Youmans composed it. In

Example 4.2: "Hallelujah!" (Ella with Chick Webb)

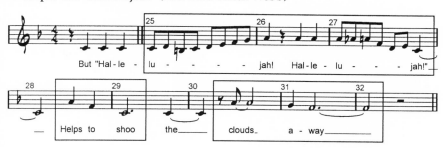

Example 4.3, the two lines are placed one above the other, clearly illustrating Ella's clever improvising skills.

What stands out about the young Ella's work with Webb was that she
established a legitimacy with whatever she sang—as she would throughout the rest of her career. While it is undeniable that there were some truly
banal selections scattered among the many sides she recorded in her early
career, she never flinched. In fact, the greatest triumph that she and Webb
enjoyed resulted from their recording of "A-Tisket, A-Tasket," a nursery
rhyme that she particularly liked. She had persuaded Van Alexander, one
of Webb's staff arrangers, to adapt it for the band and Webb immediately
programmed it for one of his radio broadcasts. He subsequently included
it in performances on the road and, as a result of its consistently positive
reception, it had become apparent that the number could be something
special.

Webb and Ella recorded "A-Tisket, A-Tasket" on May 2, 1938, and it
soon was a runaway smash hit for them, the only recording they did in
their time together to rise to number one on the charts. The nursery rhyme
tells of a young girl who drops a brown and yellow basket while on the
way to show it to her mother. It is picked up by another girl and the rest
of the story is a lament for the lost basket. The recording was an indication
of how Ella could put her stamp on virtually anything and make it a
personal success. "From coast to coast young girls were copying Ella,
sometimes note for note," related John Hammond.[19]

"A-Tisket, A-Tasket" is set in the key of A-flat major, although Ella shifts
into A-flat minor for a short stretch later in the arrangement. The first

Example 4.3: "Hallelujah!" (with Chick Webb)

eight measures of her opening chorus are shown in Example 4.4. In telling us she lost the basket, Ella converts the simple line into an infectious swinging passage.

"I dropped it, I dropped it/Yes on the way I dropped it/A little girlie picked it up and put it in her pocket," continues Ella. It is not difficult to understand the appeal of this number. It was unquestionably a novelty piece, but Ella's youthful voice, coupled with her natural and charming innocence as she delivered the uncomplicated words and catchy melody, were highly attractive to the general listening public. As a result of this recording, her popularity skyrocketed, making her one of the music world's most beloved singers.

Van Alexander's arrangement of "A-Tisket, A-Tasket" contains a full bag of tricks. Toward the end of the track, Ella engages in her first of two exchanges with the band members—EF: "Oh dear, I wonder where my basket can be."/Band: "So do we, so do we, so do we, so do we, so do we."/EF: "Oh gee, I wish that little girl I could see."/Band: "So do we, so do we, so do we, so do we, so do we" (Example 4.5).

Example 4.4: "A-Tisket, A-Tasket" (with Chick Webb)

Example 4.5: "A-Tisket, A-Tasket" (Ella with Chick Webb)

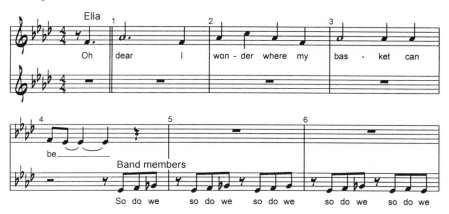

Ella continues with her lament—"Oh why was I so careless with that basket of mine?/That itty-bitty basket was a joy of mine."—and closes the take after her second exchange with the band members: Band: "Was it green?"/EF: "No, no, no, no."/Band: "Was it red?"/EF: "No, no, no, no."/Band: "Was it blue?"/EF: "No, no, no, no, just a little yellow basket/A little yellow basket."

Although Chick Webb is a somewhat forgotten figure in the annals of jazz, that does not diminish the fact that he was a superb drummer, with few rivals, who fronted one of the finest black ensembles of his time. In the course of exerting a tremendous influence on other players, he was pivotal in shaping the approach to big band drumming during the 1930s. Sadly, due to his debilitating medical problems, his time as a bandleader lasted only 13 years.

Ella Fitzgerald was undeniably the catalyst, the dominating talent without whom Webb would not have progressed as far as he did. For four years under the dynamic drummer, and for three more years as the nominal leader of the band after his death, Ella's singing captured the attention of the listening public, as well as her contemporaries on the music scene. By the end of this whirlwind seven-year run, she had established herself as an exciting and supremely talented vocalist.

Fortunately, the substantial body of recordings by Webb and Ella are readily available. More than a little of the music they made together was of a high caliber and virtually all of their output was well-crafted and entertaining. Chick Webb and his Orchestra rocked Harlem's famous Savoy Ballroom, standing proudly as champions of the legendary battles of the bands and giving the dancers who pounded the floorboards all they could hope for. Chick Webb and his Orchestra, featuring Ella Fitzgerald, rocked the whole music world—and, incredibly, Ella would continue to perform and record for another fifty years.

CHAPTER 5

The Bebop Influence

The origins of Fitzgerald's vocal improvising were rooted primarily in instrumental models, not vocal ones. And particularly the instrumentals at that point where swing and bebop meet. She coined an uncanny and remarkably abstract vocabulary ... that expressed the most subtle nuances of jazz improvisation—its attack, smears, curves, phrasing, vibrato and pulse. ... In mimicking virtuosity, she came to possess it.

—John McDonough[1]

For Fitzgerald, when the mood was upon her, scat was an opportunity to display astonishing inventiveness and startling agile and sustained vocal technique.

—Bruce Crowther and Mike Pinfold[2]

In the first half of the twentieth century American popular music consistently conveyed a sense of the positive, regardless of concurrent social or political forces at work. From World War I on, past the Depression years, and through World War II, jazz-tinged sounds endured, entertaining the public and providing welcome relief in difficult times. During this period of over twenty years, the musical messages were delivered primarily by the big bands. Sadly, the inevitable consequences of World War II, like the fuel shortage and the higher cost of living, in combination with an unstable music industry that was still recuperating from the turmoil of a major strike by the musicians' union in the early 1940s, made it a certainty that the overwhelming majority of the big bands would not survive. (For more information on the big bands see Chapters 7 and 8.)

After the war, as America's consciousness underwent wholesale changes, the musical climate was also transformed dramatically. With the demise of the big bands, it was natural for the young instrumentalists of the day, then regrouping in smaller configurations, to explore different ways of expressing themselves. The adventurous musicians were formulatng new approaches to harmony and melody. They composed original pieces or reinvented established songs, in either case adding chromatically altered pitches to the chords and designing radically contoured lead lines. Needless to say, this quickly took the music out of the general public's realm. It also met with disapproval from many older, established musicians who had cut their teeth on the tunes of the early jazz stars or the songwriters of the musical theater, and who were not interested in redefining themselves. "Early jazz and swing had been allies of popular music from Broadway and Tin Pan Alley," commented writer William G. Hyland. "Now bebop was virtually the enemy."[3]

The musicians who led the way in the development of bebop are legendary, among the finest creative artists in American, and world, cultural history. Players like trumpeter Dizzy Gillespie, alto saxophonist Charlie Parker, pianist Thelonious Monk, and drummer Kenny Clarke, as well as several other equally gifted individuals, forged a musical language with precepts and structural components that remain fundamental to all current musical expression.

Much of the rebellion against the bebop school of music was simply a manifestation of the natural reaction that occurs when radical ideas impinge on what is familiar and conventional at any particular time. The great Louis Armstrong, the most important American musician of the twentieth century, was also affected by the bebop movement. He was no longer the primary model the young musicians of the day were studying and assimilating. In retrospect though, members of the new breed were actually taking what had been passed on to them by Armstrong in the first place and expanding on it. In any event, because of his brilliance, and of the fact that he was beloved worldwide, Armstrong survived. He continued to entertain by playing his own way, but he clearly was not enamored of modern music and he was not hesitant to make his feelings known. In an article he wrote for the *Jazz Review* in 1960, he was forthright in his assessment of the developments in music:

Of course there have been many different styles in music . . . such as bop—Music of tomorrow—"progressive," "cool," etc. All these different new styles of this day doesn't do anything for the up + coming [*sic*] youngsters . . . to derive on, like the old timers did for us. . . . I myself has been . . . trying to figure out what the modern musicians trying to prove. And the only solution that I came to is, the majority of them are inferior musicians. . . . The results is a very few musicians are working nowadays. The public itself gotten so tired of hearing so much modern slop until they refused to continue paying those big checks.[4]

In fairness to Armstrong, it is important to note that he was perceptive enough to recognize a top-notch musician when he heard one—and not so set in his ways as to deny respect when it was warranted. Conversely, he was held in the highest esteem by the younger players who fully recognized his monumental importance. "Louis Armstrong was also a great innovator and a great bearer of a message," said Dizzy Gillespie, "and, at one time, every trumpet player in the world, everybody who wasn't in a classical band, had to be influenced by Louis Armstrong. Louis not only influenced trumpet players, he changed the modus operandi of music by inventing the solo."[5] Miles Davis, another superstar jazz trumpeter and a uniquely original voice, enthused that Armstrong "was just a beautiful guy. . . . I can't ever remember a time when he sounded bad playing the trumpet. Never. . . . I just loved the way he played and sang."[6]

The debate over bebop notwithstanding, there were significant numbers of critics, writers, and jazz fans, as well as musicians young and old, who were excited by the ideas and creations of the beboppers and who came to embrace them wholeheartedly. Ella Fitzgerald was among this group. She was still with Chick Webb when Gillespie and his cohorts were beginning to formulate their new methods in the mid to late 1930s. Gillespie had also worked for about a month in Boston with Ella in late 1941 when she was fronting Webb's band after Webb had passed away.

That Ella was attracted to bebop should be understandable. First of all, she had the phenomenal ear, the gift to grasp intuitively whatever she heard. Secondly, her vocal skills, her tremendous articulation and flexibility, would enable her to execute the trickier rhythms and contours of the music. "She would pick up on whether it was a Louis Armstrong or Bird [Charlie Parker] song, or whatever it was—she could duplicate it. She picked up on ideas, original ideas," commented her long-time publicist Virginia Wicks. This first became evident when, on October 4, 1945, she recorded "Flying Home" on a studio date under the musical direction of Vic Schoen. Ella's scatting on the track clearly reveals her assimilation of the bebop language. Her phrases are built on the newer, more sophisticated harmonies. She also throws in a number of quotes of other songs during her improvising.

In November 1946, Moe Gale, Dizzy Gillespie's manager, booked the trumpeter and his big band a tour and added Ella to the bill. "I think really the first experience I had of really getting to know Dizzy was when I traveled on a tour with him," she recalled. "That's actually the way I feel I learned . . . bop."[7] During the tour, she began singing a scatted version of "Oh, Lady Be Good," further demonstrating her impressive ability to sing in the bebop idiom. This exciting number became a mainstay of her repertoire for the rest of her career. "[Dizzy] was the cause, one of the reasons I started singing 'Lady Be Good,'" said Ella. "To me it's been an education with Dizzy, and I always felt close to him, and he always called me 'Sis,' you know."[8]

Ella's first tour with Gillespie was obviously a great pleasure for her, as well as an important learning experience. She heard firsthand how he and his sidemen expressed themselves in both formal concerts and jam sessions. The sounds left an indelible imprint on her and, as was always her miraculous way, it did not take her long to start incorporating the bebop nuances into her singing. Interestingly, Alyn Shipton, in his comprehensive biography of Dizzy Gillespie, downplays the impact that this first tour with the trumpeter had on Ella:

It is hard to see in terms of Ella's long-term output that there was really any lasting effect on her natural style from the tour with Dizzy's band of boppers. Claims have been made on the basis of one or two airshots that her harmonic language was irrevocably altered by the experience, but, with the exception of one or two passing notes, the main contribution of the tour was to add overtly bebop lyrics like 'Oop Bop Sh'bam' to her repertoire, and for her to shadow Dizzy's horn during scat choruses on "Lady Be Good."[9]

Ella's harmonic language may not have been "irrevocably altered" during her first short stay with Gillespie, but she certainly latched onto the bebop concepts and was moved almost immediately to begin transferring some of the unique sounds that she was hearing into her performance arsenal. The process may not have been completed, but it was well under way by the time she finished the tour. "Ella, I like for her impeccable tonality and her sense of rhythm," said Gillespie. "She thinks like we do with those licks that she sings. That's from the bebop era. She listens and she does all our licks. She learned that after she got with me, going on the road."[10]

Milt Gabler, Ella's producer at Decca, heard her sing "Oh, Lady Be Good" in a live performance and decided to bring her into the studio to record the number on March 19, 1947. Backed by a studio band under the direction of Bob Haggart, the recording was another winner, a major hit for Ella. That summer, Decca released "Oh, Lady Be Good" in a pairing with "Flying Home," Ella's earlier scat sensation, and the double treat also received rave reviews. Ella continued to tour on and off with Gillespie throughout 1947 and in September of that year, when the trumpeter made his Carnegie Hall debut, Ella was accorded a similar honor by being booked with him. Charlie Parker was also on the program as a special guest. The concert was a huge success and received positive reviews all around.

Scatting became a permanent fixture in Ella's performances over the years. "Those bop musicians like Parker and Gillespie have stimulated me more than I can say," said Ella. "I've been inspired by them and I want the whole world to know. Bop musicians have more to say than any other musicians playing today. They know what they're doing."[11]

Ella's discography contains many exciting examples of her bop-oriented scatting. Her improvising is always right on the mark, her lines adhering to the harmonies on which they are based. This is what sets Ella apart from all but a tiny handful of the other singers, past and present, who have ever scatted. Her improvising was *accurate*—not close, not pretty good, but completely accurate—and captivating. As the twenty-first century unfolds, singers on the scene tend to be stylists, some excellent, but the vast majority who include scatting in their performances are in the "close" or "pretty good" categories at best. Of those singers who scat with authority, certainly Jon Hendricks, the great veteran, and perhaps two or three others, including Darmon Meader of the New York Voices (who, significantly, also happens to be an accomplished jazz saxophonist), come to mind. Is the art of scatting dead? No, it isn't—and it shouldn't be. It is an available and valid component of singing that can be exciting and entertaining—but any singer, in addition to being blessed with a strong voice, must attain an *executable* level of musicianship, both intellectual *and* auditory, that includes the same advanced theoretical skills expected of any accomplished instrumentalist.

Ella Fitzgerald's vocal flexibility was unparalleled, and she created lines as appealing as those produced by top professional instrumentalists, despite her lack of any real knowledge of practical theory—but she heard everything, period. Even if she had not been such an overridingly private person and had occasionally opened up and been willing to try and explain her performing methods, she still would not have been able to analyze theoretically how the chord progression in a song worked, or how what she was singing fit onto the harmony. She simply had the *big ears*, and her scatting was sophisticated and precise—and hip.

Furthermore, Ella always kept her audiences entranced no matter how adventurous she got in her performances. It didn't matter whether she was playing in a club in front of jazz aficionados or in theaters for large audiences who simply loved good singing. Her skill in entertaining was such that she could program scatted numbers with standards, blues, ballads, pop ditties, Latin tunes, or whatever, and never fail to please.

It has often been pointed out that Ella had a reservoir of proven material that she could draw from as needed, specific routines or lines and passages in some songs that she could and would sing the same way, or very close to the same way, anytime she programmed the numbers in a performance. Indeed, what performer doesn't have his or her own personal bag of musical devices? What is infinitely more significant is that Ella executed her material at a level that was unattainable for virtually any other singer. Whether often repeated or completely spontaneous, her licks were breathtaking, pleasing to hear, and technically demanding, requiring an artist of her extraordinary ability for their realization. She expanded this material, not relying on it as a quick fix, but instead using it as a supplement while she conjured new and exhilarating ideas. She was constantly reworking the music she sang, applying her killer phrasing and rhythm to create mini-adventures on any tune she tackled.

Picking highlights of Ella's scatting is easy—almost any of her recorded tracks yields something wonderful. Still, there are a few solos at the top of the list that merit special consideration, tracks on which Ella achieves a magical level of accomplishment. Two early examples are the aforementioned versions of "Flying Home" and "Oh, Lady Be Good" from the late 1940s. Ella's most famous recorded example of scatting is her spectacular version of "How High the Moon" from her appearance in Berlin on February 13, 1960. This concert in the German metropolis represented a landmark performance for Ella and yielded what has become one of the seminal recordings in the annals of jazz and American popular music. The album, *Ella in Berlin: Mack the Knife*—the CD re-issue is titled *The Complete Ella in Berlin*—earned Ella the Grammy for "Best Pop Vocal Performance, Album, Female." She also won in the category of "Best Pop Vocal Performance Single Record or Track, Female" for her version of "Mack the Knife" on the same album. (For a detailed discussion of *Ella in Berlin*, see the section on Paul Smith in Chapter 9.)

In Berlin, Ella was accompanied by pianist Paul Smith, guitarist Jim Hall, bassist Wilfred Middlebrooks, and drummer Gus Johnson. After taking the first chorus of "How High the Moon" at a relaxed medium groove, Johnson's four-bar break doubles the tempo and Ella blasts off for six minutes of continuous scatting, 10 choruses and an extended vamp of sheer firepower. Her soloing is a post-doctoral clinic in the art of bebop, setting the bar so high for singers that one can only hope to be around if and when somebody ever manages to come even close to that level.

Charlie Parker based his classic "Ornithology" on the chord progression to "How High the Moon" and, in tribute, Ella uses her third chorus to quote Bird's tune, a nifty feat because of the angular lines and advanced rhythms of the bop composition. On her fourth chorus she throws in an ingenious quote of Duke Ellington's "Rockin' in Rhythm" and closes playfully with extemporaneous lyrics: "Though the words may be wrong to this song. . . . " She continues with hot riffing and never goes for too long without interjecting more quotes—it's the "Irish Washerwoman" during her sixth chorus and "Stormy Weather" in the eighth chorus. In her ninth chorus she makes up lyrics to let the people in the audience know she hasn't forgotten them: "I guess these people wonder what I'm singing. . . . " During her tenth chorus she gives a nod to her Chick Webb days by squeezing in lines from "A-Tisket, A-Tasket" before ending by crooning "I guess I better quit while I'm ahead."

Ella now segues into a prolonged vamp during which she weaves notes from the top to the bottom of her vocal range. At one point she utters some wildly buzzing, sub-toned sound effects on her lowest notes. There is also more quoting as she throws in hints of Gershwin's *American in Paris*. Next, she travels to the other side of the world, singing "High, high, high . . . " in a Middle Eastern scale. Nearing the end, she and the quartet cool down momentarily for an abbreviated version of "Smoke Gets in Your Eyes." To top off the adventure, Ella ends this astonishing vocal romp on a high B-flat above the staff. The crowd goes wild.

On March 26, 1965, Ella performed in Hamburg, West Germany, accompanied by Tommy Flanagan and his trio mates, bassist Keter Betts and drummer Gus Johnson. Ella had appeared in Hamburg several times before and was adored by the audiences there. On this particular night she was in her usual peak form and, fortunately, Norman Granz produced a recording of the concert and titled it appropriately *Ella in Hamburg*. "There's a magic about Ella Fitzgerald," wrote Jack Maher about the concert, "She has that electric quality that marks all the great ones—Chaplin, Garbo, Armstrong, DiMaggio, Valentino. . . . She creates an atmosphere that is charged with human understanding."[12] The CD reissue is currently available only as a Verve import, but it is well worth the higher price. The program is typical for Ella during this period of her career, a mix of the old and the new. There are wonderful standards, "That Old Black Magic," "Body and Soul," "Here's That Rainy Day," and "Angel Eyes"; a Duke Ellington medley; the well-known bossa nova "The Boy [Girl] from Ipanema"; a burning rendition of the children's song "Old McDonald Had a Farm"; The Beatles' "A Hard Day's Night"; and the folk song "Walk Right In."

Ella also does some scatting on the blues, in this case getting into it on Arnett Cobb's instrumental "Smooth Sailing." The specific tune, however, is really inconsequential since the chord progression would be the same on any blues, with the melody serving as a means, leading into the soloing. Her first two solo choruses are shown in Example 5.1. She bases her improvisations on the harmonies typical to the bebop progression for the blues. An indication of this occurs in both choruses in measure 8 where the A-flat pitch in her lines would function as the flatted-seventh on the B-flat chord, which would be present at this point in the more traditional swing-era progression, and as the flatted fifth or flatted ninth respectively on the D-minor and G-dominant chords of the bop progression shown here.

At the end of the first chorus, between measures 9 and 12, she nails an incredible passage, laden with sixteenth-notes, which clearly demonstrates the unsurpassed flexibility of her vocalizing. In musicians' parlance, this is called doubling up, or the practice of creating the effect of

Example 5.1: Scatted improvisation on the blues *(Ella in Hamburg)*

✗ = ghost note

speeding up by doubling the expected amount of notes in a passage. A sophisticated line built on swing eighth-notes would also have worked well here, but in this case Ella chooses to cram twice as many notes in by building the lick on sixteenth-notes. This is a device that Dizzy Gillespie, Charlie Parker, and all the great beboppers used often to add excitement to their solos. Ella does this with her voice, without faking anything, her lines very much in the idiom and completely accurate in relation to the underlying chords.

Ella's singing at the beginning of her second chorus once again demonstrates how she understood the advanced language of bebop. Her very first pitch is an E-natural, or a chromatic pitch not directly related to the key of this blues, B-flat. On a B-flat dominant chord, E-flat is the fourth degree, or eleventh of the chord, a pitch that a singer or instrumentalist would not sustain because it would obscure the intended chord sound. The E-natural that Ella sings here is the raised fourth, or sharp-eleventh, of the B-flat dominant chord. This chromatic alteration eliminates the tonal ambiguity that would occur if the natural-eleventh were used and adds some bite to the sound. In musical terms, this is known as the lydian sound and is considered a sophisticated texture. Ella also moves from the E-natural by half-step up to the fifth of the B-flat dominant chord and continues this chromatic shift of moving by half-step to chord tones four more times in succession through the descending line. The resulting pattern, having started on the sharp-eleventh, is very hip. Also in the second chorus, between measures 5 and 7, and again between measures 9 and 10, Ella uses repeated motives, or riffs, to shape her lines, a practice common to both the swing musicians and the beboppers.

CHAPTER 6

Norman Granz

Granz, more than any other single force in jazz since the war, has consistently supported those artists that form the mainstream of the jazz tradition, those artists whose roots are life-deep in jazz and without whom there could have been no modern jazz, cool or turbulent.

—Nat Hentoff[1]

Norman Granz's achievements and influence as a jazz impresario are extraordinary. Having raised jazz to unprecedented levels of acceptance on the concert stage, both in the United States and abroad, Granz's impact on America's indigenous music remains unmatched. His importance to Ella Fitzgerald in particular was enormous. Under the close supervision of the indomitable Granz, Ella performed and recorded profusely, progressing from a top jazz star to a world-renowned icon of both jazz and popular singing. "[Granz] had an undeniably keen eye and ear for great players and singers, particularly those who had not received the recognition due them," remarked singer Mel Tormé. "Ella Fitzgerald and Oscar Peterson are two examples of jazz greats who might have remained 'cult' artists had not Granz taken them under his managerial wing and guided them into becoming huge commercial successes."[2]

Granz was born in Los Angeles on August 6, 1918, and grew up in Boyle Heights, an integrated neighborhood in the city. His family was not particularly well off and moved frequently so his father could find work. Despite the difficult circumstances, Granz made it through Roosevelt High School and was accepted at UCLA. During his college years he worked in a brokerage office where he earned money to pay for his studies and where he also began acquiring the business acumen that would subsequently serve him well as a music promoter.

After a stint in the U.S. Army Air Corps in late 1941, Granz spent a short time in New York City in early 1942. During his stay there, he immersed himself completely in the city's unrivaled jazz scene and listened to as many of the leading players as possible. Returning to Los Angeles, he undertook his first efforts as a promoter by organizing jam sessions at a local club. In this regard, he was the beneficiary of considerable assistance from Nat Cole, the great pianist he had previously befriended, and the brother of Lester Young, Lee Young, a drummer and bandleader he had met recently. The three spent much time together and Cole in particular was instrumental in introducing Granz to the important personalities and inner workings of the black jazz scene in Los Angeles. As a result, Granz was able to book Cole and Lester Young, as well as other top players, for his jam sessions. However, Granz had eventually to curtail his music activities after being served his official army draft notice. When, in 1943, he was able to obtain a discharge on an obscure technicality, he went back again to Los Angeles and commenced working in earnest, organizing jam sessions.

Although an ardent jazz fan, Granz indicated to John McDonough of *Down Beat* that his primary motivation for wanting to become a promoter was "as much out of a sense of social outrage as a love of music."[3] Granz could not tolerate the prevailing attitudes of the time. "Black musicians were playing all over Los Angeles in the early '40s, but almost entirely to white audiences," he said. "This was because there were very few places that welcomed blacks as patrons."[4]

Granz soon persuaded a prosperous Los Angeles club owner to allow him to stage jam sessions weekly on the one night that the club was closed. McDonough has pointed out that Granz promised good-paying audiences, but also "attached four conditions to his offer: one, integrate the audiences; two, pay the musicians; three, put tables on the dance floor so people would listen instead of dance; and four, allow integrated crowds the other six nights of the week."[5] The weekly jam became such a hit that other club owners quickly jumped in line offering their open nights for similar events. Granz, ever the opportunist, was now maintaining a full schedule as a jazz promoter.

In 1944, Granz began presenting jazz concerts on a larger scale, featuring big name players who would already be in town playing with touring bands. It was not long before the budding impresario was intent on further broadening the scope of his musical productions. The opportunity arose when Granz staged a benefit concert at the Philharmonic Auditorium on July 2, 1944, in support of a group of young Mexican-Americans who had been arrested in connection with the notorious Sleepy Lagoon murder case. "There were so many kids accused that it smacked of a prejudice case," recounted Granz. "I didn't know what the hell was going on with the case, but it did seem to be a prejudice case, and this was a chance to try out one of my ideas."[6] The exciting concert featured several top-rank players, among them Nat Cole and Illinois Jacquet. The event was a rousing success and Granz began presenting Jazz at the Philharmonic (JATP) on a regular basis in the nation's premiere theaters and auditoriums. Thereafter, whenever and wherever he obtained bookings, he stood firm, sticking to his ultimatum that the musicians would not play if the crowd was not integrated.

In addition to staging the JATP concerts, Granz had also been recording them. When he ultimately procured an agreement with Asch Records to release Volume I of JATP, it sold approximately 150,000 copies to wide acclaim. Encouraged, Granz committed to continue presenting and touring with JATP. In 1947, he also founded his first of several record labels, Clef Records, making arrangements to be distributed by the larger and well-established Mercury Records. John Hammond, an incomparable talent scout and record producer, appreciated the achievements of Granz. "Norman, whose career in jazz and whose musical tastes in many ways match my own . . . is a business man, which I am not, a self-made millionaire through his shrewd management of jazz artists and the company he established to release records of his concerts," declared Hammond. "Norman and I first met when he was releasing his records through Mercury. He has done more to improve the lot of jazz musicians than anyone."[7]

JATP concerts featured staged jam sessions performed by consistently outstanding rosters of both swing and bop players. Audiences were usually enthusiastic, although occasionally unruly, and the music critics could be harsh. D. Leon Wolff was particularly scathing in a *Down Beat* review following one JATP concert: "Everything that is rotten in contemporary jazz was to be found in this musical catastrophe. . . . Every . . . congenital idiot in Chicago was on hand, apparently."[8] Granz, who never backed down, was quick to respond the following month: "You see, it's obvious that [Wolff] is an aesthetic snob of the worst sort . . . and is not at all really and honestly concerned with improving the audience's critical standards. . . . I'm getting sick and tired of these so-called critics who, in an effort to explain their aloneness in critical reaction, insist on belittling the public. Sure, my show is predicated on pleasing as many people as possible. I make no bones about that."[9]

Granz plowed on undaunted—and he continued to experience periodic frustrations. After a poorly attended concert in his home town in early 1947 he was very disappointed. "I'm through with Los Angeles forever," he complained. "I'll never play here again if they beg me."[10] Of course, Granz was emoting and, in spite of his exasperation, he was incapable of giving up.

Granz received a surefire career-enhancing boost when he began including Ella Fitzgerald on his concerts after initially underestimating her talent. She appeared in her first JATP performance on February 11, 1949, beginning a lifelong association with the ambitious promoter. This was a monumental step for both individuals. Granz benefitted from the appearances of a great singer and Ella started an association with someone who in the years ahead would change her life and make her a bigger star than she could have imagined.

Granz severed his ties with Mercury in 1951 and went on independently with Clef. Over the next few years he would form two more small recording labels, Norgran and Down Home. He also took JATP to Europe for the first time in 1952. "[He] went his own way through the 1950s, ignoring new trends and recording many of the best and, ironically, least well known of the older jazz stars," said John Hammond. "As impresario he assembled casts of memorable players from the 1930s and 1940s . . . putting on concerts in the finest halls and seeing to it that everyone who worked for him was well paid, well treated, and well appreciated."[11]

In early 1954, just after the expiration of Ella's latest contract with Moe Gale, her manager since the mid-1930s, she took advantage of the opportunity to move on. "Ella Fitzgerald has signed a long-term personal management contract with Norman Granz," reported *Down Beat*. "*The Jazz at the Philharmonic* impresario thus takes over the reins held for more than 15 years by Moe Gale."[12] Granz also paid off a considerable amount of Ella's taxes that Gale had let accumulate, an exceedingly generous gesture that likely eased any hesitation she may have had about changing managers. This was a big move for Ella and she no doubt anticipated the day when she would be able to record under Granz's supervision.

Granz produced JATP concerts in the United States until late 1957, completing 16 national tours in the process. From a purely artistic viewpoint, these seminal performances—highly exciting and featuring the best players of the time—left their mark on jazz and its devoted fans. Furthermore, because the concerts took place in the years following World War II, their sociological impact was highly significant. Historian Lewis A. Erenberg lauds the fact that "*Jazz at the Philharmonic* programs transported large numbers of musicians from city to city and demanded that auditoriums and halls be integrated wherever they played." He adds that, despite the sometimes smallish audiences, "they followed the music passionately and saw their interest in modern jazz as a declaration of personal independence from the tyranny of middle-class values that were buttoning down America."[13]

Granz's keen sense of what would succeed for an artist was of immeasurable benefit to Ella Fitzgerald. She had been singing jazz-oriented numbers and lighter commercial fare almost exclusively during her career to date at Decca Records, largely under the direction of Milt Gabler. Although she continued to shine in the bop-oriented concerts of JATP, Granz had other plans for her, and when the opportunity to make changes presented itself, he pounced on it. "Ella had recorded for Decca exclusively since the '30s," he explained. "This meant that I could never include her in any of the JATP concert albums. . . . Early in 1956 Decca was hot to issue the sound track of *The Benny Goodman Story*. But Benny's band included several artists under contract to me. . . . I said I wanted to buy Ella's contract, and [Decca] said okay."[14] The process, essentially a battle of egos, had actually taken several months, but Granz had the upper hand all along. Decca ultimately had no choice but to release Ella if they were to get the Goodman album out on time.

With Ella's recording activities finally in his purview, Granz intended to make her a prime attraction on Verve, a new label he founded only after signing her. Beginning in 1956 with *The Cole Porter Song Book* album, he would pair Ella with some of the top arrangers and musicians in the business and give her the opportunities to record a series of large-scale projects that featured the works of great songwriters and lyricists—Rodgers and Hart, Duke Ellington, the Gershwins, Irving Berlin, Jerome Kern, Harold Arlen, and Johnny Mercer. Some years later, Ella reiterated the significance of the exceptional series of recordings: "I had gotten to the point where I was only singing bebop. I thought that bop was IT! [*sic*] . . . But it finally got to the point where I had no place to sing. I realized then that there was more to music than bop. Norman came along then and he felt that I should do other things, so he produced the Cole Porter Songbook with me. It was a turning point in my life."[15] (See Chapter 7 for detailed information on the *Song Books*.)

Within a year of signing Ella, Granz further streamlined his operations. "Norman Granz has announced the unification of four disceries under the Verve banner," reported *Down Beat*. "The consolidation is based on a sales volume of approximately $2 million dollars in 1956 in record sales of Clef, Norgran, Down Home, and Verve. Henceforth, said Granz, all his recordings will be released on the *Verve* label."[16] In addition to the miraculous *Song Books*, Granz and Fitzgerald would also collaborate on many other live performances and recordings for Verve. Granz managed the great singer's activities completely and unswervingly. "The way Ella Fitzgerald was packaged is always really, from at least 1956 onward, filtered through Norman Granz's desire," commented Phil Schaap.

Tommy Flanagan, the master pianist, worked as Ella's musical director and accompanist for many years. "Norman Granz was always on the record dates. I put my two cents in, but he didn't like it," said Flanagan forthrightly. "I'd usually go to try to say something to Ella, and Ella would feel like she was in between. She didn't want to get that feeling, like she was uneasy with Norman or me." Flanagan stayed with Ella longer than any of the accompanists who worked with her during her career. "You know . . . [Granz] had the editing rights on recordings," added Flanagan. "He used to not use a lot of my intros, if you could believe that. Some [live] recordings . . . he would just start with maybe Ella singing . . . but I wouldn't know until after we'd hear the recording. . . . He doesn't know that much [musically]. I've told him that. [However], if Ella could put up with it, I could. She didn't lose anything by letting him have his say. She knew that he wouldn't be around for every performance." Flanagan may have been disappointed at some things that transpired, but his work with Ella was obviously of advanced artistic merit—and his association with Granz was certainly cordial and of great benefit to both men.

Moving to Switzerland in 1959, Granz stayed actively involved in the music business, thereafter working almost exclusively from his European base. He continued to promote concerts (including three JATP European tours and one more in the United States in 1967) and to manage Ella, as well as his other immensely popular superstar, pianist Oscar Peterson. In December 1960, he sold his interests in Verve to MGM for around two and a half million dollars, investing a portion of the money in the acquisition of paintings by some of the masters of modern art, including Pablo Picasso, with whom he developed a friendship.

In the early 1970s, Granz founded Pablo Records, producing several more recordings with Ella throughout the last years of her career. It has often been suggested that Granz was in reality a self-serving entrepreneur who shrewdly improved his own lot at the expense of the performers who worked for him. Indeed, if one considers the frequently grueling schedules of Ella and other Granz artists, it might be hard to argue against this. However, it should be noted that Granz, in the early 1980s, actually suggested to Ella that she ease up on her performing and recording, but she was tone-deaf to his pleas. In any event, when all was said and done, Granz's clients earned a lot of money under predominantly favorable circumstances. "Sometimes I'd read a critic who'd say I overrecorded artists," Granz commented. "But if you took away all the albums I did with Billie [Holiday], [Charlie] Parker, Lester [Young], Art Tatum, Ben Webster, and even Ella in the '50s, many would have gone totally unrecorded and most wouldn't have made more than a couple of records. . . . [M]y most profound regret is that I may not have recorded them enough."[17]

Nelson Riddle, the outstanding arranger, worked on three of the *Song Book* collections, as well as on other excellent collaborative sessions with Ella. He observed the Granz/Fitzgerald partnership in action on many occasions and made the following remarks:

Another aspect of Ella's life are her occasional tirades against [Granz], complaining sometimes about the ambitious series of personal appearances he has set up for her, other times about the choice of songs he has selected for her to record on his Pablo label. . . . [H]er petulance is very transparent and is more for effect than anything else. . . . I am told she gets restless after a few weeks of relaxation, and in spite of herself is drawn back on the road to resume her travels.

As far as the songs are concerned, Norman brings a list of songs which represent his choice of material for her to record, and Ella brings a list of tunes which she would like to sing, and they sit down, whether it be at his office or her home, and thrash the thing out.

Norman has as many complaints about her choices as she has about his, and whenever I'm present . . . I am constantly amused, because through all the fuss and feather shines the respect and affection they have for each other. It seems obvious to everyone but the two principals.

And to make it funnier and even more touching, one suspects that this has been going on for years![18]

Even the preeminent Duke Ellington, the giant of American music, was clear in his appreciation of Granz:

[In 1958] we went to Europe for Norman Granz for the first time. He . . . represented us beautifully . . . and left me feeling very much indebted to him. He took us back several times after that, and in 1966 we went with Ella Fitzgerald, which was a bang. Norman Granz is one of those guys I have spoken of as encountering at the various intersections of my road through life, guys who have been there to point out the way. . . . The representation he gave me was great.[19]

Ella Fitzgerald, for whom singing and the song were everything, was by nature humble and gracious to others. In spite of the frustrations and anxieties she occasionally felt working with a dominant personality like Norman Granz, she persisted and maintained a healthy perspective. "Certainly [her work with Granz] resulted in tension from time to time," noted Stuart Nicholson, "but it was a creative tension on which Ella thrived."[20] Ella always spoke well of Granz, pointing out that he was both a manager and a friend. She never forgot how much he had done for her. Granz died in Geneva, Switzerland on November 22, 2001.

CHAPTER 7

The Arrangers

The lofty goal of every arranger is to take notes written on paper and transform them into *live* music—a message from the arranger to the listener. In doing so, the arranger must be an orchestrator since his music must be written for the orchestra at hand, and a composer in the areas where he can be inventive.

—Sammy Nestico[1]

[An arranger's] craft is fueled by inspiration and soul power—it involves a sense of daring, spontaneity, and a considerable amount of self-confidence.

—Norman David[2]

In 1913, Art Hickman, a musician who also happened to be a baseball fan, got permission from the San Francisco Seals baseball club to stage dances as an escape from the monotony of the spring training season. He did so well that his band received bookings for the whole summer at a local hotel. Dance-band historian Leo Walker told more of the story:

[Hickman's] band consisted of six pieces: piano, trombone, trumpet, drums, and two banjos. Before long, a violin and string bass were added. . . . The band was booked back periodically . . . and all during 1915. . . . The next year while his fame continued to spread, Hickman once more enlarged the group adding two saxophones. . . . Florenz Ziegfeld was visiting San Francisco and . . . [was so impressed] that in 1919 he took the Hickman band to New York. . . . From about 1916 until the time of his own retirement the Hickman band had been a ten man organization. This was larger than most groups which started prior to 1920. . . . By 1920 quite a number of those [bandleaders] who were to be important names were becoming successfully established.[3]

When Hickman added saxophones to his band it was a significant move. He was attracted to the distinctive tonal quality of the instrument, despite the fact that up to the time it had been considered a novelty instrument. The perceptive Hickman was not deterred and other bandleaders were quick to follow his lead. Over the next decade or so the saxophone became a mainstay in the music world and the saxophone section was soon a regular component in all dance bands. In combination with trumpets and trombones, and backed by a rhythm section usually consisting of guitar, piano, bass, and drums, the instrumentation of the classic big band was taking shape. Bands were forming throughout the United States, the ones not working regularly in the major cities being referred to as territory bands.

"Sometime in the early [1920s] another important trend began," added Leo Walker. "Dancing started to move out of the Masonic Temples, Elks Clubs, and community halls into ballrooms built especially for that purpose. . . . In addition to the ballrooms, most of the country's leading hotels now found it profitable to provide dancing."[4] With a significant boost from the evolving recording industry, dancing was becoming a major industry. "Increasing numbers of single individuals of both sexes were in the cities with some spending money and leisure time but limited traditional connections for meeting people," recounts historian Thomas J. Hennessey.[5] Dancing provided a significant means of entertainment and social interaction for the masses, earning big profits for entrepreneurs in the process.

Performances by the earliest dance bands were customarily bland and not adventurous in conception. This began to change when a few bandleaders, most notably Paul Whiteman and Fletcher Henderson, started featuring written arrangements for their ensembles—pieces that were designed to be more than just repetitions of a composition's melody. In short order, the craft of arranging evolved into an important commodity and arrangers became the architects of the big-band sound. By the time the swing era was unfolding in the early 1930s, big bands contained in the neighborhood of fourteen to eighteen members. The quality of these bands ran the gamut, some highly accomplished and interesting, others mediocre at best.

RECORDINGS FOR DECCA, 1942–1954

A singer almost always got his or her start working with a band. Ella Fitzgerald got her break when she was hired to sing with Chick Webb and his band in 1935. She thrived as a result of the experience, honing her craft in the company of some of the finest instrumentalists around. She also got her first opportunities to sing within the musical landscapes designed by the outstanding arrangers who contributed to Webb's repertoire. Because of Ella's impressive talent, as well as the fact that her fast-rising popularity was such a boon to his success, Webb began looking for ways to showcase her to the widest possible audience. Consequently, Webb's arrangers were called upon to feature the amazing singer with charts that were well-conceived and entertaining, in spite of the fact that the source music provided them was often removed from the pure jazz sounds with which the band had initially been associated. In molding the raw musical material at hand, they crafted arrangements that both catered to Webb's targeted audience and took advantage of the particularly fine musicians who were playing in and singing with the band. Among these top arrangers were Edgar Sampson, Charlie Dixon, Don Redman, Will Hudson, George Bassman, and Van Alexander.

Another noteworthy arranger with ties to Ella Fitzgerald was the amazing Benny Carter. An equally accomplished composer and saxophonist, he was an emerging young bandleader and contemporary of Webb's during the 1930s. Carter became Ella's first champion after his band backed her in her legendary amateur contest win at Harlem's Apollo Theater in 1934. The two developed a lasting friendship and they eventually collaborated in 1955 when Carter penned the charts for one of Ella's last Decca recording sessions. They worked together again on several occasions in subsequent years. For example, in 1961, Carter was in the studio orchestra and took some wonderful alto saxophone solos on Ella's *Harold Arlen Song Book* album for Verve. He also supplied the charts and played on *30 by Ella*, for Capitol in 1968; wrote the arrangements for *A Classy Pair*, an album Ella made with Count Basie for Pablo Records in 1979; and played in the band that accompanied Ella on her final album, *All That Jazz*, released by Pablo in 1990. A legend who is admired worldwide, Carter maintained a full and illustrious career for over seventy years until his death in Los Angeles on July 12, 2003.

After her association with Chick Webb, either under his direction or as the de facto leader of his band, Ella continued to record profusely for the duration of her career. Historians frequently opine that the mature Ella did not emerge until she left Decca records in 1954 and began recording for Verve under the supervision of Norman Granz. While it is natural to laud the magnificent slew of albums she put out from the mid-1950s on, the fact remains that much of the work she did in the preceding dozen years must also be recognized for its exceptional quality. She recorded her first sides with Louis Armstrong, completed two beautiful duo sessions with pianist Ellis Larkins (see the section on Larkins in Chapter 9), and worked in many other settings with groups of various sizes and with musicians ranging from behind-the-scenes studio players to world-renowned stars.

The arrangers who contributed to many of her recordings throughout this period were Johnny Long, Randy Brooks, Vic Schoen, Bob Haggart, Gordon Jenkins, Sonny Burke, Dave Barbour, Leroy Kirkland, Jerry Gray,

André Previn, Toots Camerata, and Sy Oliver. Some were well-known at the time, only to fade into obscurity; others either maintained high profiles for years to come or were remembered for specific achievements. Bob Haggart, for example, stayed active through the 1990s until his death in December 1998. Among his accomplishments: he composed the well-known standard "What's New" and he played bass and co-led with Yank Lawson the successful group they called The World's Greatest Jazz Band. Gordon Jenkins, a musical director at Decca in the late 1940s and early 1950s, was the composer of "Good-bye," the engaging ballad that Benny Goodman would adopt as his closing theme. Jenkins, who remained a successful arranger and musical director through the late 1960s, working with major talents like Nat King Cole and Frank Sinatra, passed away in May 1984. André Previn has enjoyed an impressive dual career, achieving fame both as a jazz pianist and an internationally acclaimed orchestral conductor. In 1983, he recorded with Ella again, joining with bassist Niels-Henning Orsted-Pederson to accompany her on a selection of Gershwin songs for the Pablo album *Nice Work If You Can Get It*.[6]

Sy Oliver

Between 1949 and 1954 Ella worked with Sy Oliver more than with any other musical director at Decca. The two had a strong musical rapport and they recorded many sides together—all very good, many outstanding.

Born in Battle Creek, Michigan, on December 17, 1910, Sy Oliver (né Melvin James Oliver) spent most of his youth in Zanesville, Ohio. His mother, a fine pianist, and his father, a multi-instrumentalist, tried to get him to play the piano at an early age, but he resisted. In later years, when a number of his friends were already playing in different groups, his interest in music increased and he asked his father to show him the fundamentals of the trumpet. Unfortunately, his father took ill soon after, but the youngster persisted on his own. He progressed rapidly on his instrument and also began to write music. He took on his first professional work while still in high school and soon left home to tour with different groups.

In 1933 Oliver became a member of the Jimmie Lunceford band. He moved to New York and stayed with Lunceford for six years, playing, arranging, and occasionally singing. Oliver's inventive charts were largely responsible for establishing Lunceford's band as one of the finest and most exciting ensembles around. In 1939 Oliver, whose star had risen significantly by then, accepted an offer from Tommy Dorsey to join his band as his chief arranger. At this time Oliver stopped playing trumpet in order to devote all his time to composing and arranging. He stayed with Dorsey until being called into the service, and from 1943 to 1945 he was a bandleader in the Army.

After leaving the service Oliver returned to New York, worked for a short time more with Tommy Dorsey on a radio program called *Endorsed by Dorsey* and then became the musical director at Club Zanzibar. During his stay there, from late 1946 through mid-1947, Oliver took the bold step of leading a band with integrated personnel. "Sy went to considerable length to get men who were, simultaneously, top technicians and good jazz men," said Bill Gottlieb in *Down Beat*. "To his credit, he ended up with four white men 'because they were the best men available.'"[7] Ultimately, despite the recent advances in integration by Benny Goodman and a few others, Oliver could not keep the band together because many of the principal New York bookers refused to work with mixed ensembles.

Oliver had never really wanted to be a bandleader anyhow. He began doing studio work for a number of record companies and soon landed at Decca where he would work as a leading producer and also record under his name. "Unlike a number of colored musicians hired for minor jobs by record companies, [Oliver's] assignments have included all of the top names in Decca's star-studded catalog," reported *Ebony*. "He believes music transcends the color line though he himself has experienced a lot of discrimination as a working musician and band leader."[8] Among the stars Oliver collaborated with over the next few years were Louis Armstrong, Bing Crosby, Billie Holiday, the Andrews Sisters, and Ella Fitzgerald.

Oliver eventually left the studios and spent the better part of the 1960s and 1970s with different musical ensembles in the United States and abroad. He picked up the trumpet again in 1971 and played into the 1980s. He passed away on May 27, 1988. In a *New York Times* obituary Peter Watrous wrote that Sy Oliver was "one of America's great jazz composers and arrangers and a man who had a significant impact on American popular music."[9]

Decca has reissued an excellent CD sampling of the Ella Fitzgerald/Sy Oliver recordings. Titled *The Last Decca Years, 1949–1954*, 16 of the CD's 20 selections have Ella singing jazz or popular numbers in large-ensemble arrangements by Oliver. On the four remaining tracks, two of which feature duets with Louis Armstrong, Ella is backed by smaller combos.

During the brief span of years in which Ella Fitzgerald and Sy Oliver worked together the two turned out scintillating music. Although Oliver might have held back from time to time, especially when the material at hand was lighter fare that did not warrant any earth-shattering writing, the charts that he penned were first-rate, the products of his fertile imagination and sure technique. Throughout the Decca collection Oliver's distinctive style shines through, his arrangements full of rich chords and inventive passages behind Ella's consistently strong vocals.

The set opens with "In the Evening (When the Sun Goes Down)," a down-home blues that is introduced with brief licks by trombonist Henderson Chambers and an unidentified guitarist. The two players stay in the action, interjecting fills behind Ella throughout her first two heartfelt choruses. Everyone opens up on the third and final chorus, the singer crooning the lyrics with fervor as Oliver provides blaring brass lines. Although she was never closely associated with the blues, Ella demonstrates how she could handle the form convincingly when the opportunity arose.

Composed by Spencer Williams in 1928, "Basin Street Blues" became a standard of the Dixieland repertoire. First performed by Louis Armstrong, the tune, belying its title, does not follow the blues format. On her version, Ella closes by paying tribute to Armstrong with her earliest recorded impression of the legendary trumpeter and singer.

"Solid as a Rock" and "A Guy Is a Guy" are two silly ditties included in the collection. The former, introduced by muted trombone and growling trumpet, tells of the strength of love. Unindentified male voices join in to back up Ella, adding to the corniness of the proceedings. The latter, which had also been a hit for Doris Day, tells the story of how a guy gets a girl to fall for him. On each selection, Oliver obliges with an arrangement in which he throws in quotes from "Here Comes the Bride." Ella makes everything work.

"I've Got the World on a String" was composed by Harold Arlen with lyrics by Ted Koehler for the 1932 review *Cotton Club Parade*. Ella's version with Sy Oliver, recorded on March 6, 1950, is taken at a relaxed medium-slow tempo. Oliver's arrangement is to the point, simple, and tasteful, with smooth-flowing unison saxophone lines and occasional interjections by the brass. (Among the three additional recordings of the song that Ella would do in later years are wonderful versions for *The Harold Arlen Song Book* on Verve and for the duets with guitarist Joe Pass on Pablo. See the sections on the *Song Books* in Chapter 7 and on Joe Pass in Chapter 9.)

Ella is joined in duet by Louis Armstrong on "Dream a Little Dream of Me" and "Can Anyone Explain." Directing smaller ensembles for the two tracks, Oliver fills his charts with interesting key modulations and adds a tempo change in the latter. These are among the fine recordings that Fitzgerald and Armstrong made together prior to their memorable long-playing albums for Verve in the mid-1950s. As with those later collaborations we are treated to superb interplay and obvious camraderie among the two superstars.

"Because of Rain," a pretty ballad which lists Nat King Cole as one of the composers, was first recorded by Cole in 1951. Oliver's gentle arrangement opens with a bass clarinet droning a rich pedal tone, and the rest of the chart is filled with plenty of clarinet and flute lines.

"I Don't Want to Take a Chance" is one of a handful of songs composed by Ella Fitzgerald during her career. Her only recorded version is this one with Sy Oliver, originally pressed on July 18, 1951. Although it will never be mistaken for an all-time standard, the tune is nonetheless engaging and an interesting number because of the fact that the music and lyrics are Ella's. Oliver's subdued arrangement includes muted trumpet fills and an alto saxophone solo.

"There Never Was a Baby Like My Baby" and "Give a Little, Get a Little" were composed by Jule Styne, with lyrics by Betty Comden and Adolphe Green, for the 1951 review *Two on the Aisle*. Both are medium-tempo swingers taken at an easy lilt. The former has a little more depth to it and the band gets a chance to stretch out a bit midway through the chart; the latter is rather undistinguished and is cute at best.

"Goody Goody," composed by the relatively unknown Matty Malneck, but with lyrics by the great Johnny Mercer, was a popular hit recorded by several artists, including Benny Goodman and Bob Crosby. Although the song should be included in the list of lighter material that Ella covered over the years this is, nonetheless, a solid track on which she sings with strength and conviction. Oliver supplies a hard-swinging arrangement with powerful horn fills interspersed throughout. He includes a passage in which most of the band members clap hands on beats two and four, as Ella croons over some hot riffing by pianist Hank Jones. Ella recorded this version of "Goody Goody" on February 25, 1952. She recorded it again on a number of occasions over the next dozen years.

"Mr. Paganini" was composed by Sam Coslow for the 1936 Paramount film *Rhythm on the Range*. Ella first recorded the song with Chick Webb in October of the same year and some of her earliest scatting can be heard on that track. Her version with Sy Oliver is taken from a session the two did in June 1952. Ella swings effortlessly through Oliver's arrangement, easily handling a number of tempo changes and throwing in a clever quote from "A-Tisket, A-Tasket" during her scatting. Ella sang this tune frequently throughout her career. Interestingly, she sang it in F major with Chick Webb, but in A-flat major on Sy Oliver's arrangement.

Ella moves easily into "Early Autumn," a lovely ballad by Ralph Burns and Woody Herman, with lyrics again by Johnny Mercer. Sy Oliver adds some excitement in the middle of the arrangement with an explosive ensemble passage that includes a trombone solo (probably by either Bobby Byrne or Al Grey) and some screeching lead trumpet licks. Another ballad, the haunting "Angel Eyes," was composed by Earl Brent and Matt Dennis for the 1953 film *Jennifer*. Ella's version on the Decca collection stands up to any of the several versions that she would record in the ensuing years. Oliver's arrangement has a few expressive flourishes, but in general we hear some of his most understated writing. At one point tenor saxophonist Sam Taylor adds laid-back fills behind Ella's vocal line.

"Preview" was composed by Paul Quinichette and Count Basie in 1952 and, typical of much of Basie's music, it is a riff-based tune. Backed only by tenor saxophonist Taylor and a rhythm section of guitar, piano, bass, and drums, Ella scats the whole performance and everyone swings at an appealing medium tempo. Taylor's solo midway through the take reflects the influence of Lester Young.

"Careless" and "Melancholy Me" were popular songs in 1939 and 1954 respectively. Taken in a fairly straightforward manner, Ella's rich vocalizing and Oliver's appropriately subdued arrangements add considerable substance to the selections.

"Blue Lou" is a hard swinger that was composed in 1933 by Irving Mills and Edgar Sampson. Chick Webb had recorded it as an instrumental in late 1934 on the last session he did before Ella Fitzgerald started singing with his band. Oliver's arrangement starts with screaming brass chords answered by bluesy licks from the saxophones. Ella belts out her choruses and throws in some impeccable scatting.

Ella recorded George Shearing's venerable standard "Lullaby of Birdland" on June 6, 1954, her final date with Sy Oliver. She would record the song again many times in subsequent years. On this version, she is backed once more by tenor saxophonist Sam Taylor, a rhythm section that includes organist Bill Doggett, and a small ensemble of singers. Once again, the inclusion of singers in her accompaniment, intoning verbal sounds and occasionally echoing some of the lyrics, is another indication of the commercial settings in which Decca might place Ella in an effort to widen the popular appeal of her recordings. She of course transcends the needless clutter and sings beautifully as usual. Of significance is the presence of organist Doggett on the track. He worked with Ella on a few occasions during her career, and despite the fact that he was known primarily for his keyboard work, he was also a talented arranger and would pen the charts for a very nice collaborative album the two would do almost eight years later. (See the section on Bill Doggett later in this chapter.)

VERVE AND PABLO: THE *SONG BOOKS* AND MORE

Ella Fitzgerald's connection with Norman Granz began when she performed on her first Jazz at the Philharmonic concert in 1949. When she left Decca and went to work full-time with Granz in 1954, she was finally with someone who would allow her to concentrate on the type of music she had been yearning to perform and record for a long time. Except for a short period at the end of the 1960s (see "One for Prestige, Two for Reprise" later in this chapter), Granz would be her guiding force for the duration of her career. He would oversee the great and varied array of albums that she made for Verve and Pablo, as well as her seemingly endless string of live performances. Continuing to sing in all types of settings, she would again collaborate with many arrangers and musical directors.

Excluding for a moment the musical directors on the seminal *Song Book* series (and on a few other notable sessions discussed later in this chapter), three important arrangers with whom Ella worked during her years with Granz were Russell Garcia, Quincy Jones, and Erich Bulling. Among Russell Garcia's many accomplishments during a highly productive career was his work as musical director for the recording of *Porgy and Bess* featuring Ella and Louis Armstrong. (For more background on Garcia, see the section on Armstrong in Chapter 3.) Quincy Jones, a major recording and broadcast executive, is a huge force in the music world with more than twenty-five Grammies to his credit. He has served as composer, arranger, musical director, and producer for some of the world's biggest stars, including Sarah Vaughan, Ray Charles, Dinah Washington, "Cannonball" Adderley, Frank Sinatra, and Michael Jackson. Jones penned the charts for the 1963 album *Ella and Basie*. (See the section on Basie in Chapter 8.) Erich Bulling wrote charts for the 1981 album *Ella Abraca Jobim: Ella Fitzgerald Sings the Antonio Carlos Jobim Song Book*. On this unofficial addition to the *Song Book* series, Norman Granz hired both jazz and Brazilian musicians and Bulling wrote effective charts that included typical Brazilian percussion in the instrumentation.

The *Song Books* hold a special place in the history of jazz and popular music because of the astonishing scope of material performed and of the stature that Ella Fitzgerald gained from doing the recordings. "If the songbooks helped to ensconce the works of these American composers in recorded history, they also helped to create the Ella legend," summarized Fitzgerald biographer James Haskins.[10] While the standards from the upper echelon of American songwriters were already familiar to the listening public, the dignified presentation of the *Song Books*—i.e., Ella's brilliant singing, in collaboration with top musical directors, and accompanied by seasoned studio musicians—brought newfound respect for the great songwriters and their works. The concept was inspired. "What Mr. Granz did was effect a fusion at a higher level of accomplishment of [Fitzgerald's] pop and jazz instincts," said John Rockwell in the *New York Times*.[11]

Doing a collection of works from one composer was not altogether new—a smattering of similar projects had been done in the past; Ella herself had recorded a set of Gershwin tunes in her superb session with pianist Ellis Larkins in 1950—but the *Song Books* raised the bar to a new level and became the standard for any similar project that followed. Ella recorded eight collections under Norman Granz's supervision. The number of tracks on which Ella sings on the original LP releases totals a whopping 236, broken down as follows:

Cole Porter—32

Rodgers and Hart—34

Duke Ellington—37

Irving Berlin—31
George and Ira Gershwin—53
Harold Arlen—24
Jerome Kern—12
Johnny Mercer—13

The CD reissues of the first six individual sets, as well as the CD compilation of the complete series, contain additional tracks, including alternate takes, previously unreleased selections, and excerpts from rehearsals.

As part of his ambitious plans for Ella, the headstrong Norman Granz had envisioned the inclusion of a massive collection of songs from the great composers and lyricists, and he saw it through. He knew what he wanted with Ella and he was also resolute in how he would go about producing her:

When I recorded Ella, I always wanted her to be way out front. I didn't want a blend, as if she were a band singer. The reason was that I frankly didn't care what happened to the music. The music supported Ella. I've had arrangers tell me that in bar 23 a trumpet hit a wrong note. I didn't care. I wasn't interested in making perfect records. . . . If I thought she sounded great on a first take, I wasn't interested in wasting time doing six more, only to come back to the first one. I couldn't care less if there were clams here and there.

There were times when I would walk into a studio and they'd have everyone walled off for stereo. I would always see that Ella was in the middle of the musicians. The engineers would go up the wall because they couldn't get any separation. I wanted singing, not separation.[12]

Completing the remarkable body of work that constitutes the *Song Books* represents an unmatched accomplishment for all who participated. Norman Granz was certainly no musician, but his uncanny intuition was fueled by the fact that he was a formidable *appreciator* of good music. He was a strong-willed and excellent businessman with a soul. He could not have been more on the mark in devising his showcases for Ella. The consistently superior quality of the performances throughout all eight albums is astonishing. On the surface, this should not be surprising because of the exceptional artists who contributed to the recordings, but we might be reminded of the well-known cliché about too much of a good thing being bad. Herein lies the magic of Ella Fitzgerald. She belonged to the exclusive class of artists whose work never gets old. A great deal of the esteem now accorded American popular songs results from how Ella Fitzgerald sang them. It is not at all difficult to listen to very long stretches of the *Song Books* without losing interest or focus.

Buddy Bregman

Buddy Bregman was born in Chicago on July 9, 1930. Acquiring an interest in music early in life, he started formal studies at age 5, gave his first piano recital when he was 12, and attended both the Chicago Conservatory and UCLA. His musical aptitude is perhaps not so surprising in light of the fact that it ran in his family; his uncle was composer Jule Styne, whose songs included "Just in Time," "Time After Time," "Diamonds Are a Girl's Best Friend," and "Guess I'll Hang My Tears Out to Dry."

While in college, Bregman landed his first professional work at Capitol Records. In short order he was working steadily, arranging and conducting for records, television, and film. He worked with many top artists, including Dinah Shore and Frank Sinatra. One of his first triumphs occurred when he was nominated for an Emmy for his orchestrations on the 1954 NBC television production of Cole Porter's *Anything Goes* starring Ethel Merman.

A short time after hearing one of Bregman's earliest records on the radio, Norman Granz met the young orchestrator and asked him if he wanted to work for Verve. From 1956 to 1957, Bregman was both one of the company's busiest musical directors and its operations manager. Following his stay at Verve, he returned to NBC television and eventually began producing and directing. This led to television work in Europe with InterTel, as well as with the BBC and ITV networks. After several years abroad he made his way back to the United States in the early 1980s and continued his busy schedule as a producer and director.

While he was at Verve, Buddy Bregman first worked with Ella Fitzgerald when he arranged four songs and conducted the studio orchestra for a recording session she did on January 25, 1956. One of the tracks, "Too Young for the Blues," has been reissued on a three-CD set titled *First Lady of Song,* a compilation of Fitzgerald recordings predominantly from the middle 1950s (Verve 314 517 898-2). This date broke the ice for Ella and Bregman, setting the stage for their next collaboration, *Ella Fitzgerald Sings the Cole Porter Song Book.*

It has often been pointed out that the *Cole Porter Song Book* did not represent Ella's best work consistently. Recorded in February and March 1956, most of the tracks were done in one take with little rehearsal. The sessions constituted an expensive operation and it is possible that Norman Granz wanted to keep expenses down. Consequently, it is not surprising that some commentators have concluded that the album sounds hurried at times, or that Granz should have called for additional takes on some tracks, especially when there was a perception that Ella could have been stronger. Whatever the case, Granz would stick with this preferred operational procedure for the rest of his career, that of wrapping up sessions as directly as possible. He never swerved far from his philosophy that less was more. Consider Don Freeman's comments in the original liner notes to the Porter album: "Is there another singer alive today whose work, like

[Ernest] Hemingway's, is so basic and simple on the surface and yet so meaningful?"[13]

In addition to the sometimes less-than-favorable views about Ella's singing on the Porter sides, another recurring complaint concerns the quality of Bregman's arrangements. It would be easy to dwell on the fact that Granz selected Bregman for the project only after learning that Nelson Riddle, his first choice as musical director, was not available. However, the young Bregman was already a skilled and experienced practitioner of his art who approached the recordings with the utmost professionalism and who did very well under the circumstances. Granz in fact praised Bregman's work. To overanalyze the writing without considering the project in its entirety is an injustice to all concerned. Although Bregman commented that his output would have taken other shapes if he had had more time, it is no secret that the charts were designed to reflect the popular appeal of Porter's music. From the outset of the project it had been the intent of both Granz and Bregman to tailor a set of music that would satisfy a large audience. Furthermore, with regard to working with Granz in particular, and in light of the realities of the recording industry in general over the years, it has been and will always be possible to suggest that things could have been done better or have been done differently. Consider Bregman's own comments about his work on the second *Song Book*, a collection of the music of Rodgers and Hart: "This time, at least I had some time to think. It was not quite as big a hit [as the *Cole Porter Song Book*], but I think the orchestrations I did were ten times better. But it was done quickly; I wish I would have had time to orchestrate more pieces."[14]

Whatever the circumstances surrounding the production of the Cole Porter session, Ella, of course, sounds wonderful—and Bregman's writing is very good. He has an obvious strong sense of swing and a firm understanding of the different families of instruments. Having so many songs to work with, he places Ella in a variety of ensemble configurations. The fact that he at times does not take too many chances does not diminish the impact of the final product. This is, after all, one of the biggest selling jazz/popular albums of all time. "It was the 11th biggest LP of the year," recalled Norman Granz, "That was insane for me."[15] Despite the opinions, including Bregman's, that things might have been done differently, he did his job very well and Ella was magnificent. Phil Schaap summarized succinctly: "I think the goal of these [songbooks] was reverence for the style. [Fitzgerald] was to supply the jazz. . . . The goal of these arrangements was texture, reverence for the songbook, showcasing the singer, voicings—and jazz was her job." The *Cole Porter Song Book* was a memorable introduction to the Granz/Fitzgerald partnership.

On a number of the Porter tracks Bregman pens accompaniments using the classic big-band instrumentation. On "Too Darn Hot" and "Just One of Those Things" he has swinging lines in the saxophone section, powerful punches from the brass, and rich ensemble writing in which he lets the trombone section step out for short stretches. On "Ridin' High," Ella and a harmonized saxophone section play call and response for a while before the brass join in and start trading with the saxes. In the final chorus Bregman has Ella modulating in mid-chorus, up a minor third before he shifts her back down to the opening key toward the end of the chorus. "It's All Right with Me" is a medium straight-ahead swinger. The band cooks behind Ella and throughout its own half-chorus. There are some nice fills on muted trumpet, probably by Harry "Sweets" Edison, a member of the trumpet section that also includes Pete Candoli, Maynard Ferguson, and Conrad Gozzo.

For some of the songs, Bregman augments the instrumentation by adding full complements of strings. (With the exception of the Duke Ellington and Johnny Mercer albums, all the subsequent *Song Books* would have some degree of string writing.) On "Anything Goes," Bregman starts with the full orchestra backing Ella in a plaintive mood through the verse. He then shifts the tempo up into a relaxed medium swing for the opening chorus with unison strings and muted brass supporting Ella's vocal at first. The orchestra is given half a chorus, with alternating saxophone, brass, and string lines, before Ella re-enters to close out the chart. On "Begin the Beguine," Bregman's writing provides the listener with hints of the great arrangement from Artie Shaw's band in earlier years. Muted brass kick off "You Do Something to Me" with a brief intro, and Ella is supported by fills from the flutes and clarinets as she opens her first chorus. On "Love for Sale" she renders the verse freely over background licks by either Bud Shank or Herb Geller on alto saxophone. In the chorus the brass are subdued, but they have their moments. For the most part Ella is supported by drawn-out saxophone lines and the strings ride on top. To start "Night and Day," Ella croons the verse over a repetitive tom-tom pattern while plucked strings add punctuation.

Bregman arranges a few charts for a string orchestra with single flute and oboe added. For example, on "Ev'ry Time We Say Goodbye" lush cello lines at one point in the arrangement set the stage for a brief duet by Ted Nash on flute and Bob Cooper on oboe. Bregman's arrangement for "I Love Paris," taken at a slow tempo, has Ella singing through passages in which harmonized high strings alternate with low strings in unison while the two woodwinds add fills and harmonized licks.

Bregman also includes charts arranged for a trombone section of three tenors and one bass, plus rhythm section. The full, brassy sonority of the trombones contrasts nicely with Ella's singing on songs like "All of You," "What Is This Thing Called Love?," "I've Got You under My Skin," and "Don't Fence Me In."

Pianist Paul Smith worked for the first time with Ella on the *Cole Porter Song Book*. He would serve as her musical director for long stretches in later years, and the two would also record an excellent set of duets. (See the section on Paul Smith in Chapter 9.) On Cole Porter's "Miss Otis Regrets," Ella and Smith provide a preview of things to come. Their rapport is evident and Smith's accompaniment is both virtuosic and sensitive. On a few other tracks—like "I Get a Kick Out of You," "Let's Do It (Let's Fall in Love)," "Get Out of Town," and "Easy to Love"—Smith, guitarist Barney Kessel, bassist Joe Mondragon, and drummer Alvin Stoller step out from the larger orchestra to provide quartet backing for Ella.

The rendition of "From This Moment On" is a highlight of the Porter album. Everything that was good in the session, as well as in all the subsequent *Song Books,* is evident on this track: Ella's one-of-a-kind vocal clarity and sense of swing, excellent arrangements that cater to both jazz and popular music sensibilities, and the best studio musicians playing superbly.

Ella's opening chorus in "From This Moment On" is shown in Example 7.1. Cole Porter's original melody contains no eighth-note syncopation. He achieves his melodic alteration by starting phrases directly on beat two of a measure, or on beat four of a measure, and holding through the beginning of the following measure. The tune presents many interpretive possibilities and Ella plays with the melody from the outset. She attacks the first word "From" on beat one in measure 1, instead of on beat two, as originally composed. In both measures 9 and 25, she reverses the procedure and starts a phrase with the word "only" on beat two, instead of on beat one, as in the original. Between measures 57 and 60, she produces another variation by shifting the location of two words within the same phrase. She starts with "we'll" on beat two rather than on beat one in measure 57, and closes by nudging "high" from beat one to beat two in measure 59. Note how, from the end of measure 47 through measure 48, Ella stretches "good night" over five beats, bending notes nicely in the process. Between measures 49 and 51, she reverses the direction of a phrase by singing the title lyrics "From this moment on" in a descending direction, rather than ascending as expected. She ends the chorus ingeniously by attacking the first syllable of "moment" on beat one in measure 66, instead of the original phrasing of holding it over from beat four in the previous measure. She then manipulates "moment" over five beats before closing the phrase with the last word "on," starting on beat two in measure 67.

Saxophone lines, brass fills, and a brief phrase by the trombone section take up the first A section of the second chorus. Ella opens the next eight bars by reversing the direction of the original melody, descending through an elastic five-note tuplet figure on the words "From this happy day" (Example 7.2).

On the bridge (Example 7.3), Ella swings the first four bars in a straightforward manner. She then takes the next four bars up an octave and belts

Example 7.1: "From This Moment On" *(Cole Porter Song Book)*

Example 7.2: "From This Moment On" *(Cole Porter Song Book)*

Example 7.3: "From This Moment On" *(Cole Porter Song Book)*

out the words "Got the skin I love to touch." In measure 42 she plays with the lyrics "arms to hold" by jumping up a fourth to the word "to," bending it down a minor third, and then finishing with the word "hold" on beat one in measure 43. Ella closes by molding the lyrics almost exclusively onto straight quarter notes through the last four measures of the bridge.

The *Rodgers and Hart Song Book* was recorded in August 1956 and released in February 1957. Interestingly, Norman Granz chose not to include any of the songs that Richard Rodgers had written with Oscar Hammerstein II, the only other lyricist he worked with during his career. In his notes for the *Complete Song Books*, John McDonough cites Norman Granz's opinion that Hart's lyrics "affected" Rodgers in such a way that his music had a "leanness and edge" not found in the songs he did with Hammerstein II. The "edge" may have been attributable to the fact that Richard Rodgers and Lorenz Hart had completely opposite personalities. The immensely talented and outwardly assured Rodgers was obsessively focused and orderly in his work; Hart was a loose cannon. In an introduction written for the Rodgers and Hart album, Rodgers commented: "It wasn't wise to leave [Hart] alone for a moment because he would simply disappear and have to be found all over again. . . . Our fights over words were furious, blasphemous, and frequent, but . . . we both knew that we were arguing academically and not personally." The two wrote some of the most enduring standards of American song before their amazing partnership ended prematurely. Edward Jablonski, a noted scholar of American musical theater, explains: "Hart's undependability [and] acute drinking problem . . . led to the dissolution of his twenty-year collaboration with Richard Rodgers. Their last Broadway show together was *By Jupiter* (1941), after which Rodgers realized he simply could not count on the erratic Hart any longer."[16] Hart passed away in November 1943.

As with the Cole Porter album, Granz recorded and assembled the *Rodgers and Hart Song Book* quickly and frugally, but things were not quite as hectic this time around. Ella was pleased with the results. "It's so pretty. I did it mostly with strings, and I've always wanted to sing with lots of strings. Then, the average layman knows the songs better, so it should sell more than Cole Porter. Another thing is that we didn't have to rush it like we did the first album, so I think the whole feeling is more relaxed."[17] As Ella suggested, the *Rodgers and Hart Song Book* turned out to be a huge success, enjoying widespread acclaim. There were, however, some lukewarm reviews. For example, in a *Down Beat* blindfold test, famed vocalist Anita O'Day made no effort to hide her reservations after listening to "My Heart Stood Still."

Who dreamed up Ella singing "and then my heart stood still"? It's ridiculous. Here's a girl who sings good swing music. . . . All I can say is, sell it to Hollywood—and they did. The arrangement was pleasant, and Ella didn't sing badly on it. I'm not saying it's bad or good, but I think it's kind of silly—the entire tune with Ella. So much talent and how they've used it! As far as buying the record— I'm hung again as to how to class this. It wasn't so bad musically—it's a nice record, whatever "nice" is.[18]

Speaking from the perspective of someone who had listened to Ella sing jazz and swing almost exclusively, O'Day had trouble reconciling Ella's transition to the world of ballads and large, orchestrated productions. Her reservations may have been representative of purists at the time, but it is hard to imagine most traditionalists not eventually being won over to Ella's accomplishments on the *Song Books*.

The Rodgers and Hart set opens with "Have You Met Miss Jones," the sophisticated melody taken at a slow lilt and backed by strings. Among the album's other swinging arrangements, taken at various tempos, are "The Lady Is a Tramp," "Manhattan," "This Can't Be Love," "Thou Swell," and "Lover." The ballad performances are exceptional, with Ella singing magnificently on time-tested standards like "Spring Is Here," "It Never Entered My Mind," "My Romance," "I Didn't Know What Time It Was," and "Blue Moon."

For six songs—"Dancing on the Ceiling," "Where or When," "Blue Room," "Isn't It Romantic," "Here in My Arms," and "You Took Advantage of Me"—pianist Paul Smith does the arranging. His charts, scored for orchestral woodwinds and the rhythm section, are rich and streamlined. (The section on Connee Boswell in Chapter 3 includes a discussion of Ella's interpretation of "Where or When" on the Rodgers and Hart *Song Book*, as well as a discussion of her singing on "I Could Write a Book," also on the album. For an example of Ella's interpretation of "You Took Advantage of Me," in a duo with Joe Pass, see the section on Pass in Chapter 9.)

For four of the tracks, Paul Smith, guitarist Barney Kessel, bassist Joe Mondragon, and drummer Alvin Stoller step out of the larger ensemble to accompany Ella. The stellar quartet is cohesive and sensitive, providing impeccable swing on "To Keep My Love Alive" and "Ev'rything I've Got," and tasteful backing for the slower tunes, "With a Song in My Heart" and "Bewitched." On the latter, Smith's piano work during the verse is magical. Ella and Barney Kessel also perform a beautiful duo on "Wait Till You See Her," Kessel's guitar accompaniment subdued and warm.

Duke Ellington

Norman Granz decided to go with Duke Ellington as the next songwriter represented on the *Song Books*. Because Ellington was under contract to Columbia at the time, Granz had to first work out the legalities before starting the project. He was on good terms with George Avakian, Ellington's producer at Columbia, and the two succeeded in coming to an agreement in relatively short order.

For some, Ellington may have been an unexpected choice for the *Song Books*. Aficionados knew that many of the renowned songs associated with him were either collaborative works or compositions by other writers altogether, including Billy Strayhorn, Ellington's longtime and equally brilliant associate. Furthermore, the words of several lyricists would be represented. Still, the whole package would be genuine "Ellingtonia" and Granz was eager to have the great bandleader on board. (For a detailed discussion about Ellington, including examples of tracks with Ella from other albums, see the section on Ellington in Chapter 8.)

Granz knew that the combination of Ellington and Ella Fitzgerald on record would undoubtedly be sensational. "Granz may have been an admitted song freak, but jazz still came first," points out John McDonough. "Perhaps only he would have had the audacity to promote Duke Ellington over the heads of Berlin and Kern to the third position in this series. But he had his reasons, not the least of which was his desire to add the great bandleader to Verve's wall of fame."[19] Another motivating factor for Granz was the opportunity to produce a *Song Book* on which the featured composer also played.

Granz wanted new arrangements for the sessions, but Ellington arrived without having prepared anything. He ended up using several charts already in his band's repertoire, giving Ella no choice but to sing in the same keys and only at the points in the arrangements where instrumental passages or solos would have taken place. She even hummed her lines on some of the tunes that didn't have lyrics. Needless to say, the recording dates were very slipshod affairs. "I didn't know what was going on until we went into the studio. I hadn't been able to work it out with Duke," recalled Granz. "I spent more time traveling around trying to talk to Duke than we spent on the record. . . . Strays [Strayhorn] had some arrangements, but nothing close to what we needed. . . . Duke came without anything done. . . . Ella was very upset. . . . Strays spent a lot of time holding Ella's hand."[20] Four days of recording, from June 24–27, 1957, yielded only 19 master tracks with the full band. That was it for Ellington. His tight performing schedule and continuing contractual obligations to Columbia precluded him working on the album any longer. Norman Granz, however, wanted more.

To fill up the sides Granz added tracks from two small-group dates that Ella did. She recorded the first one in September 1956 with tenor saxophonist Ben Webster, violinist Stuff Smith, and the rhythm section from the first two *Song Books:* pianist Paul Smith, guitarist Barney Kessel, bassist Joe Mondragon, and Alvin Stoller on drums. Needless to say, this was an excellent session with many wonderful moments. On "Cotton Tail," Ella is on fire, scatting all the way through and trading fours with Webster. "Do Nothin' till You Hear from Me" gets the full ballad treatment with Kessel's lovely fills, Webster's lush sub-tones, and hip violin lines by Stuff Smith on the bridge. Three of the tracks—"Solitude," "Azure," and "In a Sentimental Mood"—feature Ella and Kessel in sparkling duets. Among the remaining tracks are timeless standards like "Satin Doll," "Sophisticated Lady," "Don't Get Around Much Anymore," and "Prelude to a Kiss." The second small-group date took place about four months after the Ellington *Song Book* sessions. On these tracks, Ben Webster joins Oscar Peterson, Herb Ellis, Ray Brown, and Alvin Stoller in a super quintet to back Ella. They perform wonderful takes on "In a Mellow Tone," "Love You Madly," and Johnny Hodges's "Squatty Roo." Webster drops out on "Mood Indigo," and Ella pairs with her buddy Oscar Peterson for a splendid version of Billy Strayhorn's "Lush Life."

Another addition to the Ellington *Song Book* is a long instrumental work that Ellington and Billy Strayhorn assembled as a tribute to Ella. Titled *Portrait of Ella Fitzgerald*, it is in four parts, each with an added written observation. In presenting part three, Ellington exclaims that Fitzgerald's "artistry always brings to mind the words of the Maestro, Mr. Toscanini, who said: 'There are only two kinds of musicians. Either you're a good musician or you're not.' And in terms of musicianship, Ella Fitzgerald is 'Beyond Category.'" A few months after the completion of the *Song Book* dates, Ellington was again forthright in his appreciation for the great singer. "With Ella up front . . . you've got to play better than your best," he exclaimed.[21] He was yet another of many brilliant artists to shower praise on Ella during her career.

Four of Billy Strayhorn's compositions are done with the full band on the Ellington *Song Book*. "Clementine" is a medium swinger and "Day Dream" an emotion-charged ballad. On "Chelsea Bridge," one of the album's selections for which no new chart was prepared, Ella hums all the way through, sticking closely to the melody. Strayhorn's most famous composition, "Take the 'A' Train," is also planned around an arrangement already in Ellington's book. Written in the key of C, Ella is fine as she dips into the lowest recesses of her range on the angular melody, but a slightly higher key might not have been a bad thing. In fact, the next time she recorded "Take the A Train," less than four years later in Berlin, Germany, she sang it in D-flat. Granted, this is only a half-step higher, but it is her key of choice nonetheless and, surprising as it might seem, she sounds more comfortable on the melody. In any event, she still cooks on the *Song Book* version and the key is not a factor during her scatted improvising when she is free to soar to any level of her range.

Among the album's other tracks with the full band are strong swinging versions of tunes like "Drop Me Off in Harlem," "Lost in Meditation," "Everything but You," and "Bli-Blip." All highlight both Ella's unmatched singing and distinctive solos from the sidemen. On "Rockin' in Rhythm," performed with Ellington's regular arrangement, Ella scats throughout, either on the lines from the chart or in hot solo passages. Cat Anderson's stratospheric screeching on trumpet is heard toward the end of the track. Juan Tizol's "Perdido" is another scat vehicle for Ella, and Jimmy Hamilton's clarinet playing is a particular treat among a number of fantastic solos. "I'm Just a Lucky So and So," a slow swinger, is not a strict blues, but it has a lot of the blues in it. Beginning with a date for Decca in 1946, Ella recorded this number several times during her career. Among the ballads she sings with the full band are "I Didn't Know About You," "All Too Soon," and "I Got It Bad (and That Ain't Good)." On the latter, Ellington backs Ella's rich vocals with lovely writing for the band's reed section. In the middle of the chart, alto saxophonist Johnny Hodges solos for a few measures, his incomparable tone as magical as ever.

"Caravan" was a smash hit for Ellington in 1937 and has been a favorite standard of singers and instrumentalists since then. It was composed by Juan Tizol but, as James Lincoln Collier points out, "Ellington did not like the bridge Tizol had written [and] provided one of his own."[22] In common AABA form, with sections 16 measures long, Ellington gave the minor-tinged A sections an Oriental feel, swinging only on the bridge. On the *Song Book* version, Ellington changes the formula and backs Ella with an exotic feel through the complete first chorus before shifting into swing feel for the remainder of the track. Ella's singing in the beginning of the second chorus is shown in Example 7.4. Instead of holding the word "night" through the first two measures as originally written, she repeats it on four separate attacks. Moving from measures 4 to 5, 20 to 21, and 24 to 25—

Example 7.4: "Caravan" (*Duke Ellington Song Book*)

respectively on the words "so bright," "we creep," and "may keep"—she uses one of her favorite phrasings in each case by holding the first word across the barline and attacking the following word on the second half of beat one. Between measure 11 and 13 she closes the first A section by reversing the normal contour of the line and ascending through the words "that shine upon our Caravan." Starting the second A section in measure 17, she sustains the line this time, as might be expected, but she still surprises the listener by leaping up an octave to start the word "Sleep" before dropping back down and carrying it through to measure 18.

Everyone really cooks on "I'm Beginning to See the Light," the swinging standard that Ellington wrote with Don George, Johnny Hodges, and Harry James. One of the trumpeters sets up this no-frills performance with a four-bar intro before Ella jumps in for three hot choruses. She runs through the melody in a straightforward manner and then takes off on the second chorus (Example 7.5). After a minor-sixth jump on the words "never cared" in measure 1, she uses one of Louis Armstrong's devices, that of reshaping melodies into successions of repeated pitches, by singing through the first four measures predominantly on Es and E-flats. In measures 5 and 6 she runs the words "now that the stars are in your eyes" through quarter-note triplets that culminate in two swinging eighth-notes. She uses quarter-note triplet patterns again on motives in measures 13 and 14 and in measures 29 and 30. In the former case, on the words "now when you turn the lamp down low" she arpeggiates the triplets in an ascending pattern over the distance of an octave. Note also her intricate phrasing in completing this passage, on the song's title words, as she moves from a quarter-note tuplet, with a ratio of five to three, into yet another quarter-note triplet that she carries across the barline this time. Between measures 17 and 24, she adds a leap in the middle of each of the bridge's four two-bar motives—jumping a fifth to and from the word "through" between measures 17 and 18, a diminished fifth to and from "in" between measures 19 and 20, another fifth to and from "caused" between measures 21 and 22, and an octave to and from "fire" in measure 23. Between measures 25 and 28 she again sings the words mainly on repeated pitches, in this case Cs and B-flats.

The band and Ella play call and response by trading fours for much of the third chorus. On her first response, Ella sings an incredible lick, coaxing the lyrics through a descending quarter-note-triplet line that is at once deceptively complex and ingeniously melodic (Example 7.6).

The 38 selections comprising the Ellington album gave Norman Granz his largest *Song Book* to that point. Despite the hectic recording sessions, the final product turned out to be sensational, a fact that is not surprising when considering the stature of the artists involved. The looseness and raw energy of the performances, as well as the presence of the legendary

Example 7.5: "I'm Beginning to See the Light" (Duke Ellington Song Book)

Example 7.6: "I'm Beginning to See the Light" (Duke Ellington Song Book)

Ellington sidemen, provide the album with an abundance of character and excitement.

Paul Weston

Paul Weston was born in Springfield, Massachusetts, on March 12, 1912, and raised in the nearby town of Pittsfield. Although he enjoyed music and listened to many recordings during high school, he did not harbor plans of making music his profession. This changed when, after he began studying economics at Dartmouth University, he acquired a strong interest in jazz. As a result, he was soon playing piano and leading a dance band until his graduation in 1933.

The following year, while Weston was at Columbia doing graduate studies, he sold some charts to orchestra leader Dick Haymes. After hearing his music on a radio broadcast, Rudy Vallee tabbed Weston to write some arrangements for him. In 1935, Tommy Dorsey, who had assumed the leadership of the Haymes orchestra, hired Weston as a full-time staff arranger. Weston stayed with Dorsey for five years.

After his stint with Dorsey, Weston freelanced again, eventually making his way to the west coast. The great lyricist Johnny Mercer, who was on the verge of launching Capitol Records, met Weston in 1943 and offered him the position of artist and repertoire director with the new company. Weston stayed at Capitol for six years. In 1950, he moved on to Columbia Records where he maintained his busy schedule for another seven years. In 1952 he married the well-known singer Jo Stafford, whom he had met on previous engagements.

Paul Weston enjoyed a full and successful career, racking up countless credits in the recording studios, as well as in film and television. Among the singers with whom he worked over the years were Dinah Shore, Jo Stafford, Margaret Whiting, Doris Day, Dean Martin, and Frankie Laine. Weston also teamed with various lyricists and composed a number of songs, including "Day by Day," "I Should Care," "Shrimp Boats," and "When April Comes Again." Of particular significance are the several albums he made under his own name. They were trendsetters, establishing the genre of easy listening, or mood music, a category of music that proved to be extremely popular with the public. "All I did was add strings to a dance band," explained Weston. "The reason it still swung was because I used good jazz musicians."[23]

Weston left Columbia in 1957, returning to Capitol for a while. That same year he helped found the National Academy of Recording Arts and Sciences, the organization that would establish the Grammy Awards in 1958. He spent much of the 1960s and 1970s as a television musical director and worked with many popular personalities, including Danny Kaye, Sid

Caesar, and Jonathan Winters. He also released a number of comedy albums with his wife, one of which won a Grammy, before the two retired from performing in the early 1970s. He died in Santa Monica, California, on September 20, 1996.

After finishing production of the *Duke Ellington Song Book*, Norman Granz began preparing for the next album in the series. This time around, it was the music of Irving Berlin. Because Buddy Bregman had stepped down as musical director after the *Rodgers and Hart Song Book*, Granz chose Paul Weston as musical director for the Berlin project. The sessions were recorded in March 1958 and, as usual, everything was completed in relatively short time, with as few takes as possible.

It is likely that Granz's first choice for musical director had remained Nelson Riddle—once again, the second choice, in this case Paul Weston, did an outstanding job. The recording is excellent, in large part because of the fresh-sounding and well-crafted charts that the unheralded Weston penned to accompany Fitzgerald.

There are only two speeds in the Berlin collection, medium-tempo and ballad. While Weston's charts are relatively straight ahead in formal design, his melodic sense and harmonic language are highly developed, and he is masterful in the instrumental colors he produces. He includes effective interplay between Ella and the ensemble, interspersing opportunities for short solos by the various horn players. The keyword for Weston's work is subtle; his writing is deceptively sophisticated. One of the best examples is his arrangement for "Alexander's Ragtime Band," with its deftly crafted passages in which authentic Dixieland sounds blend and alternate with cooler, boppish sonorities. Another of the album's standout tracks is the pretty ballad "Reaching for the Moon," on which Weston backs Ella's plaintive vocal with only a duo of guitar and violin.

The album obviously contains many well-known tunes by Berlin, but some of his more obscure material is also there. Included in the collection are groovers, like "Let's Face the Music and Dance," "Let Yourself Go," "Puttin' on the Ritz," "I Used to Be Color Blind," "All by Myself," "Isn't This a Lovely Day," "The Song Is Ended" (with some nice scatting by Ella), and "I've Got My Love to Keep Me Warm" (the hardest swinger on the album). Among the ballads are "You're Laughing at Me," "How about Me?," "How Deep Is the Ocean," "You Keep Coming Back Like a Song," "Now It Can Be Told," and "Change Partners."

One of Irving Berlin's most enduringly popular songs is "Cheek to Cheek," with its lengthy form and appealing harmonies. For a close look at Ella's rendition of "Cheek to Cheek" on the Berlin album, as well as additional versions by Ella, Connee Boswell, and Louis Armstrong, see the section on Boswell in Chapter 3.

Nelson Riddle

The composer/arranger with whom Ella Fitzgerald worked the most during her career was Nelson Riddle. Long considered among the very best in his field, Riddle's genius derived from a keen artistic perception that allowed him to write arrangements that both respected the spirit of the music at hand and conformed to the particular personalities and skills of the artists with whom he was working.

Riddle was born in Hackensack, New Jersey, on June 1, 1921. Influenced by his music-loving parents, he studied piano and trombone through his teen years. In his last year of high school he took his first arranging lessons with Bill Finegan, a talented local arranger who would go on to enjoy considerable success writing for Glenn Miller, as well as co-fronting a big band with Eddie Sauter.

Beginning in 1940, Riddle spent the better part of the next six years working professionally as a trombonist and arranger. Of importance was a stint he did with Tommy Dorsey, during which time he learned a great amount about the craft of arranging from Dorsey's fine staff of arrangers. Incidentally, he just missed working with the aforementioned Sy Oliver, who had recently left Dorsey to enlist in the Army.

In late 1946 bandleader Bob Crosby, who was about to relocate to California, hired Riddle to write arrangements for him. Riddle promptly moved to Los Angeles where, in addition to his work with Crosby, he took lessons in composition and began accepting additional writing jobs. He was engaged to work for Nat King Cole in 1949 and penned the arrangement for one of Cole's biggest hits for Capitol Records, "Mona Lisa." Riddle ended up staying with Capitol for the next 11 years, building a reputation as a top arranger and conductor. During that time he collaborated with Cole on several albums and wrote for many other outstanding performers. He also did well with releases of his own easy listening music.

Riddle was still a relative unknown when he first recorded with Frank Sinatra on April 30, 1953. The session was a resounding success. "Now they were on to something magical," recounts Sinatra biographer J. Randy Taraborrelli, "Riddle had injected new life into Sinatra's sound. . . . [M]any Sinatra historians still feel that the albums that resulted from Frank's next seven years at Capitol are among his best and most memorable . . . thanks to producer Voyle Gilmore and arranger-conductor Nelson Riddle."[24] One wonders how phenomenal the result would have been if Sinatra and Ella Fitzgerald had ever had the opportunity to record an album together with Riddle as musical director.

Riddle stayed active into the early 1980s. In addition to his work in the recording studio he also wrote a great deal of music for television and films; among his successes were his theme for the TV series *Route 66*, a big hit in 1962, and the scores for the films *Ocean's Eleven*, *Pajama Game*, and *Pal Joey*. He was also the musical director for the inaugural balls of Presidents Kennedy and Reagan. Riddle passed away in Los Angeles on October 6, 1985.

It should come as no surprise that the albums made by Ella Fitzgerald with Nelson Riddle as the musical director are superb and feature some of the singer's most inspiring work. There was no creative tug-of-war, no conflict of egos when these two confident and accomplished musicians worked together. "When it was Nelson Riddle, or someone else she really respected, she listened," said publicist Virginia Wicks.

She had great respect for people with talent, . . . but funnily enough, Ella, of all the artists I ever handled, was usually way ahead of everybody else in terms of her interpretation. If there was something that they felt she should emphasize more, or whatever, she'd listen, she'd do it, she'd take direction. But they didn't have to give her much. She just innately knew how to interpret the lyrics and how to sing. Nobody told her how to sing—'Let's put this part in a little faster; we can do this or that.' Unless she felt that the suggestion was a good one, Ella was the perfect one. Ella was the one who set the pace without being high-handed. She was the most modest of anyone in the room, but they followed her lead; her lead was pretty much perfection. . . . She was a true, pure musician who just knew how to sing, and knew what tempo. She very often would set the tempo and the feeling for the music. She was a great admirer of Nelson Riddle's work.

Nelson Riddle was available for Norman Granz's fifth *Song Book* extravaganza, and what a production it was—almost sixty selections from the vast catalog of the Gershwin brothers. Recorded in January, March, July, and August 1959, *Ella Fitzgerald Sings the George and Ira Gershwin Song Book* was the biggest of the collections, five disks in its original LP format. "In fifty-nine selections recorded over a period of eight months," recalled Riddle, "not a note was changed in any arrangement, no key was altered, no routine was restructured. Everything went according to plan, pleasantly and entirely satisfactorily."[25] It was a monumental achievement, by far the most ambitious and comprehensive project of the series. Only one of the final three *Song Books* to follow, the Harold Arlen set, would have anything approaching a large number of selections. "I think my favorite album I ever made with any singer is the Ella Fitzgerald Gershwin [*Song Book*] . . . of Nelson Riddle's arrangements," said pianist Lou Levy. "That was a fantastic music lesson for me. The different ways that they did the same songs—"Lady Be Good" so slow and beautiful. That was a great influence on me, and as a result I do a lot of fast ones slow now. It was like going to school."[26]

It would be an exercise in overkill to try and pick highlights of Fitzgerald's singing on the Gershwin tracks. Everything is good; the album starts at the highest level and stays there. Ella is constantly on fire, at all temperatures, as she interprets the music. The ballads are crisply articulated with feeling; her swing is powerful and hip. At the time of the Gershwin sessions Ella's interpretive skills were at peak maturity. She could throw anything into the mix of a performance and it would work. Take, for instance, her interpretation on "How Long Has This Been Going On." She floats effortlessly through the lines for most of the track before she ends by paring down the lyrics and speaking the words sensuously for added effect: "Kiss me twice/Once more/Thrice/Make it four." (For a discussion of "How Long Has This Been Going On," as recorded by Ella and Oscar Peterson on their duo album, see the section on Peterson in Chapter 9.)

Throughout the Gershwin *Song Book,* Nelson Riddle complements Ella's singing with transcendent arrangements. Applying his finely honed skills in instrumentation and orchestration, he uses clever instrumental combinations and richly structured harmonies to produce a variety of orchestral colors. Ella is so good at what she does that Riddle has the freedom on such a major project to support her with equally virtuosic instrumental accompaniment, the strong solos and ensemble work often lasting more than just a few bars. On tunes like "Strike Up the Band," "Things Are Looking Up," "'S Wonderful," "My Cousin in Milwaukee," "He Loves and She Loves," and "Our Love Is Here to Stay," Riddle's writing is at once creatively interesting for the listener and a showcase for the talented studio players. For instance, on "Strike Up the Band," from the musical of the same name, the arrangement moves back and forth seamlessly between energetic march melodies and easy-flowing swing passages. Riddle even adds a duet for piccolo and tuba. (In her 1950 recording of Gershwin songs with pianist Ellis Larkins, Ella sang "Soon," also from *Strike Up the Band.* For a discussion of this track, see the section on Larkins in Chapter 9.)

Among the other swinging tracks on the album are "My One and Only," "Let's Call the Whole Thing Off," "That Certain Feeling," and "A Foggy Day." On "Fascinating Rhythm," Ella navigates the tricky melodic rhythms with precision at a refreshingly medium tempo. "Nice Work if You Can Get It" and "They All Laughed" both have Ella crooning verses with elegant backing by guitarist Barney Kessel.

The only waltz on the Gershwin album is "By Strauss," from the 1936 revue *The Show Is On.* Riddle supplies an accompaniment that is in the best spirit of the Viennese-waltz tradition, albeit with a bunch of swing added in.

The "Real American Folk Song" is one of the more obscure songs in the Gershwin catalog, a song that was introduced by Nora Bayes in the 1918 musical play *Ladies First.* Discographer J. Wilfred Johnson points out that it was the first song on which the Gershwin brothers collaborated.[27] It was not recorded for a little over forty years until Ella Fitzgerald did her version for the Gershwin *Song Book.* True to the original nature of the number,

Nelson Riddle's arrangement includes some nimble-fingered piano rag-time to accompany Ella's spirited singing. In the book of liner notes for the *Complete Ella Fitzgerald Song Books*, Lou Levy and Vic Feldman are listed as the pianists on the session. However, in his comprehensive book written in 1959 to accompany the *Gershwin Song Book*, Lawrence D. Stewart names Lou Bush as the ragtime player.

The ballad performances alone on the Gershwin *Song Book* would en-sure the superiority of the album. On time-honored standards like "But Not for Me," "The Man I Love," "Someone to Watch Over Me," and "I've Got a Crush on You," Ella sings beautifully. Her sure vocal control, par-ticularly in her lower register, is a highlight on "Love Walked In." On "They Can't Take That Away from Me," she grooves at a medium-slow tempo, in the spirit of the best soul singers. A pleasant surprise on the album is the version of "Oh, Lady Be Good." Taken at the unexpected ballad tempo, Riddle and Fitzgerald emphasize the elegance of the me-lodic line and create one of the most engaging statements of the whole session.

"I Got Rhythm" was the logical choice as the last offering, the big finale, on the original LP releases of the Gershwin *Song Book*. The song was writ-ten for the musical *Girl Crazy*. Although the show did not become a major hit after it opened on October 30, 1930, it was nonetheless a spirited affair and it contained other outstanding numbers, such as "But Not for Me" and "Embraceable You." To ensure a suitable realization of the music for the stage performance, George Gershwin and the producers had top jazz players in the pit. "When the show opened at the Alvin," relates Gershwin biographer Joan Peyser, "the line-up included [Red] Nichols on cornet, Charlie Teagarden on trumpet, Glenn Miller on trombone, Benny Good-man on clarinet, and Gene Krupa on drums. During intermission, these men took off on jam sessions, thrilling audiences."[28]

It is not an exaggeration to say that "I Got Rhythm," or at least the harmonies on which its chorus is constructed, is required knowledge for serious instrumentalists, singers, composers, arrangers, writers, and afi-cionados. Not only one of the Gershwins' most famous songs, it is also one of the most widely performed and imitated compositions of all time. Over the years, jazz and popular performers have composed literally thousands of compositions based on its chord progression. In blowing sessions, an indication that the harmony of a tune is "rhythm changes" would be the only information the musicians would need to create their improvisations. In the 1940s, when the beboppers were working out their ideas, they added modifications to Gershwin's original harmonies, but the song has never lost its basic identity since its conception.

Most musicians aren't even aware that there is a verse to "I Got Rhythm." Ella includes the verse, something that is rarely, if ever, heard. It opens slowly, posing a question: "Days can be sunny with never a sigh/

Don't need what money can buy/ Birds in the trees sing their dayful of song/Why shouldn't we sing along?" The tempo becomes brisker and Ella croons the closing lyrics of the verse: "I'm chipper all the day/happy with my lot/How do I get that way?/Look at what I've got."

After the enlightening opening, Ella and the orchestra members continue swinging at the same comfortable, medium tempo for the choruses. The first half of Ella's opening chorus is shown in Example 7.7. Over these eight measures, she sticks closely to the original contours of the melody. The interest in the passage results from her rhythmic treatment of the principal motive. In measures 1 and 2, she sings "I got rhythm," ending on two quick eighth-notes. In measures 3 and 4, she adds "I got music" on the same lick in retrograde. In measures 5 and 6, and 13 and 14, she uses this same motive again, but holds the final note a little longer. In measures 9 and 10, and 11 and 12, she sings the principal motive, as she had done at the outset, but she ends on two quarter-notes instead of swinging eighth-notes.

Ella scats over the first half of her second chorus on "I Got Rhythm." For a discussion of this solo, including its intriguing similarities to a version by Leo Watson, one of Ella's influences, see the section on Watson in Chapter 3.

If Nelson Riddle had collaborated with Ella Fitzgerald on nothing but the *George and Ira Gershwin Song Book* his legacy with the great singer would have been firmly established. Fortunately for him, and for the listening public, he was afforded several more opportunities to record with

Example 7.7: "I Got Rhythm" *(Gershwin Song Book)*

her. "Ella Fitzgerald, one of the purest natural talents who has ever lived . . . is very relaxed and easy-going, her marvelous concept of singing entirely unconventional and instinctive," remarked an unrestrained Riddle. "Working with her . . . is utterly devoid of problems of any kind, and she is almost always cheerful, willing and cooperative."[29]

Riddle was at the helm for the final two *Song Books*, the seventh, with the music of Jerome Kern, and the eighth, showcasing songs with words by Johnny Mercer, the sole lyricist-only among the elite group of songwriters. (Billy May had written the charts for the sixth *Song Book*, featuring the music of Harold Arlen; see the section on Billy May in this chapter.)

With only 12 and 13 tracks respectively, the Kern and Mercer collections are by far the shortest of the series. By the time of the Kern recordings, the *Song Books* had already made their mark, but Norman Granz decided there was room for a little more. Although Kern and Mercer had worked respectively with several different lyricists and composers, Granz felt that the individual importance of the two masters would merit their being showcased in the last two *Song Book* projects. In his liner notes for the *Complete Song Books*, John McDonough says that the Kern and Mercer collections "lacked the sense of occasion that had surrounded the earlier albums."[30] This may have been so, but it does not diminish the fact that the two albums presented outstanding music. Furthermore, Ella Fitzgerald and Nelson Riddle were always invigorated when they collaborated. Commenting on the *Jerome Kern Song Book*, writer Martin Williams credits Nelson Riddle "with a good understanding of Ella Fitzgerald, with miraculously relevant taste in scoring for strings, and with the same coy brass figures that he has been using for the past ten years."[31]

Recorded in early January 1963, the Kern album's first seven selections are arranged with slow, freely-rendered verses followed by swinging choruses at various tempos. Ella sings effortlessly on the opener, "Let's Begin." In the accompanying chart Riddle makes good use of muted brass and also leaves room for a brief trombone solo. Brass chords and Paul Smith's piano fills open the second selection, "A Fine Romance," a take that has everyone digging in. The track is nonstop energy and Riddle adds two modulations in the process, from the opening key of F, through G-flat to G. Ella had recorded the tune in 1957 on the second of her seminal duo albums with Louis Armstrong. Interestingly, she opened similarly in the key of F on that occasion, but she also easily made the transition to B-flat in order to sing with Armstrong in his key. For a closer look at that performance, see the section on Armstrong in Chapter 3.

On "I'll Be Hard to Handle," the ubiquitous Paul Smith backs Ella with supple flourishes on the verse before the swinging choruses kick in. "I'm Old Fashioned" cooks throughout with Riddle adding a rousing, Basie-like ensemble break midway through the performance. Granz and Fitzergerald also program two of Kern's lesser-known numbers, "You Couldn't Be Cuter" and "She Didn't Say 'Yes'." On the latter, Riddle's writing includes some richly voiced passages for a combination of flutes and muted brass.

For jazz musicians, "All the Things You Are" is an all-time standard, on the exclusive short list that includes tunes like Gershwin's "I Got Rhythm," Johnny Green's "Body and Soul," and Billy Strayhorn's "Take the 'A' Train." With lyrics by Oscar Hammerstein II, Jerome Kern composed "All the Things You Are" for the 1939 musical *Very Warm for May*. Ever since, popular and improvising vocalists and instrumentalists have continuously worked out on its ingenious chord progression and appealing melody. Surprisingly, Ella's version on the Jerome Kern *Song Book* is the only one she ever recorded during her career.

While "All the Things You Are" is both a lovely and ingeniously crafted tune, its melodic rhythm, as its appears on the published sheet music, is conservative. There are only four eighth-notes in the whole piece; the rest of the music is quarter-notes and higher. The melody obviously presents innumerable possibilities for interpretation. Ella's opening chorus is shown in Example 7.8. Nelson Riddle starts the arrangement with an eight-bar intro dominated by the trombones and trumpets. In contrast to this brassy opening, Ella' s singing is relaxed, with even a hint of restraint. She stays faithful to the melody for the first four measures and is looser for the rest of the chorus. Wherever the original melody is consecutive quarter-notes, she alters the rhythms. On both the word "winter" in measures 5 and 6 and "evening" in measures 11 and 12, she swings the first syllable across the barline and lands on the second syllable on the second half of beat one. She uses the same phrasing for successive words also, on "And some" in measures 28 and 29, and "I'll know" in measures 30 and 31. In measure 7 she bends the word "long" down a half-step from B-flat to A. In measures 12 and 13 she sings the words "that trembles on the brink" with a combination of syncopated eight-notes and a quarter-note triplet. She also makes good use of quarter-note triplets on the words "You are the" in measure 16, "The dearest" in measure 20, and "are what you" in measure 22. Throughout the chorus, Ella sings in the lower end of her range, always controlled and in tune. Riddle supplies only sparse instrumental accompaniment at first. On the bridge, he gives Ella a background of strings, punctuated by the tenor saxophone fills of Plas Johnson. Although the brass re-enters strongly toward the end of the bridge, Ella reacts only minimally and maintains her predominantly subdued mood until the end of the chorus.

The orchestra takes over for a swinging half-chorus, playing mostly melody. Ella then reverses the direction of Kern's original line and comes in at the bridge on *descending* quarter-notes. Her phrasing throughout the bridge is amazing (Example 7.9). In measure 17, she shifts the rhythm

Example 7.8: "All the Things You Are" *(Jerome Kern Song Book)*

Example 7.9: "All the Things You Are" *(Jerome Kern Song Book)*

forward on the words "angel glow" by placing the second syllable of "angel" on beat three of the measure, instead of on the second half of beat two as originally written. She holds the word "glow" longer than expected, over the barline into measure 18. As a result, the next motive is now shifted forward. The words "that lights a star" normally fall on beats two, three, and four in measure 18 and on beat one in measure 19. Ella, however, starts the motive on beats three and four in measure 18, and on beat one in measure 19. This lets her swing the motive by delaying the entrance of the word "star" until the second half of beat one. Between measures 20 and 23, Ella closes out the bridge with sophisticated phrasing built mostly around quarter-note triplets.

Of the remaining five tracks on the Kern album, "Remind Me" and "Yesterdays" are both given straight-eighth-note Latin rhythms at comfortable tempos. "The Way You Look Tonight" is a no-frills ballad; minus a verse, Riddle substitutes with a peaceful two-bar intro for the strings and Ella does a single chorus. Oscar Hammerstein II was the lyricist on both "Why Was I Born," for *Sweet Adeline* in 1929, and "Can't Help Lovin' Dat Man," for *Show Boat* in 1927. Ella and Riddle opt for a dramatic treatment of the latter, the singer and instrumental accompaniment building steadily in intensity as the performance progresses.

The eighth and last *Song Book,* a collection of songs with lyrics by Johnny Mercer, was recorded in October 1964. Mercer is the only featured songwriter in the series who worked almost exclusively as a lyricist. Eleven of the album's 13 songs are products of his collaborations with different composers; he wrote the music, as well as the words, on the other 2 selections. Ella Fitzgerald had of course performed songs with Mercer's lyrics on countless occasions during her career, including on a number of tracks on both the Harold Arlen and Jerome Kern *Song Books.*

The Mercer *Song Book* is another gem. Ella is as hot as ever, as if she is sending a message to the listener: "This is the final *Song Book*—so check it out." Nelson Riddle supplies his usual exciting charts and there is plenty of terrific soloing from a number of top-notch players on the session. This time around there are no string sections in the ensemble; Riddle writes for the classic big band, with harp and a few extra woodwinds thrown in. He makes sure that everyone gets a chance to stretch out.

On the first track, Richard Whiting's "Too Marvelous for Words," the music is highly charged from the outset and Ella is obviously delighted as she belts out the lyrics. Riddle gives the band its own hot half-chorus, leaving room for pianist Paul Smith's inventive soloing throughout. On Rube Bloom's "Day In-Day Out," Babe Russin interjects hip tenor saxophone lines throughout the medium-tempo swinger. Hoagy Carmichael's "Skylark" swings slowly, at danceable tempo, but with infectious energy nonetheless. The arrangement opens and closes with avian-like flute riffs, probably played by Buddy Collette.

One of the most obscure songs in the Mercer collection—for that matter, one of the most obscure songs on any of the *Song Books*—is "Single-O," a soulful swinger composed by Donald Kahn. Discographer J. Wilfred Johnson points out that the song was copyrighted six days after Ella recorded it. "As far as can be determined," adds Johnson, "no other recording of this song exists. . . . Donald Kahn . . . is the son of the esteemed lyricist, Gus Kahn."[32]

Among the classic ballads on the album are Ralph Burns's and Woody Herman's "Early Autumn," "Laura" by David Raksin, and Victor Schertzinger's "I Remember You." Johnny Mercer's two compositions on the album are "Something's Gotta Give" and "Dream." The former is a rocking swinger with solo space for tenor saxophonist Plas Johnson; the latter, taken at a slower tempo, includes clarinetist Buddy DeFranco's impressive boppish solo.

In addition to their collaborations on the *Song Books*, Ella Fitzgerald and Nelson Riddle were teamed for four more albums together. All feature Ella in fine voice, regardless of what stage of her career she was in at the time of the recordings. Many of the tunes on these albums were staples of Ella's repertoire, but there was a large number she had never recorded.

Ella Swings Brightly with Nelson, recorded in November and December 1961 and released in March 1962, is the earliest of the non-*Song Book* albums that Fitzgerald and Riddle made together. Ten composers are represented on the 12 tracks of the original LP, Duke Ellington and Jerome Kern the composers with two songs covered. The 1993 CD reissue has three additional tracks from other writers. Of Ellington's songs, "I'm Gonna Go Fishin'" is rather obscure. Discographer J. Wilfred Johnson reports that the "music is an extension and adaptation of a theme from Ellington's score for the 1959 Columbia film *Anatomy of a Murder*."[33] The second Ellington selection, the familiar "What Am I Here For?," has lyrics by Frankie Laine. Ella is right at home on the catchy tune, as she always is with the great bandleader's music. She would record this song one more time, four years later on the album *Ella at Duke's Place*. For an illustration and discussion of her singing on that later version, see the section on Ellington in Chapter 8. The selections by Jerome Kern are "I Won't Dance" and "Pick Yourself Up." Benny Green proved to be prophetic in his liner notes to the original LP when he called Kern "a composer so prolific and so gifted that his output might have merited a Song Book all to itself."[34]

Ella Swings Brightly starts off with "When Your Lover Has Gone." Indicative of the album's intent and belying the song's title, Ella and Riddle provide a rousing rendition. Ella's phrasing in the first half of her opening chorus is shown in Example 7.10. Singing in the key of D-flat, she sticks closely to the melody on the words "When you're alone" in measures 1 and 2, adding a little swing to the motive but staying on the expected pitches of C, C, B, and B-flat. In measure 4, however, on the words "starlit skies," Ella uses one of her favorite devices, that of inserting a skip within a motive. The three pitches at this point would be a B followed by two B-flats. Ella changes the middle pitch to an F, dropping down a tritone between the syllables of "starlit" and jumping back a fourth to the word "skies." The next time she sings the words "When you're alone," in measures 5 and 6, she starts on a quarter-note triplet and ends by bending the word "lone" through an eighth-note triplet. In measures 11 and 12 she sings the words "there is no" on a quarter-note triplet and finishes the motive by swinging the word "sunrise." She completes the passage by

Example 7.10: "When Your Lover Has Gone" *(Ella Swings Brightly with Nelson)*

bending the verb "has" through an eighth-note triplet, holding it for two and a half more beats, and then swinging into the word "gone" as she slides down a major third.

For versions of "When Your Lover Has Gone," by Ella with Oscar Peterson on their album *Ella and Oscar,* and by Louis Armstrong on a recording with his big band of the early 1930s, see the section on Peterson in Chapter 9. Ella recorded the song with Peterson some 14 years after her session here with Riddle. Her non-repetitive phrasing on the two takes clearly indicates how she remained consistently inventive over the years. Incidentally, she sings the song in D-flat with Nelson Riddle but starts in C with Oscar Peterson before the two modulate up a half-step to D-flat halfway through their track.

Throughout *Ella Swings Brightly*, the two headliners stay hot, at any tempo, on songs like "Don't Be That Way," "Love Me or Leave Me," "I Only Have Eyes for You," "The Gentleman Is a Dope," "Alone Together," and "Mean to Me." (For a discussion of Fitzgerald's only other recorded version of Fred Ahlert's "Mean to Me," in a duet with Oscar Peterson some years later, see the section on Peterson in Chapter 9.)

"I Hear Music," with lyrics by Frank Loesser and music by Burton Lane, is a bright, positive song. Nelson Riddle has the band cooking right from the outset with a blaring eight-bar intro and Ella comes in swinging, already in high gear. Her opening chorus is shown in Example 7.11. She stays pretty close to the original melodic lines, but we do hear her again inserting little skips within motives a number of times. In measures 3 and 27 she attacks the word "mighty" on the second half of beat one, drops down a fifth between its syllables, and returns a fourth to the word "fine." In measure 11 she reverses direction, splitting the syllables of "mighty" on the last two notes of a quarter-note triplet and ascending a fourth before dropping back a fifth to the word "fine." She produces a variation of this latter motive in measure 25, stretching the pronoun "I" through the same direction and intervals, but adding syncopation by attacking on the second half of beat one. She adds yet another alteration to the same motive in measure 12 on the word "music,'" in measure 15 on the words "coffee right," and in measure 26 on the words "hear music." In each case, after she skips up to a B-flat, she drops back down a major sixth to a D-flat, the minor third of the key (B-flat) before she completes the motive. Ella often added chromatic pitches to her lines in order to imply alternative harmonies, but in this case the D-flats are functioning as blue notes in the key.

On her aforementioned 1975 album with Oscar Peterson, Ella sings her only other recorded version of "I Hear Music." (See the section on Peterson in Chapter 9.) Interestingly, she sings it in the key of C with Peterson, a step up from the key of B-flat that she sings with Nelson Riddle. Although her version with Peterson is still superb, one can occasionally dis-

Example 7.11: "I Hear Music" *(Ella Swings Brightly with Nelson)*

cern the slightest hints of strain when she sings her highest notes. It is curious why Ella, who was obviously older, and whose voice had deepened by the time of her recording with Peterson, didn't again sing in the key of B-flat. One explanation could be that she wanted to minimize using the *lowest* notes in her range.

Ella Swings Gently with Nelson was recorded in late 1961 (on the same studio dates that yielded *Ella Swings Brightly with Nelson*) and in April

1962. Released in November 1962, there are 13 tracks on the original LP; the 1993 CD reissue has 2 additional tracks. In addition to wonderful takes on tunes such as "I Can't Get Started," "Imagination," "I Wished on the Moon," and "Body and Soul," tunes that Ella had already recorded on previous dates, we hear her lone recorded versions of "Sweet and Slow," "Darn That Dream," "He's Funny That Way," and "My One and Only Love." Among the remaining tracks, "Street of Dreams," "Georgia on My Mind," and "The Very Thought of You" are also first-time selections, but Ella would record other versions of all three in later years.

Ella and Riddle feature the music of Cole Porter again on *Dream Dancing.* Thirteen of the LP's 15 tracks were recorded in June 1972 and, through an agreement with Norman Granz, released by Atlantic Records later that year under its first title, *Ella Sings Cole.* In February 1978, the 2 additional tracks were recorded and added to the album when it was reissued by Pablo that year. Seven of the selections were repeats from the *Cole Porter Song Book.* Of the remainder, 6 belong to the group of songs that Ella had not previously done in the studio. These are the 2 numbers added in 1978, the title track and "After You," as well as "So Near and Yet So Far," "Down in the Depths (on the Ninetieth Floor)," "At Long Last Love," and "Without Love." Ella's version of "C'est Magnifique" on *Dream Dancing* remains her only recording of the song released to date although she first recorded it during some live Los Angeles club dates she made with Paul Smith and his trio in 1962. Similarly, Ella had also made one previous recording of "My Heart Belongs to Daddy," but that was the 1954 version on *Songs in a Mellow Mood,* the second of her superior albums with pianist Ellis Larkins.

The Best is Yet to Come, recorded in early February 1982, was the last album on which Ella and Nelson Riddle worked together. Among its 10 selections are "Don't Be That Way," "You're Driving Me Crazy," and "Deep Purple," songs that Ella had recorded often on previous dates. She also does "Autumn in New York," the lovely Vernon Duke number that she first pressed with Louis Armstrong in 1957, and "Somewhere in the Night," identified by discographer J. Wilfred Johnson as the theme from *The Naked City,* a television show in the early 1960s.[35] The album's remaining tracks feature songs not covered by Ella on any other recordings: the title track, a Carolyn Leigh/Cy Coleman tune that had been a hit for both Tony Bennett and Frank Sinatra, in 1959 and 1964 respectively; "I Wonder Where Our Love Has Gone," first recorded by Lou Rawls in 1958; "Good-bye," the melancholy ballad composed by Gordon Jenkins in 1935 and later adopted by Benny Goodman to be his closing theme; and two songs linked to Billie Holiday, "Any Old Time" and "God Bless the Child."

The Best is Yet to Come continues to elicit mixed reactions, primarily because of the combination of Ella's occasionally shaky voice and the dark textures of Riddle's unorthodox orchestrations that, in some cases, employ the unusual instrumentation of flutes, French horns, and cellos. In any event, while Ella is not consistently at the top of her game this time around, she is still Ella, and magnificent in many instances—and Riddle, the craftsman, produces plenty of wonderful music.

Billy May

Billy May, a first-rate arranger and trumpeter, was born in Pittsburgh, Pennsylvania, on November 10, 1916. His has been a long and multifaceted career during which he remained active through the mid-1990s.

Whatever training he may have had, May's inventive, panoramic, and occasionally humor-filled arrangements indicate the influence of Duke Ellington. May's originality was evident early in his career as a result of a famous arrangement of "Cherokee" that he penned in 1939 for Charlie Barnet's band.

Following his stint with Barnet, May went with Glenn Miller from 1940 to 1942. In addition to his writing at the time, May was blowing a hot trumpet, so much so that George T. Simon, in his comprehensive book *The Big Bands*, recounts that "the real excitement came from the horn of big, broad-shouldered-and-bellied Billy May, who not only played excellent lead but also emoted some of the best jazz that ever came from the Miller ranks."[36]

May also worked with Les Brown and Alvino Rey for short periods before doing studio work on the west coast for a number of years. In the late 1940s, he began working steadily as a musical director, arranging and conducting on the staffs of NBC and Capitol Records. *Down Beat* reported that "Billy hits a mad pace of penmanship and conducting, carrying out such assignments as the scoring job for John Scott Trotter's ork [*sic*] . . . on the Bing Crosby transcriptions; conducting and writing music for the *Ozzie and Harriet* Sunday night radio stanza; scoring and conducting a string of kiddie albums for Capitol; and similar chores for other recordings and transcriptions."[37]

Over the years May provided scores for television and film and served as musical director for many great artists, including Peggy Lee, Nat King Cole, Bing Crosby, Rosemary Clooney, Frank Sinatra, and Ella Fitzgerald. His sides with Sinatra in particular were big hits. He also recorded several albums under his own name for Capitol, most of this output coming during the 1950s.

For the sixth *Song Book*, Norman Granz chose to feature the music of Harold Arlen, the highly inventive composer whose achievements include one of the twentieth century's greatest songs, "Over the Rainbow." Arlen began working professionally in the 1920s and was already experienced as a pianist, arranger, and singer by the time his first song of note, "Get Happy," was published in 1930. Over the next five decades, well into the 1970s, he composed more than four hundred songs. In the process, he worked with a number of master lyricists, most notably Johnny Mercer, Ted Koehler, E. Y. Harburg, Leo Robin, and Ira Gershwin.

Norman Granz considered Arlen's music to be considerably blues oriented and he engaged Billy May as the musical director for the *Song Book* sessions. May wrote most of the charts, but it is known that a few were contracted out to other arrangers, two of whom were Russell Garcia and Walter Sheets. "Norman was a pain," recalled May. "I remember he was upset when I didn't write a whole lot of jazz things in there as improvisations. So we made room for some solos by Benny Carter. As for Ella, she was always very sweet and cooperative."[38] May's negative impression of Granz aside, the resulting album is a tour de force. In commenting about the Arlen *Song Book,* Will Friedwald, in his book *Jazz Singing,* describes May as "an arranger as bodacious as [Nelson] Riddle is subtle."[39] There is obviously a lot of high energy on the album, but that appears to have been Norman Granz's intention in the first place. It should be noted that there are also many instances, particularly in the ballads and slower swinging numbers, when the versatile May provides writing that is sensitive, subdued, and elegant.

For the better part of the album, May backs Ella with the standard big-band instrumentation. The opening track, "Blues in the Night," is a burner, over seven minutes of down-in-the-gut jazz with emotion-packed singing by Fitzgerald, powerful ensemble writing, and a great alto saxophone solo by Benny Carter. Surprisingly, the track ends with a fade out, an extreme rarity for an Ella Fitzgerald recording. Among the other big-band tracks, "Stormy Weather" and "When the Sun Comes Out" are two selections that corroborate Norman Granz's comment about the bluesiness of Arlen's tunes. Ella sings with a lot of soul on each and May throws in some effective double-time passages in the arrangement for the latter. "That Old Black Magic" grooves straight-ahead at medium tempo and includes some brief but effective solo work by tenor saxophonist Plas Johnson. "Hooray for Love," "Let's Take a Walk around the Block," and "Ac-cent-tchu-ate the Positive" are also spirited swingers, the latter showcasing Ella's strong command in the lower end of her range. Ella puts a lot of feeling into "One for My Baby (and One More for the Road)," a tune that would also be a hit for Frank Sinatra. "Get Happy" is a fiery up-tempo romp.

For some of the tracks, May pares down the big band, using only one trumpet and one trombone in combination with a full complement of saxophones and a rhythm section with vibraphone added. Ella does nice takes on tunes like "Let's Fall in Love," moving aside momentarily for solos by Benny Carter and trombonist Milt Bernhart; "Between the Devil and the Deep Blue Sea," an appealing swinger that also includes a short solo break by vibraphonist Emil Richards; and "Come Rain or Come Shine," taken straight-ahead in a medium-tempo groove. (For a discussion of Ella's version of "Come Rain or Come Shine" with Oscar Peterson, see the section on Peterson in Chapter 9.)

There are many nice moments on the tracks with strings added to the ensemble. May provides an appealing laid-back groove on "My Shining Hour" and Milton Bernhart's muted trombone solo adds a nice touch. On "This Time the Dream's on Me," Ella sings with a gorgeous tone and much sensitivity. The track opens with some hip licks by guitarist Herb Ellis and Benny Carter takes a lush alto saxophone solo a little later on. "Over the Rainbow," taken at a relaxed medium tempo, is given a jazzier treatment than might be expected. Because Judy Garland's rendition in *The Wizard of Oz* was so established in the public's consciousness, this might have been the most logical way to let Ella put her own personal stamp on it. Whatever the case, her singing is radiant and convincing.

What is astonishing about the Ella of the 1950s and 1960s, when she was at the absolute height of her powers, is that she was constantly out-doing herself when it appeared that it could not be humanly possible to be any better. If one listens to nothing else but the *Song Books*, in the order of their releases, it is downright uncanny how with each successive album Ella's performances attain new levels. Quoted in the liner notes for the original LP release of the *Harold Arlen Song Book,* the great composer him-self leaves no doubt about his admiration for Ella's singing: "She is unique. Her style is unlike anyone else's—she stands alone while most everybody else is derivative. She has sung songs and made them irresis-tibly attractive. . . . Her voice, her style are pure unadulterated American, her phrasing impeccable—she improvises playfully and with more flu-idity than most instrumentalists."[40]

Ella's interpretations on any of the album's songs substantiate Arlen's comments. Take, for example, her version of "I've Got the World on a String." Ted Koehler's lyrics in the verse could serve as Ella's personal motto: "Joy you may define in a thousand ways/but a case like mine needs a special phrase/to reveal how I feel." Ella definitely has the world on a string—and she's also sitting on top of it. Her "case" needs a "special phrase" because of the sublime quality of her voice and of the way she sings with sensitivity, conviction—and "joy." The opening of her first cho-rus is shown in Example 7.12. Swinging at a medium tempo, she produces such a feeling of relaxed confidence that it is easy to overlook the com-plexity of her phrasing as she develops the passage gradually from motive to motive. She starts simply in measure 1 with a quarter-note triplet/half-note combination on the words "world on a string." In measure 2 she takes "sittin' on a rainbow" through an eighth-note triplet and eighth-notes. In measure 3 it is sixteenth notes tied to an eighth-note triplet on

Example 7.12: "I've Got the World on a String" (*Harold Arlen Song Book*)

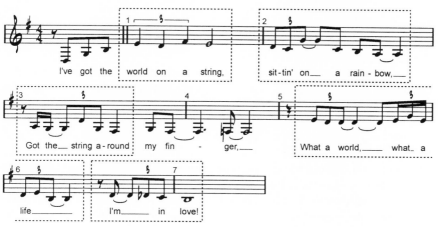

"Got the string around." In measures 5 and 6, on the words "What a world, what a life," note her agility, especially in the way she bends the words "what" and "life," respectively on a sixteenth-note triplet at the end of measure 5 and on an eighth-note triplet in measure 6. She completes the passage with a chromatically descending eighth-note triplet as she sings "I'm in love." Throughout these measures we have another example of the fullness of Ella's voice and her controlled intonation in the lower reaches of her range.

After the opening chorus, the band takes a half-chorus during which there is a brief alto saxophone solo, perhaps by Ted Nash, although he is listed as playing tenor saxophone in the credits for this track. Ella returns at the bridge and once again manhandles the melodic motives with incredibly elastic phrasing (Example 7.13). In particular, note how she starts by stretching the word "beautiful" through a tricky tuplet figure, holding momentarily across the barline into measure 17, and ending on descending sixteenth-notes. Because this arrangement is based in the key of G major, the lyrics "as long as I hold," in measure 18, would normally all be sung on successive Bs, the root of the B-dominant chord that occurs at this point in the harmonic progression; the words "the string" would then be sung in measure 19 on successive C-sharps, the thirteenth of the subsequent E-dominant chord. Ella starts the motive on a B, as expected, but she reshapes the line by ascending the distance of a minor sixth to a G-natural on the word "I" and then descending the distance of a diminished fifth back to the two C-sharps. Here, in addition to her ingenious melodic manipulation, she also demonstrates her strong ear by altering the harmony, the G-natural at the top of the motive being the flatted thirteenth of the B-dominant chord. In measures 20 and 21, Ella uses a combination

Example 7.13: "I've Got the World on a String" *(Harold Arlen Song Book)*

of eighth-note triplets and swinging eighth-notes on the words "I'd be a silly so and so."

OTHER RECORDINGS FOR VERVE

Frank DeVol

Frank DeVol was a prolific composer and arranger who worked professionally for an amazing 70 years. When he passed away in Lafayette, California, on October 27, 1999, he left behind a vast and impressive list of credits.

DeVol was born in Moundsville, West Virginia, on September 20, 1911, and spent most of his childhood in Canton, Ohio, where his father was the director of the pit orchestra in the city's opera house. He exhibited an aptitude for music at a young age and by the time he reached his early teens he could play violin, piano, and a number of other instruments. He also assisted his father in maintaining the theater's music library and in preparing musical scores for the silent films that were being shown.

At Miami (Ohio) University, DeVol was involved in both music and acting. After graduating he spent the next few years with a number of bands, at various times arranging, playing, singing, and conducting. His work eventually led him to re-locate to California in the mid-1930s and for most of the next twenty-five years he maintained a full schedule as a music director on radio and in the recording studios. The list of outstanding singers with whom he worked includes Peggy Lee, Rosemary Clooney, Tony Bennett, Nat King Cole, and Ella Fitzgerald. *Down Beat* once lauded DeVol as the fastest arranger in the business: "An early riser, he says he will pen one arrangement each morning before reporting to the

CBS studios at 1:30 P.M., from which time they rehearse, play, and transcribe the show for later re-broadcast. He will leave the studio at 4 P.M. and before retiring will write another score and a few bridges."[41]

From the late 1950s on, most of DeVol's work was for television and the movies. He composed or orchestrated the music for over fifty films— among them *Cat Ballou, Pillow Talk, Guess Who's Coming to Dinner, The Brady Bunch Movie,* and *Parent Trap*—as well as several of director Robert Aldrich's movies, such as *Kiss Me Deadly, The Dirty Dozen,* and *Flight of the Phoenix.* His theme songs for some of TV's most popular sitcoms, in particular *My Three Sons* and *The Brady Bunch,* were recognized and loved by millions of listeners. Furthermore, he also had acting roles on these and several other top-rated comedies, including *The Jeffersons, Petticoat Junction, I Dream of Jeannie, Get Smart,* and *My Favorite Martian.*

Like Someone in Love was recorded in October 1957 and released in 1958. Indicative of its title, the album is comprised of ballads with themes related to love. As such, it becomes another magnificent showcase for Ella, who often commented about the joy she got from singing ballads. Frank DeVol' s arrangements are suitably sensual and subdued. The strings are predominant, with romantic lines in the different sections and rich writing for the full complement, but there are also tasteful doses of celeste, flute, French horn, and other assorted instruments. Backing everything is a rhythm section to provide the right pulses at the right times. As an added treat, the great tenor saxophonist Stan Getz solos on four of the tracks: "There's a Lull in My Life," "What Will I Tell My Heart," "Midnight Sun," and "You're Blasé." Among the rest of the selections are "More Than You Know," "I Never Had a Chance," "We'll Be Together Again," "Then I'll Be Tired of You," "Like Someone in Love," and "I Thought About You." All are accorded lovely renderings.

"Close Your Eyes," composed by Bernice Petkere in 1932, is one of the lesser known numbers on the album. In his arrangement, DeVol establishes a dreamy mood with singing strings and the repetitive beating of bongos in the background. He adds an effective change of pace by interspersing slow swing passages that groove nicely while still maintaining the ethereal mood of the performance.

"What's New" is perhaps the jazziest track on the album. This was the only version of the Johnny Burke/Bob Haggart song that Ella recorded during her career. Frank DeVol keeps the strings in the arrangement, but he lets Ella go for stretches with just the rhythm section. Toward the end, she comes about as close as she does on the whole album to improvising, adding a brief flourish on the song's final words. Incidentally, the saxophone lines on this track are the first we hear that are not performed by Stan Getz. Altoist Ted Nash takes the brief solo, as he does on "How Long Has This Been Going On." He also solos on extra tracks that were added to *Like Someone in Love* when it was reissued on CD in 1991: "I'll Never Be the Same," "Lost in a Fog," "Everything Happens to Me," and "So Rare." The four performances were heard originally on *Hello Love,* another album with Ella and Frank DeVol.

Released in 1960, *Hello Love* is an album comprised of selections from sessions that Ella did with DeVol in the late 1950s. In addition to the aforementioned songs added to *Like Someone in Love,* Ella sings brilliantly on "You Go to My Head," "Willow Weep for Me," "I'm Through With Love," "I've Grown Accustomed to His Face," "Spring Will Be a Little Late This Year," "Tenderly," "Stairway to the Stars," and "Moonlight in Vermont."

Ella Wishes You a Swinging Christmas was recorded in July and August 1960, and released for the holiday season that year. DeVol wrote the charts for the date but shared the conducting duties with Russell Garcia. (For information on Garcia, see the section on Louis Armstrong in Chapter 3.) Intended to reflect the happiness of Christmas, the album contains most of the beloved numbers that one would expect to find on such a release. With the exception of the ballad "What Are You Doing New Year's Eve," everything is upbeat, on "Jingle Bells," "Santa Claus Is Coming to Town," "Sleigh Ride," "Let It Snow," "Rudolph the Red-Nosed Reindeer," "Frosty the Snowman," and a few other chestnuts. Not surprisingly, Ella also sings "White Christmas," the all-time classic that was a huge hit for Bing Crosby in the 1940s. Verve twice reissued *Ella Wishes You a Swinging Christmas* on CD, in 1988 and 2002, adding to the latter a number of alternate takes and previously unreleased tracks that include "The Secret of Christmas" and a medley of "We Three Kings of Orient Are" and "O Little Town of Bethlehem."

Marty Paich

Marty Paich, a multifaceted musician known primarily for his work as an arranger and musical director, was also an accomplished pianist and bandleader. Born in Oakland, California, on January 23, 1925, he became interested in music early in life after hearing a local accordionist. In fact, he was so intrigued that he asked his parents to buy him an accordion and he was soon playing the instrument. During high school he played the trumpet, developed an affinity for jazz, and put together his own band. By his mid-teens he was already gigging, as well as writing arrangements for the Oakland bandleader Gary Nottingham. From 1943 to 1946, Paich was a bandleader and arranger while in the Army—during this period he began to play piano full time—and he studied composition at the Los Angeles Conservatory of Music from 1946 to 1950.

Beginning in the early 1950s Paich was one of the west coast's most active musicians. He wrote and produced recordings for a who's-who of artists, put out his own albums, and played live engagements. Among those with whom he worked were Shelley Manne, Peggy Lee, Shorty Rogers, Terry Gibbs, Dave Pell, Art Pepper, Ernestine Anderson, Mel Tormé, and Ella Fitzgerald. He also fronted his own 11-member band, the Dektette, which he used on recordings with Tormé and Fitzgerald. The dates with Tormé in particular brought him considerable recognition.

Talking about an album he did with Gary Crosby, Paich's fervency for the music he loved was evident: "A lot of [teen-agers] will buy the album to hear Gary. They'll also hear some modern jazz by such guys as Bud Shank, Claude Williamson and Mel Lewis. And I'm sure that a good many of the younger listeners will like the music enough to follow it up. That's my way of getting jazz to them."[42]

In later years Paich would work more in the realm of commercial music and the visual media, writing arrangements for singers like Carly Simon, Aretha Franklin, and Barbra Streisand, and serving as the musical director on a number of television shows, including those of Glen Campbell and Sonny and Cher. His credits as an orchestrator of film scores include *Pretty Woman* and *The Fugitive*. Paich passed away in Santa Ynez, California, on August 12, 1995.

Several sides that Ella made under the musical direction of Marty Paich have not yet been reissued on CD. Fortunately, three albums are available: *Ella Swings Lightly, Ella Sings Broadway,* and *Whisper Not.*

Ella Swings Lightly was recorded in late November 1958 and released in the spring of the following year. In his liner notes to the 1992 CD reissue of this album, James Gavin comments that the recording "follows no other formula other than to match [Ella] with the repertoire she loved most—Tin Pan Alley and Swing Era standards."[43] Marty Paich backs Ella on the session with his working group of the time, the Dek-tette. A collection of topflight musicians—among them alto saxophonist Bud Shank, tenor saxophonist Bill Holman, trumpeters Don Fagerquist and Al Porcino, pianist Lou Levy, and drummer Mel Lewis—they were players with roots in the big-band tradition who knew how to give the music its due and how to back a great singer in the process. Lou Levy was also Ella's regular accompanist at this time. (See the section on Levy in Chapter 9.)

On the album's opening track, Walter Donaldson's "Little White Lies," the compatibility among everyone is quickly evident. Ella and the band are, to use musicians' vernacular, "in the pocket," establishing a great mood as they swing at a relaxed tempo. Don Fagerquist adds some nice colors with muted-trumpet licks behind Ella's vocals.

On "You Hit the Spot," a hard swinger, Bud Shank and trombonist Bob Enevoldsen take solos and Ella coasts effortlessly through two half-step modulations toward the end of the arrangement. "Moonlight on the Ganges," was first recorded by Paul Whiteman in the late 1920s; Ella and the Dek-tette go easy at first before shifting gears and taking it out up-tempo. On the laid-back "My Kinda Love," written by Jo Trent and Louis Alter in 1929, Ella provides lots of soul and there is some excellent ensemble playing by the band. Another tune from 1929 is "Just You, Just Me," written by Raymond Klager and Jesse Greer. Paich opts for a high-speed arrangement that is all bebop and Ella sizzles throughout, alternating between the lyrics and impeccable scatting. Cooking along with her, the horns punctuate with hip licks that include hints of Dizzy Gillespie's "Woody 'n You."

"You Brought a New Kind of Love to Me" and "You're an Old Smoothie" are unhurried swingers, from 1930 and 1932 respectively. "720 in the Books" was first a successful instrumental for Jan Savit in 1939. From the 1940s come "Knock Me a Kiss," a tongue-in-cheek novelty loaded with amorous innuendo that was a hit for Louis Jordan; "What's Your Story, Morning Glory," a bluesy number first recorded by Andy Kirk and his band; and "It's Gotta Be This or That," a tune sung by Benny Goodman, of all people, when he first recorded it in April 1945.

There are two songs by Harold Arlen, "As Long As I Live," composed in 1934 to lyrics by Ted Koehler, and the well-known "Blues in the Night," composed in 1941 by Arlen in partnership with the legendary lyricist Johnny Mercer. Ella would record both songs again about two years later for her Arlen *Song Book*.

"If I Were a Bell," was written by Frank Loesser for *Guys and Dolls* in 1950. Ella's only other recorded version is on *Ella Sings Broadway*, also under the musical direction of Marty Paich. "Teardrops from My Eyes" is a popular hit from the 1950s. "Little Jazz," an instrumental composed in 1957 by Buster Harding and the great trumpeter Roy Eldridge, is another of the countless compositions based on the chord progression of George Gershwin's "I Got Rhythm." Ella is totally at home on this scat vehicle and she soars through the chart. Beginning in the key of C, Paich adds an effective half-step shift up to D-flat and rounds out the arrangement with richly harmonized ensemble licks. (For a detailed discussion on the importance of "I Got Rhythm," see the section on Nelson Riddle in this chapter.)

Ella Swings Lightly is a strong album, with a good mix of selections and solid performances all around. When it was reissued on CD in 1992, four extra tracks were added: two versions of "Oh, What a Night for Love," an alternate take of "Little Jazz," and the Mack David/Jerry Livingston ballad "Dreams Are Made for Children."

Ella and Marty Paich recorded *Ella Sings Broadway* in early October 1962. When the album was released the following year, it appeared to have been planned like a theme album, but it was definitely not meant as another *Song Book*. Whatever the case, it is comprised of principal songs and lighter fare from Broadway musicals staged between 1947 and 1956. As such, the music is decidedly associated with some of the next slew of songwriters who came after those represented on the *Song Books*. There are selections by Richard Rodgers and Oscar Hammerstein II, Alan Jay Lerner and Frederick Loewe, Richard Adler and Jerry Ross, and Frank Loesser. Richard Rodgers's had already been featured on an earlier *Song Book*, but all the songs on that album were written with his previous partner, Lorenz Hart.

Commenting that *Ella Sings Broadway* is "not bad . . . at all," biographer Geoffrey Mark Fidelman also adds that the album "lack[s] the inspiration and chemistry that made her other collections such winners."[44] (Fidelman was also referring to the album *Rhythm Is My Business;* see the section on Bill Doggett in this chapter.) It is of course unreasonable and unrealistic to expect that every album by Ella, or by any top artist, would be a monstrous achievement. In Ella's case, this is especially true because of the lofty standards she set with the *Song Books* and some of the sides she made with her great accompanists. Still, *Ella Sings Broadway* is fantastic, a typically excellent performance. That her articulation is always marvelous is no secret, but the clarity with which Ella sings on this album is downright amazing. Supporting her, Marty Paich reaffirms his talent with excellent arrangements that befit the music. He writes for what sounds like the standard big-band instrumentation, although there may be a few extra players thrown in. The musicians are not identified in the album's liner notes, but it is obvious that all are seasoned professionals and that some are accomplished soloists.

Of the Adler and Ross selections, "Hernando's Hideaway," replete with castanets and tuba providing counterpoint to Ella's opening lines, and "Steam Heat," with Ella digging in on the title words, "S-s-s-s-steam Heat," were written for *Pajama Game*. "Whatever Lola Wants," the novelty number from *Damn Yankees,* has an appropriate exotic feeling to it, with plenty of screeching blasts from the brass, but there are also a few nice swing passages thrown in.

Among Frank Loesser's tunes are two from *Guys and Dolls,* "If I Were a Bell" and the musical's title number. Ella sang the former on her previous album with Marty Paich, *Ella Swings Lightly,* and the arranger again supplies an engaging, relaxed groove for the arrangement. The harmonmuted trumpet solo in mid-chart is very nice, despite the "oohs" and "aahs" of some background vocalists who have been popping in and out of the action. On "Guys and Dolls," Ella and the band tear it up, swinging infectiously at medium tempo on the catchy melody and obviously enjoying themselves. Loesser's other two songs, from *The Most Happy Fella,* are "Warm All Over" and "Somebody Somewhere." Both are pretty ballads that swing slowly; Marty Paich's writing for the woodwinds on the latter is especially effective.

There are two selections by Rodgers and Hammerstein on the album. "Dites-Moi," from *South Pacific,* swings easily without any wasted energy.

The title words are French for "tell me" and Ella certainly tells us by singing a chorus in French, her pronunciation impressively accurate. "No Other Love" from *Me and Juliet* is brief and to the point, a gentle song with some of Marty Paich's sparser writing on the session.

Among the three numbers by Lerner and Loewe is "Almost Like Being in Love" from *Brigadoon*, an energetic swinger with Ella grooving so well that the background vocalists who have returned to add their "aahhs" and "buh, buh, buhs" are actually palatable. "I Could Have Danced All Night," an up-tempo romp, and "Show Me" are from *My Fair Lady*. On the latter, Marty Paich alters the normal 3/4 waltz rhythm in some passages by shortening every second measure to two beats and creating a six-against-five feel. The incredible Ella burns throughout, navigating effortlessly through the irregular pattern whenever it pops up.

Whisper Not, the last album on which Ella and Marty Paich collaborated, was recorded in July 1966. It features some adventurous writing by Paich and a very fine performance by Ella. Biographer Geoffrey Mark Fidelman points out that "Norman Granz allowed several hours of rehearsal time for the orchestra, which usually was not part of his recording equation."[45] The album's potpourri of selections includes the standards "Sweet Georgia Brown," "Whisper Not," "Spring Can Really Hang You Up the Most," "Time After Time," "You've Changed," and "Lover Man"; two big hits of the early 1960s, "Wives and Lovers," the Burt Bacharach/Hal David ditty with roots in the film of the same name, and "Matchmaker, Matchmaker," from *Fiddler on the Roof*; "I've Got Your Number," from the 1962 musical *Little Me*; "I Said No," a Frank Loesser song from the early 1940s; "Ol' MacDonald," the venerable children's song that Ella sang often; and "Thanks for the Memory," adopted by Bob Hope as his theme song after he first crooned it on screen in the late 1930s.

Bill Doggett

Bill Doggett is perhaps an unexpected name in a discussion of arrangers who worked with Ella Fitzgerald. To fans of rhythm and blues he is remembered as a grooving organist who had a big hit in 1956 with a tune called "Honky Tonk." He had, in fact, first made a name for himself as an accomplished and modernistic jazz pianist and arranger.

Born in Philadelphia on February 16, 1916, Doggett played trumpet and piano as a youngster. When he settled on the latter he developed quickly and was gigging by the time he was in high school. In 1939, he recorded his first of several sides with Lucky Millinder and in 1942 he began a two-year stay with the Ink Spots, playing piano, arranging, and recording with the well-known singers. In subsequent years he played with or arranged for many top-rank musicians, among them Lionel Hampton, Illinois Jacquet, Count Basie, and Coleman Hawkins.

In late 1947, Doggett became the pianist in Louis Jordan's band. He took over from Wild Bill Davis who was leaving to concentrate on playing the Hammond organ full-time with the goal of establishing the instrument in the jazz world. Doggett, influenced by Davis, developed his own interest in the organ and later began practicing it diligently whenever he was not touring with Jordan.

Doggett first played piano with Ella Fitzgerald in the mid-1940s, serving for a time as her musical director. Phil Schaap, in his Fitzgerald discography, notes that Doggett "confirmed the existence of eight EF [sic] radio broadcasts during the period that he was her regular accompanist."[46] His first studio date with Ella was in early 1949, when he was still with Louis Jordan. On the recommendation of Wild Bill Davis, Doggett recorded with her again in mid-1951 and early 1952, these times playing organ in small-group sessions that included Hank Jones, Teddy Wilson, Ray Charles, and the Ray Charles Singers. Sy Oliver was the musical director on the former session and one of his arrangements, "Smooth Sailing," was a hot scat feature for Ella that did very well on the charts. The track also brought Doggett's impressive organ playing to the attention of the listening public. "Smooth Sailing" and two more exciting selections from the 1952 session, "Air Mail Special" and "Rough Ridin'," have been reissued by Decca.[47]

Spurred by the success of "Smooth Sailing," and intent on exploring new musical avenues, Doggett left Louis Jordan's group in 1951 and formed his own organ trio. In short order, he was signed by King Records and over the next eight years he recorded often for the company. He would never lose his love of jazz, but his success with the aforementioned "Honky Tonk" firmly established him as a big star of rhythm and blues. After leaving King Records in 1960, Doggett continued recording with other companies through the early part of the decade. From the 1970s on, he enjoyed a resurgence on the jazz scene, and he continued performing in the United States and abroad into the 1990s. He passed away in New York on November 13, 1996.

Rhythm Is My Business was recorded on January 30 and 31, 1962. This is one of the Ella albums about which it is absolutely impossible to even infer something could have been better. The great singer is on fire, at any tempo, and Bill Doggett's equally burning charts constitute an outstanding collection of down-in-the-gut big-band sounds. To top it all off, the top-notch roster of players in the band includes trumpeters Taft Jordan and Ernie Royal, trombonists Kai Winding and Britt Woodman, saxophonists Jerry Dodgion and Phil Woods, pianist Hank Jones, and drummer Gus Johnson.

The album starts with "Rough Ridin'," one of the exciting numbers that Ella and Doggett had recorded together in 1952. Next come "Broadway," from the Count Basie book of the 1940s, and "You Can Depend on

Me," first recorded by Earl "Fatha" Hines in 1932. "Runnin' Wild" dates from 1922 and is an up-tempo blast, Ella belting out the lyrics like only she can. On "Show Me the Way to Go Out of This World," Ella lets us know right from the outset that she's not going to pull any punches. She exclaims "I wanna go now," the band members yell "Go ahead," and she cooks on the medium-tempo number. The blues-flavored "I'll Always Be in Love with You" is taken medium tempo in 6/8 time. The bass line at the beginning of the chart, taken up later by the saxophones, pays homage to Miles Davis's widely admired "All Blues," one of the compositions on the trumpeter's astounding 1959 album *Kind of Blue*.

On "Hallelujah, I Love Him So," Bill Doggett opens with a few gospel-like chords on the organ before Ella and the band groove through the number that had been an R & B hit for Ray Charles in early 1956. Doggett was of course completely familiar with the tune, his own "Honky Tonk" having been a smash success in the same year. Incidentally, the original title of the song is "Hallelujah, I Love Her So." Ella changed the gender in the title words, something she did often during her career when she wanted the message of a song to reflect a woman's perspective—"Have You Met *Sir* Jones" and "The *Boy* from Ipanema" are two other well-known examples.

"I Can't Face the Music," first sung by Mildred Bailey in 1938, is the first slow number on the album. Ella croons soulfully and Phil Woods is all over his alto saxophone on a brief but exciting solo. "No Moon at All" was a popular tune of the late 1940s recorded by, among others, Nat King Cole. Ella's fondness for the tune is apparent from her spirited singing. There are nice tenor saxophone and trumpet solos before the great pianist Hank Jones takes a few bars. Jones was Ella's regular accompanist from 1948 to 1953. (See the section on Hank Jones in Chapter 9.) "Laughin' on the Outside" is a pretty ballad, Ella radiant on the popular number from the mid-1940s and Phil Woods once again cooking on his solo break. On "After You've Gone," Doggett lets Ella open it as a ballad and then kicks up the tempo. Ella and the band take turns on hip licks throughout before cooling off toward the end and putting the finishing touches on a fantastic album. When Verve brought out *Rhythm Is My Business* on CD in 1999, two previously unissued tracks were added: "Taking a Chance on Love" and "If I Could Be with You."

TWO YEARS AT CAPITOL

In late 1967, Norman Granz decided to take a break from the rigors of his work, including producing the many recordings of Ella Fitzgerald. No definitive reason has ever been established as to why Granz made such a move, but Geoffrey Mark Fidelman points out that a few of the people he interviewed "mentioned the constant friction between [Ella and Granz] coupled with Granz's growing legal, financial, and tax problems as some of the reasons."[48] Granz signed Ella with Capitol Records for a four-record deal and relinquished his role as her producer, although he remained her manager. Dave Dexter was now in charge of Ella's recording activities. He and Capitol had specific ideas of how they wanted to present Ella that, as it turned out, simply did not take advantage of the fact that they were working with the greatest singer around.

The first album, recorded in February 1967 and called *Brighten the Corner*, had Ella singing 14 religious songs, backed by a studio chorus and orchestra under the direction of Ralph Carmichael. Ella was a very spiritual person, but the album was bland and uninspired as she sang her way through songs like "Abide With Me," "Just a Closer Walk with Thee," "The Old Rugged Cross," "What a Friend We Have in Jesus," and "Rock of Ages, Cleft For Me."

Ella's next album for Capitol was *Ella Fitzgerald's Christmas*, recorded in July 1967, and also under the musical direction of Ralph Carmichael. This was the second collection of Christmas songs Ella made in her career. The first, *Ella Wishes You a Swinging Christmas*, recorded for Verve seven years before (and arranged by Frank DeVol), was still in the stores. The two recordings differ completely in tone. Whereas the earlier album is a jaunty affair, with "Rudolph," "Frosty," and "Santa" all taking part in the festivities, her later project is comprised of more solemn and religious songs like "O Holy Night," "It Came Upon a Midnight Clear," "Hark the Herald Angels Sing," "Silent Night," "Sleep, My Little Lord Jesus," "O Come All Ye Faithful," and a few more.

In light of Dave Dexter's misguided efforts, Ralph Carmichael was a highly appropriate choice as musical director for Ella's first two projects at Capitol. His has been a varied career with numerous credits in film and television, as well as in the recording studios. However, Carmichael's primary calling has always been in the field of Christian music, a genre in which he is undoubtedly talented and with which he has enjoyed tremendous success. Still a major figure, he was inducted into the National Religious Broadcasters Hall of Fame in 2001.

Ralph Carmichael was born in Quincy, Illinois, on May 27, 1927. Influenced by his father, he began taking lessons on several instruments at a young age and acquired interests in a number of musical styles, including gospel music. While studying at Southern California Bible College in the mid-1940s he led a big band that performed religious selections on a local television station, and in 1950 he began a lengthy run as a film scorer for evangelist Billy Graham's World Wide Pictures. In short order, his activities branched out and he was also serving as musical director for a number of the day's top television programs. Toward the end of the 1950s, Capitol Records hired him and he was the musical director for singers like Nat King Cole, Bing Crosby, Rosemary Clooney, and Perry Como.

During the 1960s he worked with musicians as diverse as bandleader Stan Kenton and pop pianist Roger Williams.

Although Carmichael missed the mark in how he framed Ella's singing, he was not totally to blame in that he was catering to the production goals of Dave Dexter and, in doing so, he worked in the same manner that he did on his other religious recordings. Ella was not afforded a reasonable opportunity to shine on the two albums. She sang well enough, of course, but in the company of sizeable choruses and within the frameworks of the cumbersome arrangements she was weighted down by the large forces involved in the recordings.

For her next album at Capitol, and third in 1967, Ella was pointed in yet another direction. *Misty Blue* featured her singing country and western songs, perhaps the last thing one might have expected from her. Recorded toward the end of December, this was certainly a departure from the norm for the great singer, albeit a project that worked out a lot better than the previous two did. There are some nice moments on the recording, despite the obvious commercial bent of the production. While Ella is accompanied again by a studio orchestra, as well as the ubiquitous chorus, the recording quality is superior to that on the two previous albums. A sampling of the track list reveals Ella doing versions of "Walking in the Sunshine," "Evil on Your Mind," "Don't Let the Doorknob Hit You," "Turn the World Around (the Other Way)," "Born to Lose," "This Gun Don't Care," and "Don't Touch Me."

Ella's musical director on *Misty Blue* was Sid Feller, who was well-known for his lengthy association with Ray Charles—and who had had a big hand in guiding Charles through his highly successful forays into country and western. Born on December 24, 1916, in New York City, Feller played trumpet in his early years, gigging around his home town. While in the Army during World War II, he continued playing and also did some conducting. He began his career as a musical director at Capitol in 1951, staying there until 1955 when, as Ray Charles's biographer Michael Lydon recounts, ABC "hired . . . [the] portly arranger who had made his name producing Jackie Gleason's easy-listening albums."[49] Feller had worked with a number of top stars and began working with Charles in 1960. He left ABC in 1965 and moved to Los Angeles where he freelanced successfully, doing a lot of work for television. He retired in 1991.

For her fourth and final album at Capitol, Ella collaborated with her longtime friend Benny Carter. Titled *30 by Ella* and recorded in late May and early June 1968, the project was all jazz this time around, Carter penning the charts and playing alto saxophone with, among others, trumpeter Harry "Sweets" Edison, tenor saxophonist Georgie Auld, pianist Jimmy Jones, and drummer Louis Bellson. The tunes are grouped into six medleys, each with Ella singing five of the selections and the band doing an instrumental version of the sixth. This was the best album Ella recorded for Capitol, the only one that showcased her properly. The band plays at a high level, as would be expected, and Ella's singing is strong throughout. Included among the selections are "Everything I Have Is Yours," "Goodnight, My Love," "At Sundown," "It's a Wonderful World," "On Green Dolphin Street," "You Stepped Out of a Dream," "Once in a While," "The Lamp Is Low," "All I Do Is Dream of You," "720 in the Books," "Deep Purple," and "You're a Sweetheart." *30 by Ella* was reissued on CD three times, in 1998, 1993, and 1999; the latter includes a bonus track of "Hawaiian War Chant."

ONE FOR PRESTIGE, TWO FOR REPRISE

Norman Granz was back again producing Ella on *Sunshine of Your Love,* an LP she cut for Prestige in February 1969. (Verve reissued the album on CD in 1996.) The album's title was taken from Eric Clapton's rock song of the same name. Recorded at San Francisco's Fairmont Hotel, Ella is backed on 6 of the 12 tracks by the Ernie Hecksher Big Band, singing to arrangements by Marty Paich, Frank DeVol, Tee Carson, and Bill Holman. On the remaining tracks, pianist Tommy Flanagan accompanies her in a trio, with bassist Frank De la Rosa and drummer Ed Thigpen. The brilliant Flanagan had started gigging with Ella again in late 1968 and he would stay with her for the next 10 years after this San Francisco date. (See the section on Flanagan in Chapter 9.) In addition to singing the title track, Ella tackled the day's biggest hits, like the Beatles' "Hey Jude" and the Hal David/Burt Bacharach songs, "This Girl's [Guy's] in Love with You" and "A House Is Not a Home," as well as some jazzier numbers, among them "Don'cha Go 'Way Mad," from Ella's time at Decca Records; "Alright, Okay, You Win," a winner in 1955 for Joe Williams with Count Basie; and "Ol' Devil Moon," the catchy song from the musical *Finian's Rainbow.*

Although Norman Granz had supervised the recording of *Sunshine of Your Love,* he had not yet made the decision to resume a regular schedule as a producer. Consequently, Ella decided to go with Reprise Records. The musical director and producer for her first album was Richard Perry, described by Geoffrey Mark Fidelman as "a rock 'n' roll wunderkind, whose specialty was to make contemporary albums for singers who were not particularly known for that kind of music."[50] Recorded in late May 1969 and released later that year, Perry titled the album after the great singer with whom he had collaborated. *Ella,* however, did not do very well, but that was most likely because of limited promotion, a pity in that the recording turned out well. In putting the album together, Perry demonstrated his impressive competence and resolve. Ella's singing is very good and Perry's charts are appropriate and not overbearing on songs of the time like The Temptations' "Get Ready," Randy Newman's "Yellow Man,"

The Beatles' "Got to Get You into My Life," Smokey Robinson's "Ooo Baby Baby," and Harry Nilsson's "Open Your Window."

Ella's second album for Reprise, *Things Ain't What They Used to Be (and You Better Believe It)*, is comprised of tracks from dates she had done under the musical direction of Gerald Wilson in January, November, and December 1970. Released the following year, the recording was supervised by Norman Granz, who was back with Ella again after resuming a full-time schedule as a record producer. The selections on the album constitute a curious mix of styles. There are tunes that might normally be expected from Ella, like "Days of Wine and Roses," "Willow Weep for Me," "Black Coffee," "Tuxedo Junction," and the title track. Among the other tracks are two Latin numbers: "Mas Que Nada," a hit for Sergio Méndez and Brasil '66 in the mid-1960s, and "Manteca," from Dizzy Gillespie's big band book in the 1940s; as well as "Sunny" and "I Heard It through the Grapevine," recent pop ditties at that time for Bobby Hebb and Gladys Knight and the Pips respectively.

Notwithstanding the program, Ella's singing is excellent throughout. She is also in superior company with Gerald Wilson, an accomplished and original voice in the music world. Born in Shelby, Mississippi, in 1918, Wilson spent parts of his youth in Memphis, Tennessee, and in Detroit. He studied music diligently and was already a talented trumpeter and arranger by the time he finished high school. His monumental first break came when he joined Jimmie Lunceford's band in 1939, replacing the recently departed Sy Oliver. (See the section on Oliver in this chapter.) Wilson enjoyed four productive years as a player and arranger in Lunceford's outstanding unit. After serving in the Navy during World War II, he moved to Los Angeles full-time and continued his professional musical activities. He led a successful big band for three years, making appearances in New York and other places, and then abandoned the project in 1947 to undertake formal studies in composition. A prolific composer and arranger, Wilson has been one of the busiest and most revered musical directors and composers in the business since then. The list of top artists with whom he has worked includes Duke Ellington, Ray Charles, Count Basie, Bobby Darin, and Nancy Wilson. He has also written extensively for television and film, and has enjoyed success as a "classical" composer with several distinguished premieres to his credit. Among Wilson's many awards and honors are five Grammy nominations, the two most recent coming in 1999.

Warner Brothers, the parent company of Prestige, reissued *Things Ain't What They Used to Be (and You Better Believe It)* in 1989, keeping the title but coupling it with Ella's previous album for the company, *Ella*.[51] This makes for an interesting combination, one of the more unusual CDs in the Ella discography, but an excellent listen nonetheless.

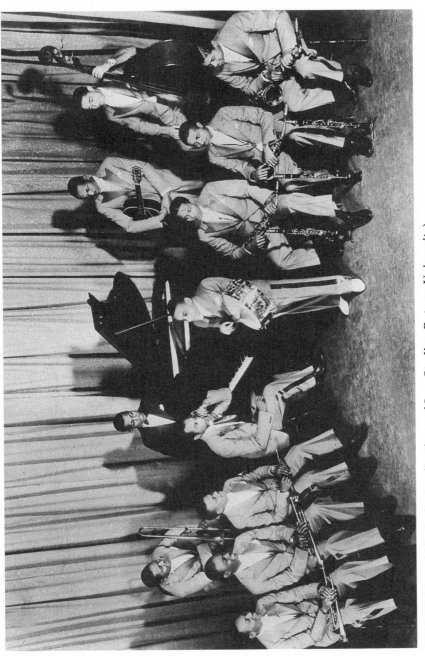

Chick Webb and his Orchestra. (Institute of Jazz Studies, Rutgers University)

Chick Webb jamming with Benny Goodman and pianist Joe Bushkin. Looking on at far left is Milt Gabler. (Institute of Jazz Studies, Rutgers University)

Publicity photo, early 1940s. (Institute of Jazz Studies, Rutgers University)

ELLA FITZGERALD "The First Lady of Song"

Personal Management: GALE, INC., 48 West 48th Street · PLaza 7-7100

Norman Granz, early 1950s. (Institute of Jazz Studies, Rutgers University)

Ella performing on a CBS-TV special, April 1959. Peggy Lee watches and Benny Goodman plays in the background. (Institute of Jazz Studies, Rutgers University)

Always singing (1960s). (Institute of Jazz Studies, Rutgers University)

The two headliners during recording sessions for *Ella at Duke's Place,* October 1965. (Institute of Jazz Studies, Rutgers University)

A fashionable Ella at London's Heathrow Airport, April 12, 1970. (Institute of Jazz Studies, Rutgers University)

Joe Pass (left), Ella, and Oscar Peterson, Denver Auditorium Theater, March 31, 1979. (Photograph by Tad Hershorn)

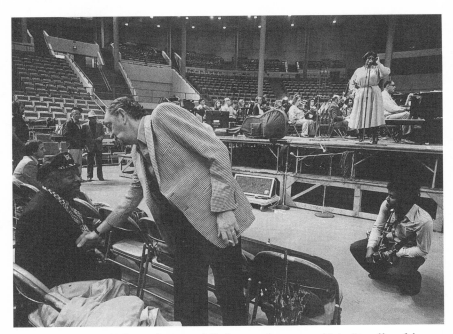

Ella rehearses with the orchestra while her road manager Pete Cavello whispers something to Count Basie, San Antonio Arena, December 12, 1979. (Photograph by Tad Hershorn)

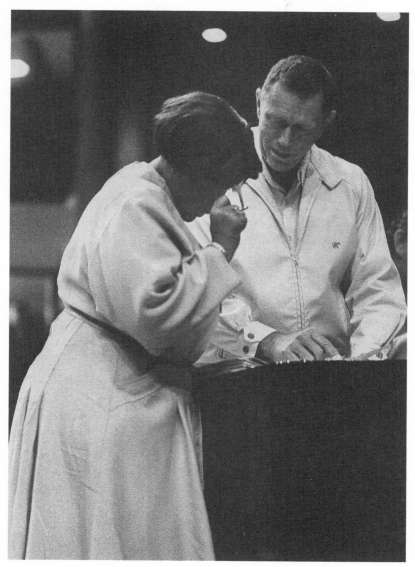

Ella and Paul Smith, San Antonio Arena, December 12, 1979. (Photograph by Tad Hershorn)

Quincy Jones (left), Ella, Bobby McFerrin, Lena Horne, and Al Grey at *Hearts for Ella* tribute, Lincoln Center, New York City, February 12, 1990. (Photograph by Tad Hershorn)

Tommy Flanagan (1998). (Institute of Jazz Studies, Rutgers University)

CHAPTER 8

Benny, Duke, and Count

The big-band sound was purely American. The phenomenon of a male or female vocalist dreamily singing in front of a large band whose conductor—and not the singer—was really the star was an art form that was completely unique to America. . . . Fronting a band was every struggling vocalist's great ambition.

—J. Randy Taraborrelli[1]

When Ella Fitzgerald began working with Chick Webb in 1935 the big-band explosion was just getting under way. There had of course been many bands on the scene for well over a decade, but none that had overwhelmingly captivated the public at large.

There were also no racially integrated bands; society's distinct line between white and black was equally prevalent in the music world. The top black bands of the time included those of Fletcher Henderson, Bennie Moten, Duke Ellington, and Jimmie Lunceford. With the exception of white bands led by Ben Pollack and Jean Goldkette, the black bands were generally more adventurous in that they reflected the jazz idiom and allowed their soloists to be an important feature of their performances.

All big bands had singers, men only, until Paul Whiteman opened the door for women by hiring Mildred Bailey in 1929. The quality of vocalists ran the gamut; some singers could really croon and others would have been better suited staying off the bandstand.

BENNY GOODMAN AND THE SWING ERA

Born in Chicago on May 30, 1909, clarinetist Benny Goodman started his professional career in his hometown in the 1920s, performing as a sideman with area bands. He was soon working with more prominent bandleaders, including Red Nicholls and Ben Pollack. In 1934 the ambitious Goodman organized his first big band in New York and, with the support of impresario John Hammond, the clarinetist slowly began to find his way. Foremost among Hammond's initial contributions was his assistance in bringing drummer Gene Krupa into the mix, a move of critical importance to Goodman. Krupa's impressive talent and energy immediately transformed the band from a good functional ensemble into a hard-swinging, exciting unit.

Goodman's fame began to grow as a result of his performances on *Let's Dance*, NBC radio's weekly Saturday evening broadcast of live dance music. However, what really pushed Goodman to the next level was his legendary appearance at Los Angeles's Palomar Ballroom in August of 1935. Jazz historians have long speculated as to why exactly the Palomar performances were such a smashing success; Goodman was already known through his radio broadcasts. Whatever the case, his Los Angeles performances served to skyrocket him to the status of superstar. "The crowds kept getting bigger and bigger, and Benny's contract was extended for another three weeks," recounts Goodman biographer, Ross Firestone. "Along with the musicians and kids, the band also began to draw movie stars and the rest of the Hollywood set, who may or may not have understood what Benny was up to but knew it was the place to be. Remote broadcasts from the Palomar helped spread the word up and down the coast."[2] Goodman was soon dubbed "The King of Swing."

The combination of Goodman's superb clarinet playing and the tight ensemble swing of his accomplished players enthralled the listening public. It also did not hurt that the band performed music by outstanding writers. For instance, the aforementioned and brilliant Fletcher Henderson contributed many charts to Goodman's book. Henderson had recently stopped fronting a big band and Goodman, who loved his music, was fully aware of the fantastic contributions he could make to the overall sound and success of the band. Another important writer for Goodman was Edgar Sampson, a member of Chick Webb's band, whose same arrangements could never have achieved as much success with Webb.

In terms of sheer numbers and boundless vitality the swing era remains one of the most exciting periods in the history of American music. It was certainly the last period during which jazz, or music closely related to the jazz idiom, was the popular sound of the day. Goodman's phenomenal success opened the door for numerous other bandleaders, including Glenn Miller, Artie Shaw, the Dorsey brothers, Count Basie, and Woody Herman. Of course, established bands, like those of Ellington and Lunceford, continued to thrive.

Two significant events took place in the early 1940s that would spell the beginning of the end for the era of the big bands. First and foremost,

America went to war, taking many of the musicians away from their primary engagements. Many continued to play in the service, but the music scenes in New York and other areas in America were seriously affected by the war movement. Some bands did maintain respectable schedules but, for the most part, the supply of top talent had been depleted. The shortage of fuel, increased taxes, and the implementation of curfews further exacerbated the situation. The second event contributing to the demise of the big bands, and to the general malaise in the music scene, was the ban on recording implemented by the American Federation of Musicians [AFM] on August 1, 1942. "From today on, there will be no recording of music, classical or jazz, in this country by union musicians," reported *Down Beat.* "The record firms, transcription firms, radio networks, and small stations are sizzling. Executives of all pointed out that at no time had the AFM indicated what terms it wanted—merely had casually sent out some carbon copies of a rubber-stamped order putting them out of business."[3]

By the beginning of 1947, the final curtain had fallen on the big band era, most of the best groups having disbanded. Some would manage to persist for a while, but they eventually fizzled out. On the other hand, many of the top vocalists did survive, going on to carve out strong careers for themselves.

Among the few bandleaders who were able to carry on for the rest of their lives were three great superstars—Duke Ellington, Count Basie, and Benny Goodman. They, of course, had their ups and downs over the following decades, including having to contend with the excesses and frequently mediocre output of the rock movement, but they made it. Goodman died in New York on June 13, 1986.

Ella Fitzgerald performed with Benny Goodman on a number of occasions during her career. The two first collaborated on a November 1936 recording date when the clarinetist's vocalist at the time, Helen Ward, had taken two weeks off to attend to personal affairs. Ella laid down three tracks with Goodman for Victor records—"Goodnight, My Love," "Oh, Yes, Take Another Guess," and "Did You Mean It." Because Ella was under exclusive contract to Decca, the company almost immediately disapproved of the records. "Decca howled when these hit the street, so they were withdrawn," commented Goodman discographer Donald R. Connor.[4] "Goodnight My Love" did stay on the charts for about three months at the beginning of 1937, reaching and staying at number one for four weeks. The recordings were put out again on LP in the 1960s and have been reissued on CD on the Classics label.[5]

Less than a week after the studio session, Ella guested on Goodman's extremely popular radio show, *Camel Caravan.* There are no recordings of the event. Fitzgerald and Goodman would not perform together again until April 1958 when they appeared on an NBC television special called *Swing into Spring*, a show hosted by Dave Garroway that also featured, among others, Red Norvo, Jo Stafford, and Harry James. A year later on CBS, Ella again performed with Goodman on a similar special, hosted this time by the clarinetist and featuring Lionel Hampton and Peggy Lee among the other guests. LP recordings were made of the two network specials, the one for CBS a much more limited edition. A CD reissue of the NBC show was released in 1991, but it is very difficult to find.[6] Segments of both broadcasts are available on VHS video.[7]

On the little work they did together, Fitzgerald and Goodman proved to be a wonderful team, producing intriguing and highly rewarding music. It is unfortunate that, other than the three now-rare sides of 1936, the great singer and "The King of Swing" never had another opportunity to collaborate in the studio.

DUKE ELLINGTON

Duke Ellington's stature and importance in the history of American music places him with Louis Armstrong, Dizzy Gillespie, Charlie Parker, Miles Davis, John Coltrane, and perhaps two or three other musicians, in the first tier of the jazz hierarchy. Moreover, Ellington and Armstrong are the only masters who, in redefining the art and raising the music to unprecedented levels of sophistication, reached mainstream listening audiences in the process. Interestingly, Ellington is also the only member of jazz history's most important personalities who, although he was an accomplished pianist, is remembered predominantly for his writing and bandleading.

A brilliant orchestrator and arranger, Ellington is often cited as America's greatest composer. Many musicians and historians are careful to qualify this opinion. Despite being an absolutely gifted artist who created many musical works of the highest caliber, the reality is that a significant portion of the compositions often credited to Ellington alone were either collaborative works or brilliant adaptations of ideas from fellow musicians. Consequently, the contention that Ellington was the best of the best remains a controversial issue. Bearing this in mind, the fact remains that the body of music *associated* with Ellington is gigantic and impressive. James Lincoln Collier provides the following assessment:

Ellington's recorded music is simply awash with melody, tens of thousands of measures of it, much of it memorable, some of it masterly. There can be no doubt that Ellington wrote a huge proportion of this enormous body of melody. . . . If Ellington was not a great songwriter, he was certainly a melodist of genuine power. . . . The men in the [band's] sections worked out a lot of the voicings, although in the main from chords supplied by Ellington. . . . [H]e, and nobody else, created the musical machine that produced the great compositions we know as "Ellington."

We thus have to see Duke Ellington as . . . a master chef. The chef does not chop all the vegetables himself or make the sauce . . . But he plans the menus, trains the assistants, supervises them, tastes everything, adjusts the spices . . . And in the end we credit him with the result. So it was with Duke Ellington: wherever he got the ingredients, it was his artistic vision that shaped the final product.[8]

Alec Wilder commented that Ellington was "the judge and jury. Without his personal taste, his sense of fitness and aptness, the vast library of Ellingtonia would not exist."[9] In that library are many great songs—standards like "Sophisticated Lady," "In a Sentimental Mood," "Prelude to a Kiss," "Satin Doll," and "I Got It Bad and That Ain't Good"—as well as large-scale works, music for film, and liturgical music. The issue of composer credit aside, Ellington's best bands were comprised of outstanding and often legendary players whose performances of the music were fabulous. An observation proffered on countless occasions is that Ellington's instrument was really his orchestra, that he used his unique compositional methods to create passages tailored to the talents and personalities of the key players who worked with him.

Ella Fitzgerald met Ellington during her time with Chick Webb. Ellington had done the groundwork to get Webb his first engagement as a bandleader. Ella and Ellington worked together on many occasions in subsequent years. The relaxed communication they enjoyed, coupled with the respect they held for each other—not to mention their exceptional talent—guaranteed that their pairing always made for a wondrous event.

Ellington was born in Washington, D.C., on April 29, 1899. His parents, James and Daisy, were reasonably well-off and respected in their community. They were good parents, instilling in their son refined values and an outward respect for people.

The young Ellington's first love was baseball; for a time he worked as a vendor at Washington Senators's games. He also took some piano lessons and, although his musical interests were not permanently sealed at the time, he continued to dabble at the keyboard on his own. A short time before starting high school, Ellington acquired his lifelong nickname. "I had a chum, . . . a rather fancy guy who liked to dress well," recalled Ellington. "He was socially uphill and a pretty good, popular fellow . . . I think he felt that in order for me to be eligible for his constant companionship I should have a title. So he named me Duke."[10]

In high school Ellington was not a very good student, although he did demonstrate an above-average aptitude for drawing and painting. More significantly, he also began to take the piano seriously. He listened mostly to the best ragtime players in his hometown, one of whom, Doc Perry, took him under his wing and taught him plenty about music and the

piano. The young Ellington was soon doing well enough to play professionally. During his senior year he turned down a scholarship to an art
institute and dropped out instead to pursue music full-time.

Ellington moved to New York in 1923 and spent the next few years
strengthening his musical skills and doing what he could to establish himself. During much of this time, he led a band called the Washingtonians
at the Kentucky Club in Times Square. Writer Mark Tucker, who has examined Ellington's Washingtonian experiences in-depth, relates that "Ellington had his hands full. . . . He was just learning how to balance
composing with leading the band, playing piano, and dealing with record
companies."[11] Ellington met the challenges head on, ultimately transform-
ing the Washingtonians into a widely popular group and completing several recordings along the way. Furthermore, his distinctive compositional
skills were maturing rapidly and his music was drawing attention. As the
1920s drew to a close Ellington's stock had risen significantly.

One of the most important boons to Ellington's career occurred in late
1927 when he was hired at the Cotton Club in Harlem, a top New York
venue that featured the cream of the black entertainers, as well as hot jazz.
Ellington expanded the size of his ensemble, adding outstanding players
like alto saxophonist Johnny Hodges and trumpeter Cootie Williams. By
the time Ellington's prolonged stay at the Cotton Club ended in February
of 1931, he had composed and recorded profusely and his fame had
skyrocketed.

The Duke Ellington Orchestra made its first visit to Europe in mid-1933,
touring England, Holland, and France. Returning to the United States, the
group went on with its whirlwind schedule without missing a beat. The
rest of the 1930s were extremely productive for Ellington. In addition to
constant touring and recording, he continued to compose wonderful music at a prolific rate. He also added new stars to his group, among them
cornetist Rex Stewart and bassist Jimmy Blanton. The band appeared in
two Hollywood movies.

With the 1940s just around the bend, Ellington met the multitalented
Billy Strayhorn, a man who would become central to Ellington's dynamic
career. Hired as a lyricist by Ellington in 1939, Strayhorn subsequently
began penning compositions and arrangements for the band. He had an
exceptional and distinctive voice as a composer and pianist, yet he was
also familiar with Ellington's musical style and compositional methods.
Strayhorn was soon an indispensable member of the Ellington operation,
in essence a right-hand man, remaining in that capacity until his death on
May 31, 1967. Ellington and Strayhorn developed a deep friendship during their years together. "He was my listener, my most dependable ap-
praiser, and as a critic he would be clinical" said Ellington. "In music . . .
there are many points at which direction must be decided, and any time
I was in the throes of debate with myself, harmonically or melodi-

cally, I would turn to Billy Strayhorn. We would talk, and then the whole world would come into focus."[12] Among his many accomplishments, Strayhorn composed "Take the 'A' Train," a tune that would become one of the most revered musical standards in American popular culture, as well as Ellington's de facto theme song.

Ellington debuted at Carnegie Hall in 1943, becoming the first black composer to present a program of his works at the renowned venue. For the ambitious program—it would last three hours—he composed an extended piece entitled *Black, Brown, and Beige* to include among the selections. Subtitled *A Tone Parallel to the History of the Negro in America*, the almost sixty-minute work did not impress the critics, its apparent lack of cohesiveness cited as one of its principal weaknesses. Henceforth, the debate about whether a jazz musician could compose serious works for the concert hall would take on a life of its own. Undeterred, Ellington composed many more large-scale works over the following years.

For the rest of the 1940s and through the 1950s, Ellington maintained a seemingly nonstop schedule, replete with recordings, live concerts, movie appearances, and international travel. He managed all this despite the fact that the big band era had gradually fizzled out after World War II. Like the handful of prominent bandleaders who were still on the scene, Ellington was often faced with changes in his personnel, although some players stayed with him for lengthy uninterrupted periods. He also benefited when a few top players from previous bands returned.

During the 1960s and early 1970s, Ellington's ambition and motivation remained strong. He composed as much as he could, recorded, and often toured internationally. "We . . . play in a much greater variety of places than we used to. It's like being in 10 different businesses," said Ellington.[13] He spent much of this period composing religious music, the most notable works being his three Sacred Concerts. As with previous attempts at longer works, the music drew mixed reviews, frequently with a negative slant. However, Ellington was wholly committed to these works. The first two received many performances, premiering respectively in San Francisco on September 16, 1965, and in New York on January 19, 1968. The Third Sacred Concert, much to Ellington's pleasure, was premiered at London's hallowed Westminster Abbey on October 24, 1973.

Sadly, Ellington had been diagnosed with cancer in 1972 and he was very sick by the time of the Third Sacred Concert. However, he continued his relentless schedule until he could no longer go on. He died on May 24, 1974, in New York City. During his funeral at St John's Cathedral, Ella Fitzgerald sang an emotional rendition of Ellington's "Solitude," as well as the spiritual "Just a Closer Walk with Thee." In a *New York Times* article, Ella spoke about the great friend she had known for almost forty years: "He used to tell me a lot of things that made a lot of sense. Once I had a big problem with a love affair . . . He told me, 'Ella, it's like a toothache.

If it hurts bad enough, you get rid of it. You miss it for a while, but you feel better afterwards.' . . . Duke never had anything bad to say about anyone. I don't think people realize even yet how great the man was."[14]

Ella Fitzgerald first recorded with Duke Ellington in late June 1957 on the sessions for her *Song Book* of his music. (See the section on Ellington in Chapter 7.) The two did not record again until the middle of October 1965 when they went into the studio in Hollywood, California, to press the album *Ella at Duke's Place*. Unlike the disorganized sessions for the *Song Book*, things were considerably more orderly this time around. Ella's accompanist at the time, Jimmy Jones, wrote arrangements for four lovely tunes—Billy Strayhorn's "Something to Live For," "A Flower Is a Lovesome Thing," and "Passion Flower," and Ellington's "I Like the Sunrise." Gerald Wilson added one arrangement, and Ellington came in fully prepared for what he wanted to do on his scores and on the session as a whole. From the outset, Ella's singing is sensational. "She is possibly the only singer who, by lending her personal beauty to a melody and lyric, can somehow make it appear that she is adding her own subtle alterations when actually she is singing the prescribed theme note for note and word for word," wrote Leonard Feather, commenting about Ella's rendition of "Something to Live For."[15]

Gerald Wilson's contribution to the album is "Imagine My Frustration," a rock and roll-type tune of his that was originally titled "When I'm Feeling Kinda Blue." Wilson had performed and recorded it with his own big band and Ellington liked the number. "Duke took the arrangement I did for my band," recounted Wilson. "Duke said he wanted Strayhorn to add lyrics, which he did. Strayhorn came up with a new title, and he wrote a set of lyrics, . . . and we had a song: my music and Billy's lyrics."[16] Ella belts out those lyrics soulfully and Johnny Hodges is transcendent, his wailing alto saxophone solo completely in the spirit of the music. (For more information about Gerald Wilson, see the section "One for Prestige, Two for Reprise" in Chapter 7.)

Ellington's well-known blues, "Duke's Place" (a.k.a. "C-Jam Blues"), opens with trumpeter Cootie Williams's high-energy, plunger-muted solo. Ella enters in great voice, stepping aside during her choruses for more solos by Johnny Hodges, Paul Gonsalves, and Jimmy Hamilton. Incidentally, this arrangement, belying the composition's title, is actually in the key of E-flat. On "Brownskin Gal in the Calico Gown," Ella and the rhythm section start in ballad tempo before the band charges in, doubling the tempo and cooking behind Ella as she swings through the rest of the chart. "Cotton Tail" is Ellington's great tune built on the chord progression to Gershwin's "I Got Rhythm." Ella's scatting and the band's playing are absolutely scorching on the up-tempo romp. The standard key for this tune is A-flat, but Ella and the band do it in B-flat.

"What Am I Here For?," Ellington's tune with lyrics by Frankie Laine, swings at a relaxed medium tempo. The opening of Ella's first chorus is shown in Example 8.1. She takes it fairly straight ahead, but there are some interesting points. After sticking closely to Ellington's line in the first four measures, she modifies the rhythm on the words "That was my fear for" in measure 5 and "there was no reason to part" in measure 7, starting the motive in both cases on a quarter-note triplet. On the words "Still I hope you'll change your mind" in measures 9 and 10, she starts with a syncopated rhythm and then lays off the swing by ending the motive on two quarter-notes and a half-note, directly on beats one, two, and three, respectively. She does the same thing in measures 11 and 12, on the words "and that somehow you will find," swinging at first before ending strictly on the beat.

The first eight measures of Ella's second chorus are shown in Example 8.2. She starts by re-shaping the contours of the motives into a series of thirds: on the title lyrics in measure 1, she alternates the words on Ds and B-flats, the distance of a major third; in measure 2, on the words "living in mis'ry," she conforms to the harmony by changing the alternating pitches to D and B-natural, a distance of a minor third. In measures 3 and 4, on the words "now that you've gone from my heart," she soars upward, starting on middle C, ascending through a quarter-note triplet, and land-

Example 8.1: "What Am I Here For?" (*Ella at Duke's Place*)

Example 8.2: "What Am I Here For?" *(Ella at Duke's Place)*

ing on the D, a major ninth above. She holds for a beat and a half at the top of the motive, then drops back down a major sixth on swinging eighth-notes. Note also, in measure 4, that she attacks the word "my" directly on beat one before singing "heart" on the second half of the beat. Here is another example of one of Ella's favorite devices, that of shifting the stress points in a melody. The word "my" is normally expected to fall on beat four, or the least stressed beat, of measure 3; "heart" would then follow on beat one, the beat most stressed in measure 4. In measures 5 and 6, Ella alternates thirds again, this time reversing the pattern in the former instance by moving up and down. In measures 7 and 8, she closes the passage by singing the words "there was no reason to part" on a lick that links a quarter-note triplet to a five-note tuplet.

Following their recording date for *Ella at Duke's Place,* the two great headliners would perform together and tour again a number of times over the next couple of years. A good amount of their work was recorded and is available on CD reissues. Ella's repertoire with Ellington consisted of a select group of songs that would make up the programs in varying combinations from performance to performance and recording to recording. Indicative of the brilliance of all concerned, the different versions of the same songs are consistently fresh and interesting.

Ella's next album with Ellington is *The Stockholm Concert, 1966,* recorded in the Swedish capital in early February before a highly enthusiastic crowd. Another superb affair, the program includes "Imagine My Frustration," "Duke's Place," "Something to Live For," and "Cotton Tail," four tunes that Ella sang on her previous album with Ellington. There is also the Hal David/Burt Bacharach tune "Wives and Lovers," with an arrangement that lets everyone swing buoyantly in 3/4 time. On "Let's Do It," a tune she first sang on her *Song Book* of Cole Porter's music, Ella swings infectiously and really digs into the lyrics while Ellington's band grooves right along. Ella's first recorded version of the ballad "Lover Man" came from her performance in Carnegie Hall on September 29, 1947, when she was accompanied by another hot big band, that of Dizzy Gillespie. On the Stockholm concert, she is backed only by the rhythm section and one of the trumpet players who provides quiet, muted fills. She gets the same pared-down accompaniment on "Só Danço Samba," the catchy Latin number composed by Antonio Carlos Jobim and Vinícius de Moraes and known in English as "Jazz Samba." Ella recorded this tune several times in various settings during her career. Here she adds some hip scatting on one of her choruses.

"Satin Doll," composed by Ellington and Billy Strayhorn, with lyrics by Johnny Mercer, is one of the best known standards of all time, a tune that, without question, is expected to be in the repertoire of popular singers and jazz instrumentalists. Ella recorded "Satin Doll" over a dozen times during her career. (For a version with Tommy Flanagan, see the section on Flanagan in Chapter 9.) Ella's first chorus on the Stockholm concert is shown in Example 8.3. The band screams out some introductory licks and Ella enters relaxed, taking it straight ahead for a bit before closing the first A section by stretching the words "my satin doll" through three measures. Normally, "my satin" would be sung in measure 6 and "doll" would fall on the first downbeat in measure 7. Instead, Ella hits "my" on the second half of beat one in measure 6 and works her way through quarter-note triplets and swinging eighth-notes before attacking "doll" on the second half of beat three in measure 7 and holding it through the first half of measure 8. She does something similar in the second A section, prolonging "my satin doll" between measures 14 and 16, using only one quarter-note triplet in the motive this time. On the words "Baby shall we go" in measure 9, and "you're flippin'" in measure 12, she flattens out the motives, singing on repeated Es and Fs respectively, instead of on the consecutive major seconds of the original melody. From the end of measure 10 through measure 11, she plays with the melodic rhythm, placing the second syllable of the word "careful" on the first of four sixteenth-notes and adding "amigo" on the last three. In measures 19 and 20, she draws out the word "be" through seven beats, using another motive that links a quarter-note triplet to swinging eighth-notes. From the end of measure 20 into measure 21, she sings "I'll give it a whirl" on a tricky rhythm, embedding an eighth-note triplet within the first two beats of measure 21. She closes the chorus by once more elongating the words "satin doll," ascending on a chromatic line on the first syllable of "satin" and then dropping a major sixth to add the second syllable and the word "doll." As she often does, Ella shifts the stress points of the melody, placing the second syllable of "satin," instead of "doll," on the downbeat of beat three.

In late July, 1966, Ella and Duke Ellington appeared at the Antibes-Juan-

Example 8.3: "Satin Doll" *(EF/Duke Ellington: The Stockholm Concert, 1966)*

les-Pins Jazz Festival, recording a large number of selections during four evenings of performances. The first reissue by Verve, in November 1997, was a two-CD set of 18 tracks that was similar to the original two-LP release. Verve put out a second reissue in September 1998 that was a much more comprehensive eight-CD collection. It contains most of the selections that Ella performed with Ellington during the festival, as well as an extremely interesting afternoon rehearsal by Ellington.[17]

Other European concerts by Ella and Ellington in 1966 have been issued on hard-to-find CDs from a number of obscure labels. Selections of Ella singing from her appearance with Ellington in Los Angeles on September 23, 1966, are included on the CD *Live at the Greek Theater, Los Angeles,* released on the Status label (DSTS 1013). Ella can also be heard with Ellington on a three-CD Pablo reissue of a four-LP set called *The Greatest Jazz Concert in the World* (PACD-2625-742-2). Recorded at Carnegie Hall in New York on March 26, 1967, the recording also contains selections by Coleman Hawkins and the Oscar Peterson Trio.

Ella and Duke Ellington made fabulous music together, their recordings constituting one of the greatest bodies of work in American music. Ellington biographer Derek Jewell commented on a European tour by the bandleader in early 1967:

Ella Fitzgerald appeared with the band at some concerts, and the collaboration had by now become a mature masterpiece. "Don't Be That Way," from the days she'd enjoyed in the 1930s with Chick Webb, summed up the way she involved herself sympathetically with the textures of the band. First, she used her warmest, richest voice against a quiet muted obligato from Cat Anderson's trumpet; then there were intensely rhythmic passages during which her personal accompanists, Sam Woodyard and Jimmy Jones, both former Ellington associates, sustained her; finally, she rocketed into thrilling high note choruses, her voice outsoaring the orchestra, from which the bass trombone of Chuck Connors could be heard stabbing out a low-down counterpoint.[18]

COUNT BASIE

Pianist Lou Levy, one of the finest pianists to accompany Ella Fitzgerald, once remarked that she was "probably the hardest-swinging singer I've ever heard, and I think most people agree on this."[19] Many might also agree that Count Basie's big band may well have been the hardest-swinging ensemble of its time—or at least the band that most consistently epitomized no-nonsense, driving swing. It should then follow that the combination of Ella and Basie would be sensational—and it was.

At any tempo or dynamic, whether on pretty ballads and relaxed numbers or on red-hot blazers, Count Basie and his musicians were, as writer Francis Davis once remarked, "a machine whose motor purred."[20] The band featured exciting ensemble sound and top-notch soloists. It is not surprising that the recordings with Basie are often cited as among the finest in Ella Fitzgerald's output. The singer and the band members fed off each other's creativity and energy, exchanging miraculous phrasing and exhilarating solos. At the core of these performances, as with all of Basie's output, was a continually swinging pulse, what John S. Wilson in the *New York Times* called "a built-in flowing intensity."[21] Up front, Basie would direct the ensemble with his uniquely minimalistic style, nodding here, smiling there, dashing off hip licks and punches that were often no more than small melodic fragments or a few well-placed notes.

Count Basie was born in Red Bank, New Jersey, on August 21, 1904. Red Bank was a thriving resort at the time and Basie's parents were hard workers; his father was a caretaker and his mother a laundress. The young Basie was enthralled by the exciting carnival shows that passed through town, often dreaming about going on the road with them. He also loved hanging around the Palace Theater where he would work various chores in order to watch the movies and listen to the vaudevillians performing there. He had been taking some piano lessons and was keen to hear how professional pianists accompanied the silent movies shown at the theater. When the regular pianist didn't show up one day, Basie snuck down and played for the movie. The manager liked what he heard and asked Basie to do the evening show.

Thrilled by his impromptu entry into the music business, Basie continued playing around, eventually making the big move to New York City. He gigged more, did some travelling with a Burlesque show in 1924, and eventually landed a steady gig at Leroy's, a Harlem nightspot where it's likely he first met two of his idols, Fats Waller and Willie "The Lion" Smith. Basie had long loved the practitioners of stride piano, masters like James P. Johnson, Smith, and especially Waller. "Really the main guy that influenced me is Thomas, that's Fats, Waller," recounted Basie. "That was the man that I really did idolize, ... I used to watch him, lay around him long enough to style a little piano after him, which was quite difficult."[22] Waller, who was also an organist, worked often at another Harlem venue, the Lincoln Theater, and it was there that he additionally influenced Basie by teaching him the fundamentals of organ playing.

In 1926, Basie began an engagement with a vaudeville act called Gonzelle White and her Jazz Band. During his travels, while in Tulsa, Oklahoma, in 1927, Basie first heard Walter Page's Blue Devils, an exciting band of 10 players. "Anyway, the Blue Devils was the first big band I had ever had a chance to get close to and really listen to," enthused Basie, "and it was the greatest thing I had ever heard."[23] Basie got to know some of the band members, who in turn had their first opportunities to hear him play. Not long after, while in Oklahoma City, Basie got a call to sit in with the Blue Devils when their regular pianist had taken ill. "So I went to the place where I was staying and put on a coat and tie," Basie reminisced, "and I was the happiest guy in the world."[24] Following his unforgettable experience, Basie returned to Kansas City and subsequently received a letter from Walter Page asking him to join the Blue Devils full-time. Basie played with them over the next several months.

Returning to Kansas City in 1929, Basie was soon attracted to the sounds of Bennie Moten's outstanding and renowned band. Basie was so moved by the group's playing that he became determined to land a position with it, despite the fact that Moten himself was a very good pianist. Through careful planning, including befriending Eddie Durham, one of Moten's band members, Basie was asked to accompany the band on its next road trip in order to work out some charts with Durham. Furthermore, after hearing Basie play, Moten was soon inviting him to sit in on occasion. Basie progressed to being a regular member of the ensemble, even leading it for a while when the players and Moten had a temporary falling-out. It was during this brief stint as leader that Basie was officially billed as Count, although he had been using the moniker probably as far back as the early 1920s. Basie stayed with the band until Moten's untimely death in 1935.

Shortly after Moten's passing, Basie had the chance to take over the leadership of a group that was playing at the Reno Club in downtown Kansas City. He set about getting the best personnel he could, including some of Moten's former sidemen. The nine-piece band was soon loaded with top players, including Walter Page on bass, alto saxophonist Buster Smith, tenor saxophonist Lester Young, and the groundbreaking swing-master, drummer Jo Jones.

In January of 1936, John Hammond, in Chicago to produce a number of recordings, was listening to his car radio one night when he happened to pick up a live broadcast of the Count Basie band on a Kansas City station. Hammond had known of Basie from his earlier work with Bennie Moten. Hearing Basie now with his own group, the unprepared Hammond was immediately bowled over. "And what I picked up from Kansas City was amazing," he raved. "Basie had developed an extraordinary economy of style. With fewer notes, he was saying all that [Fats] Waller and [Earl] Hines could say pianistically, using perfectly timed punctuation—a chord, even a single note—which could inspire a horn player to heights he had never reached before."[25] Hammond became a huge fan of Basie's, even traveling to Kansas City to hear the band in person. He raved about the ensemble to anyone who would listen. The people at Decca Records were certainly listening and beat everyone to the punch by signing Basie to his first recording contract. Soon after, MCA, a giant among management companies, was representing the pianist. Next, with Hammond's assistance, Basie was headed east, his group now expanded to 13 members with a fuller complement of horns.

The first group that Basie brought to New York in 1936 was an outfit that played loosely and with occasionally questionable intonation. "[Trumpeter Buck] Clayton and [Lester] Young and tenor saxist [saxophonist] Hershal Evans and drummer Jo Jones and Walter Page were there," noted George T. Simon, "but there were also several soon-to-be-forgotten musicians, . . . and no sign yet of some of the stars that were soon to [further] strengthen the band."[26] Although some listeners may not have been overly impressed initially, Basie's band was in fact a sensation for anyone who had the musical experience or insight to hear through its imperfections. The ensemble possessed a sound and style that were highly promising and exciting. Writer Stanley Dance suggests that the band's "success resulted not so much from what it did as the way in which it did it. . . . It took the big-band mixture as before and shook it in a newly effective way. . . . [The] band's performances were rhythmically intoxicating—and lean. . . . The essence of the big-band idiom was presented unadulterated, without equivocation. And miraculously, it was accepted."[27] In other words, Basie did not succumb to the show business mindset that was evident with many of the bandleaders of the time, a result of the keen competition to attract and maintain audiences. He and his players did not resort to any tricks to entertain, the hard-swinging unit letting its music speak for itself. "[For] me there has never been anything like the early Basie band," said John Hammond. "It had shortcomings. Its sound was occasionally raw and raucous, but you expected it to erupt and sooner or later it did."[28]

With the exception of the period from 1949 to 1952, when financial considerations led him to tour with a septet, Basie would continue to lead swinging big bands for the better part of almost fifty years. During the last 10 years of his life, he also appeared and recorded for Pablo in a number of small-group settings, trading licks with top colleagues like Ray Brown, Zoot Sims, Louis Bellson, Roy Eldridge, Johnny Griffin, and Milt Jackson. Basie died in Hollywood, Florida, on April 26, 1984.

Throughout his five decades of bandleading, Basie's groups maintained their trademark characteristics of strong ensemble work and exceptional soloing. The earlier big bands were more a collection of individual stars who performed wonderfully as a unit, but with a looser and more spontaneous feel; from the early 1950s on, the groups swung just as much, but primarily within the frameworks of outstanding compositions and arrangements by top-flight writers like Neal Hefti, Frank Foster, Sammy Nestico, and Quincy Jones. "No other big band comes close to the Basie band in swing, jazz sound, and feeling, and that rare kind of section work that is both precise and relaxed," raved *Down Beat* in 1954.[29] Joe Williams, the outstanding singer who enjoyed great success with Basie, once commented that "in all our performances the band members would strive for their finest peak of excellence."[30]

Over the years, Basie worked with a number of top-rank singers. In addition to Williams, the list includes Billie Holiday, Billy Eckstine, Frank Sinatra—and Ella Fitzgerald, who first heard Basie and his band while she was with Chick Webb. She didn't sing with Basie until some years later, after which the two performed together often during the rest of their careers. With the Basie band, Ella was in her element, participating in spirited sessions, swinging purely without excessive frills. Regardless of whatever arrangements they might be using, the end performances always felt spontaneous and unaffected. Basie, like the other legendary artists who worked with Ella, fully enjoyed his times with her. "The only thing Ella knows how to do is just go out there and be wonderful," he enthused.[31]

Ella and Basie was the first album that the singer and bandleader made together. Recorded on July 15 and 16, 1963, with charts by Quincy Jones, the session proved to be a mutually rewarding and refreshing encounter. At this time in history, when the Beatles and rock were starting to overtake America and the world, Ella and Basie demonstrated that they were still two of the hippest musicians around and that they still had a lot to say. Producer Norman Granz remarked that the "album has been recorded today in the welter of nonsense that unfortunately has found wide acceptance—and who knows, it might bring some people 'round [sic] to swing again."[32] Basie was enthusiastic about the recording, remarking that "as usual, when you're working with Ella, it was more like a ball than a job."[33]

Ella and Basie cooks from the first note of the first track and never lets up. The album leads off with "Honeysuckle Rose," Fats Waller's time-honored composition with lyrics by Andy Razaf. Ella's first chorus is shown in Example 8.4. Her opening is incredible. If she sang no more than the first five measures the performance would still be sensational. Accompanied only by bassist Buddy Catlett, she modulates in every measure, starting in the key of D-flat on the words "Ev'ry honeybee," shifting up to E-flat on "fills with jealousy," changing direction back to D on "when they see you out with me," and returning to the home key of D-flat on "I don't blame them goodness knows." Basie and the rest of the rhythm section, as well as trumpeter Joe Newman playing muted licks, sneak in at measure 7, and remain the only accompaniment until the second half of measure 22, when the whole band finally comes in out of nowhere with two supercharged chords. In measures 9 and 10, Ella sings the words "When you're passin' by" and "flowers droop and sigh" on identical motives that descend on swinging eighth-notes and return upward on quarter-note triplets. She uses identical motives on the words "When I'm takin' sips" in measure 25, and on the words "from your tasty lips" in measure 26, but reverses direction for the most part and sings within a shorter span. Note the elasticity of her phrasing on the words "and I know the reason why" in measures 11 and 12, and twice on the title words beginning in measures 14 and 30, in all three cases, on sophisticated tuplet rhythms.

The blazing opening track establishes the spirited character of the album. The other Fats Waller number included in the session is "Ain't Misbehavin'," given a medium-slow groove by Quincy Jones. Ella sings passionately while the ubiquitous energy of Basie's band bubbles just be-

Example 8.4: "Honeysuckle Rose" *(Ella and Basie)*

low the surface. One can only imagine the joy that Basie must have always felt when performing the music of Waller, his biggest idol.

"Into Each Life Some Rain Must Fall" was composed by Allan Roberts and Doris Fisher in 1944. The only other time Ella recorded the song was when she introduced the appealing swing number in late 1944 on a side with the Ink Spots, the popular vocal quartet. That recording is available on a CD reissue.[34] Bill Doggett, the piano player on the session, and later a very successful organist, recorded several times with Ella over the next few years. (See the section on Doggett in Chapter 7.) On this version with Basie, Quincy Jones provides lots of soul with a hard-grooving, gospel-like chart. For the last minute and a half, Ella and the band settle into a prolonged vamp, riffing with intense, toe-tapping energy. The track ends with a fade-out, a rarity on Ella's recordings.

"Shiny Stockings" is a catchy swinger by Frank Foster, his original arrangement adapted by Quincy Jones for the recording with Ella. She digs in on the tune, singing lyrics that she wrote. Ella delivers a lovely rendition of "My Last Affair," Haven Johnson's ballad from 1936. Jones's arrangement is tasteful and engaging; the sustained unison high C played by the muted trumpets in the intro is especially inspired.

Among the other selections on the album are "Tea for Two," composed by Vincent Youmans to words by Irving Caesar for *No, No, Nanette* in 1925; "'Deed I Do," Walter Hirsch and Fred Rose's popular number of a year later; and "On the Sunny Side of the Street," written by Dorothy Fields and Jimmy McHugh in 1930, but whose definitive recording, according to discographer J. Wilfred Johnson "is the 1945 Tommy Dorsey and his Orchestra rendition with the Pied Pipers (Victor), the arrangement for which, by Sy Oliver, is considered by many to be the finest arrangement for a popular song ever devised."[35]

Basie and the rhythm section team up with tenor saxophonist Frank Foster, trumpeter Joe Newman, and trombonist Urbie Green to back Ella on two tracks. On "Them There Eyes," a hit for Billie Holiday at one time, Ella sings and scats inventively and the horn players take nice solos, trumpeter Newman trading fours with Ella along the way. Basie's piano solo is ingenious, a marvel of economy. "Dream a Little Dream of Me" is a very pretty ballad from the early 1930s. Basie plays organ on the track, Ella croons gently, and the band plays with sensitivity.

"Satin Doll" is, of course, from the Duke Ellington repertoire. Basie and the band play the tune like it is their own, their affinity for the music of Basie's great colleague both obvious and exciting. Ella's singing is dazzling on Jones's laid-back arrangement, the band blaring only a few times for punctuation. (For discussions of two versions of "Satin Doll" by Ella, see the section on Ellington in this chapter and the section on Tommy Flanagan in Chapter 9.)

Don George, Johnny Hodges, and Harry James teamed with Ellington to write the music and lyrics of "I'm Beginning to See the Light," another wonderful tune from his book to be included on *Ella and Basie*. Everyone grooves through the first chorus straight ahead, the fairly subdued band throwing in big blasts only at the end of the three A sections. Ella does some scatting, trading fours with the band for half of the second chorus before Basie takes the bridge on piano and the band cooks on the last eight measures. Instead of singing a full chorus again, Ella comes back in at the bridge (Example 8.5). The original two-bar motives that open the bridge are simple first-inversion triadic arpeggiations, descending from fifth to root to third and ascending back. Ella starts instead with a descending lick that covers the span of an octave on the words "Used to ramble through the park" in measures 17 and 18. She follows, in measures 19 and 20, with a motive more closely related to the original, but reverses direction, ascending the distance of a fifth on the words "Shadow boxing" and dropping back down to add the words "in the dark" on repeated E-flats. In measures 23 and 24, she closes the bridge, drawing the words "four alarm fire" upward on a stepwise lick spanning the distance of a major seventh and dropping back down a fifth to the word "now." In the process, she stretches the word "fire" over three beats. She starts the last eight measures of the chorus, as she often does in hard-swinging numbers, by singing the motives in a higher range than would normally be expected. Even at this late stage in her career, Ella still sang quite a bit in an instrumental manner, and at this point in the chorus, between measures 25 and 27, she belts out the lyrics much the same way the brass might do it. At

Example 8.5: "I'm Beginning to See the Light" *(Ella and Basie)*

the end of measure 27, she begins to cool down and, starting on the word "rainbows," she descends the distance of a major tenth on the words "in my wine," landing on consecutive A-flats back in the lower end of her range.

A CD release of a 1971 concert that Ella did with Basie in Holland was released in late 1994 on the Jazz Band label (EBCD 2121-2), but it is almost impossible to find and has not yet been reissued by a major label. On June 2, 1972, Ella appeared at the Civic Center Auditorium in Santa Monica, California, in a concert with her trio—pianist Tommy Flanagan, bassist Keter Betts, and drummer Ed Thigpen—plus the Count Basie Orchestra and the Jazz at the Philharmonic All-Stars. Ella was in fine voice and this is clearly evident on the resulting Pablo album, *Jazz at the Santa Monica Civic '72*. The program contains standards and pop selections, although this was about the last time that Ella would record such a varied mix of tunes. Almost all of her recorded output for the rest of her career would be comprised of jazz treatments of songs from the standard repertoire.

The Santa Monica concert features arrangements by Marty Paich, Gerald Wilson, and Nelson Riddle, among others. Ella sets the mood with a spirited version of "L-O-V-E," Bert Kaempfert's tune that had gone on to be a winner for Nat King Cole in the mid 1960s. Also on the program are "Begin the Beguine," "Indian Summer," "Shiny Stockings," and a Cole Porter medley of "Too Darn Hot" and "It's All Right with Me." Ella is accompanied by her trio on "Night and Day," "Spring Can Really Hang You Up the Most," "Little White Lies," and "Madalena."

The pop songs that Ella covers are Carole King's "You've Got a Friend," a number that was a smash hit for both King and James Taylor in 1971; "Street Beater," the theme from the television sitcom *Sanford and Son*, composed by Quincy Jones and with lyrics by Ella; "I Can't Stop Loving You," the country and western tune that had been a Grammy winner for Ray Charles in 1962; and Marvin Gaye's "What's Going On?" Ella sounds wonderful on these selections, once again demonstrating her uncanny ability to put her personal imprint on almost anything she sings. A couple of years later, Ella told *Down Beat*: "When I sang [Marvin Gaye's] 'What's Goin' On?' some people said 'Why are you doing that? It's a protest song!' I told them, 'I don't find it that way. To me, it's good music.'"[36]

The Santa Monica concert closes with a rousing jam session on Duke Ellington's "C-Jam Blues." Joining Ella and the Basie band are the Jazz at the Philharmonic All-Stars, among them trumpeters Harry "Sweets" Edison and Roy Eldridge, and tenor saxophonists Eddie "Lockjaw" Davis and Stan Getz.

On February 15, 1979, Ella and Count Basie were in Los Angeles to record *A Classy Pair* for Pablo. Providing the arrangements for the recording was Benny Carter, Ella's long-time friend and colleague. Leonard Feather comments that the session "is marked by a total lack of ego. . . .

The highest compliment that can be paid Ella and Basie is that they de-
serve each other's company."[37] Ella sings brilliantly and it would be difficult to find another performance on which Basie himself plays any better.
By this time in their respective careers, the two stars were so tuned into
each other that it was impossible for them not to be great together.

If there was any tune that could be deemed the perfect theme for Ella
and Basie, a selection with which the two stars felt a deep connection, it
had to be "Honeysuckle Rose." It therefore comes as no surprise that *A
Classy Pair* opens with Fats Waller's engaging composition. This version
is a masterpiece, an even greater rendition than the one on the *Ella and
Basie* album. Basie opens the track with an extraordinary solo, over two
minutes of easy, finger-snapping swing. As he often does, he stays close
to the melody and does not play a lot of notes, but his deft touch and
soulful drive produce two choruses that are fresh and the epitome of hip-
ness. Ella comes in seamlessly, taking over from Basie in the same relaxed
mood. Before getting into the particulars of her musical interpretation, it
is interesting to see how she changes the lyrics, either from forgetfulness
or simply as a lark, or maybe a combination of both:

Original—first A section:

Ev'ry honeybee fills with jealousy/when they see you out with me,
I don't blame them, goodness knows/Honeysuckle Rose.

Ella—first A section:

Ev'ry honeybee fills with jealousy/when they see you walk with me,
I don't mind them goodness knows/you're my Honeysuckle Rose.

Original—second A section:

When you're passin' by flowers droop and sigh/and I know the reason why,
You're much sweeter goodness knows/Honeysuckle Rose.

Ella—second A section:

Flowers droop and sigh when they pass you by/and I know the reason why,
Goodness knows/you're my Honeysuckle Rose.

Original—third A section:

When I'm takin' sips from your tasty lips/seems the honey fairly drips,
You're confection, goodness knows/Honeysuckle Rose.

Ella—third A section:

Say the honey drips from your tasty lips/and I know the reason why,
You're much sweeter goodness knows/Mmm, Honeysuckle Rose.

The first half of Ella's chorus is shown in Example 8.6. She toys with the melody, re-shaping every motive. In measures 2, 5, 9, and 10, she floats through the lyrics effortlessly on five-note tuplet figures. In measure 4, note how she bends the word "me" by dropping a major sixth, soars up a ninth to the pronoun "I," and then drops back down an augmented fourth to the word "don't." Between measures 6 and 8, on the words "You're my Honeysuckle Rose," she starts with a quarter-note triplet rhythm, dissects "Honeysuckle" with an octave leap between the two halves of the word, and then drops back down a sixth to complete the phrase. Throughout this half chorus, Ella also adds a blues element, singing the flatted third of the key, D-flat, in her lines in measures 4, 5, 6, 7, 12, and 14.

Ella was hot on her first chorus, but her second chorus is something else (Example 8.7). Because it is always so easy to praise her, it can become comically redundant to compare her performances. That said, her second chorus of "Honeysuckle Rose" on *A Classy Pair* has to be deemed one of the finest accomplishments of her recorded output. Both her melodic and rhythmic conception are downright scary, her technical execution superior. Once again, she is very liberal with the lyrics, re-inventing them to fit the contours of her miraculous lines. In measures 1 through 4, on the words "Flowers droop and sigh when they pass you by," she runs up to a high F and then descends on a series of thirds, stretching some of the

Example 8.6: "Honeysuckle Rose" (*A Classy Pair*)

Example 8.7: "Honeysuckle Rose" *(A Classy Pair)*

words and putting others in places where you wouldn't expect them to be. Between measures 6 and 8, on the words "You're my Honeysuckle Rose," she starts with repeated motives that incorporate chromatic C-sharp approach notes and leaps of a sixth, both ascending and descending. Between measures 12 and 16, on the words "You're much sweeter goodness knows my Honeysuckle Rose," note her wild phrasing as she links together a series of quarter-note triplets for most of the line. From the end of measure 16 through measure 20, on the words "You don't buy sugar you just have to touch my cup," she sings a typically boppish line, ghosting an E-flat in measure 18 and adding a descending run in measure 19. Beginning at the end of measure 22, she stretches the word "when" through most of measure 23, adds the words "you stir it up" to complete the line in measure 24, then flies up a whopping octave plus a minor sixth to exclaim "Ooh!" Between measures 25 and 28, she descends gradually, strictly on the beat, playfully singing "Drip drip drip from your tasty lips" on half-notes and quarter-notes. Note how she breaks up the word "goodness" in measure 29, leaping down a sixth between syllables. Beginning on the second half of beat two in measure 30, she ends the chorus, first singing "You're my Honeysuckle" on a line that links quarter-note triplets and swinging eighth-notes, and then hitting "Rose" directly on beat four in measure 31 and stretching it for four beats into measure 32.

The rest of *A Classy Pair* is filled with gems. "My Kind of Trouble Is You" is a soulful, medium-slow tune that Benny Carter composed in 1955 and performed with his orchestra. The lyrics are by Paul Vandervoort II and Ella really gets into the song, her tone rich and warm as she croons with plenty of feeling. "Teach Me Tonight" was written by Sammy Cahn and Gene DePaul in 1953 and Ella burns on the medium-tempo swinger. "Organ Grinder's Swing" dates from Ella's early days with Chick Webb, an example of her interpretations of children's songs. This the longest track on the album, six minutes of all-out swing, Ella riffing for the last three with the band and pushing all concerned to keep grooving. Evidently, everyone is having such a grand time that they don't want to stop and the track fades out, a rarity on Ella's albums that is reminiscent of her performance on "Into Each Life Some Rain Must Fall" on the *Ella and Basie* album 16 years earlier.

Ella swings easily on "Don't Worry 'bout Me," first sung by Cab Calloway in 1939, and she and the band cook on "I'm Getting Sentimental over You," taking it considerably faster than Tommy Dorsey did and sounding just right in doing so. That "Ain't Misbehavin'" is included on the album is no surprise. The real treat of the track, however, is Basie's beautiful piano solo, a chorus during which he sticks closely to the melody, adding a few embellishments here and there, but nonetheless swinging magnificently in his inimitable sparse style. "Just a-Sittin' and a-Rockin'" is Billy Strayhorn's easy-swinging number from Duke Ellington's book. Basie takes another mesmerizing solo and bassist John Clayton adds a few solo measures of his own. Basie, who seems to be outdoing himself on each successive track, turns out yet another great solo to open "Sweet Lorraine" and Ella, obviously moved, sings beautifully to put a close to a wonderful album.

Five months after they recorded *A Classy Pair*, Ella and Count Basie performed at the Montreux International Jazz Festival on July 12, 1979. The resulting album, *A Perfect Match*, marked the last time the two superstars would record together. Ella's trio at the time—pianist Paul Smith, bassist Keter Betts, and drummer Mickey Roker—also served as the rhythm section in Basie's band. Included on the album are "Please Don't Talk About Me When I'm Gone," "Sweet Georgia Brown," "Some Other Spring," "Make Me Rainbows," "After You've Gone," "You've Changed," "St. Louis Blues," "Basella," and, of course, "Honeysuckle Rose."

On "Fine and Mellow," Ella is backed by her trio only, and on Thelonious Monk's "'Round Midnight," alto saxophonist Danny Turner switches to flute and joins the trio in the accompaniment. Two other numbers from the concert, "(I Don't Stand) A Ghost of a Chance (with You)" and "Flying Home," were held off *A Perfect Match* and included on the album *Fitzgerald/ Basie/Pass: Digital III at Montreux,* released the following year.

CHAPTER 9

The Principal Accompanists

What you're doing is weaving carpets for the singer to stand on, and maybe you do little things that fit into the open spots. Don't play too much, don't play too loud, and don't play the melody.

—Jimmy Rowles[1]

The majority of Ella Fitzgerald's accompanists during her career were pianists who performed with her either in duos or as leaders of trios or quartets. On occasion, some of them also participated as members of larger ensembles assembled for specific recordings. A few were with her for lengthy periods over the years, others for much shorter stays.

A discussion of the most important pianists to accompany Ella logically starts from the time of her first engagements under Norman Granz's direction. Beginning with her appearances on his Jazz at the Philharmonic (JATP) concerts in the late 1940s, the impresario guided her closely as she progressed through a brilliant solo career and achieved the status of international superstar. Because it was critical that she have an accompanist who could stand up to her all-encompassing professionalism, Granz saw to it that there was always a first-rate pianist to back her. Each was a seasoned professional and, in some cases, a brilliant soloist.

The following list names the pianists and includes a general chronology of the periods they spent with Ella accompanying her in small group or duo performances. Names in boldface designate the most significant players with respect to longevity or recording legacy, or a combination of both. While it is always possible that a name or two, prominent or not, may be missing, the list is nonetheless comprehensive and provides an accurate overview.

Note that Paul Smith recorded with Ella in 1956 as a member of the studio orchestras on the first two of her *Song Books* (Porter, Rodgers and Hart). On both albums, Smith and the rhythm section step out from the larger ensemble to provide quartet accompaniment on several tracks. On the second album, Smith performs in duo with Ella on one track. With the exception of the Ellington *Song Book*, Smith performed on the rest of the albums in the series, but only within the larger ensembles. Lou Levy was also an orchestra member on two *Song Books* (Gershwin, Arlen) that were recorded during his time with Ella.

Fitzgerald's accompanists on piano:

Hank Jones 1948–1953

Oscar Peterson 1949–1993

Ellis Larkins 1950, 1954

Ray Tunia 1953–1954

John Lewis 1954–1955

Don Abney 1955–1957

Paul Smith 1956, 1960 (6 months), 1962–1963, 1978–1981, 1983–1989

Lou Levy 1957–1962

Ray Bryant 1959 (3 months)

Tommy Flanagan 1956 (1 month), 1963–1965, 1968–1978

Jimmy Jones 1966–1968

Tee Carson 1968 (2–3 months)

Jimmy Rowles 1981–1983

Mike Wofford 1989–1992

Although the guitarists who performed with Ella Fitzgerald were usually members of small groups led by pianists, they did on occasion accompany her in duo sessions, both live and on recordings. Of particular note are a few wonderful tracks with Barney Kessel and Ella on two of the *Song Books* (Rodgers and Hart, Ellington). Because of the numerous combinations of players comprising the small groups that backed Ella during her career, a compact chronology for guitarists is not possible. Joe Pass, however, concertized and recorded with her on a regular basis during the latter years of her career. He is the only guitarist whose name is highlighted and for whom his important years working with Ella are indicated.

Fitzgerald's accompanists on guitar:

Barney Kessel

Herb Ellis

Jim Hall
Joe Pass 1973–1986

HANK JONES

Hank Jones was born in Vicksburg, Mississippi on July 31, 1918, and raised in and around Detroit, Michigan. He began studying piano at a young age, becoming a strong player by his early teens. His principal early jazz influences were Fats Waller, Teddy Wilson, and Art Tatum. During the 1940s, when Detroit was a big center for jazz, Hank and his brothers, trumpeter Thad and drummer Elvin, were among the remarkable number of the city's musicians who would become accomplished and celebrated stars. Also included in this group were Tommy Flanagan, Kenny Burrell, Pepper Adams, Yusef Lateef, and Barry Harris.

After gigging throughout Michigan for a number of years, Jones moved to New York in 1944. A strong advocate of bebop music, he played around town, all the while practicing and listening diligently to absorb the new music. He developed into an exquisite musician. Throughout a brilliant career spanning into the early years of the new millennium, Jones who, as writer Nat Hentoff said, "is a melodist, a lyrical storyteller . . . a joyful swinger,"[2] has performed or recorded as a leader or sideman with the cream of jazz musicians, including Charlie Parker, Dizzy Gillespie, Coleman Hawkins, Benny Goodman, Lester Young, Ray Brown, Dave Holland, and Wynton Marsalis.

In late 1947, Jones joined Norman Granz's Jazz at the Philharmonic. This, in turn, led to his becoming Ella Fitzgerald's first regular accompanist of note. He worked with her for the most part between 1948 and 1953. Jones was like Oscar Peterson (another superb pianist to perform with Ella) in that he did not conform to the generally accepted mold of an accompanist. Although each of Ella's accompanists during her career was also a soloist, most of them would supply more integrated and seamless backing behind her. Jones, on the other hand, was a hard bopper not averse to interjecting flourishes of punctuation and sidestepping the commonplace when accompanying Ella. "[H]e breaks the rules and makes it work," explained Phil Schaap. "He's busy when spare or nothing is called for; he fills in those spaces that have to be left empty. So, that's really breaking the rules. But it's glorious. I know the singers don't get mad at him—so I know they dig it."

A few years after leaving Ella Fitzgerald in 1953, Jones commented: "I think she's the greatest singer of them all . . . I had four and a half years to listen to her under all conditions, and I recently played for her [again]. . . . It was a great experience. She was even greater than before. She does so many things so well."[3] Jones recorded on a number of occasions with Ella, both in small groups and in larger ensembles, conducted by Sy Oliver, Bill Doggett, and others. Fortunately, a good amount of this work has been reissued on CD. Hank Jones leads off the list of Ella's important accompanists because, in addition to his stature as one of the jazz world's great pianists, he was the first in a succession of prominent accompanists who could only have spurred Ella to greater heights as she progressed through her miraculous career.

OSCAR PETERSON

Oscar Peterson was born in Montreal on August 15, 1925, the fourth of five children. His parents were from islands in the Caribbean, his father from the British Virgin Islands and his mother from St. Kitts. Gene Lees, in his biography of Peterson, summarizes that "Oscar Peterson was part of a minority within a minority, an English-speaking black in a white city whose primary language was French."[4]

Peterson's father was a stern but caring parent. A self-taught pianist of reasonable ability, he wanted all his children to play music. Oscar Peterson explained how his father accomplished this: "He taught the older children, and then he expected them to pass on what they had learned step by step by step. Daisy [Peterson's sister] did a lot of teaching in the house, and she helped me tremendously."[5]

Peterson was obsessed with his piano studies, practicing for hours on end and taking breaks only to eat and to complete schoolwork. Throughout high school, Peterson took serious private lessons, learned as many songs as he could, and entertained his classmates whenever the opportunity arose. At the age of 14 he won an amateur competition sponsored by the Canadian Broadcasting Corporation. Almost immediately, he was pegged to perform on several radio broadcasts, continuing to do so for the next few years. In addition, with the aid of older musicians who recognized his talent, he would sneak into the area's top jazz club to listen and to play occasionally. From about age 17, Peterson began working professionally on a regular basis.

Norman Granz, the jazz impresario who would be so central to the career of Peterson, as well as Ella Fitzgerald, heard the young pianist performing in Montreal in the late 1940s and decided that he had to introduce the remarkable musician to audiences in the United States. Granz, never one to underplay an opportunity, arranged for Peterson to make his U.S. debut at a Jazz at the Philharmonic concert in, of all places, New York's revered Carnegie Hall. From all reports, it is known that Peterson astonished all present with his incredible playing.

Oscar Peterson has had a marvelous career, dazzling audiences around the world. Among the great musicians who have played in his trios and quartets have been drummer Ed Thigpen, bassists Ray Brown and Niels-

Henning Orsted-Pedersen, and guitarists Barney Kessel, Herb Ellis, and Joe Pass. "[Norman] Granz launched the pianist, who became virtually the house pianist of his various record labels," summarized Lewis Porter, Michael Ullman, and Ed Hazell. "Peterson, an extraordinarily fluid and adaptable artist, toured with Granz's Jazz at the Philharmonic troupes, and recorded for Granz with scores of musicians . . . (It is likely that Peterson has recorded more than any pianist in jazz.)"[6]

Although he was never Ella Fitzgerald's official accompanist per se, Peterson would appear with her on many occasions during her career, either as a member of the Jazz at the Philharmonic troupe or as part of a twin-billing—or as the leader of the trio or quartet accompanying her. "Very often, Norman Granz would have a plan and he'd have penciled in certain numbers," remembered Virginia Wicks, Ella's publicist. "[Ella and Oscar] would come in on what they liked or they didn't like. They all thought more or less alike."

Norman Granz was a highly successful producer because of his unswerving resolve, strong business sense, loyalty to his musicians, and uncanny ability to know what would play. Ella Fitzgerald and Oscar Peterson, Granz's two huge stars, certainly played. In 1957, on the last JATP American tour before Granz moved to Switzerland (he tried one more tour in the United States in early 1967), selections from recorded concerts at the Chicago Opera House and the Shrine Auditorium in Los Angeles were released on a Fitzgerald album entitled *Jazz at the Opera House*. Accompanied brilliantly by Peterson, Herb Ellis, Ray Brown, and Jo Jones, Ella is superb on the recording, absolutely in top form. Phil Schaap remarked:

There's no doubt that the idea that the two defining jazz artists of a whole generation, and the absolute climax of what would be the reigning concert and tour of the period, was Norman Granz's idea. If you had taken any other brain, whether it was a genius like Norman Granz, or just somebody who is a fan, and say "I want to have the jazz event of the fifties to conclude with two artists on stage, and they could be anybody," they wouldn't have been Ella Fitzgerald and Oscar Peterson. These are his two definite champions. But musically, it's a very successful thing. They almost always leaned towards her ability to be a spirited horn and that's a good way to do it. . . . So, it works. . . . And [Granz] really saw in his mind's ear a concert ending with the two of them tearing it up. And they did it for him with no misses. So, he was right.

Bassist Bill Crow, a fine player and seasoned veteran of the jazz scene, recounted the following story:

On a Jazz at the Philharmonic tour of Japan in 1953, Oscar played [a] trick on [Ray] Brown, loosening the G string of his bass several turns and then distracting him with conversation while Norman Granz announced the trio and Ella Fitzgerald. When they took the stage and began to play, Ray's G string was so loose it didn't make any notes at all, just thwacks and buzzes. Ella gave him a dirty look as he cranked his string taut again, while Oscar and Norman laughed with delight.[7]

Ella was a genuinely humble genius, but that did not stop her from intimidating even seasoned professionals when something was not right. Peterson's prank was obviously harmless and pretty humorous, but in this case, when it affected the opening of Ella's performance, anything could have happened. However, the lifelong friendship that they enjoyed, as well as the utmost professional respect that they commanded from one another, had been cultivated during these early days working together. There was no problem. "Oh, marvelous. They were completely in tune, completely harmonious," said Virginia Wicks. "The two of them were like one song. [Ella] loved him personally, and also had great pride working with him. It was like a gift to her to work with Oscar. And, of course, Oscar felt the same."

After working together on and off for over twenty-five years, Fitzgerald and Peterson went into the studio to make a long-playing duo album in May 1975. Aptly titled *Ella and Oscar,* the fantastic performance is an invaluable document of the two stars' work together. Ray Brown, by this time a legendary veteran of Peterson's small groups, played bass on four tracks. Benny Green, who wrote the liner notes for the album, had this to say about Peterson: "I had meant to compose a really quite ingenious and exhaustive account of his consummate tact as an accompanist as well as his amazing melodic richness and rhythmic strength. . . . [I] finally realized that there was nothing to say about it. Except that there is no other jazz musician alive who could get within a mile of it."[8]

Peterson's prodigious talent, coupled with his star-power and strong personality, contributed to his being an unconventional accompanist. Consequently, and maybe not surprisingly, the *Ella and Oscar* album garnered mixed reactions. Geoffrey Mark Fidelman noted that "Ella and Oscar were two tremendous talents each used to the limelight. This album had both vying for it."[9] It is certainly undeniable that the electrifying pianist was a dynamo throughout the recording, offering breathtaking solos on all the tracks. "Peterson, the consummate piano virtuoso, was also a superb accompanist," said Stuart Nicholson. "But his role was that of accompanist *and* soloist. His darting in and out of the limelight gave the album an unbalanced feeling."[10] This last sentiment might also have been inevitable, if considered strictly from the perspective of the generally expected function of a traditional accompanist. However, Fitzgerald and Peterson did not constitute a typical partnership. Their performances were always showcases for the both of them. Regardless of his aggressive tack in backing up Ella, Peterson was an exceptional accompanist who was also one of the *two* stars of the show—and the two created remarkable music to-gether. "Working with Oscar Peterson, like working with Art Tatum, is a very complex issue," commented Phil Schapp. "And it can work out, even for all of its density, musically. And does work out. Obviously, [Ella and Oscar] enjoyed doing it."

Fitzgerald and Peterson were great friends who continually welcomed the challenges and stimulation generated by their musical exchanges. "She never called me her accompanist. She used to call me her lawyer," related Peterson. "I was with her until practically the very end of her singing career. . . . I have never truthfully played with a musician—and that in-cludes an awful lot of them—who frightened me as much as playing for Ella. Because she has the kind of gift you can't describe."[11] Coming from Peterson, this was quite a statement.

When the album *Ella and Oscar* was pressed, Ella was at the stage in life when her voice was in a process of gradually deepening. On the recording, her rounded sound, coupled with her inventive phrasing, was a solid match for Peterson's pyrotechnics. On "Mean to Me," the opening track, Peterson sets the mood with a relaxed four-bar introduction, going into a stride-piano feel when Ella enters. She starts out equally at ease, the strong rapport with her brilliant collaborator quickly apparent. Staying relatively faithful to the original melody, her phrasing is nonetheless elastic and she adds enough nice touches to let the listener know that this will be an extraordinary session. As she coasts through her chorus she intersperses flatted thirds (blues notes), effortless intervallic skips, and motives built on triplets and swinging eighth-notes.

On the next track, Fitzgerald and Peterson open the Gershwins' "How Long Has This Been Going On?" with a engaging rubato chorus. Peterson then throws in a brief piano fill, establishing a medium-tempo swing groove. The first sixteen measures of the second chorus are shown in Ex-ample 9.1. In measure 5, Ella speaks the word "wow," but not too vehe-mently since it is a "little wow." In measures 9 and 10, her amazing flexibility is displayed as she leaps an octave to a high F on the word "chill," holds it just long enough for good effect, and then jumps back down a major seventh to the G-flat below. In measure 13, she speaks the word "sweet" for emphasis, then ends the passage on a descending eighth-note lick, tagging the words "how long" three times in succession so there is no doubt that she really wants to know how long everything *has* been going on.

Peterson follows this chorus with a virtuosic solo that is flawless and beautiful to hear. As he nears the end of the bridge, he downshifts as Ella is about come in. They modulate up a half-step to the key of A and Ella sings the last eight measures freely and peacefully on top of Peterson's gentle backing.

Next up is one of Ella's four recorded versions of "When Your Lover

Example 9.1: "How Long Has This Been Going On?" *(Ella and Oscar)*

Has Gone." (For a version she did four years prior to this recording, on the album *Ella Swings Brightly with Nelson*, see the section on Nelson Riddle in Chapter 7.) Ella and Peterson swing easily on E. A. Swan's engaging melody. The first half of Ella's opening chorus is shown in Example 9.2. Whereas the original melody consists of a series of two-measure figures, usually starting on the second beat of the measure, Ella alters the entrances of these figures, in most cases coming in on the second half of beat two. She does this four times—in measures 1, 5, 7, and 9—and, in measure 11, she anticipates the figure by a half-beat. She also executes a sudden leap of an octave between the words "At" and "break" in measure 9.

Peterson solos after Ella's chorus, modulates up a half-step to the key of D-flat, Ella re-enters scatting, and the two trade fours for one and three-quarter choruses. Ella's scatting is fairly subdued, maintaining the overall relaxed feeling of the track. For the final eight measures she reverts to the lyrics, closes out the chorus, and improvises a tag ending to complete the selection.

For an intriguing comparison with Ella's interpretation, Example 9.3 shows the opening of Louis Armstrong's chorus on "When Your Lover Has Gone," as recorded with his big band on April 29, 1931.[12] In measures 3, 5, and 7 he attacks the song's two-measure signature figure on the

Example 9.2: "When Your Lover Has Gone" *(Ella and Oscar)*

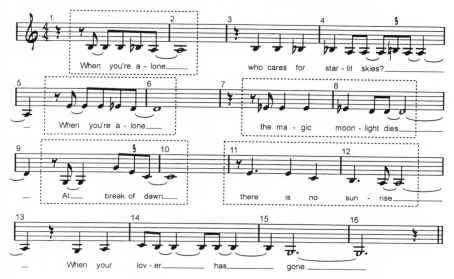

Example 9.3: "When Your Lover Has Gone" *(Louis Armstrong: Big Band Recordings)*

second half of beat two—Ella does this in her excerpt on four occasions. In addition, both singers use identical phrasing in measure 7, an eighth-note followed by two quarter-notes. Armstrong's rhythmic concept in this excerpt is astounding, an example of how his freshness and originality were ahead of the times. Notice especially the incredible passage he creates between measures 13 and 16 in which he improvises devilishly on the title lyrics, attacking words on or off the beat only if he is not pushing them through intricately placed triplet figures.

On the next two tracks, Fitzgerald and Peterson present lovely ballad renderings of "More Than You Know" and "There's a Lull in My Life." On the former, Ella has the spotlight most of the way through while, on the latter, Peterson opens with a solo before any singing occurs. Next comes "Midnight Sun" in an easy groove. Ella draws out Johnny Mercer's lyrics with deep feeling, maintaining a soulful mood throughout. On this track, bassist Ray Brown has joined in for the rest of the session.

"I Hear Music" is a gem among the many highlights of the album. Oscar Peterson and Ray Brown provide exceptional drive at a medium tempo on the Frank Loesser/Burton Lane standard. Throughout the first chorus Ella remains mostly faithful to the original melody. On the second chorus she really goes to town (Example 9.4). She starts by scatting a boppish six-beat pick-up to the chorus. Her amazing ability to redesign melodies then comes into play immediately in measure 1. She manipulates the tune's signature phrase by dropping down an octave between the words "I" and "hear" and then, turning on a dime, she shoots up a major seventh to the word "music." Additionally, she suggests a re-harmonization of the line, singing the pitches B-flat to A on the pronoun "I," instead of just holding on an A, and A-flat to G on "music," instead of the expected A to G. She does the latter again in measure 10. In measure 3, she shifts directions on the words "mighty fine," descending on the syllables of "mighty" and returning to "fine," instead of going in the opposite direction as expected. In measure 5, on the words "murmur of a morning," Ella again reverses the contour of the original melody by descending through the motive; a comparison of the two motives is shown more closely in Example 9.5. In measure 13, when the same melodic fragment occurs at a later point in the chorus, she blares the words "singing of the sparrow" on identical pitches, similar to how a lead trumpet player might emphasize a phrase in a big-band arrangement. Ella moves into the bridge at measure 17 with another of her trademark octave leaps. In measure 19 she adds a nice twist on the word "melody," with a neat drop of a sixth, before finishing. Starting the last eight measures of the chorus, Ella restates the "I hear music" motive by descending through a triplet figure from a high E. She ends the chorus on held notes in the last four measures.

Oscar Peterson follows Ella with two scorching solo choruses. Using a favorite device of theirs, the musicians then modulate the key up a half-

Example 9.4: "I Hear Music" *(Ella and Oscar)*

Example 9.5: "I Hear Music" *(Ella and Oscar)*

step and Ella returns for one more inventive chorus. (For a version of "I Hear Music" that Ella did with Nelson Riddle, also on the album *Ella Swings Brightly with Nelson,* see the section on Riddle in Chapter 7.)

The next track, "Street of Dreams," is a nice change of pace. The slow swinger starts with short solo breaks by Peterson and Ray Brown. The session ends with "April in Paris," taken at a slightly faster tempo. After Ella sings the verse, she and Peterson each take two choruses before she returns to scat one more. The two trade licks on an extended vamp to end the take.

On the back cover of the CD reissue of *Ella and Oscar,* there is a short blurb lauding the session. Part of it reads: "Their individual genius for blending virtuosity and sensitivity and for infusing every note with a spirit of affirmation was reinforced when they held this intimate meeting." The recording was certainly one of the great highlights to come during the latter years of Ella's career.

ELLIS LARKINS

Ellis Larkins, the eldest of six children, was born in Baltimore on May 15, 1923. His parents, both good amateur musicians, gave him his initial musical training, first on violin and ultimately on piano. Progressing quickly, the young Larkins soon began serious private classical studies which in turn led to a number of recitals. As a result, he became a local celebrity, recognized for his impressive talent at such a young age. He eventually attended the Frederick Douglass High School, a prominent and distinguished institution in the black community, where he continued his musical development. Larkins also studied privately with instructors at the Peabody Institute—black students at this time were still not accepted officially at the conservatory.

Larkins was listening to as much jazz as he could, trying to incorporate it into his playing. In addition, he was becoming adept at accompanying singers. His interest in jazz would pay off when, after graduating from high school in 1940 and going to New York City to study at Julliard on a scholarship, he had to start playing around town to support himself. John Hammond, the impresario important to the careers of so many prominent musicians, helped Larkins get his union card.

Larkins began a busy playing schedule that included, among his first string of gigs, a stay with guitarist Billy Moore. By the time Larkins graduated from Julliard in 1940 he was an accomplished pianist who performed regularly, often in New York leading his own trio. He also appeared or recorded with many top performers, including clarinetist Edmond Hall; singers Mildred Bailey, Helen Humes, Sylvia Syms, and Joe Williams; and the legendary tenor saxophonists Coleman Hawkins and Lester Young. Of note are a series of recordings that Larkins made with cornetist Ruby Braff in 1955, 1972, and 1994, pressings that have become classics to aficionados. In 1988 Larkins returned to his home town, assuming the rank of Baltimore's elder statesman of jazz. He passed away on September 30, 2002.

Ellis Larkins and Ella Fitzgerald recorded duo sessions for Decca in 1950 and 1954. Because of the exceptional musicianship from the two performers, both recordings are landmark achievements for Ella. Larkins remembered that "John Hammond and Milt Gabler [Fitzgerald's producer at Decca] wanted to do a record with Ella, and I got the call. . . . With her, there was no rehearsal, you just did it. . . . She had everything, phrasing, intelligence, and warmth."[13]

The first session with Larkins, *Ella Sings Gershwin,* was also the first long-playing album that she made in her career.[14] This was a project that wholly appealed to her, a recording that gave her the opportunity to team up with an outstanding accompanist and to finally stretch out on a selection of tunes by a great composer. Ella had been longing for some time to sing more music of substance, choice standards by the top songwriters. The following excerpt from a *Down Beat* review of a club appearance she made in Chicago two years prior to the Gershwin recording is indicative of her frame of mind:

"I don't like to sing bop." It was no one less than Ella Fitzgerald saying that, and if she hadn't qualified it with a "most," it would have shattered the illusions of thousands of her fans. . . . What Ella sang . . . was mostly sweet, though the songs themselves easily could have had a jump treatment. . . . By "sweet," don't think we mean without experimentation and interpolation and the constant musicianship she exhibits when she sings. But you can't be gentle with a jump tune, and Miss Fitzgerald was feeling very gentle indeed. How long this will last, we have no way of knowing.[15]

On the second album with Larkins, *Songs in a Mellow Mood,* Ella sang 12 of her favorite tunes, once again with remarkable backing by the pianist.[16] However, there had been a gap of three and a half years between the two sessions, during which time Ella's output with Decca had still consisted of predominantly commercial fare (although there were certainly some nice moments). Ella continued to make known her desire to upgrade her repertoire. For example, a few months after completing the second recording with Larkins, she expressed her feelings to writer Nat Hentoff while recounting how Frank Sinatra would come to hear her when he was in New York at the same time. "Sinatra came into Basin Street often while he was at the Copa," related Ella, "and he asked for ["The Man That Got Away"] every time. And he also asked, 'How come, Ella, you don't have a number like *that* to record?' I don't know why myself. . . . They give me something by somebody that no one else has, and then they wonder why the record doesn't sell."[17] It would not be until 1956, when she did the first of the *Song Book* series (of Cole Porter songs) for Norman Granz and Verve, that her career would take the artistic turn that she desired so much.

Ella's singing on the sides with Ellis Larkins is wondrous, showcasing her at the peak of her powers. In Larkins, she had the consummate partner, an exceptional player with exquisite taste. "Ellis Larkins is a great accompanist because he has dealt with the whole issue of submergence without it messing up his art," remarked Phil Schaap. "You have to just totally delete a lot of your personality and needs and ego—or you're not an accompanist. It's an incredibly difficult thing to do. . . . If you only think of it as a subtraction, it will never work." Jimmy Rowles, another top-rank pianist and a later accompanist of Ella, once said that "Ellis Larkins . . . is a great accompanist, and you could take a real lesson by paying him some attention."[18]

Larkins was fully aware of the issues that one faces when working with a vocalist. He realized how important it was to have a heartfelt understanding of the song being performed. "The good standards—Gershwin, Kern, Rodgers and Hammerstein, Ellington—are in most cases very pianistic," said Larkins. "The melody lines are good, and they have good lyrics. I prefer to know the lyrics when I play a song, because when you play a tune that has a beautiful lyric it gives you more to work with. You can become a singer."[19]

In 1994, GRP Records, the parent company of Decca Jazz, reissued the Fitzgerald/Larkins sessions as a CD compilation, calling it *Pure Ella*. James Gavin commented in the liner notes that the "duets brought together two artists who could hear around the same corners, anticipating each other's subtlest shifts of mood."[20]

Ella Sings Gershwin opens with "Someone to Watch over Me." After Larkins's brief chordal intro Ella enters with the verse. It is immediately apparent that this type of project, so long in coming for her, was more than worth the wait. She sings freely around the time, confident yet unaffected, her voice crystalline and her delivery understated. The exquisite chorus that follows is remarkable for its refined simplicity. Ella is straightforward, adding little embellishment and just the right touch of vibrato. The breathiness in her voice highlights the poignant lyrics as she progresses through the melody, with no wavering on the sustained notes that end the sections. She picks up the tempo slightly and is a bit freer with the time during the bridge before she closes out the chorus much as she started. All the while, Larkins shines through with his sensitive and tasteful backing. This streamlined opener sets the stage for all that follows. Throughout the session, Ella continues in similar fashion, immaculate in her delivery and staying true to each tune without any flashiness or excessive emotion. Larkins accompanies with a matching economy of style, breaking out occasionally to solo.

The two performers establish a relaxed medium groove on the second track, "My One and Only." After Ella's opening chorus Larkins takes a half-chorus in which he alternates fragments of the melody with his own inventive figures. Ella returns with a final chorus and adds lyrics—"It's time you woke up/It's time you spoke up"—to create a brief tag before the final line, "When I'm so crazy over you."

Next up is "But Not for Me." Larkins's four-bar intro paves the way for Ella, who sings her first chorus freely and slowly. Larkins takes over by shifting into a medium-tempo lilt and soloing for a half a chorus, sticking closely to the melody and adding a flourish or two. Ella then retakes the lead for the second half of the chorus (Example 9.6). Entering with a nice eighth-note pick-up phrase, she proceeds to leap down a sixth between the words "so" and "well" before swinging through the next six measures to complete the section.

Ella slows the pace and sings the last A section freely. Once again, she adds a tag to close the chorus: "And there's no knot/I guess he's not for me." Larkins ends the take tinkling a few quiet notes.

Example 9.6: "But not for Me" *(Ella Sings Gershwin)*

On "Looking for a Boy" Ella follows her swinging first chorus by going into a free rendition of the verse. She returns to the second A section swinging again and, after the bridge, the musicians modulate up a half-step to the key of D-flat for the final eight measures of the chorus. Ella throws in a tag with impromptu lyrics—"Won't you find that boy?/Help me find a boy who's looking for a girl to love"—to emphasize the song's underlying message as she brings the track to a close.

Ella treats the first chorus of "I've Got a Crush on You" very freely, playing with the tempo, Larkins locked in with her seamlessly. As on the previous track, she segues into the verse before returning to another chorus. She closes with the lyrics "cause I've got a crush, my baby, on you," holding the last word for six or seven seconds, the sustained pitch ringing true in the air before she gently cuts it off. The beautiful track fully demonstrates Ella's approach to the entire session, how she is completely committed to the material, singing directly into the microphone so that her voice is clearly out front. She addresses the listener point-blank—and she is completely on target.

Larkins's brief intro escorts Ella into "How Long Has This Been Going On?" She sings the first half of her opening chorus slowly in time. "I could cry salty tears/Where have I been all these years," she starts, leaving it to the listener to work on an interpretation or to call up deeper feelings. She frees up on the bridge and then takes the last A back in tempo. Larkins goes into the bridge again, freely at a faster pace, playing hints of the melody accompanied by soaring arpeggiated chords. Ella returns in measure seven of the bridge and finishes the take in the original slower tempo. (For Ella's version of this song with Oscar Peterson, see the section on Peterson in this chapter.)

On the pretty tune "Maybe" the unpretentiousness with which Fitzgerald and Larkins have approached this recording session is perhaps more marked than on any other track. The two artists take the first chorus with a half-time feel. Larkins follows with a solo, doubling up into a medium-tempo swing groove and generating his ideas without any histrionics. Ella returns, maintaining the tempo for three-quarters of another chorus before slowing the tempo and singing the last eight measures freely to a simple ending.

Ella concludes her Gershwin set with "Soon," from the musical *Strike Up the Band*. The first chorus is taken at a medium tempo, Ella wistful in her vocalizing, Larkins playing it straight. The two musicians then up the tempo a little and swing through a second chorus in which Ella's phrasing and manipulation of melody are at their absolute best (Example 9.7). Going into the first four measures, she sings the word "soon" three times to set up a line in which she employs sophisticated, highly syncopated rhythms, placing the lyrics before or after the beat, or across the barlines. Note also her effective use of triplet figures in measures 6, 8, 14, and

Example 9.7: "Soon" *(Ella Sings Gershwin)*

particularly in measures 18 and 19, where she runs the figure over the barline, and in measures 23 and 24, where she links two quarter-note triplets. The performers also add a good touch by modulating up a half-step to the key of A for the second half of the chorus. Ella throws in a boppish lick to launch the new key in measure 17 and she tags the final line, "Let's make that day come soon," holding the last pitch for over three measures to finish the track.

The *Ella Sings Gershwin* session provided clear proof of how ready and focused Ella was for an undertaking of this nature. She sang beautifully and she had the perfect partner in Ellis Larkins, a first-class pianist with exquisite taste and a profound understanding of the project at hand. Given this first-time opportunity, her tremendous respect for the music shone through. On each track she gave the listener the essence of the song, without superfluous emoting. She established the interpretive parameters and gave no more, or no less, than was necessary—and she would sing in like fashion for years to come. Such was her genius, a manner of expression that was, despite any appraisal, rightfully or wrongly, that it lacked substantive emotional content, one of the most direct and purposeful singing styles that the music world would ever know.

For the *Songs in a Mellow Mood* album, Ella chose 12 of her favorite selections by various songwriters. Ellis Larkins again provided brilliant accompaniment, although, with the exception of a few brief breaks, he did little soloing this time around. In any event, the end result was another exemplary collaboration by the two virtuosos.

Ella was undoubtedly excited to go another round with Larkins on a new batch of tunes. She is assured and concise on "People Will Say We're in Love," "Please Be Kind," and "Baby, What Else Can I Do." Another Gershwin number, "Nice Work If You Can Get It," gets a lively, swinging treatment. On "I'm Glad There Is You" and "What Is There to Say" her renditions are slow and luscious, the lower part of her range highlighted. "Imagination" can't be interpreted more succinctly, Ella working the pretty tune at a slow lilt, giving us a single, richly toned chorus before Larkins's gentle closing lick. On "You Leave Me Breathless" the two artists, in the spirit of the song's title, have some fun near the end of the track by lapsing into silence for almost five seconds before Ella comes back in to tell us that she has definitely been left breathless.

Although Cole Porter's "My Heart Belongs to Daddy" is not a blues number, we hear Ella's most blues-inflected singing of the session on her single-chorus treatment of the song. She bends notes, lays back on the beat, and draws out the final lyrics, interspersing deliberate pauses and hanging onto each word. She also takes several liberties with the lyrics, a notable instance occurring when she begins the second half of the chorus by substituting "Yes, I'm gonna marry Daddy" for the title phrase.

Ella sings beautifully on "Star Dust," composed by Hoagy Carmichael in 1927. In J. Wilfred Johnson's monumental Ella Fitzgerald discography the author reports that the time-honored song "has been recorded more than 700 times with at least 50 different arrangements for every possible instrument or combination of instruments; the lyric [sic] has been translated into forty languages."[21] (For a discussion of Ella's take on this venerable standard, and of a version by her prime singing model, Connee Boswell, see the section on Boswell in Chapter 3.)

On "Until the Real Thing Comes Along" Ella follows Larkins's brief opening flourish by humming an improvised intro as a lead-in to her first chorus (Example 9.8). When she delves into the opening lyrics her voice is rich and clear and her feeling for the message convincing, leaving no doubt that she will wait for the real thing.

On the jauntiest track of the session, "Makin' Whoopee," a bright four-bar intro by Larkins sets the mood for Ella's exuberant first chorus. Larkins follows with a half-chorus solo, maintaining the mood with licks that are both inventive and unpretentious, his left hand providing a steady bass pulse as he perhaps nods in the direction of the great stride pianists. Approaching the bridge he modulates up a step to the key of C and Ella comes in with a new chorus instead of continuing from the bridge. This is the closest she comes to really letting loose on the session and we hear some of her most inspired phrasing and vocal dexterity.

Example 9.9 shows the first eight measures of Ella's second chorus of "Makin' Whoopee," as well as the opening of Louis Armstrong's chorus from *Ella and Louis Again,* the album the two recorded three years later for Verve. While we see Ella's own formidable style and interpretive tendencies, the two passages still exhibit intriguing rhythmic and melodic similarities, an indication of Armstrong's ever-present influence. For instance, Armstrong often took motives that had moving pitches and altered them to motives with repeated pitches. Both Fitzgerald and Armstrong open their choruses in exactly this manner by singing repeated pitches on the word "another," instead of the original stepwise figure. This is illustrated in more detail in Example 9.10. In Ella's take we see, in addition to

Example 9.8: Humming an improvised intro *(Songs in a Mellow Mood)*

Example 9.9: "Makin' Whoopee" (*Songs in a Mellow Mood* **and** *Ella and Louis Again*)

Ella (*Songs in a Mellow Mood* **w/Ellis Larkins)**

effortless octave leaps in measures 3 and 7, her effective syncopation of the melody in these same measures, as well as in measures 5 and 6. Notice also how in measure 7 she delays starting the word "whoopee" until the second half of beat one. This displacing of the attack on a lyric, especially later than might be expected, was a favorite device of Armstrong's. In his passage, truly a lesson in inventive phrasing, he anticipates a triplet figure in measure two and delays starting the word "maybe" until the second eighth-note of the triplet. Both singers also add blues inflections, Ella using the flatted third of the key on the word "can't" in measure 3 and Armstrong sticking with the flatted third when he sings "of makin' whoopee" in measures 6 and 7. In measures 3 and 4 of his passage, Armstrong speaks lyrics rather than singing them and ends with an impromptu chuckle: "What's this I hear? Well can't you guess? Ha ha." On her take with Larkins, Ella speaks lyrics in her second chorus after the

Example 9.10: "Makin' Whoopee"—motive comparison

pianist's solo. Just before the bridge she speaks the question in the following line: "He says he's busy, but she says: 'Is he?'" At the end of the track she tags the last line—"You'd better keep her, I think it's cheaper than makin' whoopee/You'd better keep her, I know it's cheaper than makin' whoopee"—speaking the words "I know it's" to add emphasis to her interpretation.

Songs in a Mellow Mood did not garner as much attention as *Ella Sings Gershwin*. It might be tempting to explain this by saying that the Gershwin set, because of its purity and sheer beauty, was a more effective collaboration. It is more likely that *Songs in a Mellow Mood* suffered from poor distribution and promotion. In fact, Ella commented that the record "got such wonderful write-ups, and I remember when I was on the coast it seemed like everybody was playing it. But the disc jockeys claimed that the company didn't give them the record. In fact, we had to go out and buy the record and give it to those disc jockeys that didn't have it . . . but maybe it's because that record company is mainly interested in pictures now."[22]

Although she performed and recorded a few numbers with Larkins when he participated, along with many other musicians, at a 1973 Carnegie Hall celebration concert in her honor, the two studio recordings Ella made with the virtuoso pianist stand alone as definitive documents of their work together, and of the art of the American song. Gary Giddins commented that "she achieves a sensuousness and command of the material that is, note for note, enthralling. Her voice had never sounded quite as resplendent before."[23] During a career that spanned almost sixty years, Ella worked with many of the greatest musicians of the twentieth century—and the sessions with Larkins remain among the very best of her achievements.

PAUL SMITH

Paul Smith was born in San Diego, California, on April 17, 1922, to parents who had previously been vaudeville performers for over twenty years. Influenced by his parents' musical backgrounds, he commenced studying piano when he was eight. He landed his first professional engagements in his mid-teens and had developed into a talented player by the time he left home at age 19 to pursue a full-time music career.

During the early 1940s, including while he was in the service, Smith worked steadily. He compiled an impressive list of credits that featured stints with Les Paul and with Tommy Dorsey. After serving as staff pianist for Warner Brothers Studios in the late 1940s, Smith moved to Los Angeles in 1949. During the 1950s and early 1960s, he was a successful west coast studio performer and NBC's staff pianist for 10 years, regularly playing for radio and television productions. He also appeared in clubs and theaters with many top popular entertainers and jazz musicians, in the process becoming a first-rate accompanist. "The roster of headliners with whom Paul worked would comprise an all-time Who's Who of modern entertainment," reported *Disc & That Magazine*. "Among them were Dinah Shore, Bing Crosby, . . . Frank Sinatra, Tony Bennett, . . . Sarah Vaughan, . . . Gordon MacRae, Jimmy Durante, . . . Jo Stafford, Carol Burnett, Nat 'King' Cole, [and] Johnny Mercer. . . . What other performer can boast of having musically associated with such an impressive list!"[24]

Smith first worked with Ella Fitzgerald in 1956, playing in the studio orchestras for both the Cole Porter and Rodgers and Hart *Song Book* sessions. He also played with her briefly in 1960 and for much of 1962 to 1963. He went to work with her again in 1978, taking over from the brilliant Tommy Flanagan who, after his lengthy association with Ella, was stepping down to pursue a full-time solo career. Although Flanagan was a hard act to follow, the multifaceted Smith would complement Ella beautifully, backing her for much of the following 12 years. "Ella was always very consistent in what she did," enthused Smith. "She never did anything that wasn't very musical. . . . Ella was so musical she made it easy to play for her. She wasn't always the same, but the general continuity was always very easy to follow."[25]

Paul Smith was a wonderful musical director for Ella Fitzgerald. He provided her with first-rate accompaniment and loyal friendship. "This is a man who has decided that being a great accompanist is a great achievement. . . . He loved Ella, loves her," remarked Phil Schaap. "I think he understands there's more to rhythm than just swinging. You know, Rachmaninoff is a great piano player, and Smith knows that. I find a lot of jazz people. . . . indifferent to that, because they don't understand. . . . rhythm existed before jazz, and rhythmic wonder and strength existed before swing. . . . Paul Smith really understands that."

Smith was also very thoughtful in organizing Ella's music after Tommy Flanagan had left. Geoffrey Mark Fidelman, in his biography of Fitzgerald, explains: "Unfortunately for Ella, Tommy was such a genius that he didn't need music—he just learned a piece and then played it from memory. Any new pianist didn't have a clue to Ella's 'book,' the lead arrangements for all the songs she did in her live concerts. Paul took great pains to write Ella such a book, using many of the Flanagan arrangements or embellishments and then adding more of his own as they toured."[26]

Although Lou Levy was Ella Fitzgerald's regular accompanist for most of the period between 1957 and 1962, Norman Granz had hired Paul Smith to tour with her for the first six months of 1960 while Levy was off doing another engagement with Peggy Lee. Consequently, Smith was the pianist on the *Ella in Berlin* album, recorded on February 13, 1960, and generally regarded as one of her greatest releases. This concert in the German metropolis was Ella's opening performance on a JATP tour in Europe that year. The 1993 CD reissue, *The Complete Ella in Berlin: Mack the Knife*, which contains selections not on previous editions (including "Love for Sale" and "Just One of Those Things," which were actually from a 1956 Hollywood concert), provides the entire documentation of the wonderful event. Guitarist Jim Hall, bassist Wilfred Middlebrooks, and drummer Gus Johnson teamed with Smith in the accompanying group.

Ella starts the program with three staples from the standard repertoire: "That Old Black Magic," "Our Love Is Here to Stay," and "Gone with the Wind." In her usual top form, she has the audience in a festive mood in short order and, although the renderings on these opening selections are straightforward with few frills (for Ella), her vocal work could constitute a master class in swing.

Next up is Errol Garner's classic composition "Misty," a lovely ballad that took its place as a mainstay of the standard repertoire soon after Garner recorded it in 1954. He introduced it as an instrumental, but Johnny Mathis's recording in 1956, with lyrics supplied by Johnny Burkes, also established it as a showcase for vocalists. Ella's rendering is a highlight of her Berlin performance—and also the earliest of her several recordings of the song. She sings assuredly with a slight huskiness to her voice, modulating from the key of B-flat up to B after only eight measures. This shift in tonality is a nice touch because it happens so unexpectedly early in the take. Jim Hall's sparse fills on the ensuing bridge are tasteful and inspired. Example 9.11 shows the opening of the selection with the modulation taking place in measure 9. In measure 2, Ella follows the contour of the original melody by singing up a major seventh on the word "helpless." However, whereas the conventional phrasing would have this take place on the downbeat of the measure, she has shifted the lyrics so

Example 9.11: "Misty" *(The Complete Ella in Berlin)*

that she attacks on the second half of beat one. In measure 3, she begins the rising triplet figure on a low D, an indication, when considering that she could sing close to three octaves higher, of her amazing range at this point in her career. In measure 4, she holds the slightest bit until the second note of the triplet before letting out the lyrics "clinging to a cloud." She uses this manner of delayed phrasing again in measure 10, starting the word "violin" on the second half of beat two. If Louis Armstrong had been listening, he most certainly would have been smiling. Note the impressive shift up of a major ninth between the words "misty" and "just" in measure 6, as well as how Ella sustains on the word "hold" in the next measure, truly in the spirit of the lyrics, before completing the phrase. The manner in which Ella sings the lyrics "sound of your hello" in measure 12, descending on a sixteenth-note figure, only to leap back up a major seventh on the last syllable, is typical of boppish phrasing.

Next is "The Lady Is a Tramp," the Rodgers and Hart song that had been a major hit for Frank Sinatra. Ella starts by singing the verse loosely, out of time, complemented by Paul Smith's tasteful backing. Her exuberance is obvious from the outset, indicating that she is going to thoroughly enjoy digging into the popular number. Everyone then takes off on two up-tempo choruses. Ever playful, Ella invents the lyrics in the second chorus, even sticking in references to the occasional concerns she has about her weight: "Girls get massages, they cry and they moan:/'Tell slender Ella to leave me alone.'/I'm not so hot, but my shape is my own." The piece swings on and, just before coming to a close, the music modulates from F to G major and Ella adds her usual tribute, "For Frank Sinatra, I whistle and stamp." The audience roars its approval for the hot rendition while Ella laughingly proclaims: "Thank you, Frank Sinatra fans."

The next selection on the concert is the Gershwin ballad "The Man I Love." From the outset, Ella's rich voice and heartfelt singing provide emotional tinges that are suggestive of Billie Holiday. When she reaches the bridge, Ella sings freely while Paul Smith fills in with a gentle touch behind her. She ends the chorus back in tempo and then returns to the bridge instead of going to the top of another chorus, a common practice for musicians on slow ballads. Coming out of the bridge, she modulates up a half-step to the key of A to finish the selection.

After substantive takes on "Summertime," "Too Darn Hot," and "Lorelei," Ella prepares to sing "Mack the Knife," the first of two showstoppers with which she will conclude the set. The song had been a major success for Louis Armstrong in 1956, as well as a huge winner for Bobby Darin two years later. Ella, who had never performed "Mack the Knife" prior to the Berlin concert, pointed this out to the audience. "We'd like to do something for you now. We haven't heard a girl sing it," she announced. "And since it's so popular, we'd like to try and do it for you. We hope we remember all the words."

Ella swings magnificently, despite the fact that, true to the uncertainty she expressed in her opening remarks, she starts having trouble with the lyrics seemingly as early as the second chorus. She, of course, does not miss a beat, manipulating her phrasing so she can fit in what words she can remember. By the time the fourth chorus arrives, Ella, now soaking the moment for all its worth, starts improvising whole choruses of alternate wording for the rest of the piece:

Oh, what's the next chorus to this song now?/This is the one now I don't know.

But it was the swinging tune, and it's a hit too./So we tried to do *Mack the Knife*.

Oh, Louis Miller, oh something about cash./Yes, Miller, he was spinning that trash.

And Mac Heath, dear, he spends like a sailor./Tell me, tell me, tell me, could that boy do something right?

Oh, Bobby Darin and Louis Armstrong,/they made a record, oh but they did.

And now, Ella, Ella and her fellas, /we're making a wreck, what a wreck of *Mack the Knife*.

Ella even throws in an impersonation of a scatting Louis Armstrong for half a chorus before ending the take. She absolutely floors her Berlin fans, dazzling them with her spontaneity and inventiveness. This version of "Mack the Knife" has attained legendary status in the world of recorded music. Ella went on to win two Grammies for a number that remains one of the foremost treasures in the entire jazz discography.

Incredibly, Ella still has one more blockbuster to present to the Berlin audience. "How High the Moon" is a perfect vehicle for her unmatched scatting. The great singer produces an astounding tour de force, a prolonged scatting romp that floors her listeners again. The stunning finale is a second true landmark of her career—from the same concert. (For more about this performance of "How High the Moon," see Chapter 5.)

Two months after their Berlin triumph, Ella Fitzgerald and Paul Smith were in the studio to do an album of duets. Recorded on April 14 and 19, 1960, the session was comprised of numbers that Ella had sung on the soundtrack album for the movie *Let No Man Write My Epitaph*. In the liner notes to the CD reissue, titled *The Intimate Ella*, Imme Schade van Westrum supplies background information about both the film and the recording: "In this somewhat bizarre film about corruption and drug addicts we see and hear Ella Fitzgerald (alongside Burl Ives, Shelley Winters and Jean Seberg) sing the songs while giving the impression that she accompanies herself on piano. In reality it is Cliff Smalls who plays the piano parts on the soundtrack.... [On *The Intimate Ella*], Fitzgerald and Paul Smith sound exceptionally subdued and in some places even melancholic."[27] A far cry from the fireworks of the "Ella in Berlin" recording, but equally inspired, listeners are treated to a tremendous performance in which the two musicians are completely attuned to each other. The session is in the same league with the Fitzgerald/Ellis Larkins collaborations of the early 1950s.

The Intimate Ella opens with Ella's take on "Black Coffee," a number first introduced by Sarah Vaughan in the late 1940s. It is in the form of a blues song with an added bridge and Ella, as she did so often during her career, demonstrates how wonderfully she can handle the genre, despite the fact that she was often perceived as having little or no connection to the blues. On the next track, "Angel Eyes," Ella's voice is resonant and pure. In a dramatic conclusion that is particularly beautiful, Smith lays out at one point so that Ella can ad-lib a mini-cadenza before the two bring the piece to a tranquil close. Smith's tasteful four-bar intro opens "I Cried for You," Ella singing the first chorus freely as the pianist shadows her brilliantly. The two modulate up a half-step to A major and take a second chorus in a medium-slow groove.

"I Can't Give You Anything but Love" is a tune Ella performed many times, both live and in the studio. (For her version with Lou Levy, see the section on Levy in this chapter; for a version by Connee Boswell, see the section on Boswell in Chapter 3.) Ella's version on *The Intimate Ella* is exceptional. As in her duo recordings with Ellis Larkins, Ella is up front in the mix, her voice projecting directly into the microphone, openly exposed so that every nuance, every breath, every turn of phrase is clearly defined—and it's perfect. Behind her, Paul Smith's accompaniment is equally exquisite and relaxed as he maintains the slow swing and fills in the nooks seamlessly. Following his two-bar intro and Ella's customary freely rendered verse, her chorus that follows is a masterpiece of phrasing and pacing (Example 9.12). Part of her genius derived from her ability to deliver such a sophisticated, at times complex, interpretation on ballads while still respecting the spirit of the lyrics and maintaining an appropriate mood. From the end of measure 4 through measure 5, she stretches the word "baby" over four and a half beats, producing a boppish motive during which she squeezes five eighth notes into the space of four. Between measures 6 and 8, on the lyrics "I've plenty of, Baby," she waits until the second half of beat two in measure 6 to start the phrase and then uses the jump of a major sixth to split up the word "plenty." This parrots the original contour of the line, but Ella does it with more agility, the original being a simpler succession of quarter notes. In measure 8, she completes the line with a blues inflection on "Baby," adding a D-flat, the flatted thirteenth of the harmony. In measures 15 and 16, on the lyrics "all those things you've always pined for," we see her flexibility in her lower range, the line spanning the distance of a major ninth and including neat downward leaps of a sixth on "you've" and "for." Ella's melodic alteration on lines spanning measures 17 through 20 and 21 through 23 is exceptional. Note how she attacks the word "Gee" off a sixteenth-note rest in measure 17, following it immediately with a quarter-note triplet figure. In measure 19, she sings "my little baby" on three sixteenth notes and then jumps an octave to the word "Baby" in the next measure. On the lyrics "Woolworth doesn't sell," in measure 22, every word is displaced as she once again incorporates a five-against-four tuplet figure.

To close the track Ella adds an eight-bar tag in which the flexibility of her vocalizing is once again on display (Example 9.13). She executes an effective octave jump between the words "darn" and "well" between measures 2 and 3. In measure 6, she sings the word "but" over two syllables, descending quickly down a sixth off a sixteenth-note attack.

After lovely versions of "Then You've Never Been Blue," "I Hadn't Anyone till You," and "My Melancholy Baby," Ella next does a take on Errol Garner's "Misty," a song that she included on many of her albums. It is interesting to contrast this interpretation with the one she sang two months earlier in Berlin (Example 9.11). The first 16 measures of the duet with Paul Smith are shown in Example 9.14. Once again, Ella starts out in B-flat and modulates up to B after only eight bars. Within only six beats, from the end of measure 1 through the first half of measure 3, her phrasing

Example 9.12: "I Can't Give You Anything but Love" *(The Intimate Ella)*

on "I'm as helpless as a kitten up a tree" is a marvel. In a line that spans a major ninth, she begins and ends in the lower region of her range and includes two triplet figures and a jump of a major seventh to split up the word "helpless." In measure 4, she delays the lyrics "clinging to a cloud," much as she did on her Berlin concert, by holding until the second note of a triplet before her attack on the first syllable. Between measures 6 and 7, on the lyrics "just holding your hand," she executes a beautiful octave jump and lets the last word resonate for four beats. In measure 10, she

Example 9.13: "I Can't Give You Anything but Love"—tag ending (*The Intimate Ella*)

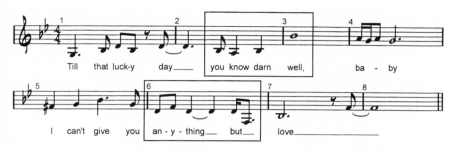

Example 9.14: "Misty" (*The Intimate Ella*)

sings "thousand violins begin to play" by rising and falling effortlessly through a span of a minor tenth. On "sound of your hello," in measure 12, she sings the phrase over a triplet figure, whereas in Berlin she had sung these lyrics on descending sixteenth-notes.

We next hear the only version of "September Song" that Ella recorded during her career. Delivering her most straightforward rendition of any track on the album, it is hard to imagine that she can sing any better. Her voice is clear and rich and at times she almost whispers. The opening half of her chorus (Example 9.15) indicates how she stays relatively faithful to the song's original melody, adding only a few subtle alterations, and how she is in complete control at the lower end of her range.

"One for My Baby," "Who's Sorry Now," "I'm Getting Sentimental over You," and "Reach for Tomorrow" round out this memorable album. *The Intimate Ella* is a magical recording, a stand-alone performance of rare beauty. Although Ella would enjoy many successes with Smith for long stretches in later years, they would not record another duo session.

LOU LEVY

Born in Chicago on March 5, 1928, Lou Levy was exposed to the piano at an early age by his father, an amateur pianist who encouraged his son to take an interest in music. Consequently, the youngster began serious piano lessons at the age of 12 and was soon immersed in his practicing.

Levy listened to and absorbed the music of the late swing masters although, like many musicians of his generation, he was swayed heavily by the emerging bebop movement. His attentiveness and diligence paid off and he began gigging steadily in 1944. "Through high school I started working with local big bands and playing big-band arrangements," he recalled. "Then . . . a guy . . . played me a record of Dizzy Gillespie. . . . Then Lee Konitz [who] lived in Chicago . . . took me to [a] record store . . . and played a [recording] . . . of Charlie Parker . . . and I knew what

Example 9.15: "September Song" (*The Intimate Ella*)

kind of music I wanted to play. Throw in all the little decorations in later life like Hindemith and Bartok, but it's still . . . Parker and . . . Gillespie."[28] Not surprisingly, the pianists who influenced Levy the most were Bud Powell and Art Tatum initially, and Oscar Peterson later on.

In a relatively short time Levy had established himself as one of the leading new pianists on the jazz scene. "Levy, though young in years, is one of the old men of the bop era," said Sharon A. Pease in *Down Beat,* "and, along with other talented musicians who are sincerely interested in this idiom, is making an important contribution toward its development."[29]

Levy enjoyed a full and successful career during which he played with, among others, Georgie Auld, Woody Herman, Tommy Dorsey, Shorty Rogers, Benny Goodman, Stan Getz, Johnny Hodges, Al Cohn, and Supersax. He was also accompanist to a number of leading singers, including Sarah Vaughan, Peggy Lee (with whom he did countless engagements during an 18-year stretch from 1955 to 1973), Anita O-Day, Nancy Wilson, Frank Sinatra, and Ella Fitzgerald. He died in San Clemente, California, on January 23, 2001.

Lou Levy worked with Ella Fitzgerald, for the most part, between 1957 and 1962. Although he already had significant experience, having accompanied Sarah Vaughan and Peggy Lee, the Fitzgerald engagement presented new challenges. "Now with Ella, either you swing or you don't swing," exclaimed Levy. "This woman romps; yet she can sing the tenderest ballad you ever heard—usually with the verse. And this can throw you, too, when you're new. Just the other night she called a tune; I went into the intro, she took off on the verse—which I didn't expect—and wow, for a moment I was really guessing."[30]

Like Ellis Larkins in previous years, Lou Levy worked with Ella during the years of her career when she was at the unquestioned pinnacle of her powers. Consequently, the albums on which he accompanied the great singer—*Ella in Rome: The Birthday Concert, Ella in Hollywood* (released on CD in Japan only, but obtainable in the United States as an import), *Ella Returns to Berlin,* and *Clap Hands, Here Comes Charlie*—are recognized universally as among the cream of her vast output. In fact, these recordings are so good that it is difficult to avoid overkill with respect to the number of superlatives that may pop up in describing the performances.

Ella in Rome: The Birthday Concert was recorded during a 1958 European tour for which Norman Granz was booking double bills of Ella and Oscar Peterson with their respective trios. Lou Levy had bassist Max Bennett and drummer Gus Johnson with him to back Fitzgerald. Because her date of birth had long been believed to be April 25, 1918, the concert, which took place on April 25, was billed as her fortieth-birthday celebration. This was before Stuart Nicholson had discovered, while doing research for his 1993 biography of the singer, that she was actually born in 1917. The discrepancy aside, the concert was still a celebration, a fantastic performance by a supreme singer. Amazingly, the tapes of the concert were neglected for almost thirty years in the Polygram vaults. Phil Schaap, who had the great fortune to find them in 1987, subsequently prepared the material for release. The album came out in 1989 and did very well on the charts.

On the opener, "St. Louis Blues," Ella belts out a couple of down-home choruses before shifting into high gear for a blistering up-tempo roller coaster ride. For the next four minutes she pulls out all the stops in chorus after chorus of virtuosic scatting. We hear hip boppish lines; nonsense syllables; glissandos swooping from high to low through her broad range; sustained, wailing altissimo pitches; and a full chorus of makeshift lyrics—"Yes, these people wonder what I'm singing/Yes, they wonder what I'm swinging/Believe it or not, it's still St. Louis Blues." She also quotes parts of other blues melodies—"Jumpin' with Symphony Sid" and "Swinging Shepherd Blues"—and even manages to throw in a line from "Only You." The audience roars at the conclusion.

"These Foolish Things" is next and, as on the program's other ballads, "Angel Eyes," "Midnight Sun," and "Sophisticated Lady," Ella's voice is clear and rich, her mood appropriately melancholy. She is particularly brilliant on "I Loves You Porgy," one of the tour de forces in her huge repertoire. On all these numbers, the trio is consistently gentle and solid behind her, Levy interspersing fills and flourishes in all the right places.

"That Old Black Magic," "It's All Right with Me," "A Foggy Day," and "Caravan" are hard swingers at various tempos. "The Lady Is a Tramp" is taken up-tempo and, toward the end of the take, Ella, as was her wont whenever she sang this number, nods in the direction of another master vocalist and her good friend: "For Frank Sinatra, I whistle and stamp."

Ella kicks off "Just One of Those Things" with a free treatment of the verse before settling into a relaxed medium tempo for the remainder of the track. In the opening of the chorus, shown in Example 9.16, we see her sophisticated approach to melody. She stretches the word "crazy" for over five beats in measures 7 and 8, and, in singing "One of those bells that now and then ring," she delays the start of the phrase until the third beat of measure 9 before displacing all the words to complete the line. She croons everything in the rich lower end of her range, particularly between measures 9 and 16.

After completing the chorus, Ella returns to the bridge and continues more of the same inventive phrasing (Example 9.17). Note especially how she handles the words "painting the town" from the end of measure 37 through the first half of measure 40, first ascending through an off-the-beat pattern and then dropping an octave to complete the line.

Example 9.16: "Just One of Those Things" *(Ella in Rome)*

Example 9.17: "Just One of Those Things" *(Ella in Rome)*

Ella's long-time favorite, "I Can't Give You Anything but Love," is taken here as another medium swinger. As with several of the selections on this concert, she sings in the lower reaches of her range, her voice full-bodied and sure. Her first chorus, shown in Example 9.18, is loaded with inventive phrasing; almost every measure could be singled out for study.

Example 9.18: "I Can't Give You Anything but Love" *(Ella in Rome)*

starting way down on a low E, and running through some nice eighth-note licks on the song's title line, she ends the phrase by extending the word "baby" over six beats in measures 3 and 4. On the words "Dream awhile scheme awhile," in measures 9 and 10, she ascends gradually on similarly contoured four-note groupings. In measures 15 and 16, on the words "all those things you've always pined for," Ella's bebop leaning comes through. The lick contains a number of chromatic passing tones and there is a typical boppish pattern in measure 15, the two four-note groupings identical in intervallic content and sequenced in whole-steps. Note Ella's sophisticated subdivision of the beats in the beginning of measure 18, her spelling out the word "baby" in measure 20, and her syncopated line in measure 22 that leads to a triplet spanning beats 2 and 3 in the following measure. She closes the chorus with another running eighth-note line in measures 29 and 30, leading to off-the-beat attacks on the words "but" and "love."

Ella does an amusing impersonation of Rose Murphy on her second chorus. Murphy was a talented jazz singer and pianist who worked professionally from the early 1930s into the 1980s. Her jazz background notwithstanding, she regularly included humor in her performances, laughing quietly and breathlessly as she sang, as well as producing an array of different vocal effects. She had what could be described as a sensual baby voice (a style that did not go unnoticed by Marilyn Monroe) and, because she often incorporated what sounded like the syllables *chee chee* into the lyrics she was singing, she became known as the "Chee Chee Girl." At present, Murphy is a little-known figure, ignored in studies of jazz history, although CD reissues of a number of her best recordings are available. In accurately mimicking Murphy, Ella provides yet another example of how she could duplicate almost anything she heard. As if to reinforce this, she follows her Murphy bit by singing a third chorus sounding like Louis Armstrong, an impersonation she often did.

In an exciting finale to the Rome concert, Oscar Peterson and his trio members, Herb Ellis and Ray Brown, plus Gus Johnson from Ella's group, join forces to back the singer on "Stompin' at the Savoy." Over the next seven minutes Ella scats up a storm, Peterson throws in a hot piano solo, and the quartet cooks in a blazing take that brings down the house.

On February 11, 1961, Ella appeared in Berlin for the second time, almost exactly one year after her first triumph in the German city. Because Paul Smith had been the pianist on the earlier concert while Lou Levy was away for a while playing with Peggy Lee, this was Levy's first exposure to a raucously enthusiastic German audience that genuinely loved Ella. Guitarist Herb Ellis, bassist Wilfred Middlebrooks, and drummer Gus Johnson made up the rest of the quartet. The program consisted of a wonderful selection of standards and Ella was on fire. Ironically, for whatever reasons, the tapes for this concert, like those for Ella's Rome concert in 1958, were subsequently ignored for almost three decades. Once again, Phil Schaap resurrected the vintage material and the resulting album, titled *Ella Returns to Berlin* and released in 1991, is the magnificent result.

The concert's opener is "Give Me the Simple Life." Ella swings straight ahead for a quick two choruses on the lively number, establishing a happy mood and warming up the audience. Next up is the time-honored classic from the Ellington repertoire, Billy Strayhorn's "Take the 'A' Train." The audience applauds in approval as Ella takes off for several choruses, singing and scatting as only she can. To end the take she exhorts to all who are listening: "Get on board, get on board, get on board!/Hurry, hurry! Hurry, hurry! Hurry, hurry!/Get on board the A train!" The atmosphere is charged now and, with no intent of letting up just yet, Ella goes into Frank Loesser's "On a Slow Boat to China," another infectious tune. During the take she enthusiastically encourages Lou Levy and Herb Ellis when they take brief four-bar breaks: "Play pretty for the people, Lou"; "I hear you, Herbie."

Ever the master of pacing, Ella has established a buoyant mood after the high-energy selections—in similar fashion, she had opened her previous Berlin performance with three hard-swinging numbers. Shifting down now, she begins a medley of three songs, all with lyrics by Oscar Hammerstein II. The first two are lovely ballads composed by Jerome Kern: "Why Was I Born," on which Levy is the sole accompanist; and "Can't Help Lovin' Dat Man," with Ellis taking over on the accompaniment. Wilfred Middlebrooks's walking bass sets up the final song of the medley, "People Will Say We're in Love," composed by Richard Rodgers. Ella and the quartet groove at a relaxed tempo to put the finishing touches on an engaging trio of tunes.

Reaching into a Latin bag for a moment, Ella and the quartet take the first chorus of "You're Driving Me Crazy" in a cha cha rhythm. After that the musicians swing into overdrive and Ella blazes through three uptempo choruses. She belts out machine-gun torrents of lyrics, at times soaring into her upper range, her articulation incredibly precise at such high speed. Everyone slows it down for the last few measures and the singer croons a few blues-tinged licks to round out the action.

When Ella recorded "Rock It for Me" with Chick Webb in late 1937 she performed it as a medium-tempo swing number. On this Berlin performance, Herb Ellis's soulful guitar intro gives the song almost a rhythm and blues feeling and Ella grooves more slowly this time around. Incidentally, she sang the tune in A-flat with Webb, whereas she is taking it in B-flat here.

"Witchcraft" was composed in 1957 by Cy Coleman with words by Carolyn Leigh. Frank Sinatra recorded it that year and the following year it became a smash hit, garnering him a Grammy nomination. Ella first recorded the song on a gig in Chicago with Lou Levy and his trio in August 1958. The swinging version she presents here on her return engagement in Berlin is a highlight of the evening's performance. After opening freely with the verse, she is at her inventive best on the likeable tune, her chorus illustrated in Example 9.19. In measures 3 and 4, on the words "that sly come hither stare," she uses a quarter-note tuplet with a five-to-three ratio in a line that is intricate yet fluid. Between measures 5 and 8, on "that stops my conscience bare, it's Witchcraft," she attacks every word off the beat. Note, in measures 11 and 12, the triplet rhythm embedded in the middle of the phrase on the words "The heat is too intense for it." Ella pauses until the second half of beat one to exclaim "Witchcraft" in measure 17 and again in measure 19. She phrases the words "strictly taboo" by starting in measure 22 on a quarter-note triplet, holding the first syllable of "taboo" from the end of the triplet into measure 23, and hitting the second syllable on the second half of beat one. She combines syncopated attacks with triplet figures on "But one I'd never switch," in measures 35 and 36, and on "'Cause there's no nicer witch than you," between measures 37 and 39.

Following her opening chorus of "Witchcraft," Ella grooves through the bridge once more. She then adds an interesting twist to the arrangement by modulating three times over the last eight measures of the form (Example 9.20). She shifts a half-step up from the opening key of C to D-flat in measure 33, ascends the same distance to the key of D in measure 35, and jumps a final half-step to the closing key of E-flat in measure 37.

Ella and the quartet take the opening chorus of Cole Porter's "Anything Goes" in the key of G, swinging at a medium up-tempo. On stretches of the second chorus they shift into a rumba rhythm, at times in the parallel key of G minor. On Irving Berlin's "Cheek to Cheek," Ella grooves solidly at a moderate tempo. She sang this song often during her career and two of her takes, as well as interpretations by Connee Boswell and Louis Armstrong, are illustrated and discussed in the section on Boswell in Chapter 3.

Ella included Errol Garner's "Misty" on her first Berlin concert and she programmed it again on her return to the German city. Her version here is a gem, a pretty rendering that is also a display of amazing vocal control. Two examples that illustrate her interpretive approach to the popular ballad appear earlier in this chapter in the section on Paul Smith.

Ella's version of "Caravan," Duke Ellington's standard, is a tour de force. She flies through two up-tempo choruses, darting from one end of her range to the other, at times twisting the melody into any number of different shapes. (For a discussion of Ella's version of "Caravan" from her Ellington *Song Book,* see the section on Ellington in Chapter 7.) Next up is "Mr. Paganini," a song that she first recorded with Chick Webb in October 1936. Having subsequently performed it countless times over the years,

Example 9.19: "Witchcraft" *(Ella Returns to Berlin)*

Example 9.20: "Witchcraft" *(Ella Returns to Berlin)*

Ella informs her listeners that she will do a number for which she receives "so many requests to repeat." Further keeping her German audience in mind, she jokingly revises the opening line for the verse: "The concert was over in Deutschlandhalle." She soon settles into a slow groove and glides through the first chorus, punctuating it with occasional scatted fills and also quoting "I'm Beginning to See the Light" for good measure. Her intricate four-bar scatted lick then launches everyone into double-time for an exciting final chorus.

The moment has come for Ella to reprieve her monster hit from the previous year. "And now we'd like to do the song that started right here in Berlin," she announces. As she utters the first words to "Mack the Knife" the audience roars its approval. Ella knows the lyrics this time, but that certainly doesn't stop her from taking liberties. When she goes into her impression of Louis Armstrong she can't resist ribbing the singer whose recording of "Mack the Knife" had overtaken Armstrong's—"Look out there Bobby Darin, me and you both singin' the same song." Toward the end of the take she continues with impromptu lyrics, including some comments that recall her singing the year before: "Bobby Darin/and Louie Armstrong/They made a record/Ooh-ooh, what a record of this song/And now Ella/Ella and her fellas/We're makin' a wreck/What a wreck, such a wreck of this same old song." Although this version of "Mack the Knife" could not be expected to have the overwhelming magic of its predecessor, it is still a sparkling climax to the program and an exciting lead-in to the inevitable encores.

As the prolonged applause of the audience subsides, Lou Levy's subdued intro leads Ella into "'Round Midnight," perhaps Thelonious Monk's most revered composition. After singing lyrics for the first eight measures she scats the rest of the chorus, albeit very gentle scatting that stays close to the haunting melody. Levy's piano fills throughout reveal his exquisite taste and sensitivity, an indication of why he was such a wonderful accompanist for Ella. All in all, this is a beautiful number.

Ella next takes off on "Joe Williams Blues," her up-tempo tribute to the outstanding vocalist and yet another example of her ability to meld lyrics and scatting to create a virtuosic showstopper. In the midst of the action she throws in references to some of Williams's well-known blues features, shows off the incredible span of her range, and squeezes in a bunch of quotes, including "Here Comes the Bride," "Stormy Weather," and "Volare." The crowd still can't get enough and another round of wild applause leads to the evening's final climax, a romp through "This Can't Be Love," for which Ella is joined by Oscar Peterson, Ray Brown, and Ed Thigpen. The tireless singer is still electric, Peterson burns through three choruses, and a fantastic concert comes to a close.

Clap Hands, Here Comes Charlie was recorded on June 23 and 24, 1961, in Los Angeles. Joining Lou Levy in Ella's accompanying quartet were guitarist Herb Ellis, bassist Joe Mondragon, and drummer Stan Levey. This recording is another blockbuster, every track a gem. The CD reissue includes three bonus tracks from a recording session on January 23 in New York earlier that year. For that date bassist Wilfred Middlebrooks and drummer Gus Johnson were with Levy and Ellis in the quartet.

Ella opens the session with "Night in Tunisia," Dizzy Gillespie's bebop classic. She sails through the first chorus, effortlessly laying down the lyrics on the angular lines. Levy then takes the interlude, after which she scats over the famous four-bar break and grooves solidly for the rest of the track. The session's other treasure of the bebop era is the aforementioned "'Round Midnight." In the original liner notes for this album, Benny Green says: "Whatever debates rage about the head of Thelonious Monk, his *Round About Midnight* [sic] always stands as irrefutable proof of the logic of his thought and the beauty of his conception."[31] Ella is radiant on Monk's masterpiece.

On "You're My Thrill," Ella sings slowly and passionately, intoning the sensuous lyrics almost at whisper level. Levy and Ellis open and close "My Reverie" with a pretty ostinato figure to create, per the title, a dreamlike mood; in between, Ella swings at a relaxed tempo.

"Good Morning Heartache," "I Got a Guy," and "Spring Can Really Hang You Up the Most" are appealing ballads that Ella makes her own, her voice ringing clearly on all three. On the latter, Ellis adds a nice touch by taking over as the sole accompanist for a few moments. Throughout these tracks, Lou Levy is brilliant, as he is on the whole album. Never seeking the limelight, he supplies a rock-solid pianistic foundation above which Ella can float in whichever direction she desires. He is like the referee in a sporting contest; you don't really pay him much attention most of the time, but if he was not there the action would come to a halt.

On "Cry Me a River," Ella alternates moments of blues-tinged emoting with swinging double-time-feel passages and Herb Ellis throws in some tasteful guitar fills. Irving Berlin's "This Year's Kisses" has an uncommon form, its first two A sections each six measures long. Swinging through her chorus without a hitch, Ella then drops out to let Levy and Ellis ex-change brief solos before she closes the take.

The album's title track, "Clap Hands, Here Comes Charlie," swings at breakneck tempo. Ella rips through her lines on the first two choruses and then trades four-bar breaks with drummer Levey and bassist Mondragon on the next two choruses. Later on, Levey takes a longer solo before ev-eryone slows the pace to take it out.

"Stella by Starlight," "Signing Off," "Music Goes 'Round and Around," "The One I Love Belongs to Somebody Else," and "This Could Be the Start of Something Big" are easy swingers at various tempos. The quartet in-troduces "Born to Be Blue" with a six-eight feel that crops up again from time to time and Ella's commitment to both the appealing melody and the somber lyrics is obvious.

For the medium-tempo intro to "Jersey Bounce," Ella scats "boop-boop-dee-dooya-da/boop-dee-dooya-da" above the hard-swinging quartet. Following her straight-ahead opening chorus, she churns out a second chorus alternating between scatting and snatches of lyrics. The group modulates up a step to the key of G and Ella really goes to town. She sings the first half of her third chorus (Example 9.21) entirely in the middle of her range, wailing with such passion that it sounds like she is singing higher. She often induced this impression during her performances. The sheer intensity of her voice, as well as her total immersion in what she was singing, was something to behold. She could produce blazing pas-sages, often with little or no overly complex phrasing, as in this example, that would have audience members rocking in their seats. That said, she

Example 9.21: "Jersey Bounce" *(Clap Hands, Here Comes Charlie)*

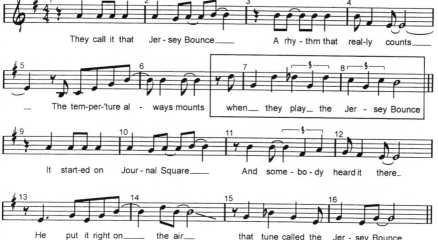

does throw in, between measures 7 and 8, a hip chromatic motive built on descending quarter-note triplets.

Ella drops down lower in her range for the bridge (Example 9.22), producing an effective contrast to the preceding action while staying relatively faithful to the original melody. She uses effective glissandos at the end of the motives in measures 18 and 20, closes out the bridge, and everyone swings through to the end of the track.

Years later, Lou Levy reminisced about his time with Ella. "Ella is the most wonderful natural person you could ever want to work with," he enthused, "and . . . no one can swing like her, no one can sing more in tune than her, and nobody knows more tunes than she does. . . . Most of the material I play now, I learned . . . from working with Ella."[32]

TOMMY FLANAGAN

Tommy Flanagan was born on March 16, 1930, in Conant Gardens, a northeast suburb of Detroit. When he was 6, his musically inclined parents introduced him to the clarinet. The young Flanagan would play clarinet through high school, but he was really more interested in the piano. Highly encouraged by his mother, he began formal piano lessons at the age of 11 and, by the time he was 15, he was playing professionally around town.

Flanagan was one of the many outstanding players who developed in Detroit's thriving jazz scene of the 1940s. In a *Down Beat* article many years later, Flanagan reminisced: "I was friends with most of the guys. . . . There was always a place to play in Detroit, little workshop things . . . there was [also] pretty good music right in the school system. Roland Hanna, Donald Byrd, Sheila Jordan, Sonny Red, and Doug Watkins all went to the same school I did."[33]

Among Flanagan's primary influences, whom he usually first heard on records, were Fats Waller, Teddy Wilson, and Nat Cole. However, the two pianists who moved him the most were Art Tatum and fellow Detroiter Hank Jones. "All I wanted to hear was Art Tatum," he said, "because his

Example 9.22: "Jersey Bounce" *(Clap Hands, Here Comes Charlie)*

approach tied up with my studies. He was so gifted that I felt he was really a genius. . . . [Hank Jones's] playing was in the same mold, I felt, as Teddy Wilson's, but updated. And I always felt that, after Tatum, Hank was the second piano player."[34] In addition to his favorite pianists, Flanagan, like many musicians of the time, was also swayed by the innovations of Charlie Parker, Dizzy Gillespie, and the other original masters of bebop.

After serving in the army from 1951 to 1953, Flanagan returned home and continued to play for the next three years. Finally, in 1956, when things had begun slowing down in Detroit, he and his close friend, the accomplished guitarist Kenny Burrell, made the important decision to move to New York City. Some of Flanagan's Detroit friends who were already in New York started mentioning his name in musical circles. It was not long before he began playing with many of the best musicians around. Among the recordings in which he participated was John Coltrane's legendary and groundbreaking "Giant Steps" session.

By the time that Norman Granz, Ella Fitzgerald's manager, asked Flanagan to join her full-time in 1963 (Flanagan had worked with her previously for a few weeks in 1956), he was an established player on the New York City jazz circuit. He would go on to serve as Ella's musical director from 1963 to 1965, and again from 1968 to 1978. Gus Johnson, the fine drummer who worked with the two great musicians for many years, remembered that even a pianist as accomplished as Flanagan felt the pressure to be at the top of his game when backing Ella. "When Tommy Flanagan came with the group, we were playing some club in Cleveland, and the first night . . . [Ella] turned around and like to scared him to death," recounted Johnson. "I . . . just told her, 'Turn around!' . . . afterwards I [waited] to hear 'You're fired!' But she had evidently gotten over it. 'This is his first night,' I told her. 'He doesn't know the numbers and he's nervous.'"[35]

Flanagan proved to be a superb accompanist for Ella, applying his already prodigious talent to the challenges of backing up the great singer. The two stars developed a solid rapport with one another, progressing to the point where they seemingly could anticipate each other's moves. "[If] it was something we had never done," related Flanagan, "I'd follow her and let her be free. It was funny—about the original key—a lot of times—I don't know if she did it on purpose, but it would be a half-step from the original key. She used to do things in A [for instance]. She used to just start singing sometimes, and I'd catch her. So she felt like: 'Hey, I can do anything.'"

An indication of the respect that Flanagan and Fitzgerald held for each other, and of their musical compatibility, is that they maintained a high creative output, as well as a stable camaraderie through their more than twelve years together. Flanagan has stated that he and Ella never had a vindictive or demoralizing argument. "We had differences of opinion," he noted. "[However], after a while, I felt I had the freedom to tell her what I thought." Phil Schaap summarized Flanagan's work with Ella as follows:

He's perfect for Ella Fitzgerald. . . . You have to know: 'Hey, there's really a genius in front of this band, and spurring [her] on at the right moment might actually make music happen that would be delightful for everybody—the lay audience, us up here on the bandstand, the artists themselves, and, if recorded, posterity.' Tommy Flanagan has that insight on how to do that—how to nuance [a song] precisely the same, so that it almost sounds as though it's identical. It would take a very discerning ear to hear any difference in the articulation of the notes, the chord choices, the arpeggiation of the chord as it's played. And then the times he changes it. He knows when to make Ella move in a different direction.

Eventually, after countless engagements and seemingly nonstop traveling, Flanagan decided to take his leave from Fitzgerald to pursue his own solo career full-time. Interestingly, he had had self doubts previously (in addition to his initial nervousness backing Ella), but they were now dissipated. "For a long time, mostly when I was accompanying Ella Fitzgerald, I never thought I had enough technique for a soloist," he said. "But then I found I liked to put myself out there. . . . Improvising gives you a great sense of freedom. When you find that out—that you're making your own song—you can go on endlessly . . . you learn something each time you play the same song . . . [that] keeps you away from the clichés."[36]

Although she knew she was losing a first-class accompanist, Ella Fitzgerald was nonetheless encouraging to Flanagan. "Ella was sorry that I was leaving," he said, "but she told me shortly afterwards that I *should* be on my own, not always backing her up. She said that I had too much talent to be in an accompanying role."[37] Flanagan, a humble gentleman, looked forward to moving on. He had been a superb accompanist for Ella, in the process demonstrating that he was a polished, completely versatile musician of great beauty. He had the wonderful gift of being able to swing and be attractive concurrently. Flanagan maintained a sensational career, constantly re-affirming his place among the first tier of jazz pianists, until his death in New York on November 16, 2001.

"Perhaps the most amazing thing about this performance is that something very much like it happened night after night, for nearly half a century," remarked Joe Goldberg, with no small amount of awe, in his liner notes for the CD reissue of *Ella in Budapest*.[38] This concert was recorded in May of 1970, in front of a large and enthusiastic crowd in the Hungarian capital city. Pianist Tommy Flanagan, in the third year of his longest run with Ella, had bassist Frank De la Rosa and drummer Ed Thigpen in the trio.

The selections for the performance clearly indicate Ella's penchant at this period in her career for eclectic programming. Among the 19 selections were pop hits of the time, like Burt Bacharach's "I'll Never Fall in Love Again" and "Raindrops Keep Falling on My Head," as well as the Blood, Sweat, and Tears rocker "Spinning Wheel." There were also luscious ballads, swinging standards, and one of her favorite numbers from her days with Chick Webb, "Mr. Paganini." Although purists may have viewed this type of programming as overstepping the boundaries for a legitimate jazz artist, the open-minded Fitzgerald never offered excuses for her song selections. More to the point, it was really another affirmation of her ability to incorporate anything she liked into her repertoire, her interpretation of any tune becoming a substantial statement.

In "Crazy Rhythm," the sizzling opening track of just over three minutes, Ella rewards us with astonishing examples of her inventiveness and showmanship. She is in complete control, her vocal work executed crisply and with tremendous energy. After charging through the first chorus at a rapid tempo, Ella and the trio introduce an 8-measure interlude passage, modulating up a half-step from the opening key of C to D-flat. In the second chorus, Ella's virtuosic display in the first 16 measures alone is astounding as she zigzags through a range of two octaves (Example 9.23). She starts by wailing on sustained mid-range notes, stretching the word "crazy" over the first 6 measures. Next, she shifts into high boppish phrases, maintaining impeccable articulation and intonation as she executes the busier, angular motives. At measure 12, she takes a quick breath and nails an altissimo A-flat that she holds dramatically before dropping to the end of the phrase to put the finishing touches on a passage that very few singers could even hope to approach.

Example 9.23: "Crazy Rhythm" (*Ella in Budapest*)

Toward the end of the selection, Ella and the trio introduce a new vamp in which she does a bit of scatting and then, taking on the additional role of emcee, she starts riffing on lyrics that talk about the program for this concert:

> We got rock, we got roll,/we want to try to satisfy you so.
> We like to try to do the kind of song,/you know, the songs you'd like to
>   hear.
>
> Old songs, new songs,/sad songs, blue songs
> Good songs, bad songs,/true songs, new songs.

Predictably, Ella has the crowd in her hand after the exciting opening number. She proceeds to perform one gem after another, to the ever-brilliant accompaniment of Flanagan and the rhythm section. Flanagan solos very little throughout the concert, but his fills behind Ella, as well as the masterful touch with which he punches out the harmonies, are wondrous.

On "Open Your Window," by songwriter Harry Nilsson, Ella surprises the listener by interjecting a quote of "It Might as Well Be Spring." In the intro to "The Girl from Ipanema," she settles into a relaxed vamp, throwing off a succession of rhythmically tricky nonsense syllables—perhaps a bow to Leo Watson. On the aforementioned "Raindrops Keep Falling on My Head," Flanagan outdoes himself, applying his jazz sensibilities to this commercial ditty and providing inventive fills that result in a beautiful and fitting accompaniment. In her rendition of "Summertime," Ella sings with a depth of feeling that belies the fact she was never associated to any extent with the blues. Her commitment to the song is total and heartfelt; she even cuts loose with a funky passage toward the end of the selection. On the popular "Cabaret," the signature tune from the musical of the same name, Ella starts with an inventive first chorus and then shifts into a faster tempo. She cleverly throws in a quick quote based on "Hello Dolly," after which the musicians complete the piece by modulating to a new key near the end.

On Duke Ellington and Billy Strayhorn's venerable "Satin Doll," Ella's singing is elastic, at times weaving forward freely in passages that are both relaxed and complex. In the opening chorus, Ella uses sophisticated phrasing to float the word "satin" from the second half of measure 6 through the beginning of measure 8 before ending the line (Example 9.24).

Later in the take, Ella modifies Johnny Mercer's lyrics and goes through a repeating eighth-note pattern (Example 9.25). Taking the role of horn player, she sings with ease and grace, producing a lick that a tenor saxophonist or trumpeter might have thrown in at this point. Reverting to Ellington's original line, she completes a passage that is jazzy, seamless in its succession of motives, and accessible. In their book *Singing Jazz,* authors Bruce Crowther and Mike Pinfold are fervid in their explanation of this

Example 9.24: "Satin Doll" *(Ella in Budapest)*

Example 9.25: "Satin Doll" *(Ella in Budapest)*

type of performance: "[Fitzgerald's style] needs no understanding of the special ways of a jazz improvisor, the using of a song as raw material to be shaped into a personal statement."[39]

Although any of their several other recordings would be worthy of inclusion in this discussion, the album entitled *Montreux '77: Ella Fitzgerald with the Tommy Flanagan Trio* is particularly noteworthy. Recorded on July 14, 1977, at the famous French jazz festival, Ella was on fire during the concert. Norman Granz, in a producer's note for the album, exclaimed that, "when appearing with a lot of great jazz musicians around, her singing reaches new heights."[40]

At the time of the concert, Tommy Flanagan was in the ninth year of his 10-year run with Fitzgerald. The telepathic communication of the two masters had reached magical proportions. With his trio, Flanagan was not merely an accompanist, but an extension of Ella. The two artists were together long enough that Flanagan even had to adapt, albeit with relative ease, to the physical changes in Ella's voice that were brought on by the natural aging process. He recalled that her voice had been getting progressively deeper throughout the years they worked. "Her voice—I was with her so long—the pitch had dropped, kept getting lower," he reminisced, smiling at the memories. "She had a big range, but [it] started getting lower as she got older. When I first joined her, she was doing a song like "Body and Soul"—she used to do it in F. Then through the years, she ended up singing it in D-flat [the original key]."

Ella opens her performance with a rousing rendition of "Too Close for Comfort," a tune from the 1956 musical *Mr. Wonderful.* After a 10-bar intro by the trio, she sings a short verse before swinging through a first chorus of the catchy melody. It is immediately apparent that this concert is going to be something special. In the world of sports, athletes say they are in the zone when everything seemingly goes perfectly. Ella and the trio are in the zone on this recording. Her second chorus of "Too Close for Comfort" is a masterpiece of phrasing, virtually every musical motive reinvented (Example 9.26). She starts the first A section by appealing to her heart to "be wise, be smart" before she tells it to "behave," three times, on a bluesy, syncopated line in the third measure. "Don't upset your cart when he's so close," she concludes, running through a boppish scalelike lick in measures 7 and 8. Ella moves into the second A section, in the eighth and ninth measures, using a repeating four-note pattern on the lyrics "be soft, be sweet." In the bridge, she exclaims "too close for comfort" and stipulates "please not again" by manhandling three quarter-note triplets in measures 19 and 20. Coming out of the bridge, the music modulates up a half-step to the key of G-flat as Ella talks to her heart again, telling it to "be firm, be fair, beware." Her amazing control and vocal dexterity are on display here as she ends the phrase with a leap down a minor seventh in measure 27. Note the tricky rhythms in measures 37 to 40 as she closes the chorus by stretching the word "comfort" through six beats.

Unlike the eclectic Budapest performance, Ella, on this night in Montreux, fills out the program mostly with selections from the jazz world, adding only Paul Williams's "Day by Day" and Stevie Wonder's "You Are the Sunshine of My Life" from the pop charts. She includes Charlie Parker's bop classic, "Billie's Bounce," the standard "Day by Day," a Latin favorite by Antonio Carlos Jobim, "One Note Samba," and a couple of Ellington numbers, "I Ain't Got Nothin' but the Blues" and "I Let a Song Go Out of My Heart."

On Harold Arlen's "Come Rain or Come Shine," Ella again follows a favored route, through a straightforward opening chorus and into an adventurous second chorus. The first two sections of the opening chorus are shown in Example 9.27. At the outset, Ella is obviously amused at something and can be heard suppressing chuckles. It's possible that she has momentarily forgotten the lyrics. Beginning in measure 4, she repeats herself, saying "deep as a mountain/high as a mountain," instead of "high as a mountain/and deep as a river." Her singing is, of course, still wonderful and, despite the generally straight-ahead rendering of the chorus, she dashes off three interesting triplet-based figures in measures 9, 13, and 15–16.

Example 9.26: "Too Close for Comfort" (*Montreux '77*)

In the second chorus, Ella is very horn-like in her delivery (Example 9.28). As she wails through the first 16 measures, she is like the lead trumpet in a big band, pulling everyone along in an arrangement's closing shout chorus. She churns out the lyrics with gusto, propelling herself to an exciting high G on the word "deep" in measures 5 and 6. Ella continues with unabated energy, taking us to the other end of her range by swooping

Example 9.27: "Come Rain or Come Shine" *(Montreux '77)*

Example 9.28: "Come Rain or Come Shine" *(Montreux '77)*

to a low C-sharp in the eleventh measure while singing "I guess when you met me/just was one of those things" [*sic*].

Ella Fitzgerald and Tommy Flanagan made superb music together. Their many recordings make up a body a of work that is timeless in its beauty and importance and a lasting document for both emotional fulfillment and musical study.

JIMMY ROWLES

Jimmy Rowles was born in Spokane, Washington, on August 18, 1918. In his early years he would often listen to his mother, a self-taught pianist, and he was moved to start playing. His first private lessons, however, didn't amount to much. "I was almost a self-taught player," he said. "The first teacher I had in Spokane didn't even teach me the value of the notes. I had to stand behind her and watch her play."[41]

Rowles was also becoming interested in the popular songs he was hearing. "What changed me was listening to Guy Lombardo's pianist; in fact, I liked the whole orchestra. I was the guy who wouldn't even listen to Benny Goodman. . . . I found a [teacher who] had me go through all the chords and the keys, throw my hand to the bass notes, and practice a stride that was built on tenths, not single notes."[42]

Rowles went on to study at Gonzaga College and during his time there he started listening to Teddy Wilson. He was deeply moved and began working diligently to absorb Wilson's playing style. He also began studying the other important musicians who had become significant models for him, among them, Art Tatum, Earl Hines, Fats Waller, Duke Ellington, Ben Webster, and Roy Eldridge.

Rowles commenced playing professional engagements around Spokane while he was still in college. He sought out any opportunities that would aid in his development. "I used to hang around the after-hours joints and play with all the black cats, which is where I got my first real jazz experience" Rowles reminisced. "Not long afterwards [in the early 1940s], I went to Los Angeles . . . and I ended up with Lester Young. . . . Billie Holiday came out to sing with us."[43] Rowles, throughout this early part of his career, also played with Benny Goodman, Woody Herman, Ben Webster, and Harry "Sweets" Edison.

As an outcome of his first appearances with Billie Holiday, Rowles later worked with her regularly for a number of years. He commented that "making albums with her was how I really learned to accompany."[44] Indeed, already recognized for his outstanding jazz soloing, he would go on to be remembered as an exceptional accompanist as well, one of the best ever. He further established his versatility through many years of work in the Los Angeles studios. However, as with many serious jazz musicians, New York City beckoned. Moving there in 1973, he continued to maintain a busy and successful playing schedule.

In 1981, Ella Fitzgerald's accompanist at the time, Paul Smith, decided to take a break for a while. When Norman Granz asked Rowles if he would take over he accepted and ended up staying with Ella for the next couple of years. The two had worked together twice briefly in the past. Rowles had recorded once with Ella in 1966, on an album arranged and directed by Marty Paich, and had made one other club appearance with her in Los Angeles in late 1956. They would record little more during their time together; two or three tracks have been reissued on compilations. Nonetheless, it is important to mention Rowles because he was a first-rate musician, at the upper end of the list of outstanding pianists who worked with Ella.

Interestingly, Rowles engendered differing opinions on his work with Ella. "Jimmy Rowles understands singing better than all the other ones," said Phil Schaap. "That's why he's so great for Fitzgerald and for any singer. He really understands singing." Biographer Stuart Nicholson refers to Rowles as "one of the great, but sadly underappreciated, pianists in jazz," adding that "he fell easily and successfully into the role of Ella's accompanist."[45] One who would disagree is another biographer, Geoffrey Mark Fidelman, who had the opportunity to hear Ella with Rowles live on a number of occasions. "Unfortunately, this was not the best musical marriage for Ella," claims Fidelman. "As talented as Rowles was, he could not totally relinquish the spotlight to Ella. He often extemporized during concerts, and changed rhythms or chord structures without rehearsal."[46]

In any event, Rowles was definitely a fantastic player and, despite the varying opinions of his accompanying style, he was caringly conscientious about his role in backing vocalists. He had even had limited success composing music for songs during his career, at one point working briefly in collaboration with the legendary lyricist Johnny Mercer. Rowles was very certain of what he needed to do for a singer. "I'd say there are two rules. Anticipation of the singer is one of them, and the other is subduing yourself."[47]

Eventually, the grind of many performances and constant travel with Ella took its toll. As had Tommy Flanagan in earlier years, Rowles decided to leave the gig. Nevertheless, the experience had been gratifying, an opportunity to contribute significantly in producing music of superior quality. "I like [Ella] very much," enthused Rowles. "Outside of the natural, nice feeling of playing for her and listening to her sing, absorbing her personality and everything, I get a big boot out of the fact that those people won't let her stop. She usually gets standing ovations at the end of every performance . . . She's great."[48]

Rowles returned to Los Angeles for good in 1985 and continued to perform in small group settings. Joe Goldberg, in an article for *Musician*, talked about one of Rowles's L.A. engagements: "When Rowles plays, the presentation is absolutely no-nonsense. . . . The music is not flashy. It is, rather, intense. The job is to get inside a song, to see what it has to offer."[49] Rowles carried on for over a decade, despite suffering from emphysema, a problem that had started while he was still working with Ella. He passed away on May 28, 1996.

JOE PASS

For many years prior to his death in Los Angeles on May 23, 1994, Joe Pass was widely recognized as one of the jazz world's premier guitar virtuosos. Constantly active with many of the leading players of the day, he was also matchless as an unaccompanied solo guitarist. "You can step out of bounds [when playing alone]," said Pass. "Sometimes I change key in the middle of a chorus when I get bored. I change the tempo, add a bar here, subtract one there."[50] Although he played in large ensembles and big bands at times during his career, Pass always maintained a preference for small-group or solo playing. It is not surprising, therefore, that Pass was an exceptional accompanist for singers.

Born Joseph Passalaqua on January 13, 1929, in New Brunswick, New Jersey, and raised in the Johnstown area of Pennsylvania, Pass's attraction to the guitar began at an early age when he saw the cowboy Gene Autry playing in a film. Pass was given a guitar by a family friend at age nine and, although he took a few basic lessons from other friends in the community, he spent the following years predominantly teaching himself. His enthusiasm was intense and he absorbed anything he could get from recordings and the radio. Pass's biggest influences on guitar were Django Reinhardt, Charlie Christian, and Wes Montgomery. He was also moved by pianists Bud Powell and Art Tatum, as well as by the bebop giants, trumpeter Dizzy Gillespie and alto saxophonist Charlie Parker.

Pass was already playing local gigs by his early teens. He moved to New York City in 1949 and continued to perform steadily during the 1950s. Finally, after the rigors of more than a decade of playing and touring, he relocated to Los Angeles in 1960. He began working regularly in the studios—and he also sought help to overcome a lingering drug problem. In 1962, with the release of his first album, Pass was back on track and working a full schedule, either with many of the best west coast musicians or on the road for two years with pianist George Shearing.

Pass joined pianist Oscar Peterson's trio in 1973. With Bassist Niels-Henning Orsted-Pedersen, the three musicians were an electrifying unit, one of the finest jazz groups of the time. In short order, Norman Granz signed Pass to the Pablo label and the guitarist went on to record on a number of excellent albums, both as leader and sideman.

Granz would often team Pass with Ella Fitzgerald. In addition to their many concert appearances together, the pair recorded four memorable duo sessions: *Take Love Easy* (1973), *Fitzgerald & Pass . . . Again* (1976), *Speak Love* (1983), and *Easy Living* (1986). Additionally, in 2001, Pablo released a CD of previously unissued live performances of the two artists, titled *Sophisticated Lady* and dating from 1973 and 1986. Listening to any of these recordings, it becomes immediately apparent that Ella and Pass connected beautifully in their music-making. On one occasion, Ella told writer Leonard Feather that "in London I did part of the show with just Joe Pass. When the two of us started improvising, he would catch every little thing I did."[51]

It has often been pointed out that Ella Fitzgerald was in the latter part of her career when she did her recordings with Joe Pass and, as such, was not always in her best voice on these sessions. Although this is certainly undeniable from a purely technical viewpoint, it must be remembered that Ella was essentially being compared to herself. At the top of her game she was exceptional; in later years, when her vocal quality was declining, she was . . . still exceptional. She possessed a resourcefulness, honed from years of experience and an unwavering love of her craft, that enabled her to transcend the limitations that were creeping up on her. A Fitzgerald at ninety percent capacity, or at eighty percent capacity, remained the standard to which singers aspired. She could still deliver masterful performances, remolding melodies and making them her own—in any voice. After a Carnegie Hall concert in 1985, Stephen Holden wrote in the *New York Times*: "When Ella Fitzgerald was joined by the guitarist Joe Pass . . . at the singer's Carnegie Hall concert . . . one had the thrill of watching two supreme virtuosos engaging in an impromptu musical frolic. . . . The pair . . . make a wonderfully harmonious match."[52]

On *Fitzgerald & Pass . . . Again,* one of the earlier recordings the two stars made together, Ella sings with exuberance and assuredness, her vocal clarity and articulation marvelous throughout the session. She opens with Duke Ellington's "I Ain't Got Nothin' but the Blues," a song in the form of chorus/chorus/bridge/chorus. Although the choruses are not in the standard 12-bar blues format, the dominant-flavored harmonies nonetheless provide Ella with ample opportunities to bend notes and to throw in blues-tinged pitches and phrasing. She delivers the selection with gusto, digging into Don George's lyrics with plenty of feeling, her vocal flexibility in evidence.

Next, "'Tis Autumn" is given a pretty, no-frills rendering. There are a few moments when it is possible to discern that Ella has lost some depth of sound in her lower range, but this is not a detraction at all. She sings beautifully and Pass matches her with an equally appealing half-chorus solo.

Ella swings at a relaxed tempo on "My Old Flame" and Pass is a mini-orchestra, his accompaniment and solo built on beautiful combinations of inventive melodic motives, rich chords, and solid bass lines. "That Old Feeling" is a straight-ahead swinger at a faster tempo that closes with Ella wailing on an extended tag ending. On "Rain," Ella eschews the lyrics and hums the melody throughout. In his liner notes to the album, Benny Green remarked that the lyrics "could not conceivably be sweeter, or more emotionally charged, than the wordless poetry which Ella gives us in their place."[53] On "I Didn't Know about You," Ella offers a streamlined and heartfelt rendition of Duke Ellington's pretty tune.

"You Took Advantage of Me" is a stand-out track on the album, Ella and Pass highly charged on the Rodgers and Hart standard. After Ella's predominantly straightforward opening chorus on this lively swinger, Pass solos beautifully for his own full chorus. An energized Ella returns for a brilliant second run-through that features some of her most imaginative phrasing of the session (Example 9.29). Furthermore, to spice up the chorus, Ella and Pass throw in two half-step modulations, going from the key of F to G-flat after the first A section and up again to the key of G following the bridge. On the opening lyrics in measures 1 and 2, "I'm a sentimental sap, that's all," Ella starts with a descending eighth-note figure and ends by bending the word "all" down a step. Indicative of her endless variety of ideas, note the three ways that she phrases the lyrics "took advantage of me," rising chromatically in measures 7 and 8, arpeggiating downward in measures 15 and 16, and descending through a chromatic lick at the conclusion of the chorus in measures 31 and 32. In measures 13 and 14, Ella sings the lyrics "what's the use you've cooked my goose" on a repeated quarter-note triplet/quarter-note pattern, phrasing the triplet across the bar line in the second instance. In measure 27, where the original melody would have had a jump of an augmented-fourth between the words "arms" and "where," she instead swoops up a minor sixth before dropping down a step to the expected pitch on the word "you're." Ella was always masterful in reversing the contour of motives. Rather than the original jump of an augmented fourth between the words "shake" and "me," followed by a repeated pitch on the word "down," in measures 11 and 12 of the chorus, she drops a minor third between "shake" and "me" before ascending a fifth and attacking the word "down" on the second half of beat four. In measure 25 of the original melody, the intervals between the words "with," "all," and "my" are a descending half-step and an ascending major seventh. Ella changes the shape of the motive dramatically by first leaping up a major sixth between the words "with" and "all," and then dropping back down again to the word "my." These latter two instances of reversed contours are illustrated more closely in Example 9.30.

The rest of the album has many additional highlights, including the slowly lilting "All Too Soon," Duke Ellington's luscious ballad "Solitude,"

Example 9.29: "You Took Advantage of Me" *(Fitzgerald & Pass . . . Again)*

and medium-tempo swingers "The One I Love" and "I've Got the World on a String." (For a discussion of Ella's version of "I've Got the World on a String" on her Harold Arlen *Song Book* album, see the section on Billy May in Chapter 7.) Joe Pass opens "Nature Boy" with almost a minute of introspective musings on his guitar that are at once virtuosic and elegant. Ella follows with a single chorus of the hauntingly beautiful melody. The two virtuosos lay on the soul for "Tennessee Waltz," Ella almost gospel-like in her delivery, Pass maintaining the mood much of the time with a

Example 9.30: "You Took Advantage of Me" (*Fitzgerald & Pass ... Again*)

bluesy ostinato riff. The final track of the session, Antonio Carlos Jobim's "One Note Samba," is intriguing in that Ella scats the whole time, giving us a rare opportunity to hear her vocal improvising on a Latin beat.

Ella Fitzgerald and Joe Pass recorded *Speak Love*, the third of their four classic duo recordings, in March of 1983. Even though a relatively short span of seven years had passed since their *Fitzgerald & Pass ... Again* session, the diminishing quality of the great singer's voice was now at times more evident. Still, as always, her unmatched talent and strong will were significant equalizers and, with the support of Pass's ever-brilliant accompaniment, she came through magnificently, providing many magical moments.

The session opens with "Speak Low," composed by Kurt Weill with words by Ogden Nash for the 1943 musical *One Touch of Venus*. Pass sets it up with a relaxed four-bar intro in a bossa nova vein and Ella cruises through the first chorus. The two artists shift into swing for the next chorus, the first half of which is shown in Example 9.31. Ella opens with the words "Speak low" on a stepwise eighth-note figure, pauses for a couple of beats, sings "when you speak" on a quarter-note triplet, and hits the word "love" on the second half of beat one in measure 3. Compare how she handles the same phrase, "too soon, too soon, Speak low/I feel," first from the end of measure 6 through measure 9 and again from the end of measure 22 through measure 25. In the former instance, she remains on the same pitch for the words "too" and "soon"; holds the second "soon" for four and a half beats, executing a glissando down an octave in the

Example 9.31: "Speak Low" (*Speak Love*)

process; and waits until beat two in measure 9 to leap up a minor seventh and add "Speak low." In the latter instance, she jumps up a fifth between the words "too" and "soon"; drops down an octave with no glissando, to the second "soon," and holds it for three beats; and stays on the same pitch for the word "I" on beat one of measure 25 before she swoops up to the word "feel," again over the interval of a minor seventh. In measure 10, she sings the lyrics "when you speak low" by combining a triplet figure with off-the-beat attacks. In measure 17, she delays the word "Speak" until the second half of beat one, stretches the word "darling" over two and a half beats and the span of a minor sixth in measure 18, and ends with additional syncopated attacks on the words "speak" and "low" from the end of measure 18 through measure 19. In measure 30, she sings the word "always" on beats three and four and then delays until the second half of beat one in measure 31 to complete the phrase with the words "too soon."

The album's second track, "Comes Love," swings at an easy clip. Ella starts out relaxed, somewhat understated, and opens up as the take progresses. Pass is superb, never overplaying as he injects fills and flourishes. The two artists modulate up from the opening key of G to A-flat halfway through and, as Ella is tagging the last line, the piece ends surprisingly on a fade-out. The pretty ballad that follows, "There's No You," is rendered plain and simply, Ella crooning with feeling on both sides of Pass's solo.

"I May Be Wrong" swings at a medium tempo and Ella, after her opening chorus, scats through a complete second chorus. This is not the best scatting she has ever done, but she gets stronger as she goes along and, just for good measure, she doubles up and throws in a brief sixteenth-note lick in the last A section. Pass solos and Ella takes it out with a final chorus. This is an interesting cut in that the listener can clearly discern the two artists trying to anticipate each other's intentions, especially on Ella's spontaneous tag ending.

"At Last" is taken at a relaxed tempo and Ella sings with much emotion. In spite of the vocal limitations that were besetting her at this time in her career, her lower register is rich and controlled on this track, perhaps at its strongest on the album. Pass accompanies with equal passion and plays some of his most bop-oriented licks of the session on his short solo.

"The Thrill Is Gone" medley is the most intriguing track on the album in that it pairs two tunes of completely opposite character. The title is originally from the lovely ballad composed by Lew Brown and Ray Henderson in 1922. J. Wilfred Johnson points out that it was introduced in the 1931 review *George White's Scandals of 1931*.[54] Producer Norman Granz, in the liner notes for *Speak Love,* points out that Joe Pass, who was a fan of B. B. King, had suggested seguing from a chorus of the aforementioned standard into King's song of the same title. Granz goes on to say that "you can hear Ella virtually shifting gears as she goes from one chorus to the next."[55]

Ella recorded "Gone with the Wind" several times during her career. Following Pass' four-bar intro, she swings through the first chorus at a medium-slow tempo, digging into the lyrics with conviction. Pass ups the tempo considerably for his solo, a chorus loaded with hip licks and inventive phrasing. He is a marvel who seemingly never runs out of ideas, every solo fresh and new-sounding. Ella is obviously moved by her colleague's superb playing and her second chorus is inspired.

"Blue and Sentimental" was composed by Count Basie in 1938 and lyrics were added almost a decade later by Jerry Livingston and Mack David. Ella scats the opening chorus, alternating between snatches of the melody and improvised licks, and adds one more chorus with the lyrics.

Pass opens "Girl Talk" with some from-the-gut blues licks. Ella, in her best feline impersonation, twice exclaims "meow, meow" for added effect. Settling into a solid medium-swing groove, she sings her first chorus with fervor and Pass follows by modulating up a half-step into the key of A for his solo. Ella returns, modulates to the key of B-flat after half a chorus, and takes it out by purring "meow, meow, meow."

Pass digs into his blues bag again for his four-bar intro to "Georgia on My Mind." Ella comes in with her most impassioned singing on the album as she belts out two high-powered choruses. Pass is dynamic yet unobtrusive in his accompaniment, producing licks that would be the envy of any rock guitarist. He pulls back a little for his half-chorus solo and Ella returns at her previous high-energy level. The two virtuosos calm down only at the end, closing in effective contrast to all that has gone on before.

APPENDIX 1

Complete Interviews

VIRGINIA WICKS

(Publicist)
Interviewed on September 30, 2000

Because Virginia Wicks was Ella Fitzgerald's good friend, as well as her publicist, her comments often reflect her obvious love for the incomparable singer. In any event, Wicks is a direct connection to Ella and, as such, her information is accurate—and she offers a few tidbits that only a publicist would know.

How did Ella select her repertoire?

They didn't come to her and give her a song—and she didn't like it—but she'd sing it anyway because she'd get a payoff or something. Some of the artists did that—she didn't. It was very important to her what she sang. I don't think she ever recorded anything she didn't like.

After Norman [Granz] really began to handle her, it was Ella's choice, more than what Nelson Riddle or somebody would decide to arrange. They would never arrange a tune or have a tune ready for her without her total approval. And it wasn't that she was high-handed. It was because she didn't sing songs unless she cared for them. If some composer would come to her, some well-known composer with a beautiful song, with a song she liked, that would be wonderful—some she liked better than others, but nobody forced her to do anything.

Can you talk about Ella's work with Nelson Riddle?

When it was Nelson Riddle, or someone else she really respected, she listened. She had great respect for people with talent, and also somebody such as Norman [Granz]. But funnily enough, Ella, of all the artists I ever handled, was usually way ahead of everybody else in terms of her interpretation. If there was something that they felt she should emphasize more, or whatever, she'd listen, she'd do it, she'd take direction. But they didn't have to give her much. She just innately knew how to interpret the lyrics and how to sing. Nobody told her how to sing: "Let's put this part in a little faster; we can do this or that." Unless she felt that the suggestion was a good one, Ella was the perfect one. Ella was the one who set the pace without being high-handed. She was the most modest of anyone in the room, but they followed her lead. Her lead was pretty much perfection. This isn't because I handled her. It was because this is true. She was a true, pure musician who just knew how to sing, and knew what tempo. She very often would set the tempo and the feeling for the music. She was a great admirer of Nelson Riddle's work.

Did Ella leave any old charts or lead sheets?

She had charts, charts with lyrics. They were for sale suddenly, some of Ella's old charts. A lot of people got a hold of these things. There was a store in kind of a sleazy part of Los Angeles that had some of her clothes, some of her jewelry— mostly costume jewelry—but jewelry, personal effects, shoes. They had racks and racks of shoes. She loved shoes, and nightgowns. And they had musical things, such as charts and old sheet music.

Any comments on Ella's influences?

Billie Holiday was one. She listened to Billie. Maxine Sullivan, I think, was one. Sinatra, of course, but that came later. Yes, she had favorites. She idolized some performers, she really did, such as Sinatra and Oscar Peterson.

What did you observe when Ella recorded with Louis Armstrong?

I'm sure she had a good relationship [with Louis Armstrong]. I don't remember her speaking of him a great deal, but she would have been very respectful. I was present at some of those [recordings with Armstrong]. I was in the sound booth when she did some of those—she would pick up on whether it was a Louis Armstrong or Bird song, or whatever it was, she could duplicate it—she picked up on ideas, original ideas. I remember they had a wonderful camaraderie during the recording sessions of which there were about three or four. I was there on, I think, two of them. Ella was good the first time, most often. They didn't have to say "We'll do this one over." Once in a while Ella would stop and say "Let's do this again," but almost apologetically.

Can you comment on how Ella practiced or vocalized?

I'm sure everyone else told you the same thing. I never heard her say "I have to go in the other room and practice." I never heard her do that. Sometimes she would have a cold and she'd be concerned about how it would come out. But did she try it first? No. I don't remember anything—other people may have—but I don't recall anything like that. She would just go do it. She was an amazing lady. If anyone tells you something differently than what I'm saying, they possibly heard something I didn't hear. So I don't say she never did. The thought of Ella standing in a room and going up and down the scales is something I don't think that ever happened. Maybe in the very early part of her career, but I wouldn't say so. She might sing a song around the house as she walked around dusting or something, just to sing it and to feel it. But I don't believe she practiced per se, sit in a room and practice. I can't imagine it.

How did you meet Ella?

I was a great fan of hers but I didn't know her. I met her through Norman [Granz] and began handling her immediately. We became friends. It was 1951.

Who were Ella's closest friends in the business?

Ella didn't very often have personal relationships. I never knew of her to say "Well, we'll go to lunch." I never knew of her to say "Let's get together over the weekend." I never heard her use those words with any of these people. She would perhaps attend something that they had, but she didn't go to very many concerts. She'd slip into a club to hear somebody. And I suppose she went to a concert now and then, but she didn't socialize particularly. She was always in awe of people, most people, but I never knew her to say "Let's go to lunch." She would call [Nelson Riddle] Mr. Riddle. She called most people by their last names. And, once in a while, if they'd force her, she'd call them by their first name. She'd call Louis [Armstrong] by his first name. She called [Norman Granz] Norman.

Did Ella like the work of Buddy Bregman?

I don't think she was as enamored or as completely respectful or as completely in awe of [Buddy Bregman] as she was of Nelson [Riddle].

Describe the relationship of Ella and Oscar Peterson.

Oh, marvelous. They were completely in tune, completely harmonious. The two of them were like one song. She loved him personally, and also had great pride working with him. It was like a gift to her to work with Oscar. And, of course, Oscar felt the same. And another one would be Herb Ellis.

I handled Oscar as well—not for as long a period—but I handled Oscar. Very often, Norman would have a plan and he'd have penciled in certain numbers. [Ella and Oscar] would come in on what they liked or they didn't like. They all thought more or less alike.

How did Ella relate to musicians in general?

For fine musicians such as an Oscar [Peterson] or Herb Ellis, she had a feeling of awe and also there were never arguments. I never heard Ella argue. She might pout but that was never with someone she respected musically.

Ella had a super ear. Do you have any comments about that aspect of her genius?

Very often—they'd say: "Ella, give me E-flat," or whatever, and . . . it was auto-matic. [She had] perfect pitch. More perfect probably than almost anyone ever. She had that kind of God-given perfect pitch. Very often pianos would be out of tune and Ella could not work with an out-of-tune piano. They'd have to imme-diately tune it on the spot because she knew the difference. Absolutely. I've seen that happen. They usually were quite careful with Ella knowing that she had perfect pitch, but I very often saw them come in with the tuning fork—whatever, I don't know if they still do that. But they'd come in and do that, go up and down the scale, and Ella would listen. And it was Ella that [was] perfect out of every-body, everything.

Say a few words about Ella's rehearsals or recordings.

The musicians didn't know necessarily, certainly not in every case, what Ella was going to do in a live performance—or I'm talking about a recording. They didn't know exactly. Naturally, they had to discuss tempo and all of that, but they didn't know where she would suddenly scat. Nor did Ella. As I say, it wasn't always the same every time. Ella would just stand there and sing and the musicians, very often, would be in awe because she had not rehearsed exactly what she was going to do there and it would just happen. It was never wrong. She never sang out of tune or out of tempo or anything. She might not like something she did, but I don't recall anybody saying "Now wait a minute, Ella, let's go with the other part," or whatever. I don't recall that."

She would have gone over the lyrics. She was always afraid she'd forget the lyrics—not always—but very often, particularly with some new tune, not a stan-dard, but some new tune. So that troubled her. But in terms of interpretation, I think she surprised herself.

Did Ella like rock and pop music?

She didn't care about being today's singer. She only knew how to be Ella. If she did, it wasn't something I was aware of. Did she play it on her record player or on the radio or anything that I know of—no. I never heard her play anything she didn't like herself.

It would be the tune. I think she appreciated the Beatles. She appreciated the Hi-Los, for instance, with their innovations, and she listened to them. And then it would be a tune that the Beatles did, but she wasn't in that world. She never went to a Beatles performance.

Did Ella know John Coltrane, or study his music?

I don't know about Coltrane. She certainly was aware of what Dizzy [Gillespie] and Charlie Parker were doing. She loved them, of course. Just adored and wor-shipped and had fun and laughed, with Dizzy particularly. She loved to sit around and gab, but it had to be informal. She was very quiet when she was in the com-pany of [Richard] Rodgers, or someone like that, and they had to pull her out.

Did Ella ever want to appear on Broadway?

She may have been asked [to appear in a Broadway show] but she would never have done that—too shy, oh my goodness. No, she would have never done that. Well, she appeared in a couple of movies—but singing, only singing. No, she could not take on the part of someone else, other than in a moment's joke—singing with Sinatra or someone like that—or Louis Armstrong.

How did Ella relate to movie stars?

She was also in awe of certain movies stars. I happened to handle Rock Hudson. Somehow or other, it came up that I handled him and she just went into—you know, she said: "You handle Rock?"—I think she never respected me more than when I told her I was handling Rock Hudson. She said: "Oh, do you think I could meet him?" I did bring him, and, of course, he was the same way. When I mentioned that I handled Ella, he was the same way. They both had a kind of purity about them that might sound strange for me to say about Rock. I took him backstage to meet Ella and both of them were overwhelmed with the occasion. She watched old movies all the time—the romantic ones, beautiful ones—the Fred Astaires, the Gary Coopers. She had great idols and she loved watching the old movies.

How was Ella viewed in the classical world?

A lot of classical people—Isaac Stern [for example]—a lot of classical people [loved Ella]. I'm sure—of course, at times—that many of them met her and told her how much they appreciated her. She would have been speechless probably. "Oh, thank you"—I can just hear her—"Oh, thank you so much." She didn't consider herself in that world. She didn't consider herself to be that important. I've never known anyone as humble as Ella was. She gained a little bit more confidence as the years went by. I knew her after that but the 1950s was the time I saw her all the time because she was living in the New York area and she was working in New York. She'd go on tour—I'd often see her on tour, but we spent a lot of time together. So I know what happened during that period. I can't speak too much of the later periods.

She was a great fan of talent and a great respecter of other people. There was never any jealously—ever, ever, ever—between herself and another singer. If she liked the singer's work, then she was like a fan. If that wasn't her cup of tea, she was just very polite or respectful of their fame. She never would say anything she didn't mean. She might not say a great deal, but if she wasn't a fan of that person she would just be extremely respectful of their accomplishments, but not ever say: "I love your singing" or "I love your music." She was very pure.

How did Ella communicate with aspiring singers?

She would just say—something like, I don't want to be quoted exactly: "Honey, you have to love what you're doing and you have to like the words. Think about the words and what they mean to you. You have to practice. You just have to think what the words are telling you to sing and it will come automatically." She thought everybody had the ability she had (*chuckling*), somewhere inside them, like it was so easy for her that it would be the same for anyone else if they opened their mouth and tried to sing. If I'd said to her "Ella, help me learn how to sing," I don't know if she'd call me honey—ha, ha.

How did Ella react to smoke and other general discomforts in clubs?

I do know what was very hard for her and what would make her cross—and the word "cross" is used as "pouting." She'd go out on stage at a club and right down below her there would be a table with four smokers [for instance]. The smoke, you could see it, would go right up into her face. She had a little white hankie and she'd blow it away. Finally, after a couple of years of this, that I observed, she would say: "I really would appreciate it if you didn't smoke. It's hard for me to sing," or something. And sometimes they would stop, and sometimes they wouldn't. It was incredible during those years how people didn't realize how terribly hard it was for a singer to sing with smoke, a lot of smoke coming up at them. I can still see Ella's face, almost covered with smoke from smokers at the tables in the nightclubs. With this little hankie, she would blow it away. You could see she was annoyed, but never did she make a pronouncement like: "If you don't stop smoking, I'll go off the stage." Never, whereas some singers would have done that. She never did. But she had her own little temper. She had her own likes and dislikes. She wasn't without annoyance. If somebody would annoy her, I mean really annoy her in her dressing room, she would sit there quietly and say "s—." *(chuckle)* I can hear her, but it was always quiet.

TOMMY FLANAGAN

(pianist)
Interviewed on October 4, 2000

Tommy Flanagan was a brilliant pianist and an engaging gentleman. Having been Ella Fitzgerald's accompanist for many years he was often asked for interviews about her. He was always gracious and forthright.

When rehearsing with Ella, how would you decide on the songs to be performed?

Well, usually she picked them because a lot of the things she ended up doing I wouldn't think of. It was strictly up to her. We worked on how the arrangement would feel and how we would approach it, and how to get out of it.

If you were doing the same or similar sets each night of an engagement, were the arrangements the same each time, or did you more or less see where it would go?

I tried to keep it like that because all of her arrangements—that's how she keeps them in her head. She had so many songs. I played some intros to three or four tunes, and I don't know which one she might go into—she wouldn't either. Unless she tells you what she's going to sing—and then, whatever: "Give me two bars— not too free."

Are there differences on how you would prepare if you were leading one of your trio gigs? How about your recent appearance at the Village Vanguard with Peter Washington and Tootie Heath?

We hadn't been together that long. My repertoire with them is not that big. [In these cases] we'd get a chance to feel each other out. Get a chance to get the arrangements, how I want them to go. Where to give them space. I believe in that; I don't like to work that much myself *(smiling)*. I like if you can get musicians who can solo. It takes me a while to get into it before I feel like soloing *(chuckling)*.

Do you still enjoy gigging?

Oh yeah, I like that.

Does it make a difference to you whether you're in a club or in a theater?

I like clubs. It's more intimate, and I see more people that can come and see me—kind of collective eye contacts. In a small place I like to speak to the people—not a lot—just to let them know I'm not a standoffish guy.

Back to your work with Ella. In some pieces that you played with her you would modulate to a new chorus, sometimes more than once. How did that come about?

She likes to do that stuff. Usually we'd do that beforehand. Unless it was something we had never done, then I'd just follow her and let her be free.

When Ella did standards, did she usually sing them in the standard keys or in the keys that suited her best?

In her keys. In fact, it was funny—about the original key—a lot of times, I don't know if she did it on purpose, but it would be a half-step away from the original key. She used to do things in A. In fact, she used to just start singing sometimes, and I'd catch her. So she felt like: "Hey, I can do anything."

Did she ever sing the same song in a different key?

Yeah, she's done that. Because, her voice—I was with her so long—the pitch had dropped, kept getting lower. She had a big range, but her range started getting lower as she got older. I think, when I first joined her, she was doing a song like "Body and Soul"—she used to do it in F. Then, through the years, she ended up singing it in D-flat [the standard key].

Did Ella have any knowledge of harmony?

She had a lot of knowledge of harmony. She could scat, improvise.

Could Ella have sat down and analyzed herself?

No. It was just a natural thing with her. She had a great ear—and her ideas, she could duplicate what she heard, which is amazing.

If you come across a song that you haven't seen before how do you prepare to play it?

I just try to learn the song—keep everything in its place. Start out with the right changes [chord progression] like the composer wrote. You have to work with it. There's guys who just wrote those things as a guide for jazz musicians—some of those composers really wrote the songs to improvise themselves. Harold Arlen—he could sing his songs and make them so different sounding. He took a lot of liberties. Why not? They're his songs.

On a recording session, did Ella ever read the lyrics?

Yes. She had huge lyrics written out.

When you're doing a recording session, either with a vocalist or an instrumental group, do you ever read something while you're playing it?

I usually have the tune in my head. I don't like reading while I'm playing or recording anyway.

Do you ever arrange, either for a small group or for a large ensemble?

No. I love to do it, but it's just so tedious for me. I wrote an arrangement for Ella once, and she was wondering when I was going to finish. When she wanted to do a song—you know, she had a staff of arrangers, cats who could just knock them out—Quincy Jones, Marty Paich, Nelson Riddle—and some of the jazz arrangers, like Oliver Nelson.

When you were in a recording studio with Ella, was her preference to do it in as few takes as possible?

She did it until she was comfortable with it—Norman Granz was always on the record dates.

Did you ever disagree with Norman Granz's conception of a session?

Mostly. I put my two cents in, but he didn't like it. I'd usually go to try to say something to Ella, and Ella would feel like she was in between. She didn't want to get that feeling, like she was uneasy with Norman or me.

If you ever totally disagreed would you let him know? Were you ever able to get your way on this stuff if it made sense musically?

You know, I would, but he had the editing rights on recordings. He used to not use a lot of my intros, if you could believe that. Some recordings, if they were live, he would just start with maybe Ella singing.

Did that ever tick you off?

Yeah—but I wouldn't know until after we'd hear the recording.

Did you respect Norman Granz?

No. Not very much—musically. He doesn't know that much. I've told him that. If Ella could put up with it, I could. She didn't lose anything by letting him have his say. She knew that he wouldn't be around for every performance.

Did you play differently if Norman Granz was in the audience?

No. It wouldn't make any difference. It didn't matter to Ella either, after she got her program together. I don't think she liked so much that he used to make out her programs.

Were you at liberty to hire the bass player and drummer?

I chose them. Everybody after [drummer] Gus Johnson, who was already there.

Did you like the way Oscar Peterson backed up a vocalist—Ella, or whoever it was?

I'd rather hear somebody else behind a vocal. I think he was trying to do [Art] Tatum too much. Tatum didn't always have the freedom, and who would say anything to him. Let him go—singers and soloists—he'd be playing that stuff behind them.

What are your views now on the jazz scene in Europe, as opposed to in the United States?

They're pretty hip in Europe now. They're getting very cocky and arrogant, because they think their musicians are—and they've come up quite a bit and the musicians have an attitude now.

Have you ever considered in your life moving to Europe?

No, not really. There are some cities over there I like a lot. I love Paris. There are a couple of cities in Italy I like.

Is New York still as vibrant now? Do you feel good still being in New York? Can you still work and do your own thing without compromising it here?

I like New York. The only thing I miss about it from when I first came here is that the caliber of the old guys that I—not that they were that old—I just missed all those great players. When I came here it was just loaded with a who's-who, every time you turned around. I just remember the day I walked into Beefsteak Charlie's and I said "Wow, I hope nothing happens in here," and there's Coleman Hawkins, Lester Young, and Ben Webster standing at the bar together—and Jo Jones, Sonny Greer.

What's your view of the younger musicians playing today? Do you think the music is going in the right direction?

I think so. The ones that are really trying to keep preserved what came before, they're really doing it, giving it a lot of respect.

What do you think about rap music and hip-hop?

When I first heard it I hated it. I couldn't stand to listen to it.

Do you think jazz is as vibrant as it was thirty or forty years ago? Is jazz still a big force on the music scene?

Oh yeah, I really do. I think it's the youngsters who really want to be as good as what came before them. There are some good young players out there.

If you weren't a musician, is there anything else you'd like to do? What would have been the other profession you would have done if you weren't a musician?

I used to like to take pictures, but I started having trouble with cameras. The better they got, they were harder for me to get them to work. They just stopped working, and I kind of stopped taking pictures.

Would you comment on Paul Smith's piano playing?

He's kind of a strange guy. He can be very robotic—he plays well, though. He knows the piano. But he's kind of cold when he's improvising. Sounds like it's written—to me.

What about Jimmy Rowles?

I loved Jimmy. He had a great feeling, conception.

How was playing at the White House?

The first time I went to the White House [to perform for President Ford], I was with Ella. I knew Ford just did it for something [politics or whatever]. They were killing some time because they had a country singer on—Loretta Lynn or one of those girls. She did almost a set, two or three songs. And they introduced Ella, and Ford comes up before she had finished the first tune. "O.K., thank you, Ella." I'm sure Clinton would have done better—most people.

Do you set a limit now on how much time you want to tour?

Sometimes I don't have a choice. I have a guy that looks out for work, but I have to cancel a lot of stuff that he recommends. I mean, I don't want to go to Idaho in February.

How does a gig like the Village Vanguard gig come along?

Well, we have an understanding. Almost like a contract, but it's an understanding that I'll be there two weeks in the fall and two in the spring—usually around my birthday in March and two weeks in September.

When you were touring with Ella, every once in a while she'd do a Beatles tune, or a tune by Blood, Sweat, and Tears—a commercial tune or a pop tune. If you were going to do that, and you hadn't done the tune before, would you try and find a lead sheet, or would you just listen to the recording and hear it?

We'd find the lead sheet and find out where the song is really going and what they really meant by writing the song.

How do you pick music for your own recordings?

Take a company like Blue Note. They might give me suggestions. Bruce Lundvall, he's pretty hip. He doesn't want anything that's too disagreeable. For instance, he likes Strayhorn's stuff if I like it. He usually goes along with the artist.

Do you still experience any prejudice anywhere? Is that still an issue in entertainment?

Not as big as it used to be. They do know you're old enough to see through things. But it's still out there.

In the 1950s and 1960s, was there really a difference for black and white musicians? How tough was it?

It wasn't hard working. I don't know how much anybody made. The more seniority you had, the older you were, you could demand a little more. Otherwise, when I first came here, I was just happy to be working. I was working all over the place.

There came a point, though, when you were known, when you were really a successful musician. Did you ever feel you were getting short-changed?

Yeah. I would have known. It ruined doing business with the people I had to deal with. That stopped after I went on the road with Ella.

Being on the gig with Ella, because she was such a big star, could you pretty much count on being treated the right way?

To a point.

Did you ever have an argument with Ella, a musical disagreement?

Not really an argument. We had differences of opinion. After a while, I felt I had the freedom to tell her what I thought.

Does it ever bug you getting the same questions all the time?

No. I just give different answers *(laughing)*. There's always a little more you can add.

O.K. Then I have only one question about the "Giant Steps" session with John Coltrane. You didn't know that tune when you went in there, did you? When he gave you the lead sheet, that was the first time you'd seen it, wasn't it?

No. He brought it by my pad, but I had no idea. He sat down and played the chords like it was a ballad almost. Of course, it's not bad as a ballad. In fact, Jimmy Rowles made a bossa nova out of it.

When you're performing now, is your preference the trio setting?

Yeah, I really like that.

Do you like working with horn players?

Not too much. No.

Why? Because they're all egotistical and want to take twenty-five choruses every time?
[The author is a saxophonist and clarinetist.]

Yeah, the guy in front. *(laughing)*

Are you into the avant-garde? Any free music you like? What about Cecil Taylor?

I like Cecil. I like his music. There's something there—and how he does it. I go to
see him. The last time I heard him he was with Elvin Jones, just the two of them.

Do you know Ornette Coleman?

I don't know Ornette.

Did you ever listen to his music?

When I first heard it I don't know why they made such a big deal out of it. I
thought he was very interesting for not really playing on changes [chord progres-
sion]. It's kind of the way I look at music: staying within the sound of the
instrument.

PHIL SCHAAP

(archivist, historian, writer, radio personality)
Interviewed on November 8, 2000

Phil Schaap is one of the jazz world's most respected personalities, a multifaceted authority
possessed of an incredible wealth of knowledge and insight. His research and expertise
encompass a broad spectrum of styles and personalities. Consequently, his comments are
always highly informed and interesting—and he often includes some wonderful asides.

Comment on Ella Fitzgerald's rehearsal techniques and procedures, and the general per-
ception that she just came in and did things on one take.

Ella could circumvent rehearsal by using familiar repertoire and routines. I was
at the rehearsals at Carnegie Hall in 1973 and that, of course, became a recorded
album that came out on Columbia. She was very much involved with that. There
was, of course, some new repertoire, and the band wasn't a working band. They
were, in some instances, Chick Webb alumni; in other instances, Ella Fitzgerald

alumni. They did the songs she was going to do once. [Eddie] Barefield had arranged [the music]. First, Barefield had gone over the passages that wouldn't be involved with her. The retakes were between him and all the musicians. And then they did it once with her. She's not comfortable about being in the dark about what's going to happen. My experience as an archivist doesn't match that experience of seeing a rehearsal in person. The tapes I've uncovered of record dates are rife with rehearsal. I reiterate that the routines and using the working bands are de facto rehearsals. They can replace rehearsal.

Name association: I'll name a singer central to Ella Fitzgerald's development. Provide whatever comments come to mind.

• *Connee Boswell*

Major influence—articulation and the rhythm of a syllable and maintaining swing. That confluence of three thoughts is a real challenge to the jazz singer. Ella Fitzgerald synthesized Boswell's success in doing it and made it her own. But it's rooted in that.

• *Louis Armstrong*

I think that Ella is one of the second liners in this regard, that her Armstrong influence is profound but filtered through a preceding genius, or preceding artists, like Connee Boswell, like Chick Webb's band. Taft Jordan is Louis Armstrong, but she doesn't know that. She knows he's Taft Jordan. I would say Louis Jordan, who was after all her boyfriend for a while in that band. He thought Louis Armstrong was the greatest thing that ever happened. Armstrong was a tremendous vocal influence on him. A lot of people forget that Louis Jordan was a singer even in the Chick Webb period. I think that Armstrong is the most under-acknowledged Ella Fitzgerald influence.

• *Leo Watson*

I think her scatting approach is different than his, is more instrumental and less humorous—Leo Watson is an excellent musician and can do many things, but the humor of the situation is still why he does it. Ella is not doing it for humor at all.

• *Bing Crosby*

Clearly, it would be impossible to avoid knowledge of Crosby. I don't think Ella copped anything from Bing, except maybe some stage rapport and repertoire.

• *Mildred Bailey*

Ella listened to Mildred Bailey. If you want an analogy, and this is conjecture to an extent—the way Lester Young said: "I listened to Jimmy Dorsey and I listened to Frank Trumbauer, and then I had to make a choice"—I can see Ella

Fitzgerald, not as systematically, having to make a similar thing. The rhythmic punch that Connee Boswell found a way not to delete says something to Ella and that's the way she went. Not that Mildred doesn't swing, except that Mildred Bailey isn't concerned. She thinks the fact that she does swing will take care of itself and she's not looking for the avenue, of the meeting of phrasing to contact of the rhythmic punch. Connee Boswell was. This perception of difference, however intuitive and unsystematic in terms of the study, is a real reason why Ella would like Connee Boswell more than a Mildred Bailey.

• *Ethel Waters*

I think Ethel Waters is a huge influence on Ella Fitzgerald, but not as much as she is on Billie Holiday. And I think neither properly recognized the Waters [influence]. I think the storytelling need of a song's delivery is understood by Ethel Waters. Ella Fitzgerald delays grasping that at the same profound level that Billie Holiday did. But I think for diction, and for its relationship to where the notes are, and what you've got to do to make those two be married, I think Ethel Waters is a huge influence on Ella Fitzgerald.

If I had to pick the two [biggest influences on Ella], I'd pick Connee Boswell and Louis Armstrong—and Ethel Waters is a profound influence on Billie Holiday, to the extent that she is, with Louis Armstrong, the second most important influence on Billie. But not on that level [with Ella]. I would say Connee Boswell and Louis Armstrong are the people who sang the real story to Ella in my understanding of it.

Was Connee Boswell that heavy an influence on Billie Holiday?

No.

Talk about the relationship between Billie Holiday and Ella Fitzgerald.

I think that Ella learns about the rhythmic breakthrough of the 1930s through a variety of musical episodes, including as an under-acknowledged one, [drummer] Jo Jones. There is no acknowledgement of Jo Jones being an important musician in Ella Fitzgerald's career, but I'm telling you otherwise. Jo's rhythmic sensibility is part of a change in rhythmic elasticity in jazz in the 1930s, which is a very profound thing, and Ella grasps that and gets it from a number of people. One of them would be Billie Holiday. She sees how Billie Holiday has applied the rhythmic breakthrough of the 1930s to singing per se and jazz singing in a more specific way and she goes there. She learns a lot about relaxation at any speed.

Jo Jones was my baby-sitter and he told me Ella Fitzgerald seemed to like him. All the Basie-ites—Earl Warren for instance—mentioned the Jo Jones connection to Ella. Every Basie-ite. Haywood Henry was one of my primaries—they were engaged. I got a lot of very important men in her life talking to me much later and giving me insights into the younger Ella Fitzgerald, which I think was one of my blessings.

• *Maxine Sullivan*

I think that Maxine's understanding of relaxation is unique to Maxine and that Ella admired it and used what she could, but that it just wasn't the way she did things.

Let's go back a little. How about Bessie Smith?

Billie Holiday says she got a lot from Bessie Smith. I don't even hear that. What she did was she synthesized the blues tradition and, having completely synthesized it, expanded some of its effects and its general feeling into American popular songbook singing. To a certain extent, Ella Fitzgerald did the same thing, but completely differently. If you want to root that in Bessie Smith—the Bessie Smith records are icons of that generation, so it would have been impossible for Ella to tiptoe around them. So she had to have heard them. But I don't hear it if you're talking about a real musical impact. I hear Louis and Connee Boswell.

Comment on Ella's association with the arranger Nelson Riddle.

I don't understand Ella Fitzgerald's motivation in terms of the class pop arrangers—I don't understand what's motivating her. I'm not sure any of us do. It seems to me that she's often interested in pushing such collaborations back in a jazz direction. Norman Granz's hand here and hers can only be separated clearly by them. Neither of them were very forthcoming with information and, of course, Ella is dead now. And Nelson Riddle is dead now. So, the pop arrangers who did not do as good a job as Nelson Riddle, and Russ Garcia, and Frank DeVol—the arrangers who did the Decca stuff in the 1940s—Ella doesn't seem to say that they are bad or good, or make any huge effort for a specific quality. In short, what I'm saying is that the quality of arranging doesn't show an aesthetic on Ella Fitzgerald's part until Norman Granz emerges. It says to me that the heavy hand belongs to Granz. I can't say that Ella cared one way or the other, unless her motivation is explained to me.

Are you insinuating that the reason she ended up doing anything with Nelson Riddle was that she wasn't going to argue anything Norman Granz put in front of her?

Well, that's too strong. She has an appreciation for music. I'm just saying: "Where are these people in 1951? Where are these people in 1943?" Why aren't the first chair pop-slash-jazz arrangers writing for Ella Fitzgerald until Norman Granz, and why did they go away after Norman Granz?

Do you have an answer for that?

No, except to say that I perceive it to be something that Norman Granz thought would be good for her, and so she agreed because there is much to agree to. There's nothing wrong with Granz making these choices for her. His redirecting her career is pivotal to our having so much magnificent music. I'm just saying that if it was Ella's idea, her motivation and delay until Granz directs her sessions goes unexplained.

But it wasn't her idea?

No, I don't think so.

We've heard some people say they tend to prefer the Billy May arrangements because they are a little jazzier. Is that just a comfortable thing to write and say?

Here, I'm going to take the opposite side. I think the goal of these [songbooks/ large studio orchestra format] was reverence for the style. She was to supply the jazz. When they brought in Marty Paich and they did the Dek-tette things, and then they're going to have Stan Getz be a guest soloist—that's when it's an issue. Otherwise, expressing a preference on jazz issues other than Ella's performance is really telling me more about your feelings about jazz and what rhythm section was on call that day. Alvin Stoller is a great swing jazz drummer, on top of reading the hell out of parts and holding bands together. So, you're really telling me more about the listener's jazz leanings. The goal of these arrangements was texture, reverence for the songbook, showcasing the singer, voicings—and jazz was her job.

Do you have a favorite of the Song Books?

Duke. Now I'm illustrating my doing precisely what I just said. The preference is based on my jazz leanings. I like Duke Ellington and Billy Strayhorn above the American popular songbook writers. I like the fact that there are solos on those records. I like [drummer] Sam Woodyard—I love Sam Woodyard. I love Sam Woodyard more than I love Alvin Stoller, so I mean I've just told you a lot. I also like the success Ella had with some songs you don't hear too often—"Azure" comes to mind immediately. But I find the *Song Books* important, independently and collectively. And I do acknowledge that each one does sound a tad different. The Cole Porter, which is [Buddy] Bregman—that is really the introduction, not the first. "This is the way we do it" is the whole point. The Gershwin is more than that, in other words, that's trying to gild the lily.
   A lot of that material is pre-milked. Ella understood that. "Summertime"—I'm switching the direction of my comment—that song is pre-milked. If a soul singer did it, they don't understand. Janis Joplin messed up "Summertime." She thought she had to add Janis Joplin to "Summertime." "Summertime" is pre-milked. Everything that is extended, in terms of what you can do with a word, a syllable, a note, fermatas, vibrato—it's already done. If you add to it, you spoil it. It's pre-milked. And Louis Armstrong and Ella Fitzgerald understood that. Most people don't. Much of Gershwin is pre-milked. You know who understood that? Whoever arranged "Summertime" for the Bob Crosby band. There's a profound understanding of how to approach "Summertime." I don't want to over-build it up. When you get there you're going to find out: "Gee, they almost did nothing." But it's a smart nothing. Gil Evans, you know, he was the musical director for Bob Hope. He wrote a lot of straightforward music. Tadd [Dameron] is the other guy. Those two. Did you ever listen to "Poor Little Plaything" with Pres [Lester Young] and Earl Warren? *(singing)* "You're just a phony guy." It's such a weird song. It's written foolishly because whoever wrote the lyrics—and I think it's really one composer, music and lyrics is the same person—there seems to me, and you're

obviously drawing out some harsh thoughts on my part—this person doesn't understand what you've got to do between the syllables and the notes. And Tadd Dameron and the singer Earl Warren, they worked their asses off to fix it, and they almost did.

How do you view the work of the great pianist Tommy Flanagan with Ella?

He's perfect for Ella Fitzgerald because—they used to talk a lot about this when Jack Teagarden was playing in the sixties. You see, Teagarden had this incredible ear, this incredible music invention. But he'd also come down to playing a fixed repertoire and people expected his band to be a Dixieland band. You know, five sets is a lot of sets, and a lot of tunes are going to be played four times, three times, maybe even five times, and you have to develop routine. You also have to know: "Hey, there's really a genius in front of this band, and spurring them on at the right moment might actually make music happen that would be delightful for everybody—the lay audience, us up here on the bandstand, the artists themselves, and, if recorded, posterity." Tommy Flanagan has that insight on how to do that— how to nuance "Black Coffee" precisely the same, so that it almost sounds as though it's identical. It would take a very discerning ear to hear any difference in the articulation of the notes, the chord choices, the arpeggiation of the chord as it's played. And then the times he changes it. He knows when to make Ella move in a different direction. Absolutely a brilliant accompanist for Ella Fitzgerald, while also a complete musician of very, very great beauty. I was speaking of Tadd Dameron a moment ago—Flanagan's understanding of having to swing and be pretty at the same time, from the musical scene he comes from, which is bebop-slash-hard bop, is unusual and makes him all the more commendable.

Do you think Flanagan would have played as well with another vocalist?

Who's the other vocalist? Buddy Holly? No! *(laughing)* It would have had to be someone with the chops that Ella has. So, Sarah [Vaughan] comes to mind. Sarah Vaughan and Tommy Flanagan would have built up an interesting rapport.

Contrast Sarah Vaughan and Ella.

Harmony. It's sort of like the difference between Benny Goodman and Artie Shaw—with Ella being Goodman and Sarah Vaughan being Shaw. Ella Fitzgerald thinks about the lay of the line and how she's going to get there as "steps forward"—Sarah Vaughan thinks about the lay of the line and how she's going to find it as "how I'm going to get to the second and third story, how I'm moving up." It's just a word picture for chords. Ella Fitzgerald hears chords and can translate them into their notes and play them rhythmically—very, very quickly—which you'd think is total chordal knowledge. But it's really an illustration of a great ear. The knowledge part is the part about: "Why leave that note out? Why leave this note out? Why pick this interval as it lays, as it's defining things?" And that's something that the "steps forward" take as an option, so it's there. But it hasn't been perused and finalized the way it would be with Sarah Vaughan. The Benny Goodman/Artie Shaw thing is an apt analogy. It tells its own story.

How about the pianist Ellis Larkins?

Ellis Larkins is a great accompanist because he has dealt with the whole issue of submergence without it messing up his art. You have to just totally delete a lot of your personality and needs and ego—or you're not an accompanist. It's an incredibly difficult thing to do. Bill Doggett, who was [at one time] Ella's accompanist—it took him years to understand why you had to do that and want to do that. If you only think of it as a subtraction, it will never work.

Could someone accompany Ella well if he wasn't really into it? In other words, he's a professional and it's a gig.

If you're Hank Jones. I don't know how he does it—and I'm not a good enough musician to explain it—he breaks the rules and makes it work. He's busy when spare or nothing is called for; he fills in those spaces that have to be left empty. So, that's really breaking the rules. But it's glorious. I don't know how he does it, but I know he does it. I know the singers don't get mad at him—so I know they dig it. I know I love it.

Well, Hank Jones is one hell of a piano player.

Earl Hines is a great piano player. If you heard Earl Hines with Ella Fitzgerald, you wouldn't have a good time.

And the pianist Paul Smith?

This is a man who has decided that being a great accompanist is a great achievement. He loved Ella, loves her. I think that that's very important. I think he understands also, better than I do, that there's more to rhythm than just swinging. You know, Rachmaninoff is a great piano player, and Paul Smith knows that. I find a lot of jazz people would be indifferent to that, because they don't understand—and I'm saying I'm guilty of this—they don't understand that there's more to rhythm—rhythm existed before jazz, and rhythmic wonder and strength existed before swing. There's nothing wrong with any of those statements of rhythmic contour and clarity of the articulation of the musical line, rhythmically by an instrument providing pitches. Paul Smith really understands that.

Jimmy Rowles?

Jimmy Rowles understands singing better than all the other ones. That's why he's so great for her and for any singer. He really understands singing.

Contrast Jimmy Rowles and Tommy Flanagan.

I'm willing to risk my life with either player. Send them in—let them save me. *(laughing)*

Talk about Ella's work with Oscar Peterson.

I think that it's an area, like many of the musical areas, where there's an unfortunate absence of information from Ella Fitzgerald's side of it. Working with Oscar

Peterson, like working with Art Tatum, is a very complex issue. And it can work out, even for all of its density, musically. And does work out. Obviously, they enjoyed doing it. There's no doubt that the idea that the two defining jazz artists of a whole generation, and the absolute climax of what would be the reigning concert and tour of the period, was Norman Granz's idea. If you had taken any other brain, whether it was a genius like Norman Granz, or just somebody who is a fan, and say: "I want to have the jazz event of the fifties to conclude with two artists on stage, and they could be anybody," they wouldn't have been Ella Fitzgerald and Oscar Peterson. These are his two definitive champions. But musically, it's a very successful thing. They almost always leaned towards her ability to be a spirited horn and that's a good way to do it. You get the same mixing it up as you do when you get Oscar Peterson with Stan Getz, or Roy Eldridge, or any of the—Sonny Stitt, even, was with the JATP. So, it works. Even though some are not an "Ella-type" musician. The way Ella Fitzgerald was packaged is always really, from at least 1956 onward, filtered through Norman Granz's desire. And he really saw in his mind's ear a concert ending with the two of them tearing it up. And they did it for him with no misses. So, he was right.

Is Ella Fitzgerald still important?

Yes. First of all, I don't think that her musical skills, her voice have been equaled, and certainly not surpassed, that there's no singer, certainly no jazz singer who has anything like those chops. She also swings. Swing isn't doing as well as people think it is. That level of rhythmical energy, while delivering music that precisely, with fixed words and notes—absolutely high level! And if you want to do it again on a live stage—we can't have her—listening to her is a good way to get there. It certainly is something I would strongly suggest. Her records are exquisite. She lived in the age of hi-fi—a lot of people have trouble with the Armstrong Hot Fives, but the musical information is there—but here with Ella, the music is gloriously recorded. Her impact, in terms of her influence—you really have to have a lot of technique and an unerring ear if you're going to derive a lot from her. To set out to be—you can synthesize some singers' essence—and I guess you could with Billie Holiday—as far as range is concerned, Holiday had an exceedingly limited range—I don't think she could sing a tenth. I think Ella has three octaves and a minor third, the spread. I didn't listen to every record, but I have documented that spread. And that's uncommon. She rarely uses her little—that voice she does on that "Frosty the Snowman," that fake voice—those are some incredibly high notes. I don't know how she hit them. She extends her range even a little bit more into her altissimo. Still, for the delivery of the elements that a singer is to deliver, she's unsurpassed. She's the voice of the century in that regard—in the century that recording began. So, we can't compare anything earlier, but we will compare in the future. If you really want to be the singer of the twenty-first century, or the singer of the twenty-second century, somebody's going to pit them against Ella Fitzgerald doing Porgy in Rome on April 25, 1958, and say: "Well, can you do this—and then come back and scat 'Stompin' at the Savoy' with Oscar Peterson? Go ahead, you got it." I hope someone does it again. It will have to sound different. It won't be like Elvis Presley clones standing on stage. They're not Elvis Presley, anyway.

So you agree, as I do, that Ella is the greatest non-operatic singer of the twentieth century?

I don't need the operatic qualification. For vocal chops, the greatest vocal chops of the twentieth century. Best for chops, no doubt about it. Retire the award. She cuts everybody. I like Rosa Ponselle, I really love Rosa Ponselle—and I have all those early records—I play them on Louis's birthday—Galli-Curci—and John Mc-Cormick's a genius—I don't know if anybody cares anymore about phrasing and breathing, but if they want to re-learn it, just get John McCormick out of the 78s dust bin and you'll be just tightened up wonderfully. I bet you Ella Fitzgerald knew about John McCormick.

APPENDIX 2

A Selection of Ella's Honors and Awards

MISCELLANEOUS

1967

- Woman of the Year *(Los Angeles Times)*
- Pied Piper Award of the American Society of Composers, Authors and Publishers (ASCAP)

October 1974

- Dedication of the Ella Fitzgerald Center for the Performing Arts, University of Maryland Eastern Shore

October 17, 1976

- Award of Distinction of the National Association of Sickle Cell Diseases

December 1979

- Inducted into *Down Beat* Hall of Fame

December 2, 1979

- Kennedy Center Honors Medal (Washington, D.C.)

March 7, 1980

- Will Rogers Memorial Award (Beverly Hills Chamber of Commerce & Civic Association)

October 10, 1980

- Lord & Taylor Rose Award—Presented to "the person whose outstanding contribution in her field has enriched all of our lives"

February 17, 1982

- Hasty Pudding Club (Harvard University) Woman of the Year

May 27, 1983

- George Peabody Medal for Distinguished Contributions to American Music (Johns Hopkins University)

March 1984

- Whitney M. Young, Jr. Award (Los Angeles Urban League)—Presented annually to individuals who make outstanding contributions toward racial and economic equality

June 19, 1987

- National Medal of Arts

1988

- Lincoln Center Medallion (New York City)

April 28, 1989

- The Society of Singers names its annual award for lifetime achievement the "Ella"

April 29, 1989

- George & Ira Gershwin Award for Outstanding Achievement

May 30, 1990

- Commander of Arts and Letters (France)

April 13, 1991

- Cole Porter "You're the Top" Centennial Award—Crystal sculpture engraved "In recognition of outstanding achievements for sustaining the Cole Porter legend, and for winning new audiences to appreciate his genius."

1992

- Magnum Opus Award for Lifetime Achievement (University of Southern California)

May 17, 1993

- New School Beacons in Jazz Award (New York)—Honors living musicians whose careers and achievements are central to the evolution of jazz

HONORARY DOCTORATES

Dartmouth College
Howard University
Princeton University
Talladega College
University of Maryland Eastern Shore
Washington University (St. Louis)
Yale University

GRAMMIES

1958
Best Jazz Performance (Individual)
Ella Fitzgerald Sings the Duke Ellington Song Book

Best Pop Vocal Performance
Ella Fitzgerald Sings the Irving Berlin Song Book

1959
Best Jazz Performance, Soloist
Ella Swings Lightly (Vocal)

Best Pop Vocal Performance, Female
"But Not for Me"

1960
Best Pop Vocal Performance Single Record or Track, Female
"Mack the Knife"

Best Pop Vocal Performance, Album, Female
Ella in Berlin: Mack the Knife

1962
Best Solo Vocal Performance, Female
Ella Swings Brightly with Nelson

1967
Lifetime Achievement Award

1976

Best Jazz Vocal Performance

Fitzgerald & Pass ... Again

1979

Best Jazz Vocal Performance

"Fine and Mellow"

1980

Best Jazz Vocal Performance, Female

A Perfect Match: Ella & Basie

1981

Best Jazz Vocal Performance, Female

Digital III at Montreux

1983

Best Jazz Vocal Performance, Female

The Best is Yet to Come

1991

Best Jazz Vocal Performance, Female

All That Jazz

DOWN BEAT READERS POLL

First Place—Female Vocalist

1937–1939, 1953–1970

DOWN BEAT CRITICS POLL

First Place—Female Vocalist

1953–1971, 1974

Notes

FOREWORD

1. Johnson, *Ella Fitzgerald.*

PREFACE

1. *Time,* November 27, 1964.
2. Lees, *Singers and the Song II,* p. 150.
3. *Down Beat,* November 18, 1965.
4. Giddins, *Visions of Jazz,* p. 197.
5. Lydon, *Ray Charles: Man and Music,* p. 396.
6. *Newark Star-Ledger,* May 4, 1994.

CHAPTER 1: THE ELLA MYSTIQUE

Author's interviews with Tommy Flanagan and Virginia Wicks.

1. *Down Beat,* September 1995.
2. Crowther and Pinfold, *Singing Jazz,* p. 136.
3. *New York Times,* April 25, 1993.
4. *Home News,* May 22, 1980.
5. "Ella: A Voice We'll Never Forget," *Down Beat,* September 1996.
6. *New York Times,* November 24, 1974.
7. "The Ella Fitzgerald Legacy," *Down Beat,* September 1996.
8. *Ebony,* May 1949.
9. *Melody Maker,* May 10, 1958.
10. Nicholson, *First Lady of Jazz,* p. 191.
11. *New York Times,* November 24, 1974.
12. Johnson, *Ella Fitzgerald,* p. 205.
13. Interview with Lou Levy by Steve Voce, Jazz Institute of Chicago, 1981.

CHAPTER 2: OVERVIEW

1. Gourse, *Seven Decades of Commentary,* p. xvi.
2. *Newark Star-Ledger,* April 26, 1997.
3. Lees, *Singers and the Song II,* p. 152.
4. *Jazz Times,* November 1983.
5. Fidelman, *First Lady of Song,* p. 4.
6. *Los Angeles Times,* January 30, 1983.
7. *New York Times,* June 23, 1996.
8. *Biography*—"Ella Fitzgerald: Forever Ella," A&E/New Video.
9. Nicholson, *First Lady of Jazz,* p. 22.
10. Maher, introduction to *American Popular Song: The Great Innovators, 1900–1950,* p. xxxvi.
11. Stuessy and Lipscomb, *Rock and Roll,* p. 31.
12. Ibid., p. 103.
13. O'Neill, *Coming Apart,* p. 23.
14. *Variety,* March 12, 1980.
15. *Variety,* March 28, 1984.
16. *Newark Star-Ledger,* June 13, 1990.

CHAPTER 3: THE INFLUENTIAL SINGERS

Author's interviews with Virginia Wicks and Phil Schaap.

1. *New York Times,* April 25, 1993.
2. Collier, *Louis Armstrong,* pp. 99–100.
3. Bergreen, *Louis Armstrong,* p. 267.
4. In his Fitzgerald biography, Stuart Nicholson points out that both Brian Rust and Will Friedwald have cited several recorded scat solos by other singers—among them, Cliff Edwards, Don Redman, Johnny Marvin, Gene Austin, and Lee Morse—prior to Armstrong's version of "Heebie Jeebies." (Nicholson, *First Lady of Jazz,* pp. 89–90.)
5. Bergreen, *Louis Armstrong,* p. 274.
6. Collier, *Louis Armstrong,* p. 203.
7. Friedwald, *Jazz Singing,* p. 29. Bing Crosby (1904–1977), the most popular singer of the swing era, was among the first white vocalists to absorb the Louis Armstrong style. Although his scatting and rhythmic invention were not at the lofty level of Armstrong's, Crosby was nonetheless very talented and highly influential. "During his most prominent years, from 1934 to 1954, Crosby held a nearly unrivaled command over all three key entertainment media, racking up legendary phonograph sales, radio ratings, and motion-picture grosses," noted Gary Giddins (Giddins, *Bing Crosby,* p. 8). Crosby had begun forging his fame when Paul Whiteman hired him to sing with his orchestra in 1926. Crosby also sang with Alton Rinker (brother of Mildred Bailey) and Harry Barris in The Rhythm Boys, a trio put together by Whiteman about a year later in New York. Henry Pleasants has concluded that "Bing's career suggests rather an assimilative, adaptive disposition. . . . [H]e was a creature of his time. He was influential not so much because he was original, but because he reflected or embodied, both in his singing and his person, his own social and musical environment" (Pleasants,

The Great American Popular Singers, p. 128). Crosby represented the common man and this undoubtedly contributed to his immense appeal. With a cool and easygoing demeanor that balanced nicely with his fluid baritone voice, his singing style was at once effortless and spirited. "Bing Crosby . . . sounded like a nice young fellow singing with his pals over a beer," remarked James Lincoln Collier, "and he made himself a fortune" (Collier, *Benny Goodman,* p. 131).

8. Collier, *Louis Armstrong,* p. 240.

9. Liner notes, *The Complete Ella Fitzgerald and Louis Armstrong* (Verve 314 537 284-2).

10. Ibid.

11. *Playboy,* November 1957.

12. Nicholson, *First Lady of Jazz,* p. 164.

13. Ibid., p. 140.

14. *New York Times,* June 15, 1986.

15. Gourse, *Sassy,* p. 207.

16. Harrison, *Black Pearls,* p. 51. Ma Rainey (1886–1939), whose given name was Gertrude, was born on April 26, 1886, in Columbus, Georgia. While she was still in her early teens a minstrel show performer, Will Rainey, heard her singing at a talent show and fell for her. The two wedded in 1904 and subsequently traveled for several years under the moniker of Ma and Pa Rainey. Ma Rainey often sang the blues during her shows. In 1923, Paramount Records signed her and she recorded for the label for the next five years. "Ma Rainey . . . was the first of the giants and the mother of them all," said Barry Ulanov. "She was thirty-seven . . . and a veteran of the tent shows, the cabarets, and the meeting houses, all the places where one sang on the Negro circuit" (Ulanov, *History of Jazz,* p. 95). Rainey recorded with some of the top musicians of the day, including Louis Armstrong. Her talent was admired by all with whom she worked and it is likely that even the great Armstrong picked up a few tricks from her. Rainey also taught and inspired Bessie Smith at the beginning of her career. Author Daphne Duvall Harrison has described Rainey as "a versatile singer who sang variety songs and blues in a voice with a gravelly timbre and a range of approximately one octave. . . . Her singing retained those characteristics most admired by Africans and Afro-Americans—buzzing sound, huskiness, satirical inflections, ability to translate everyday experiences into living sound. Her dynamism fueled with empathy drew her listeners into the mood of a blues" (Harrison, *Black Pearls,* p. 39).

17. Hammond and Townsend, *John Hammond on Record,* p. 46.

18. Harrison, *Black Pearls,* p. 52.

19. Collier, *Louis Armstrong,* p. 137.

20. Finkelstein, "Jazz: A People's Music," p. 143.

21. Schuller, *Early Jazz,* pp. 237, 237n.

22. Hammond and Townsend, *John Hammond on Record,* p. 119.

23. Erenberg, *Swingin' the Dream,* p. 19.

24. Liner notes, *Ethel Waters Souvenir Album* (Decca A-348). This was a compilation on five 10-inch records that Decca released in 1943. The selections were comprised of eight tracks by Waters from previous recordings, as well as two previously unreleased tracks.

25. Pleasants, *The Great American Popular Singers,* pp. 91–92.

26. A number of writers have mentioned Waters and Armstrong, as well as Bing Crosby, in the same breath with respect to their influence on jazz-inflected popular singing.

27. Feather, *The Passion for Jazz,* p. 64.

28. *Village Voice,* October 10, 1977.

29. Waters and Samuels, *Sparrow,* p. 261.

30. *Village Voice,* October 10, 1977.

31. *New York Times,* September 2, 1977.

32. *Swing,* June 1940.

33. Ibid.

34. Pleasants, *The Great American Popular Singers,* p. 144.

35. Friedwald, *Jazz Singing,* p. 72.

36. *Down Beat,* August 1, 1940.

37. Friedwald, *Jazz Singing,* p. 76.

38. Giddins, *Bing Crosby,* p. 122.

39. *Down Beat,* January 25, 1952.

40. *Down Beat,* October 15, 1944.

41. Ibid.

42. *Storyville,* June–July 1977.

43. *Jazz Journal,* January 1974.

44. Schuller, *Early Jazz,* p. 642n.

45. *Down Beat,* November 1, 1944.

46. *Storyville,* June–July 1977.

47. *New York Times,* October 12, 1976.

48. Ibid.

49. *Down Beat,* October 15, 1944.

50. Nicholson, *Billie Holiday,* p. 27.

51. Delannoy, *Lester Young,* p. 55.

52. Erenberg, *Swingin' the Dream,* p. 171.

53. *Down Beat,* February 1938.

54. Nicholson, *Billie Holiday,* p. 231.

55. *Esquire,* June 1945.

56. Liner notes, MJCD 803. *Masters of Jazz Series: Anthology of Scat Singing,* vol. 3, 1933–41. Released in 1995 by Média 7, Nanterre, France.

57. *Esquire,* June 1945.

58. *Pre-Bop: Leo Watson, Earl Fatha Hines, Shorty Sherock,* Bob Thiele Music BBM1-0940. Bob Thiele Music, Ltd. was manufactured and distributed by RCA Records. This album, released in 1975, contained reissues of original 78 rpm recordings provided by Leonard Feather.

59. *Down Beat,* June 16, 1950.

60. *Metronome,* July 1950.

61. *Pre-Bop,* Bob Thiele Music BBM1-0940.

CHAPTER 4: THE CHICK WEBB YEARS

1. *Modern Drummer,* January 1988.

2. Korall, *Drummin' Men,* p. 11.

3. Ibid., p. 14.

4. Tormé, *Traps*, p. 185.

5. *Down Beat*, September 1938.

6. Giddins, *Visions of Jazz*, p. 138.

7. Simon, *The Big Bands*, p. 440.

8. Nicholson, *First Lady of Jazz*, pp. 34–36.

9. *Biography*—"Ella Fitzgerald: Forever Ella," A&E/New Video.

10. Liner notes, *Ella Fitzgerald: The Early Years—Part 1* (Decca Jazz GRD-2-618).

11. Ellington, *Music Is My Mistress*, p. 100.

12. Nicholson, *First Lady of Jazz*, p. 50.

13. *Down Beat*, March 1937.

14. *Down Beat*, June 1937.

15. Gillespie and Fraser, *To Be or Not to Bop*, p. 133.

16. Pleasants, *The Great American Popular Singers*, p. 175.

17. *Ella Fitzgerald: The Early Years—Part 1* (Decca GRD-2-618) and *Ella Fitzgerald: The Early Years—Part 2* (GRD-2-623). On her first studio date with Chick Webb and his Orchestra, on June 12, 1935, Ella sang two songs: "I'll Chase the Blues Away," by Edgar Sampson and Ken Harrison, and "Love and Kisses," by Sonny Curtis.

18. Liner notes, *Ella Fitzgerald: The Early Years—Part 2* (Decca Jazz GRD-2-623).

19. Hammond and Townsend, *John Hammond on Record*, p. 195.

CHAPTER 5: THE BEBOP INFLUENCE

1. *Down Beat*, September 1996.

2. Crowther and Pinfold, *Singing Jazz*, p. 146.

3. Hyland, *Song Is Ended*, p. 293.

4. Armstrong, *His Own Words*, pp. 174–75.

5. Gillespie and Fraser, *To Be or Not to Bop*, p. 486.

6. Davis and Troupe, *Miles: The Autobiography*, p. 316.

7. Gillespie and Fraser, *To Be or Not to Bop*, pp. 272–73.

8. Ibid., p. 273.

9. Shipton, *Groovin' High*, p. 193.

10. Gillespie and Fraser, *To Be or Not to Bop*, p. 350.

11. *Ebony*, May 1949.

12. Liner notes, *Ella in Hamburg* (Verve LP V 4069).

CHAPTER 6: NORMAN GRANZ

Author's interviews with Phil Schaap and Tommy Flanagan.

1. "Writer Underlines Granz's Top Jazz Accomplishment," *Down Beat*, December 15, 1954.

2. Tormé, *Traps*, p. 95.

3. *Down Beat*, October 1979.

4. Ibid.

5. Ibid.

6. Lees, *Oscar Peterson*, p. 76.

7. Hammond and Townsend, *John Hammond on Record*, pp. 293–94.

8. *Down Beat*, November 18, 1946.

9. *Down Beat*, December 16, 1946.

10. *Down Beat*, April 1947.

11. Hammond and Townsend, *John Hammond on Record*, p. 341.

12. *Down Beat*, May 19, 1954.

13. Erenberg, *Swingin' the Dream*, p. 253.

14. *Down Beat*, October 1979.

15. *New York Times*, November 24, 1974.

16. *Down Beat*, February 20, 1957.

17. *Down Beat*, November 1979.

18. Riddle, *Arranged by Nelson Riddle*, p. 173.

19. Ellington, *Music Is My Mistress*, p. 238.

20. Nicholson, *First Lady of Jazz*, p. 180.

CHAPTER 7: THE ARRANGERS

Author's interviews with Phil Schaap and Virginia Wicks.

1. Nestico, *The Complete Arranger*, p. 1.

2. David, *Jazz Arranging*, p. 1.

3. Walker, *Dance Bands*, p. 15.

4. Ibid., p. 16.

5. Hennessey, *From Jazz to Swing*, p. 80.

6. *Nice Work If You Can Get It*, (Pablo PACD-2312-140-2).

7. *Down Beat*, January 15, 1947.

8. *Ebony*, June 1951.

9. *New York Times*, May 28, 1988.

10. Haskins, *Life through Jazz*, p. 140.

11. *New York Times*, June 15, 1986.

12. "A Voice We'll Never Forget," *Down Beat*, September 1996.

13. Liner notes, Verve LP MG V-4001-2. Reproduced on CD reissue. See *Ella Fitzgerald Sings the Cole Porter Song Book* (Verve 314 537 257-2) and *The Complete Ella Fitzgerald Song Books* (Verve 314 519 832-2) in CD Discography.

14. Liner notes, *The Complete Ella Fitzgerald Song Books*, (Verve 314 519 832-2).

15. *Down Beat*, October 1979.

16. Jablonski, *Alan Jay Lerner: A Biography*, pp. 22–23.

17. *Down Beat*, November 28, 1956.

18. *Down Beat*, April 4, 1957.

19. Liner notes, *The Complete Ella Fitzgerald Song Books*, (Verve 314 519 832-2).

20. Hajdu, *Lush Life*, p. 168.

21. *Playboy*, November 1957.

22. Collier, *Duke Ellington*, p. 185.

23. Clarke, *Penguin Encyclopedia*, p. 1868.

24. Taraborrelli, *Sinatra: A Complete Life*, pp. 162–63.

25. Riddle, *Arranged by Nelson Riddle*, p. 173.

26. Interview with Lou Levy by Steve Voce, Jazz Institute of Chicago, 1981.

27. Johnson, *Ella Fitzgerald*, p. 263.

28. Peyser, *George Gershwin*, pp. 172–73.

29. Riddle, *Arranged by Nelson Riddle*, p. 173.

30. Liner notes, *The Complete Ella Fitzgerald Song Books*, (Verve 314 519 832-2).

31. Williams, "Ella and Her Critics," in *Jazz Heritage*, p. 41.

32. Johnson, *Ella Fitzgerald*, p. 267.

33. Ibid., p. 239.

34. Liner notes, Verve LP V6-4054. Reproduced on CD reissue. See *Ella Fitzgerald Sings the Jerome Kern Song Book* (Verve 825 669-2) and *The Complete Ella Fitzgerald Song Books* (Verve 314 519 832-2) in CD Discography.

35. Johnson, *Ella Fitzgerald*, p. 269.

36. Simon, *The Big Bands*, p. 360.

37. *Down Beat*, October 7, 1948.

38. Liner notes, *The Complete Ella Fitzgerald Song Books*, (Verve 314 519 832-2).

39. Friedwald, *Jazz Singing*, p. 150.

40. Liner notes, Verve LP V-4046-2. Reproduced on CD reissue. See *Ella Fitzgerald Sings the Harold Arlen Song Book* (Verve 817 527-2 and Verve 817 528-2) and *The Complete Ella Fitzgerald Song Books* (Verve 314 519 832-2) in CD Discography.

41. *Down Beat*, November 3, 1948.

42. *Oakland Tribune*, December 28, 1958.

43. Liner notes, *Ella Swings Lightly* (Verve 314 517 535-2).

44. Fidelman, *First Lady of Song*, p. 151.

45. Ibid., p. 172.

46. Discography by Phil Schaap in Nicholson, *First Lady of Jazz*, p. 270.

47. *Ella Fitzgerald: 75th Birthday Celebration* (Decca GRD-2-619).

48. Fidelman, *First Lady of Song*, p. 183.

49. Lydon, *Ray Charles: Man and Music*, p. 166.

50. Fidelman, *First Lady of Song*, p. 195.

51. *Things Ain't What They Used to Be (and You Better Believe It)* (Warner/Reprise 9 26023-2).

CHAPTER 8: BENNY, DUKE, AND COUNT

1. Taraborrelli, *Sinatra: A Complete Life*, p. 37.

2. Firestone, *Swing, Swing, Swing*, p. 150.

3. *Down Beat*, August 1, 1942.

4. Connor, *Off the Record*, p. 138.

5. *Ella Fitzgerald: 1935–1937* (Classics 500).

6. *Swing into Spring: The Classic Broadcast of April 9, 1958* (Sandy Hook CDSH 2057).

7. *Ella Fitzgerald in Concert*, Video Yesteryear 763.

8. Collier, *Duke Ellington*, pp. 302–4.

9. Wilder, *American Popular Song*, p. 412.

10. Ellington, *Music Is My Mistress*, p. 20.

11. Tucker, *Ellington: The Early Years*, p. 170.

12. Ellington, *Music Is My Mistress*, p. 156.

13. *Down Beat,* July 2, 1964.

14. *New York Times,* November 24, 1974.

15. Liner notes, Verve LP V6-4070. Reproduced on CD reissue. See *Ella at Duke's Place* (Verve 314 529 700-2) in CD Discography.

16. Hajdu, *Lush Life,* p. 242.

17. *Ella and Duke at the Cote d'Azur* (Verve 314 539 030-2); and *Ella Fitzgerald/Duke Ellington: Cote d'Azur Concerts* (Verve 314 539 033-2).

18. Jewell, *Duke,* p. 175.

19. Nicholson, *First Lady of Jazz,* p. 194.

20. *The Atlantic Monthly,* August 1984.

21. *New York Times,* April 27, 1984.

22. Pearson, *Goin' to Kansas City,* p. 136.

23. Basie and Murray, *Good Morning Blues,* p. 7.

24. Ibid., p. 11.

25. Hammond and Townsend, *John Hammond on Record,* p. 167.

26. Simon, *The Big Bands,* p. 82.

27. Dance, *The World of Count Basie,* p. 4.

28. Hammond and Townsend, *John Hammond on Record,* p. 170.

29. *Down Beat,* February 10, 1954.

30. Gourse, *Every Day,* p. 74.

31. Basie and Murray, *Good Morning Blues,* p. 332.

32. Liner notes, Verve LP V6-4061. Reproduced on CD reissue. See *Ella and Basie* (Verve 314 539 059-2) in CD Discography.

33. Basie and Murray, *Good Morning Blues,* p. 347.

34. *Ella Fitzgerald: 1941–1944* (Classics 840).

35. Johnson, *Ella Fitzgerald,* p. 259.

36. *New York Times,* November 24, 1974.

37. Liner notes, *A Classy Pair* (Pablo PACD-2312-132-2).

CHAPTER 9: THE PRINCIPAL ACCOMPANISTS

Author's interviews with Phil Schaap, Virginia Wicks, and Tommy Flanagan.

1. *Contemporary Keyboard,* July 1982.

2. *Wall Street Journal,* November 9, 1992.

3. *Down Beat,* October 30, 1958.

4. Lees, *Oscar Peterson,* p. 15.

5. Ibid., p. 26.

6. Porter, Ullman, and Hazell, *Origins to the Present,* p. 279.

7. Crow, *Jazz Anecdotes,* pp. 165–66.

8. Liner notes, *Ella and Oscar* (Pablo 2310-759).

9. Fidelman, *First Lady of Song,* p. 227.

10. Nicholson, *First Lady of Jazz,* p. 222

11. *Down Beat,* September 1995.

12. JSP Records of London, England, has issued remastered recordings on a superb double-CD collection titled *Louis Armstrong: The Big Band Recordings 1930–32* (JSPCD3401).

13. *Baltimore City Paper,* February 15, 1995.

14. Decca LP DL5300. Reissued on CD. See *Pure Ella* (Decca GRD-636) in CD Discography.

15. *Down Beat*, September 22, 1948.

16. Decca LP DL8069. Reissued on CD. See *Pure Ella* (Decca GRD-636) in CD Discography.

17. *Down Beat*, February 23, 1955.

18. *Contemporary Keyboard*, July 1982.

19. *New York Times*, September 6, 1985.

20. *Pure Ella* (Decca GRD-636).

21. Johnson, *Ella Fitzgerald*, p. 270.

22. *Down Beat*, February 23, 1955.

23. *Village Voice*, December 1976.

24. *Disc & That Magazine* 1, no. 5 (1978).

25. Nicholson, *First Lady of Jazz*, p. 177.

26. Fidelman, *First Lady of Song*, p. 247.

27. *The Intimate Ella* (Verve 839 838-2).

28. Gitler, *Swing to Bop*, pp. 266–67.

29. *Down Beat*, August 26, 1949.

30. *Down Beat*, February 20, 1958.

31. Liner notes, Verve LP V6-4053. Reissued on CD. See *Clap Hands, Here Comes Charlie* (Verve 835 646-2) in CD Discography.

32. Interview with Lou Levy by Steve Voce, Jazz Institute of Chicago, 1981.

33. *Down Beat*, July 1982.

34. *Down Beat*, January 13, 1966.

35. Dance, *The World of Count Basie*, p. 295.

36. *The New Yorker*, November 20, 1978.

37. *Down Beat*, July 1982.

38. *Ella Fitzgerald in Budapest* (Pablo PACD-5308-2).

39. Crowther and Pinfold, *Singing Jazz*, p. 145.

40. Producer's note, *Montreux '77: Ella Fitzgerald with the Tommy Flanagan Trio* (Pablo 2308-206).

41. *Crescendo International*, January 1982.

42. *Contemporary Keyboard*, July 1982.

43. Ibid.

44. Ibid.

45. Nicholson, *First Lady of Jazz*, p. 228.

46. Fidelman, *First Lady of Song*, p. 259.

47. *Contemporary Keyboard*, July 1982.

48. *Crescendo International*, January 1982.

49. *Musician*, April 1988.

50. *International Herald Tribune*, August 4, 1981.

51. *Los Angeles Times*, January 30, 1983.

52. *New York Times*, June 24, 1985.

53. Liner notes, *Fitzgerald and Pass . . . Again* (Pablo 2310-772).

54. Johnson, *Ella Fitzgerald*, p. 277.

55. *Speak Love* (Pablo 2310-888).

Ella Fitzgerald—
CD Discography

Ella Fitzgerald is one of the two or three most widely recorded artists of all time. She did almost all of her dates for Decca, Verve, Pablo, and to a lesser extent, Capitol. This discography is comprised of all the recordings she made for these companies that have been reissued on CD to date, plus the best compilations derived from the original releases. Extra tracks (either previously unreleased tracks or alternate takes) on CD reissues and compilations are indicated. Also included here are a number of important releases that are available from other labels. The years in which the recordings were made are indicated for all original releases, as well as for the compilations when practical. For the few albums that were not released within one year of the recording date, or that were recorded over a number of nonconsecutive years, the year of the release will be indicated. When a CD contains more than one version of a title, the running total will appear in parentheses after each listing of the title. Catalog numbers in parentheses indicate earlier releases or imports of the same CD. The catalog numbers in bold indicate the most current or only available releases. In a few cases, the listed import is the only available CD reissue of that recording.

To include the contents of imports and new compilations by companies other than those in this discography—and the list regularly grows longer—would be redundant. This discography does not claim, nor intend, to be all-inclusive. It is a CD listing only, with no information about record singles, long-playing albums, as-yet-unreleased material, and releases from the more obscure or hard-to-obtain labels. However, this discography is up-to-date and includes every important Fitzgerald recording that is available on CD through the beginning of 2003. As such, it is a comprehensive document of the superb body of recorded work that Fitzgerald accomplished during her brilliant career.

Abbreviations

alt	alternate take	mono	monoaural
b	bass	org	organ
bs	baritone saxophone	p	piano
cl	clarinet	p.u.	previously unreleased
d	drums	as	alto saxophone
eb	electric bass	ts	tenor saxophone
EF	Ella Fitzgerald	tpt	trumpet
flgl	flugelhorn	trb	trombone
frh	French horn	tu	tuba
g	guitar	vib	vibraphone (vibraharp)
hca	harmonica	vln	violin
instr	instrumental	vtrb	valve trombone
JATP	Jazz at the Philharmonic	vo	vocal

DECCA

Ella Fitzgerald: The Early Years—Part 1: With Chick Webb and His Orchestra (1935–1938)

(2 CDs) **GRD-2-618**

I'll Chase the Blues Away/Love and Kisses/Rhythm and Romance/Under the Spell of the Blues/When I Get Low I Get High/Sing Me a Swing Song (and Let Me Dance)/A Little Bit Later On/Love, You're Just a Laugh/Mr. Paganini/Vote for Mr. Rhythm/My Last Affair/Organ Grinder's Swing/Shine/Darktown Strutters' Ball/Oh, Yes, Take Another Guess/You Showed Me the Way/Cryin' Mood/If You Ever Should Leave/ Everyone's Wrong but Me/Just a Simple Melody/I Got a Guy/Rock It for Me/I Want to Be Happy/The Dipsy Doodle/If Dreams Come True/Hallelujah!/Bei Mir Bist du Schoen/ It's My Turn Now/It's Wonderful/I Was Doing All Right/A-Tisket, A-Tasket/Heart of Mine/I'm Just a Jitterbug/You Can't Be Mine (and Someone Else's, Too)/If You Only Knew/Pack Up Your Sins and Go to the Devil/McPherson Is Rehearsin' (to Swing)/ Everybody Step/Wacky Dust/Strictly from Dixie/F. D. R. Jones/It's Foxy/I Found My Yellow Basket

Ella Fitzgerald: The Early Years—Part 2: With Chick Webb and His Orchestra (1935–1938)

(2 CDs) **GRD-2-623**

Undecided/ 'Tain't What You Do (It's the Way That Cha Do It)/My Heart Belongs to Daddy/Chew-Chew-Chew (Chew Your Bubble Gum)/Don't Worry 'bout Me/If You Ever Change Your Mind/Little White Lies/Coochi-Coochi-Coo/Betcha Nickel/Stairway

to the Stars/I Want the Waiter (with the Water)/Out of Nowhere/My Last Goodbye/
Billy (I Always Dream of Billy)/You're Gonna Lose Your Gal/After I Say I'm Sorry/
Moon Ray/Sugar Babies/The Starlit Hour/What's the Matter with Me?/Baby, Won't
You Please Come Home?/If It Weren't for You/Imagination/Deedle-De-Dum/Shake
Down the Stars/Gulf Coast Blues/Five O'Clock Whistle/Louisville, K-Y/Taking a
Chance on Love/Cabin in the Sky/I'm the Lonesomest Girl in Town/Three Little Words/
The One I Love Belongs to Somebody Else/The Muffin Man/Keep Cool, Fool/No Noth-
ing/My Man (Mon Homme)/I Can't Believe That You're in Love with Me/I Must Have
That Man/When My Sugar Walks down the Street/I Got It Bad (and That Ain't Good)/
I Can't Help Lovin' Dat Man

The War Years (1941–1947)

(2 CDs) **GRD-2-628**

Compilation: EF; The Ink Spots; The Delta Rhythm Boys; Louis Jordan; Louis
Armstrong; Bob Haggart; others.

Jim/This Love of Mine/Somebody Nobody Loves/You Don't Know What Love Is/Make
Love to Me/Mama, Come Home/My Heart and I Decided/He's My Guy/Cow Cow
Boogie/Time Alone Will Tell/Once Too Often/Into Each Life Some Rain Must Fall/I'm
Making Believe/And Her Tears Flowed Like Wine/I'm Confessin' (That I Love You)/
I'm Beginning to See the Light/That's the Way It Is/It's Only a Paper Moon/Cry You
Out of My Heart/A Kiss Goodnight/Benny's Coming Home on Saturday/Flyin' Home/
Stone Cold Dead in the Market/Petootie Pie/You Won't Be Satisfied (until You Break
My Heart)/The Frim Fram Sauce/I'm Just a Lovely So and So/I Didn't Mean a Word
I Said/For Sentimental Reasons/It's a Pity to Say Goodnight/Guilty/Sentimental Jour-
ney/A Sunday Kind of Love/That's My Desire/Oh, Lady Be Good/Don't You Think I
Ought to Know?/You're Breakin' In a New Heart/I Want to Learn about Love/That
Old Feeling/My Baby Likes to Bebop (and I Like to Bebop Too)/No Sense/How High
the Moon (alt 1)/*How High the Moon* (alt 2)

The Last Decca Years, 1949–1954

GRD-668

Compilation: EF; Louis Armstrong; Studio orchestra, arranged and conducted by
Sy Oliver.

In the Evening (When the Sun Goes Down)/Basin Street Blues/Solid as a Rock/I've
Got the World on a String/Dream a Little Dream of Me/Can Anyone Explain?/Because
of Rain/I Don't Want to Take a Chance/There Never Was a Baby Like My Baby/Give
a Little, Get a Little/A Guy Is a Guy/Goody Goody/Mr. Paganini, Parts 1 and 2/Early
Autumn/Angel Eyes/Preview/Careless/Blue Lou/Melancholy Me/Lullaby of Birdland

Pure Ella

(1950, 1954) ("Ella Sings Gershwin" LP DL5300, "Songs in a Mellow Mood" LP
DL8068) **GRD-636**

EF; Ellis Larkins, p.

Someone to Watch over Me/My One and Only/But Not for Me/Looking for a Boy/I've
Got a Crush on You/How Long Has This Been Going On?/Maybe/Soon/I'm Glad There

Is You/What Is There to Say?/People Will Say We're in Love/Please Be Kind/Until the Real Thing Comes Along/Makin' Whoopee/Imagination/Star Dust/My Heart Belongs to Daddy/You Leave Me Breathless/Baby, What Else Can I Do?/Nice Work If You Can Get It

Ella Fitzgerald: 75th Birthday Celebration: The Original Decca Recordings

(2 CDs) **GRD-2-619**

Compilation of Decca recordings 1938–1955: EF; various artists.

A-Tisket, A-Tasket/Undecided/Don't Worry about Me/Stairway to the Stars/Five O'Clock Whistle/Cow Cow Boogie/Into Each Life Some Rain Must Fall/It's Only a Paper Moon/Flying Home/Stone Cold Dead in the Market/You Won't Be Satisfied/I'm Just a Lucky So and So/I Didn't Mean a Word I Said/Oh, Lady Be Good/How High the Moon/My Happiness/Black Coffee/In the Evening When the Sun Goes Down/Basin Street Blues/I've Got the World on a String/Ain't Nobody's Business but My Own/Dream a Little Dream of Me/Smooth Sailing/Airmail Special/Rough Ridin'/Goody Goody/Angel Eyes/Mr. Paganini, Parts 1and 2/Preview/Blue Lou/I Wished on the Moon/Until the Real Thing Comes Along/Lullaby of Birdland/That Old Black Magic/Ol' Devil Moon/Lover, Come Back to Me/Between the Devil and the Deep Blue Sea/Hard Hearted Hannah/My One and Only Love

Ella: The Legendary Decca Recordings

(4 CDs) **GRD-648**

("The Best of Ella Fitzgerald" GRD-659, "Ella and Friends" GRD-663, "Pure Ella" GRD-636, and 25 additional selected tracks)

A-Tisket, A-Tasket/Undecided/Stairway to the Stars/Five O'Clock Whistle/Cow Cow Boogie/Flying Home/Stone Cold Dead in the Market/You Won't Be Satisfied (until You Break My Heart)/I'm Just a Lucky So and So/I Didn't Mean a Word I Said/Oh, Lady Be Good/How High the Moon/My Happiness/In the Evening (When the Sun Goes Down)/Smooth Sailing/Air Mail Special/Mr. Paganini, Parts 1 and 2/Blue Lou/Lullaby of Birdland/Hard Hearted Hannah/The Frim Fram Sauce/Dream a Little Dream of Me/Can Anyone Explain?/Would You Like to Take a Walk?/Who Walks In When I Walk Out?/Into Each Life Some Rain Must Fall/I'm Making Believe/I'm Beginning to See the Light/I Still Feel the Same about You/Petootie Pie/Baby, It's Cold Outside/Don't Cry, Cry Baby/Ain't Nobody's Business but My Own/I'll Never Be Free/It's Only a Paper Moon/(Gonna) Cry You Out of My Heart/(I Love You) For Sentimental Reasons/It's a Pity to Say Goodnight/Fairy Tales/I Gotta Have My Baby Back/Someone to Watch over Me/My One and Only/But Not for Me/Looking for a Boy/I've Got a Crush on You/How Long Has This Been Going On?/Maybe/Soon/I'm Glad There Is You/What Is There to Say?/People Will Say We're in Love/Please Be Kind/Until the Real Thing Comes Along/Makin' Whoopee/Imagination/Stardust/My Heart Belongs to Daddy/You Leave Me Breathless/Baby, What Else Can I Do?/Nice Work If You Can Get It/Basin Street Blues/I've Got the World on a String/Goody Goody/Angel Eyes/Happy Talk/I'm Gonna Wash That Man Right Outa My Hair/Black Coffee/I Wished on the Moon/A Sunday Kind of Love/That's My Desire/Thanks for the Memory/It Might As Well Be Spring/You'll Never Know/I Can't Get Started/That Old Black Magic/Old

Devil Moon/Lover, Come Back to Me/Between the Devil and the Deep Blue Sea/(Love Is) The Tender Trap/My One and Only Love

The Early Years—Parts 1 and 2

GRD-654 (See GRD-2-618 and GRD-2-623)

The Best of Ella Fitzgerald

GRD-659

Compilation: EF; various artists.

A-Tisket, A-Tasket/Undecided/Stairway to the Stars/Five O'Clock Whistle/Cow Cow Boogie/Flyin' Home/Stone Cold Dead in the Market/You Won't Be Satisfied (until You Break My Heart)/I'm Just a Lucky So and So/I Didn't Mean a Word I Said/Oh, Lady Be Good/How High the Moon/My Happiness/In the Evening When the Sun Goes Down/Smooth Sailing/Airmail Special/Mr. Paganini, Parts 1 and 2/Blue Lou/Lullaby of Birdland/Hard Hearted Hannah

Ella and Friends

GRD-663

Compilation: EF; Louis Armstrong; The Ink Spots; The Delta Rhythm Boys; The Mills Brothers.

The Frim Fram Sauce/Dream a Little Dream of Me/Can Anyone Explain?/Would You Like to Take a Walk?/Who Walks In When I Walk Out?/Into Each Life Some Rain Must Fall/I'm Making Believe/I'm Beginning to See the Light/I Still Feel the Same about You/It's Only a Paper Moon/(Gonna) Cry You Out of My Heart/(I Love You) For Sentimental Reasons/It's a Pity to Say Goodnight/Fairy Tales/I Gotta Have My Baby Back

Priceless Jazz: Ella Fitzgerald

GRD-9870

Compilation: EF; various artists.

A-Tisket, A-Tasket/Goody Goody/Someone to Watch over Me/Makin' Whoopee/Flyin' Home/Nice Work If You Can Get It/How High the Moon/But Not for Me/Lover, Come Back to Me/Mr. Paganini, Parts 1 and 2/Oh, Lady Be Good/My Heart Belongs to Daddy/Lullaby of Birdland/It Might As Well Be Spring/Stairway to the Stars/Old Devil Moon

Priceless Jazz: More Ella Fitzgerald

GRD 9916

Compilation: EF; Studio orchestras, arranged and conducted by Benny Carter, Sy Oliver, and Bob Haggart; Ellis Larkins; others.

Between the Devil and the Deep Blue Sea/Angel Eyes/Hard Hearted Hannah/My One and Only Love/I've Got the World on a String/Baby, It's Cold Outside/Basin Street

Blues/Airmail Special/I Gotta Have My Baby Back/Looking for a Boy/Black Coffee/A Sunday Kind of Love/Soon/Thanks for the Memory/That Old Black Magic/Stardust/ Undecided

Swingsation: Ella Fitzgerald with Chick Webb

GRD-9921

Compilation: EF; Chick Webb and His Orchestra.

Sing Me a Swing Song (and Let Me Dance)/Blue Minor/When I Get Low I Get High/ A Little Bit Later On/Don't Be That Way/Vote for Mr. Rhythm/Organ Grinder's Swing/Blue Lou/Oh Yes, Take Another Guess/I Want to Be Happy/Clap Hands! Here Comes Charlie/A-Tisket, A-Tasket/I'm Just a Jitterbug/Harlem Congo/Wacky Dust/ Undecided/Tain't What You Do (It's the Way That Cha Do It)/Liza (All the Clouds'll Roll Away)

VERVE

NOTE: A catalog number preceded by the letters "POCJ" denotes a Verve import (Japan). Most imports are readily available, usually at increased prices.

Ella Fitzgerald Sings the Cole Porter Song Book—Volume One

(1956) **821 989-2** (See also Verve 314 537 257-2)

EF; Studio orchestra, arranged and conducted by Buddy Bregman.

All through the Night/Anything Goes/Miss Otis Regrets/Too Darn Hot/In the Still of the Night/I Get a Kick Out of You/Do I Love You/Always True to You in My Fashion/ Let's Do It (Let's Fall in Love)/Just One of Those Things/Ev'ry Time We Say Goodbye/ All of You/Begin the Beguine/Get Out of Town/I Am in Love/From This Moment On

Ella Fitzgerald Sings the Cole Porter Song Book—Volume Two

(1956) **821 990-2** (See also Verve 314 537 257-2)

EF; Studio orchestra, arranged and conducted by Buddy Bregman.

I Love Paris/You Do Something to Me/Ridin' High/Easy to Love/It's All Right with Me/Why Can't You Behave?/What Is This Thing Called Love?/You're the Top/Love for Sale/It's De-Lovely/Night and Day/Ace in the Hole/So in Love/I've Got You under My Skin/I Concentrate on You/Don't Fence Me In

Ella Fitzgerald Sings the Cole Porter Song Book

(1956) (Compilation of Volumes One and Two) **314 537 257-2**

Add: *You're the Top* (alt)/*I Concentrate on You* (alt)/*Let's Do It (Let's Fall in Love)* (alt)

Ella and Louis

(1956) (825 373-2) **314 543 304-2**

EF; Louis Armstrong, vo and tpt; Oscar Peterson, p; Herb Ellis, g; Ray Brown, b; Buddy Rich, d.

Can't We Be Friends?/Isn't This a Lovely Day?/Moonlight in Vermont/They Can't Take That Away from Me/Under a Blanket of Blue/Tenderly/A Foggy Day/Stars Fell on Alabama/Cheek to Cheek/The Nearness of You/April in Paris

Ella Fitzgerald Sings the Rodgers and Hart Songbook—Volume One

(1956) (POCJ-2129) **821 579-2** (See also Verve 314 537 258-2)

EF; Studio orchestra, arranged and conducted by Buddy Bregman.

Have You Met Miss Jones/You Took Advantage of Me/A Ship without a Sail/To Keep My Love Alive/Dancing on the Ceiling/The Lady Is a Tramp/With a Song in My Heart/ Manhattan/Johnny One Note/I Wish I Were in Love Again/Spring Is Here/It Never Entered My Mind/This Can't Be Love/Thou Swell/My Romance/Where or When/Little Girl Blue

Ella Fitzgerald Sings the Rodgers and Hart Song Book—Volume Two

(1956) (POCJ-2130) **821 580-2** (See also Verve 314 537 258-2)

EF; Studio orchestra, arranged and conducted by Buddy Bregman.

Give It Back to the Indians/Ten Cents a Dance/There's a Small Hotel/I Didn't Know What Time It Was/Ev'rything I've Got/I Could Write a Book/The Blue Room/My Funny Valentine/Bewitched/Mountain Greenery/Wait till You See Her/Lover/Isn't It Romantic/Here in My Arms/Blue Moon/My Heart Stood Still/I've Got Five Dollars

Ella Fitzgerald Sings the Rodgers and Hart Song Book

(Compilation of Volumes One and Two) **314 537 258-2**

Add: *Lover* (mono)

Ella Fitzgerald Sings the Duke Ellington Song Book

(1956, 1957) (3 CDs) **837 035-2** (See also Verve 314 537 259-2)

EF; Duke Ellington Orchestra.

Rockin' in Rhythm/Drop Me Off in Harlem/Day Dream/Caravan/Take the 'A' Train/ I Ain't Got Nothin' but the Blues/Clementine/I Didn't Know about You/I'm Beginning to See the Light/Lost in Meditation/Perdido/Cotton Tail/Do Nothin' till You Hear from Me/ Just A-Sittin' and A-Rockin'/Solitude/Rocks in My Bed/Satin Doll/Sophisticated Lady/Just Squeeze Me (but Don't Tease Me)/It Don't Mean a Thing (if It Ain't Got That Swing)/Azure/I Let a Song Go Out of My Heart/In a Sentimental Mood/Don't Get Around Much Anymore/Prelude to a Kiss/Mood Indigo/In a Mellow Tone/Love You Madly/Lush Life/Squatty Roo/I'm Just a Lucky So and So/All Too Soon/Everything but You/I Got It Bad (and That Ain't Good)/Bli-Blip/Chelsea Bridge/Portrait of Ella Fitzgerald/The E and D Blues (E for Ella, D for Duke)

Ella Fitzgerald Sings the Duke Ellington Song Book

(Reissue) **314 537 259-2**

> Add: *Chelsea Bridge* (rehearsal 1)/*Chelsea Bridge* (rehearsal 2)/*Chelsea Bridge* (rehearsal 3)/*Chelsea Bridge* (rehearsal 4)/*Chelsea Bridge* (rehearsal 5)/*Chelsea Bridge* (rehearsal 6)/*Chelsea Bridge* (rehearsal 7)/*Chelsea Bridge* (rehearsal 8)/*All Heart* (rehearsal)/*All Heart* (complete take 1)/*All Heart* (complete take 2)/*All Heart* (complete take 3)

Ella Fitzgerald, Billie Holiday, and Carmen McRae: At Newport

(1957) **314 559 809-2**

EF; Don Abney, p; Wendell Marshall, b; Jo Jones, d. (Tracks with Fitzgerald listed here.)

> *This Can't Be Love/I Got It Bad (and That Ain't Good)/Body and Soul/Too Close for Comfort/Lullaby of Birdland/I've Got a Crush on You/I'm Gonna Sit Right Down and Write Myself a Letter/April in Paris/Air Mail Special/I Can't Give You Anything but Love*

Ella and Louis Again

(1957) (2 CDs) (825 374-2) **440 065 390-2**

EF; Louis Armstrong, vo and tpt; Oscar Peterson, p; Herb Ellis, g; Ray Brown, b; Louis Bellson, d. (*Fitzgerald only; †Armstrong only.)

> *Don't Be That Way/†Makin' Whoopee/They All Laughed/*Comes Love/Autumn in New York/†Let's Do It/Stompin' at the Savoy/I Won't Dance/Gee, Baby, Ain't I Good to You?/Let's Call the Whole Thing Off/*These Foolish Things/I've Got My Love to Keep Me Warm/†Willow Weep for Me/I'm Puttin' All My Eggs in One Basket/A Fine Romance/*Ill Wind/Love Is Here to Stay/†I Get a Kick Out of You/Learnin' the Blues*

Porgy and Bess—Ella Fitzgerald and Louis Armstrong

(1957) **827 475-2**

EF; Louis Armstrong vo and tpt; Russ Garcia Orchestra.

> *Overture/Summertime/I Wants to Stay Here/My Man's Gone Now/I Got Plenty o' Nuttin'/The Buzzard Song/Bess, You Is My Woman Now/It Ain't Necessarily So/What You Want wid Bess?/A Woman Is a Sometime Thing/Oh, Doctor Jesus/Medley: Here Come de Honey Man; Crab Man; Oh, Dey's So Fresh and Fine (Strawberry Woman)/There's a Boat Dat's Leavin' Soon for New York/Bess, Oh Where's My Bess?/Oh Lawd, I'm on My Way*

At the Opera House

(1957) (Two venues: Los Angeles Opera House/Chicago Opera House) **831 269-2**

EF; Oscar Peterson, p; Herb Ellis, g; Ray Brown, b; Jo Jones, d; Roy Eldridge, tpt; J. J. Johnson, trb; Sonny Stitt, as; Stan Getz; Coleman Hawkins; Illinois Jacquet; Flip Phillips; Lester Young, ts; Connie Kay, d.

It's All Right with Me (1)/*Don'cha Go 'Way Mad* (1)/*Bewitched, Bothered and Bewildered* (1)/*These Foolish Things* (1)/*Ill Wind* (1)/*Goody Goody* (1)/*Moonlight in Vermont* (1)/*Them There Eyes*/*Stompin' at the Savoy* (1)/*It's All Right with Me* (2)/*Don'cha Go 'Way Mad* (2)/*Bewitched, Bothered and Bewildered* (2)/*These Foolish Things* (2)/*Ill Wind* (2)/*Goody Goody* (2)/*Moonlight in Vermont* (2)/*Stompin' at the Savoy* (2)/*Oh, Lady Be Good*

Like Someone in Love

(1957) **314 511 524-2**

EF; Studio orchestra, arranged and conducted by Frank DeVol; *Stan Getz, ts. (Selections marked with † are from "Hello Love." See Verve POCJ-2760.)

There's a Lull in My Life/*More than You Know*/**What Will I Tell My Heart?*/*I Never Had a Chance*/*Close Your Eyes*/*We'll Be Together Again*/*Then I'll Be Tired of You*/*Like Someone in Love*/**Midnight Sun*/*I Thought about You*/**You're Blasé*/*Night Wind*/*What's New?*/*Hurry Home*/*How Long Has This Been Going On?*/†*I'll Never Be the Same*/†*Lost in a Fog*/†*Everything Happens to Me*/†*So Rare*

Hello Love

(1957) **POCJ-2760**

EF; Studio orchestra, arranged and conducted by Frank DeVol.

You Go to My Head/*Willow Weep for Me*/*I'm Through with Love*/*Spring Will Be a Little Late This Year*/*Everything Happens to Me*/*Lost in a Fog*/*I've Grown Accustomed to His Face*/*I'll Never Be the Same*/*So Rare*/*Tenderly*/*Stairway to the Stars*/*Moonlight in Vermont*

Ella Fitzgerald Sings the Irving Berlin Song Book—Volume One

(1958) (POCJ-2145) **829 534-2**

EF; Studio orchestra, arranged and conducted by Paul Weston.

Let's Face the Music and Dance/*You're Laughing at Me*/*Let Yourself Go*/*You Can Have Him*/*Russian Lullaby*/*Puttin' On the Ritz*/*Get Thee Behind Me Satan*/*Alexander's Ragtime Band*/*Top Hat, White Tie, and Tails*/*How about Me?*/*Cheek to Cheek*/*I Used to Be Color Blind*/*Lazy*/*How Deep Is the Ocean?*/*All by Myself*/*Remember*

Ella Fitzgerald Sings the Irving Berlin Song Book—Volume Two

(1958) (POCJ-2146) **829 535-2**

EF; Studio orchestra, arranged and conducted by Paul Weston.

Blue Skies/*Suppertime*/*How's Chances*/*Heat Wave*/*Isn't This a Lovely Day?*/*You Keep Coming Back Like a Song*/*Reaching for the Moon*/*Slumming on Park Avenue*/*The Song Is Ended*/*I'm Putting All My Eggs in One Basket*/*Now It Can Be Told*/*Always*/*It's a Lovely Day Today*/*Change Partners*/*No Strings (I'm Fancy Free)*/*I've Got My Love to Keep Me Warm*/*Blue Skies*

Ella in Rome: The Birthday Concert

(1958) **835 454-2**

EF; Lou Levy, p; Max Bennett, b; Gus Johnson, d; *Oscar Peterson, p; *Ray Brown. b; *Herb Ellis, g; *Gus Johnson, d.

> St. Louis Blues/These Foolish Things (Remind Me of You)/Just Squeeze Me/Angel Eyes/That Old Black Magic/Just One of Those Things/I Loves You Porgy/It's All Right with Me/I Can't Give You Anything but Love/When You're Smiling (the Whole World Smiles with You)/A Foggy Day/Midnight Sun/The Lady Is a Tramp/Sophisticated Lady/Caravan/*Stompin' at the Savoy

Ella Swings Lightly

(1958) (847 392-2) **314 517 535-2**

EF; Marty Paich Dek-Tette: Bud Shank, as; Bill Holman, ts; Don Fagerquist, tpt; Al Porcino, tpt; Bob Enevoldsen, vtb, ts; Vince DeRosa, frh; John Kitzmiller, tu; Med Flory, bs; Lou Levy, p; Joe Mondragon, b; Mel Lewis, d.

> Little White Lies/You Hit the Spot/What's Your Story, Morning Glory?/Just You, Just Me/As Long As I Live/Teardrops from My Eyes/It's Gotta Be This or That/Moonlight on the Ganges/My Kinda Love/Blues in the Night/If I Were a Bell/You're an Old Smoothie/Little Jazz/You Brought a New Kind of Love to Me/Knock Me a Kiss/720 in the Books/Oh, What a Night for Love (p.u.)/Little Jazz (alt)/Dreams Are Made for Children (p.u.)/Oh, What a Night for Love (alt)

Ella Fitzgerald Sings the George and Ira Gershwin Song Book

(1959) (3 CDs) (POCJ-2153/5) **825 024-2** (See also Verve 314 537 260-2)

EF; Studio orchestra, arranged and conducted by Nelson Riddle.

> Sam and Delilah/But Not for Me/My One and Only/Let's Call the Whole Thing Off/ (I've Got) Beginner's Luck/Oh, Lady Be Good/Nice Work If You Can Get It/Things Are Looking Up/Just Another Rhumba/How Long Has This Been Going On?/'S Wonderful/The Man I Love/That Certain Feeling/By Strauss/Someone to Watch over Me/ The Real American Folk Song/Who Cares?/Looking for a Boy/They All Laughed/My Cousin from Milwaukee/Somebody from Somewhere/A Foggy Day/Clap Yo' Hands/ For You, for Me, for Evermore/Stiff Upper Lip/Boy Wanted/Strike Up the Band/Soon/ I've Got a Crush on You/Bidin' My Time/Aren't You Kind of Glad We Did?/Of Thee I Sing (Baby)/"The Half of It, Dearie" Blues/I Was Doing All Right/He Loves and She Loves/Love Is Sweeping the Country/Treat Me Rough/Love Is Here to Stay/Slap That Bass/Isn't It a Pity/Shall We Dance?/Love Walked In/You've Got What Gets Me/They Can't Take That Away from Me/Embraceable You/I Can't Be Bothered Now/Boy! What Love Has Done to Me!/Fascinatin' Rhythm/Funny Face/Lorelei/Oh, So Nice/Let's Kiss and Make Up/I Got Rhythm

Ella Fitzgerald Sings the George and Ira Gershwin Song Book

(1959) (Reissue) **314 537 260-2**

> Add: Ambulatory Suite (instr)/The Preludes (instr)/Somebody Loves Me/Cheerful Little Earful/But Not for Me (45 rpm take)/Lorelei (alt)/Love Is Here to Stay (partial

alt)/*Oh, Lady Be Good* (alt 1)/*Oh, Lady Be Good* (alt 2)/*Oh, Lady Be Good* (alt 3)/*But Not for Me* (mono)/*Fascinating Rhythm* (mono)/*They All Laughed* (mono)/*The Man I Love* (mono)/*Nice Work If You Can Get It* (mono)/*Clap Yo' Hands* (mono)/*Let's Call the Whole Thing Off* (mono)/*I Was Doing All Right* (mono)/*He Loves and She Loves* (mono)/*(I've Got) Beginner's Luck* (mono)

Get Happy

(1959) **314 523 321-2**

EF; Studio orchestras, arranged and conducted by Frank DeVol, Russell Garcia, Marty Paich, Nelson Riddle, and Paul Weston.

Somebody Loves Me/Cheerful Little Earful/You Make Me Feel So Young/Beat Me, Daddy, Eight to the Bar/Like Young/Cool Breeze/Moonlight Becomes You/Blues Skies/ You Turned the Tables on Me/Gypsy in My Soul/Goody Goody/St. Louis Blues/A-Tisket, A-Tasket (bonus track)/*Swingin' Shepherd Blues* (p.u.)

Ella in Berlin: Mack the Knife

(1960) **825 670-2** (See "The Complete Ella in Berlin: Mack the Knife" Verve 314 519 564-2)

The Complete Ella in Berlin: Mack the Knife

(1960) (825 670-2) **314 519 564-2**

EF; Paul Smith, p; Jim Hall, g; Wilfred Middlebrooks, b; Gus Johnson, d.

That Old Black Magic/Our Love Is Here to Stay/Gone with the Wind/Misty/The Lady Is a Tramp/The Man I Love/Love for Sale/Just One of Those Things/Summertime/Too Darn Hot/Lorelei/Mack the Knife/How High the Moon

The Intimate Ella

(1960) **839 838-2** (Also available under the original title: "Ella Fitzgerald Sings the Songs from the Film 'Let No Man Write My Epitaph'" Verve POCJ 2067)

EF; Paul Smith, p.

Black Coffee/Angel Eyes/I Cried for You/I Can't Give You Anything but Love/Then You've Never Been Blue/I Hadn't Anyone 'till You/My Melancholy Baby/Misty/September Song/One for My Baby (and One More for the Road)/Who's Sorry Now?/I'm Getting Sentimental over You/Reach for Tomorrow

Ella Wishes You a Swinging Christmas

(1960) **827 150-2** (See Verve 440 065 086-2)

Ella Wishes You a Swinging Christmas

(1959, 1960) (827 150-2) **440 065 086-2**

EF; Studio orchestra, arranged and conducted by Frank DeVol, †Russell Garcia. (Tracks marked with an asterisk were not released on the first CD re-issue/Verve 827 150-2.)

Jingle Bells/Santa Claus Is Coming to Town/Have Yourself a Merry Little Christmas/ What Are You Doing New Year's Eve?/Sleigh Ride/*The Christmas Song/Good Morning Blues/Let It Snow/Winter Wonderland/Rudolph the Red-Nosed Reindeer/Frosty the Snowman/White Christmas/*The Secret of Christmas/*Medley: We Three Kings of Orient Are; O Little Town of Bethlehem/Christmas Island (p.u.)/*The Christmas Song* (alt)/*White Christmas* (alt)/*Frosty, the Snowman* (alt)

Ella Fitzgerald Sings the Harold Arlen Song Book—Volume One

(1961) (POCJ-2120) **817 527-2**

EF; Studio orchestra, arranged and conducted by Billy May.

Blues in the Night (My Mama Done Told Me)/Let's Fall in Love/Stormy Weather/ Between the Devil and the Deep Blue Sea/My Shining Hour/Sing My Heart/Hooray for Love/This Time the Dream's on Me/That Old Black Magic/I've Got the World on a String/Let's Take a Walk around the Block/Ill Wind (You're Blowin' Me No Good)/ Ac-cent-tchu-ate the Positive

Ella Fitzgerald Sings the Harold Arlen Song Book—Volume Two

(1961) (POCJ-2121) **817 528-2**

EF; Studio orchestra, arranged and conducted by Billy May.

When the Sun Comes Out/Come Rain or Come Shine/As Long As I Live/Happiness Is a Thing Called Joe/It's Only a Paper Moon/The Man That Got Away/One for My Baby (and One More for the Road)/It Was Written in the Stars/Get Happy/I Gotta Right to Sing the Blues/Out of This World/Over the Rainbow/Ding-Dong! The Witch Is Dead

Ella Returns to Berlin

(1961) (POCJ-2065) **837 758-2**

EF; Lou Levy, p; Herb Ellis, g; Wilfred Middlebrooks, b; Gus Johnson, d; *Oscar Peterson, p; *Ray Brown, b; *Ed Thigpen, d.

Give Me the Simple Life/Take the 'A' Train/On a Slow Boat to China/Medley: Why Was I Born?; Can't Help Lovin' Dat Man; People Will Say We're in Love/You're Driving Me Crazy/Rock It for Me/Witchcraft/Anything Goes/Cheek to Cheek/Misty/ Caravan/Mr. Paganini/Mack the Knife/'Round Midnight/Joe Williams' Blues/*This Can't Be Love

Ella in Hollywood

(1961) **POCJ-2647**

EF; Lou Levy, p; Herb Ellis, g; Wilfred Middlebrooks, b; Gus Johnson.

This Could Be the Start of Something Big/I've Got the World on a String/You're Driving Me Crazy/Just in Time/It Might As Well Be Spring/Take the 'A' Train/Stairway to the Stars/Mr. Paganini (You'll Have to Swing It)/Satin Doll/Blue Moon/Baby, Won't You Please Come Home/Air Mail Special

Clap Hands, Here Comes Charlie!

(1961) **835 646-2**

EF; Lou Levy, p; Herb Ellis, g; Joe Mondragon, b; Wilfred Middlebrooks, b; Stan Levey, d; Gus Johnson, d.

Night in Tunisia/You're My Thrill/My Reverie/Stella by Starlight/'Round Midnight/ Jersey Bounce/Signing Off/Cry Me a River/This Year's Kisses/Good Morning Heartache/(I Was) Born to Be Blue/Clap Hands, Here Comes Charlie!/Spring Can Really Hang You Up the Most/Music Goes 'Round and Around/The One I Love Belongs to Someone Else/I Got a Guy/This Could Be the Start of Something Big

Ella Swings Brightly with Nelson

(1959, 1961) **314 519 347-2**

EF; Studio orchestra, arranged and conducted by Nelson Riddle. (*Previously issued on *Get Happy*/Verve LP MG VS-6102; †previously issued on Verve 10248.)

*When Your Lover Has Gone/Don't Be That Way/Love Me or Leave Me/I Hear Music/ What Am I Here For?/I'm Gonna Go Fishin'/I Won't Dance/I Only Have Eyes for You/The Gentleman Is a Dope/Mean to Me/Alone Together/Pick Yourself Up/†Call Me Darling/*Somebody Loves Me/*Cheerful Little Earful*

Rhythm Is My Business

(1962) **314 559 513-2**

EF; Studio orchestra, arranged and conducted by Bill Doggett.

Rough Ridin'/Broadway/You Can Depend on Me/Runnin' Wild/Show Me the Way to Go Out of This World 'Cause That's Where Everything Is/I'll Always Be in Love with You/Hallelujah, I Love Him So/I Can't Face the Music/No Moon at All/Laughin' on the Outside/After You've Gone/Taking a Chance on Love (p.u.)/If I Could Be with You (p.u.)

Ella Swings Gently with Nelson

(1961, 1962) **314 519 348-2**

EF; Studio orchestra, arranged and conducted by Nelson Riddle.

Sweet and Slow/Georgia on My Mind/I Can't Get Started/Street of Dreams/Imagination/The Very Thought of You/It's a Blue World/Darn That Dream/She's Funny That Way/I Wished on the Moon/It's a Pity to Say Goodnight/My One and Only Love/ Body and Soul/Call Me Darling (p.u.)/All of Me

Ella Sings Broadway

(1962) **314 549 373-2**

EF; Studio orchestra, arranged and conducted by Marty Paich.

Hernando's Hideaway/If I Were a Bell/Warm All Over/Almost Like Being in Love/ Dites-Moi/I Could Have Danced All Night/Show Me/No Other Love/Steam Heat/ Whatever Lola Wants/Guys and Dolls/Somebody Somewhere

Ella Fitzgerald Sings the Jerome Kern Song Book

(1963) **825 669-2**

EF; Studio orchestra, arranged and conducted by Nelson Riddle.

> *Let's Begin/A Fine Romance/All the Things You Are/I'll Be Hard to Handle/You Couldn't Be Cuter/She Didn't Say Yes/I'm Old Fashioned/Remind Me/The Way You Look Tonight/Yesterdays/Can't Help Lovin' Dat Man/Why Was I Born?*

Ella and Basie

(1963) (821 576-2) **314 539 059-2**

EF; Count Basie Orchestra, arranged by Quincy Jones.

> *Honeysuckle Rose/'Deed I Do/Into Each Life Some Rain Must Fall/Them There Eyes/ Dream a Little Dream of Me/Tea for Two/Satin Doll/I'm Beginning to See the Light/ Shiny Stockings/My Last Affair/Ain't Misbehavin'/On the Sunny Side of the Street/ My Last Affair* (alt 1)/*My Last Affair* (alt 2)/*Robbins' Nest* (breakdown)/*Robbins' Nest* (1)/*Robbins' Nest* (2)/*Robbins' Nest* (3)

These Are the Blues

(1963) **829 536-2**

EF; Roy Eldridge, tpt; Wild Bill Davis, org; Herb Ellis, g; Ray Brown, b; Gus Johnson, d.

> *Jailhouse Blues/In the Evening (When the Sun Goes Down)/See See Rider/You Don't Know My Mind/Trouble in Mind/How Long, How Long Blues/Cherry Red/Downhearted Blues/St. Louis Blues/Hear Me Talkin' to Ya*

Ella at Juan-Les-Pins

(1964) (2 CDs) **314 589 656-2**

EF; Tommy Flanagan, p; Bill Yancey, b; Gus Johnson, d; Roy Eldridge, tpt.

> *Hello Dolly* (1)/*Day In, Day Out* (1)/*Just A-Sittin' and A-Rockin'* (1)/*I Love Being Here with You* (1)/*People* (1)/*Someone to Watch over Me* (1)/*Can't Buy Me Love* (1)/ *Them There Eyes* (1)/*The Lady Is a Tramp* (1)/*Summertime* (1)/*Cutie Pants* (1)/*I'm Puttin' All My Eggs in One Basket* (1)/*St. Louis Blues* (1)/*Perdido* (1)/*A-Tisket, A-Tasket* (1)/*Mack the Knife* (1)/*A-Tisket, A-Tasket* (2)/*Honeysuckle Rose/ Hello Dolly* (2)/*Day In, Day Out* (2)/*Just A- Sittin' and A-Rockin'* (2)/*I Love Being Here with You* (2)/*People* (2)/*Someone to Watch over Me* (2)/*Can't Buy Me Love* (2)/*Them There Eyes* (2)/*The Lady Is a Tramp* (2)/*Summertime* (2)/*Cutie Pants* (2)/*I'm Puttin' All My Eggs in One Basket* (2)/*St. Louis Blues* (2)/*Perdido* (2)/*A-Tisket, A-Tasket* (3)/*Goody Goody/The Boy from Ipanema/They Can't Take That Away from Me/You'd Be So Nice to Come Home To/Shiny Stockings/Somewhere in the Night/I've Got You under My Skin/Blues in the Night/Too Close for Comfort/Mack the Knife* (2)/*Medley: When Lights Are Low* (1); *A-Tisket, A-Tasket* (4)/*The Cricket Song/How High the Moon/ Medley: A-Tisket, A-Tasket* (5); *When Lights Are Low* (2)

Ella Fitzgerald Sings the Johnny Mercer Songbook

(1964) (823 247-2) **314 539 057-2**

EF; Studio orchestra, arranged and conducted by Nelson Riddle.

Too Marvelous for Words/Early Autumn/Day In–Day Out/Laura/This Time the Dream's on Me/Skylark/Single-O/Something's Gotta Give/Trav'lin' Light/Midnight Sun/Dream (When You're Feeling Blue)/I Remember You/When a Woman Loves a Man

Ella in Hamburg

(1965) **POCJ 2649**

EF; Tommy Flanagan, p; Keter Betts, b; Gus Johnson, d.

Walk Right In/That Old Black Magic/Body and Soul/Here's That Rainy Day/And the Angels Sing/A Hard Day's Night/Ellington Medley: Do Nothin' till You Hear from Me; Mood Indigo; It Don't Mean a Thing (if It Ain't Got That Swing)/The Boy from Ipanema/Don't Rain on My Parade/Angel Eyes/Smooth Sailing/Old McDonald Had a Farm

Ella at Duke's Place

(1965) **314 529 700-2**

EF; Duke Ellington and His Orchestra.

Something to Live For/A Flower Is a Lovesome Thing/Passion Flower/I Like the Sunrise/Azure/Imagine My Frustration/Duke's Place (C-Jam Blues)/Brown-Skin Gal (in the Calico Gown)/What Am I Here For?/Cotton Tail

Whisper Not

(1966) **314 589 478-2**

EF; Studio orchestra, arranged and conducted by Marty Paich.

Sweet Georgia Brown/Whisper Not/I Said No/Thanks for the Memory/Spring Can Really Hang You Up the Most/Ol' MacDonald/Time after Time/You've Changed/I've Got Your Number/Lover Man/Wives and Lovers/Matchmaker, Matchmaker

Ella and Duke at the Cote D'Azur

(1966) **314 539 030-2** (Reissue of original 2-LP set. See Verve 314 539 033-2)

EF/Duke Ellington and His Orchestra.

Ella Fitzgerald/Duke Ellington: Cote D'Azur Concerts

(1966) (8 CDs) **314 539 033-2**

EF; Duke Ellington and His Orchestra; Jimmy Jones, p; Jim Hughart, b; Grady Tate, d. A collection of most of the selections performed by Fitzgerald with Ellington during the Juan-les-Pins International Jazz Festival. Includes an afternoon rehearsal by Ellington. (Tracks with Fitzgerald listed here.)

Let's Do It (1)/Satin Doll (1)/Cottontail (1)/Thou Swell (incomplete)/Satin Doll (2)/
Wives and Lovers (1)/Something to Live For (1)/Let's Do It (2)/The More I See You/
Goin' Out of My Head (1)/So Danco Samba (Jazz Samba) (1)/Lullaby of Birdland (1)/
How Long Has This Been Going On?/Mack the Knife (1)/Thou Swell (2)/Satin Doll/
Wives and Lovers (2)/Something to Live For (2)/Let's Do It (3)/Sweet Georgia Brown/
Goin' Out of My Head (2)/So Danco Samba (Jazz Samba) (2)/Lullaby of Birdland (2)/
Moment of Truth/Misty/Mack the Knife (2)/Cottontail (2)/Just Squeeze Me

Sunshine of Your Love

(1969) (POCJ-2166) **314 533 102-2** (Originally released by Prestige—LP PRST 7685)

EF; Ernie Hecksher Big Band, arranged by Marty Paich, Frank DeVol, Tee Carson,
and Bill Holman; Tommy Flanagan, p; Frank De la Rosa, b; Ed Thigpen, d.

Hey Jude/Sunshine of Your Love/This Girl's in Love with You/Watch What Happens/
Alright, Okay, You Win/Give Me the Simple Life/Useless Landscape/Old Devil Moon/
Don'cha Go 'Way Mad/A House Is Not a Home/Trouble Is a Man/Love You Madly

VERVE COMPILATIONS

The Silver Collection: The Song Books

823 445-2

Selections from the Song Books.

Oh, Lady Be Good/Nice Work If You Can Get It/Fascinatin' Rhythm/All the Things
You Are/Yesterdays/Can't Help Lovin' Dat Man/Come Rain or Come Shine/It's Only
a Paper Moon/Over the Rainbow/Laura/Skylark/This Time the Dream's on Me/Puttin'
On the Ritz/Alexander's Ragtime Band/Cheek to Cheek/My Funny Valentine/Have
You Met Miss Jones?/The Lady Is a Tramp/Manhattan

Love Songs: The Best of the Verve Song Books

831 367-2

From This Moment On/Solitude/Love You Madly/All the Things You Are/I Concen-
trate on You/Out of This World/How about Me/I'm Beginning to See the Light/The
Man I Love/I Remember You/I Let a Song Go Out of My Heart/Always/Just One of
Those Things/Prelude to a Kiss/All Too Soon/Lover

Compact Jazz: Ella Fitzgerald

831 762-2

EF; Count Basie; Duke Ellington; Nelson Riddle; Oscar Peterson; Tommy Flanagan.

Mack the Knife/Desifinado/Mr. Paganini/I Can't Get Started/A Night in Tunisia/A-
Tisket, A-Tasket/Shiny Stockings/Smooth Sailing/Goody Goody/Rough Ridin'/The Boy
from Ipanema/Sweet Georgia Brown/Duke's Place (C-Jam Blues)/Misty/Somebody
Loves Me/How High the Moon

Compact Jazz: Ella Fitzgerald Live
833 294-2

EF; Duke Ellington; Oscar Peterson.

Oh, Lady Be Good/Summertime/Honeysuckle Rose/Body and Soul/Squeeze Me/These Foolish Things/Stompin' at the Savoy/Baby, Won't You Please Come Home?/You'd Be So Nice to Come Home To/The More I See You/I've Got a Crush on You/I Can't Give You Anything but Love/The Man I Love/Take the 'A' Train

Compact Jazz: Ella Fitzgerald/Louis Armstrong
835 313-2

EF; Louis Armstrong, vo and tpt; Oscar Peterson, p; Ray Brown, b; Herb Ellis, g; Buddy Rich, d; Louis Bellson, d.

They Can't Take That Away from Me/Gee Baby Ain't I Good to You?/I Won't Dance/ It Ain't Necessarily So/A Fine Romance/Stompin' at the Savoy/A Foggy Day/Don't Be That Way/Summertime/Cheek to Cheek/Can't We Be Friends?/Let's Call the Whole Thing Off

For the Love of Ella Fitzgerald
(2 CDs) 841 765-2

EF; Louis Armstrong; Duke Ellington; Count Basie; Oscar Peterson; others.

A-Tisket, A-Tasket/Oh, Lady Be Good/Stompin' at the Savoy/How High the Moon/Mr. Paganini/Sweet Georgia Brown/Mack the Knife/Caravan/A Night in Tunisia/ Rockin' in Rhythm/Honeysuckle Rose/I Got Rhythm/A Fine Romance/On the Sunny Side of the Street/Party Blues/Cottontail/Misty/Sophisticated Lady/Midnight Sun/Solitude/ How Long, How Long Blues/I Loves You Porgy/Summertime/Mood Indigo/Laura/ Stormy Weather/Autumn in New York/These Foolish Things/I Can't Get Started/See See Rider/I Love Paris/Blues in the Night

Jazz 'Round Midnight
843 621-2

EF; various artists.

The Man I Love/Reaching for the Moon/Blue Moon/Moonlight Becomes You/Love Is Here to Stay/With a Song in My Heart/How Deep Is the Ocean/September Song/Good Morning Heartache/'Round Midnight/I Got It Bad (and That Ain't Good)/One for My Baby (and One More for the Road)/Cry Me a River/Do Nothin' till You Hear from Me

The Essential Ella Fitzgerald: The Great Songs
314 517 170-2

EF; various artists.

Oh, Lady Be Good (1)/Oh, Lady Be Good (2)/There's a Lull in My Life/Little Jazz/Drop Me Off in Harlem/Angel Eyes/Ding! Dong! The Witch Is Dead/A-Tisket, A-Tasket/

Summertime/Into Each Life Some Rain Must Fall/Spring Can Really Hang You Up the Most/Pick Yourself Up/Cool Breeze/Imagine My Frustration/Mack the Knife/ Dream

First Lady of Song

(1949, 1954–1956) (3 CDs) **314 517 898-2**

EF; Louis Armstrong, tpt; Roy Eldridge, tpt; Ray Brown, b; Herb Ellis, g; Oscar Peterson, p; Count Basie Orchestra; Hank Jones, p; Lou Levy, p; Jimmy Rowles, p; many others.

Perdido/Lullaby of Birdland/Too Young for the Blues/Too Darn Hot/Miss Otis Regrets/ April in Paris/Undecided/Can't We Be Friends?/Bewitched, Bothered and Bewildered/ Just A-Sittin' and A-Rockin'/I'm Just a Lucky So-and-So/Air Mail Special/A-Tisket, A-Tasket/Baby, Don't You Go 'Way Mad/Angel Eyes/I Won't Dance/Oh, Lady Be Good/More Than You Know/Lush Life/Blue Skies/Swingin' Shepherd Blues/These Foolish Things/Trav'lin' Light/You're an Old Smoothie/Makin' Whoopee/How Long Has This Been Going On?/Detour Ahead/Mack the Knife/How High the Moon/Black Coffee/Let It Snow! Let It Snow! Let It Snow!/Get Happy!/Heart and Soul/Mr. Paganini (You'll Have to Swing It)/A Night in Tunisia/I Can't Get Started/Don't Be That Way/After You've Gone/Hernando's Hideaway/A Fine Romance/'Deed I Do/Heah Me Talkin' to You/Can't Buy Me Love/Day In—Day Out/Something's Gotta Give/Here's That Rainy Day/(I've Got) Something to Live For/You've Changed/Jazz Samba/It Don't Mean a Thing (if It Ain't Got That Swing)

Compact Jazz: Ella Fitzgerald and Duke Ellington

314 517 953-2

EF; Duke Ellington and His Orchestra.

Take the 'A' Train/Caravan/I Got It Bad (and That Ain't Good)/I'm Beginning to See the Light/I Didn't Know about You/I Ain't Got Nothin' but the Blues/Everything but You/(I've Got) Something to Live For/Duke's Place/Passion Flower/Cottontail/Mack the Knife/It Don't Mean a Thing (if It Ain't Got That Swing)

The Best of the Song Books

314 519 804-2

Something's Gotta Give/Love Is Here to Stay/Bewitched, Bothered and Bewildered/I've Got My Love to Keep Me Warm/The Lady Is a Tramp/I Got It Bad (and That Ain't Good)/Miss Otis Regrets/'S Wonderful/Between the Devil and the Deep Blue Sea/Love for Sale/They Can't Take That Away from Me/Midnight Sun/Hooray for Love/Why Was I Born/Cottontail/Ev'ry Time We Say Goodbye

Verve Jazz Masters 6—Ella Fitzgerald

(POCJ-1549) **314 519 822-2**

EF; various artists.

I Hear Music/I Ain't Got Nothing but the Blues/Ev'rything I've Got/I Loves You Porgy/Mack the Knife/I'm Putting All My Eggs in One Basket/The Man That Got

Away/Just You, Just Me/I've Got the World on a String/A-Tisket, A-Tasket/These Foolish Things/Heat Wave/I Never Had a Chance/How High the Moon/In the Evening (When the Sun Goes Down)/Signing Off

The Complete Ella Fitzgerald Song Books

(16 CDs) **314 519 832-2** (314 537 257-2; 314 537 258-2; 837 035-2; 829 534/5-2; 825 024-2; 817 527/8-2; 825 669-2; 314 539 057-2)

Add: Ellington: *Chelsea Bridge* (rehearsal)/*Chelsea Bridge* (alt.) Gershwins: *Ambulatory Suite* (instrumental)/*The Preludes* (instrumental)/*Somebody Loves Me; Cheerful Little Earful* (from Get Happy!—Verve LP MGV 4036)/*Oh, Lady Be Good* (alt)/*But Not for Me* (45 rpm—Verve 10180) Arlen: *Let's Take a Walk around the Block* (alt)/*Sing My Heart* (alt)

Verve Jazz Masters 24—Ella Fitzgerald and Louis Armstrong
314 521 851-2

EF; Louis Armstrong, vo and tpt; Oscar Peterson, p; Herb Ellis, g; Ray Brown, b; Buddy Rich, d; Louis Bellson, d.

I've Got My Love to Keep Me Warm/Isn't This a Lovely Day?/Learnin' the Blues/I Got Plenty o' Nuttin'/Moonlight in Vermont/Under a Blanket of Blue/I'm Putting All My Eggs in One Basket/Our Love Is Here to Stay/April in Paris/Tenderly/Bess/They All Laughed

Best of the Song Books: Ballads
314 521 867-2

Oh, Lady Be Good/I'm Old Fashioned/Laura/Day Dream/Easy to Love/It Was Written in the Stars/How Long Has This Been Going On?/Let's Begin/Now It Can Be Told/ There's a Small Hotel/Do Nothing till You Hear from Me/Ill Wind/You're Laughing at Me/A Ship Without a Sail/Trav'lin' Light/This Time the Dream's on Me

Best of Ella Fitzgerald—First Lady of Song
314 523 382-2

EF; Louis Armstrong; Oscar Peterson, p; Herb Ellis, g; Count Basie; Nelson Riddle; others.

Too Young for the Blues/Can't We Be Friends?/Bewitched, Bothered, and Bewildered/ Just A-Sittin' and A-Rockin' /I'm Just a Lucky So and So/Baby, Don't You Go 'Way Mad/Angel Eyes/I Won't Dance/Lush Life/Blue Skies/The Swingin' Shepherd Blues/ You're an Old Smoothie/Detour Ahead/Don't Be That Way/A Fine Romance/'Deed I Do

Ella Fitzgerald: Jazz 'Round Midnight Again
314 527 032-2

Various artists; some selections from the Song Books.

A Flower Is a Lovesome Thing/Easy to Love/Embraceable You/Midnight Sun/Misty/I Get a Kick Out of You/You've Changed/Now It Can Be Told/The Man That Got Away/ Ill Wind/The Way You Look Tonight/I Didn't Know about You/Bewitched/Early Autumn/My Shining Hour/It Might As Well Be Spring

Daydream: Best of the Duke Ellington Song Book

314 527 223-2

Take the 'A' Train/Day Dream/Everything but You/Azure/Solitude/The E and D Blues (E for Ella, D for Duke)/Bli-Blip/It Don't Mean a Thing (if It Ain't Got That Swing)/ I Ain't Got Nothin' but the Blues/I Got It Bad (and That Ain't Good)/Just Squeeze Me/Cottontail/Squatty Roo/Rocks in My Bed/ Rockin' in Rhythm/Mood Indigo/All Too Soon

Verve Jazz Masters 46—Ella Fitzgerald: The Jazz Sides

314 527 655-2

EF; various artists.

Let's Do It (Let's Fall in Love)/Caravan/They Can't Take That Away from Me/ Ev'rything I've Got/In a Mellow Tone/One for My Baby (and One More for the Road)/ You Hit the Spot/Born to Be Blue/Them There Eyes/Knock Me a Kiss/Jersey Bounce/ Black Coffee/Hear Me Talkin' to Ya/It's Only a Paper Moon/Passion Flower/The Music Goes 'Round and Around

Oh, Lady Be Good: Best of the Gershwin Song Book

314 529 581-2

Fascinatin' Rhythm/'S Wonderful/Someone to Watch over Me/He Loves and She Loves/Oh, Lady Be Good/A Foggy Day/How Long Has This Been Going On?/Let's Call the Whole Thing Off/But Not for Me/My One and Only Love/I've Got a Crush on You/Nice Work If You Can Get It/The Man I Love/Funny Face/Embraceable You/ They Can't Take That Away from Me/I Got Rhythm

Best of the Song Books: Love Songs

314 531 762-2

From This Moment On/Solitude/Love You Madly/All the Things You Are/I Concentrate on You/Out of This World/How about Me/I'm Beginning to See the Light/The Man I Love/I Remember You/I Let a Song Go Out of My Heart/Always/Just One of Those Things/Prelude to a Kiss/All Too Soon/Lover

Best of the Song Books—The Collection

314 533 247-2

(Best of The Songbooks—314 519 804-2; Best of The Songbooks: Ballads—314 521 867-2; Best of The Songbooks: Love Songs—314 531 762-2)

The Complete Ella Fitzgerald and Louis Armstrong

(3 CDs) **314 537 284-2** (Ella and Louis—825 373-2; Ella and Louis Again—825 374-2; Porgy and Bess—827 475-2)

> Add: *You Won't Be Satisfied (until You Break My Heart)* / *Undecided* (from Jazz at the Hollywood Bowl—LP MGV 8231-2)

Best of Ella Fitzgerald and Louis Armstrong

314 537 909-2

> *Let's Call the Whole Thing Off/Love Is Here to Stay/The Nearness of You/Stars Fell on Alabama/Gee, Baby Ain't I Good to You/They Can't Take That Away from Me/Autumn in New York/Summertime/Tenderly/ Stompin' at the Savoy/Under a Blanket of Blue/I Wants to Stay Here/I've Got My Love to Keep Me Warm/There's a Boat Dat's Leavin' Soon for New York/You Won't Be Satisfied (until You Break My Heart)*

Ultimate Ella Fitzgerald (Selected By Joe Williams)

314 539 054-2

EF; Louis Armstrong; Nelson Riddle; Lou Levy; Paul Smith; Hank Jones; Oscar Peterson; Count Basie; others.

> *A-Tisket, A-Tasket/Oh, Lady Be Good/Lullaby of Birdland/Angel Eyes/Imagine My Frustration/Midnight Sun/Mack the Knife/Bess, You Is My Woman Now/How High the Moon/All Too Soon/Blue Skies/Mr. Paganini/ There's a Lull in My Life/Robbins' Nest/Lush Life/Too Close for Comfort*

Pure Ella: The Very Best of Ella Fitzgerald

314 539 206-2

EF; Louis Armstrong; Duke Ellington; Paul Smith; others.

> *Mack the Knife/Blue Skies/A-Tisket, A-Tasket/They Can't Take That Away from Me/Misty/Mr. Paganini/Tea for Two/Love Is Here to Stay/Night and Day/My Funny Valentine/The Boy from Ipanema/Too Marvelous for Words/Take the 'A' Train/Summertime/How High the Moon/All the Things You Are/Over the Rainbow/Oh, Lady Be Good*

Our Love Is Here to Stay: Ella Fitzgerald and Louis Armstrong Sing Gershwin

314 539 679-2

EF; Louis Armstrong; others.

> *I Got Plenty o' Nuttin'/He Loves and She Loves/A Woman Is a Sometime Thing/You Can't Take That Away from Me/Let's Call the Whole Thing Off/Strike Up the Band/Things Are Looking Up/They All Laughed/A Foggy Day/How Long Has This Been Going On?/Summertime/Love Is Here to Stay/ There's a Boat Dat's Leavin' Soon for New York/'S Wonderful/I Was Doing All Right/Oh, Lady Be Good*

Something to Live For

(2 CDs) **314 547 800-2**

EF; many others.

A-Tisket, A-Tasket/You Showed Me the Way/Stairway to the Stars/How High the Moon/Perdido/Can Anyone Explain/Ella's Contribution to the Blues/But Not for Me/ Thanks for the Memory/Ridin' High/Ev'ry Time We Say Goodbye/Angel Eyes/Goody Goody/Oh, Lady Be Good/The Lady Is a Tramp/Body and Soul/Airmail Special/Midnight Sun/Summertime/Mack the Knife/Misty/The Man I Love/Mr. Paganini/'Round Midnight/Bill Bailey/Yesterdays/Lover Man/Duke's Place/Sweet Georgia Brown/Something to Live For

Ella Fitzgerald and Louis Armstrong: Jazz 'Round Midnight

(843 621-2) **314 557 352-2**

Can't We Be Friends/I Got Plenty o' Nuttin'/They All Laughed/I've Got My Love to Keep Me Warm/Summertime/Comes Love/Under a Blanket of Blue/I Won't Dance/ Don't Be That Way/Bess, You Is My Woman Now/I'm Puttin' All My Eggs in One Basket/April in Paris/Love Is Here to Stay/Stars Fell on Alabama

Quiet Now—Ella's Moods

314 559 736-2

EF; various artists.

Prelude to a Kiss/Detour Ahead/Let's Do It (Let's Fall in Love)/I Cried for You/I Concentrate on You/Spring Can Really Hang You Up the Most/Black Coffee/Cry Me a River/Bewitched/How Deep Is the Ocean/Dream a Little Dream of Me/Lush Life

Ella Fitzgerald: Ella for Lovers

440 065 331-2

Compilation of tracks from Verve and Decca releases.

I Got a Guy/I Hadn't Anyone till You/Please Be Kind/How Long Has This Been Going On?/With a Song in My Heart/Baby, What Else Can I Do?/I've Got a Crush on You/ My Melancholy Baby/Wait till You See Her/You're My Thrill/Misty/What Is There to Say?/Bewitched/I'm Getting Sentimental over You/Imagination/Russian Lullaby

CAPITOL

Brighten the Corner

(1967) **CDP 7 95151-2**

EF; Studio chorus and orchestra, arranged and conducted by Ralph Carmichael.

Abide with Me/Just a Closer Walk with Thee/The Old Rugged Cross/Brighten the Corner (Where You Are)/I Need Thee Every Hour/In the Garden/(God Be with You) Till We Meet Again/God Will Take Care of You/The Church in the Wildwood/Throw Out the Lifeline/I Shall Not Be Moved/Let the Lower Lights Be Burning/What a Friend We Have in Jesus/Rock of Ages, Cleft for Me

Ella Fitzgerald's Christmas

(1967) **CDP 7 94452-2**

EF; Studio chorus and orchestra, arranged and conducted by Ralph Carmichael.

O Holy Night/It Came upon a Midnight Clear/Hark the Herald Angels Sing/Away in a Manger/Joy to the World/The First Noel/Silent Night/O Come All Ye Faithful/Sleep, My Little Lord Jesus/Angels We Have Heard on High/O Little Town of Bethlehem/We Three Kings/God Rest Ye Merry Gentlemen

Misty Blue

(1967) **CDP 7 95152-2**

EF; Studio chorus and orchestra, arranged and conducted by Sid Feller.

Misty Blue/Walking in the Sunshine/It's Only Love/Evil on Your Mind/I Taught Him Everything He Knows/Don't Let the Doorknob Hit You/Turn the World Around (the Other Way)/The Chokin' Kind/Born to Lose/This Gun Don't Care/Don't Touch Me

30 by Ella

(1968) (CDP 7 48333 2) **Capitol Jazz 20090**

EF; Harry Edison, tpt; Benny Carter, as; Georgie Auld, ts; Jimmy Jones, p; John Collins, g; Bob West, eb; Panama Francis, d; Louis Bellson, d.

Medley: *My Mother's Eyes; Try a Little Tenderness; I Got It Bad (and That Ain't Good)* (instr); *Everything I Have Is Yours; I Never Knew; Goodnight, My Love*/Medley: *Four or Five Times; Maybe; Taking a Chance on Love* (instr); *Elmer's Tune; At Sundown; It's a Wonderful World/* Medley: *On Green Dolphin Street; How Am I to Know?; Just Friends* (instr); *I Cried for You; Seems Like Old Times; You Stepped Out of a Dream*/Medley: *If I Gave My Heart to You; Once in a While; Ebb Tide* (instr); *The Lamp Is Low; Where Are You?; Thinking of You*/Medley: *Candy; All I Do Is Dream of You; Spring Is Here* (instr); *720 in the Books; It Happened in Monterey; What Can I Say after I Say I'm Sorry?*/Medley: *No Regrets; I've Got a Feeling You're Fooling; Don't Blame Me* (instr); *Deep Purple; Rain; You're a Sweetheart/Hawaiian War Chant* (bonus track)

PABLO

NOTE: Norman Granz sold the Pablo catalog to Fantasy, Inc., in 1987. Fantasy, in turn, has released a number of the Pablo albums on the Original Jazz Classics label. The catalog numbers for these releases are preceded by the letters "OJCCD."

Jazz at the Philharmonic in Tokyo 1953

(2 CDs) **PACD-2620-104-2**

EF; Oscar Peterson, p; Gene Krupa, d; JATP All-Stars; others. (Tracks with Fitzgerald listed here.)

On the Sunny Side of the Street/Body and Soul/Why Don't You Do Right?/Oh, Lady Be Good/I Got It Bad (and That Ain't Good)/How High the Moon/My Funny Valentine/Smooth Sailing/The Frim Fram Sauce/Perdido

Ella Fitzgerald/Duke Ellington: The Stockholm Concert 1966

Released in 1984. **PACD 2308-242-2**

EF; Duke Ellington Orchestra; Jimmy Jones, p; Joe Comfort, b; Gus Johnson, d.

Imagine My Frustration/Duke's Place/Satin Doll/Something to Live For/Wives and Lovers/So Danco Samba/Let's Do It/Lover Man/Cottontail

The Greatest Jazz Concert in the World

(1967) (3 CDs) Released in 1975. **PACD-2625-742-2**

EF; Jimmy Jones, p; Bob Cranshaw, b; Sam Woodyard, d; Duke Ellington Orchestra; (Coleman Hawkins and the Oscar Peterson Trio also perform on other tracks).

Don't Be That Way/You've Changed/Let's Do It/On the Sunny Side of the Street/It's Only a Paper Moon/Day Dream/If I Could Be with You/Between the Devil and the Deep Blue Sea/Cotton Tail

Ella Fitzgerald in Budapest

(1970) **PACD-5308-2**

EF; Tommy Flanagan, p; Frank De La Rosa, b; Ed Thigpen, d.

Crazy Rhythm/ Medley: This Guy's in Love with You; I'm Gonna Sit Right Down and Write Myself a Letter/Open Your Window/Satin Doll/Spinning Wheel/As Time Goes By/You'd Better Love Me/ I'll Never Fall in Love Again/Hello Young Lovers/ Medley: I Concentrate on You; You Go to My Head/The Girl from Ipanema/Cabaret/ Dancing in the Dark/Raindrops Keep Falling on My Head/The Lady Is a Tramp/Summertime/Mr. Paganini/Mack the Knife/People

Ella á Nice

(1971) Released in 1983. (2308-234-2) **OJCCD-442-2**

EF; Tommy Flanagan, p; Frank de la Rosa, b; Ed Thigpen, d.

Night and Day/The Many Faces of Cole Porter: Get Out of Town; Easy to Love; You Do Something to Me/The Ballad Medley: Body and Soul; The Man I Love; Porgy/The Bossa Scene: The Girl from Ipanema; Fly Me to the Moon; O Nosso Amor; Cielito Lindo; Madalena; Agua de Beber (Water to Drink)/Summertime/They Can't Take That Away from Me/Aspects of Duke: Mood Indigo; Do Nothin' till You Hear from Me; It Don't Mean a Thing (if It Ain't Got That Swing)/Something/St. Louis Blues/Close to You/Put a Little Love in Your Heart

Jazz at the Santa Monica Civic '72

(1972) (3 CDs) **PACD-2625-701-2**

EF; Tommy Flanagan, p; Keter Betts, b; Ed Thigpen, d; Count Basie Orchestra; JATP All-Stars. (Tracks with Fitzgerald listed here.)

L-O-V-E/Begin the Beguine/Indian Summer/You've Got a Friend/What's Going On?/ Night and Day/Spring Can Really Hang You Up the Most/Little White Lies/Madalena/ Shiny Stockings/Cole Porter Medley: Too Darn Hot; It's All Right with Me/Street Beater ("Sanford and Son" Theme)/I Can't Stop Loving You/C Jam Blues

Take Love Easy

(1973) **PACD-2310-702-2**

EF; Joe Pass, g.

Take Love Easy/Once I Loved/Don't Be That Way/You're Blasé/Lush Life/A Foggy Day/ Gee Baby, Ain't I Good to You?/You Go to My Head/I Want to Talk about You

Fine and Mellow

(1974) Released in 1979. **PACD-2310-829-2**

EF; Harry Edison, tpt; Clark Terry, tpt; Zoot Sims, ts; Eddie "Lockjaw" Davis, ts; Joe Pass, g; Tommy Flanagan, p; Ray Brown, b; Louis Bellson, d.

Fine and Mellow/I'm Just a Lucky So-and-So/(I Don't Stand) A Ghost of a Chance (with You)/Rockin' in Rhythm/ I'm in the Mood for Love/'Round Midnight/I Can't Give You Anything but Love/The Man I Love/Polka Dots and Moonbeams

Ella in London

(1974) (2310-711-2) **OJCCD-974-2**

EF; Tommy Flanagan, p; Joe Pass, g; Keter Betts, b; Bobby Durham, d.

Sweet Georgia Brown/They Can't Take That Away from Me/Ev'rytime We Say Goodbye/The Man I Love/It Don't Mean a Thing (if It Ain't Got That Swing)/You've Got a Friend/Lemon Drop/The Very Thought of You/Happy Blues

Ella and Oscar

(1975) **PACD-2310-759-2**

EF; Oscar Peterson, p; *Ray Brown, b.

*Mean to Me/How Long Has This Been Going On?/When Your Lover Has Gone/More Than You Know/There's a Lull in My Life/*Midnight Sun/*I Hear Music/*Street of Dreams/*April in Paris*

Ella Fitzgerald: Montreux Jazz Festival 1975

(2310-751-2) **OJCCD-789-2**

EF; Tommy Flanagan, p; Keter Betts, b; Bobby Durham, d.

Caravan/Satin Doll/Teach Me Tonight/Wave/It's All Right with Me/Let's Do It/How High the Moon/The Girl from Ipanema/T'Ain't Nobody's Bizness If I Do

Fitzgerald and Pass ... Again

(1976) **PACD-2310-772-2**

EF; Joe Pass, g.

I Ain't Got Nothing but the Blues/'Tis Autumn/My Old Flame/That Old Feeling/ Rain/I Didn't Know about You/You Took Advantage of Me/I've Got the World on a String/All Too Soon/The One I Love (Belongs to Somebody Else)/Solitude/Nature Boy/ Tennessee Waltz/One Note Samba

Montreux '77: Ella Fitzgerald with the Tommy Flanagan Trio

(1977) (2308-206-2) **OJCCD-376-2**

EF; Tommy Flanagan, p; Keter Betts, b; Bobby Durham, d.

Too Close for Comfort/I Ain't Got Nothing but the Blues/My Man/Come Rain or Come Shine/Day by Day/Ordinary Fool/One Note Samba/I Let a Song Go Out of My Heart/ Billie's Bounce/You Are the Sunshine of My Life

Dream Dancing

(1972, 1978) Released in 1978. **PACD-2310-814-2**

EF; Studio orchestra, arranged and conducted by Nelson Riddle.

Dream Dancing/I've Got You under My Skin/I Concentrate on You/My Heart Belongs to Daddy/Love for Sale/So Near and Yet So Far/Down in the Depths/After You/Just One of Those Things/I Get a Kick Out of You/All of You/Anything Goes/At Long Last Love/C'est Magnifique/Without Love

Lady Time

(1978) (2310-825-2) **OJCCD-864-2**

EF; Jackie Davis, org; Louis Bellson, d.

I'm Walkin'/All or Nothing at All/I Never Had a Chance/I Cried for You/What Will I Tell My Heart?/Since I Fell for You/And the Angels Sing/I'm Confessin' (That I Love You)/Mack the Knife/That's My Desire/ I'm in the Mood for Love

A Classy Pair

(1979) Released in 1982. **PACD-2312-132-2**

EF; Count Basie Orchestra.

Honeysuckle Rose/My Kind of Trouble Is You/Teach Me Tonight/Organ Grinder's Swing/Don't Worry 'bout Me/I'm Getting Sentimental over You/ Ain't Misbehavin'/ Just A-Sittin' and A-Rockin'/Sweet Lorraine

A Perfect Match

(1979) **PACD-2312-110-2**

EF; Count Basie Orchestra.

Please Don't Talk about Me When I'm Gone/Sweet Georgia Brown/Some Other Spring/ Make Me Rainbows/After You've Gone/'Round Midnight/Fine and Mellow/You've Changed/Honeysuckle Rose/St. Louis Blues/Basella

Fitzgerald/Basie/Pass: Digital III at Montreux

(1979) (2308-223-2) **OJCCD-996-2**

EF; Count Basie Orchestra; Joe Pass, g; Niels-Henning Orsted-Pederson, b. (Fitzgerald, with the Count Basie Orchestra, sings only on tracks marked with an asterisk.)

> *I Can't Get Started/Good Mileage/*(I Don't Stand) A Ghost of a Chance (with You)/ *Flying Home/I Cover the Waterfront/Li'l Darlin'/In Your Own Sweet Way/Oleo*

Ella Abraca Jobim: Ella Fitzgerald Sings the Antonio Carlos Jobim Songbook

(1980, 1981) **PACD-2630-201-2**

EF; Clark Terry, tpt; Zoot Sims, ts; Toots Thielemans, hca; studio ensemble, arranged and conducted by Erich Bulling.

> *Dreamer/This Love That I've Found/The Girl from Ipanema/Somewhere in the Hills/ Photograph/Wave/Triste/Quiet Nights of Quiet Stars/Water to Drink/Bonita/Off Key (Desafinado)/ He's a Carioca/Dindi/How Insensitive/One Note Samba/Felicidade/Useless Landscape*

The Best Is Yet to Come

(1982) (2312-138-2) **OJCCD-889-2**

EF; Studio orchestra, arranged and conducted By Nelson Riddle.

> *Don't Be That Way/God Bless the Child/I Wonder Where Our Love Has Gone/You're Driving Me Crazy/Any Old Time/Good-bye/Autumn in New York/The Best Is Yet to Come/Deep Purple/Somewhere in the Night*

Speak Love

(1983) **PACD-2310-888-2**

EF; Joe Pass, g.

> *Speak Low/Come Love/There's No You/I May Be Wrong (but I Think You're Wonderful)/At Last/The Thrill Is Gone/Gone with the Wind/Blue and Sentimental/Girl Talk/ Georgia on My Mind*

Sophisticated Lady

(1975, 1983). Released in 2001. **PACD-5310-2**

EF; Joe Pass, g. (Tracks marked with an asterisk are Joe Pass only.)

> *I'm Beginning to See the Light/ Medley: I Got It Bad (and That Ain't Good); Sophisticated Lady/One Note Samba/Georgia on My Mind/Gone with the Wind/Bluesette/ *Old Folks/*Wave/*Cherokee/Take Love Easy/Mood Indigo/Satin Doll*

Nice Work If You Can Get It: Ella Fitzgerald and André Previn Do Gershwin

(1983) **PACD-2312-140-2**

EF; André Previn, p; Niels-Henning Orsted-Pederson, b.

A Foggy Day/Nice Work If You Can Get It/But Not for Me/Let's Call the Whole Thing Off/How Long Has This Been Going On?/Who Cares?/ Medley: I've Got a Crush on You; Someone to Watch over Me; Embraceable You/They Can't Take That Away from Me

Return to Happiness: Jazz at the Philharmonic, Tokyo 1983

Released in 1987. **PACD-2620-117-2**

EF; Paul Smith, p; Keter Betts, b; Bobby Durham, d; JATP All-Stars. (Tracks with Fitzgerald listed here.)

Manteca/Willow Weep for Me/All of Me/Blue Moon/Night and Day/They Can't Take That Away from Me/Medley: The Man I Love; Body and Soul/'Round Midnight/ Flying Home

Easy Living

(1983, 1986) Released in 1986. **PACD-2310-921-2**

EF; Joe Pass, g.

My Ship/Don't Be That Way/My Man/Don't Worry 'bout Me/Days of Wine and Roses/Easy Living/(I Don't Stand) A Ghost of a Chance (with You)/Love for Sale/ Moonlight in Vermont/On Green Dolphin Street/Why Don't You Do Right?/By Myself/I Want a Little Girl/I'm Making Believe/On a Slow Boat to China

All That Jazz

(1989) **PACD-2310-938-2**

EF; Harry Edison, tpt; Clark Terry, tpt; Benny Carter, as; Al Grey, trb; Kenny Barron, p; Mike Wofford, p; Ray Brown, b; Bobby Durham, d.

Dream a Little Dream of Me/My Last Affair/Baby, Don't Quit Now/Oh, Look at Me Now/The Jersey Bounce/When Your Lover Has Gone/That Old Devil Called Love/All That Jazz/Just When We're Falling in Love (Robbins' Nest)/Good Morning, Heartache/ Little Jazz/The Nearness of You

PABLO COMPILATIONS

Bluella: Ella Fitzgerald Sings the Blues

PACD-2310-960-2

EF; Count Basie Orchestra; Ray Brown, b; Roy Eldridge, tpt; Stan Getz, ts; Zoot Sims, ts; Clark Terry, tpt; others.

Smooth Sailing/Duke's Place/St. Louis Blues/C-Jam Blues/Happy Blues/Billie's Bounce/I'm Walkin'/Fine and Mellow/St. Louis Blues/Basella

The Best of Ella Fitzgerald

PACD-2405-421-2

EF; Louis Bellson, d; Ray Brown, b; Eddie "Lockjaw" Davis, ts; Tommy Flanagan, p; Joe Pass, g; Oscar Peterson, p; Zoot Sims, ts; others.

Dreamer/You're Blasé/Fine and Mellow/Honeysuckle Rose/I Wonder Where Our Love Has Gone/Street of Dreams/ I'm Walkin'/This Love That I've Found/I'm Getting Sentimental over You/Any Old Time/How Long Has This Been Going On?/Since I Fell for You/Don't Be That Way/You Go to My Head

Ella Fitzgerald: The Concert Years

(4 CDs) (Selected recordings from several albums, 1953–1983) **PACD-4414-2**

EF; Roy Eldridge, tpt; Oscar Peterson, p; Herb Ellis, g; Ray Brown, b; Duke Ellington Orchestra; Tommy Flanagan, p; Count Basie Orchestra; Paul Smith, p; others.

On the Sunny Side of the Street/Body and Soul/Why Don't You Do Right?/Oh, Lady Be Good/I Got It Bad (and That Ain't Good)/How High the Moon/My Funny Valentine/Smooth Sailing/Frim Fram Sauce/Perdido/Night and Day/The Many Faces of Cole Porter: Get Out of Town; Easy to Love; Do Something to Me/The Ballad Medley: Body and Soul; The Man I Love; I Loves You Porgy/The Bossa Scene: The Girl from Ipanema; Fly Me to the Moon; O Nosso Amor (Carnival Samba); Cielito Lindo; Madalena; Agua de Beber (Water to Drink)/They Can't Take That Away from Me/St. Louis Blues/ L-O-V-E/Begin the Beguine/Indian Summer/Too Close for Comfort/I Ain't Got Nothin' but the Blues/Day by Day/Ordinary Fool/Billie's Bounce/Please Don't Talk about Me When I'm Gone/Make Me Rainbows/After You've Gone/'Round Midnight/Imagine My Frustration/Duke's Place/Satin Doll/Something to Live For/So Danco Samba/Don't Be That Way/You've Changed/Let's Do It/On the Sunny Side of the Street/Cottontail/ You've Got a Friend/Spring Can Really Hang You Up the Most/Madalena/Shiny Stockings/I Can't Stop Loving You/C-Jam Blues/Sweet Georgia Brown/They Can't Take That Away from Me/Ev'ry Time We Say Goodbye/The Man I Love/It Don't Mean a Thing (if It Ain't Got That Swing)/Lemon Drop/The Very Thought of You/Happy Blues/ Caravan/Satin Doll/Teach Me Tonight/Wave/It's All Right with Me/How High the Moon/T'Ain't Nobody's Bizness If I Do/You've Changed/Basella/Manteca/Willow Weep for Me/All of Me/Blue Moon/Night and Day/Flying Home

CLASSICS

Ella Fitzgerald: 1935–1937

500

Compilation: EF; Chick Webb and His Orchestra; Teddy Wilson and His Orchestra; Benny Goodman and His Orchestra; Ella Fitzgerald and Her Savoy Eight.

I'll Chase the Blues Away/Love and Kisses/Rhythm and Romance/I'll Chase the Blues Away/My Melancholy Baby/All My Life/Crying Out My Heart for You/Under the Spell of the Blues/When I Get Low I Get High/Sing Me a Swing Song (and Let Me Dance)/A Little Bit Later On/Love You're Just a Laugh/Devoting My Time to You/ You'll Have to Swing It/Swingin' on the Reservation/Got the Spring Fever Blues/Vote for Mr. Rhythm/Goodnight My Love/Oh, Yes, Take Another Guess/Didja Mean It/My Last Affair/Organ Grinder's Swing/Shine/Darktown Strutter's Ball/Take Another Guess

Ella Fitzgerald: 1937–1938

506

Compilation: EF; Chick Webb and His Orchestra; The Mills Brothers; Ella Fitzgerald and Her Savoy Eight.

Big Boy Blue/Dedicated to You/You Showed Me the Way/Crying Mood/Love Is the Thing So They Say/All or Nothing at All/If You Ever Should Leave/Everyone's Wrong but Me/Deep in the Heart of the South/Just a Simple Melody/I Got a Guy/Holiday in Harlem/Rock It for Me/I Want to Be Happy/The Dipsy Doodle/If Dreams Come True/ Hallelujah!/Bei Mir Bist du Schoen/It's My Turn Now/It's Wonderful/I Was Doing All Right/A-Tisket, A-Tasket

Ella Fitzgerald: 1938–1939

518

EF; Chick Webb and His Orchestra; EF and Her Savoy Eight.

Heart of Mine/I'm Just a Jitterbug/This Time It's Real/(Oh, Oh) What Do You Know about Love?/You Can't Be Mine (and Someone Else's Too)/We Can't Go On This Way/ Saving Myself for You/If You Only Knew/Pack Up Your Sins and Go to the Devil/ MacPherson Is Rehearsin' (to Swing)/Everybody Step/Ella/Wacky Dust/Gotta Pebble in My Shoe/I Can't Stop Loving You/Strictly from Dixie/Woe Is Me/I Let a Tear Fall in the River/F. D. R. Jones/I Love Each Move You Make/It's Foxy/I Found My Yellow Basket/Undecided

Ella Fitzgerald: 1939

525

EF; Chick Webb and His Orchestra; EF and Her Savoy Eight; EF and Her Famous Orchestra.

'Tain't What You Do/One Side of Me/My Heart Belongs to Daddy/Once Is Enough for Me/I Had to Live and Learn/Sugar Pie/It's Slumbertime along the Swanee/I'm up a Tree/Chew-Chew-Chew (Your Bubble Gum)/Don't Worry about Me/If Anything Happened to You/If That's What You're Thinking, You're Wrong/If You Ever Change Your Mind/Have Mercy/Little White Lies/Coochi-Coochi-Coo/That Was My Heart/ Betcha Nickel/Stairway to the Stars/I Want the Waiter (with the Water)/That's All, Brother/Out of Nowhere

Ella Fitzgerald: 1939–1940

566

Compilation: EF and Her Famous Orchestra.

My Last Goodbye/Billy (I Always Dream of Billy)/Please Tell Me the Truth/I'm Not Complainin'/You're Gonna Lose Your Gal/After I Say I'm Sorry/Baby, What Else Can I Do?/My Wubba Dolly (Rubber Dolly)/Lindy Hopper's Delight/Moon Ray/Is There Somebody Else/Sugar Blues/The Starlit Hour/What's the Matter with Me?/Baby, Won't You Please Come Home?/If It Weren't for You/Sing Song Swing/Imagination/ Take It from the Top/Tea Dance/Jubilee Swing/Untitled Instrumental/Deedel-De-Dum

Ella Fitzgerald: 1940–1941

644

Compilation: EF and Her Famous Orchestra.

Shake Down the Stars/Gulf Coast Blues/I Fell in Love with a Dream/Five O'Clock Whistle/So Long/Louisville, K-Y/Taking a Chance on Love/Cabin in the Sky/I'm the Lonesomest Gal in Town/Three Little Words/Hello Ma! I Done It Again/Wishful Thinking/The One I Love (Belongs to Somebody Else)/The Muffin Man/Keep Cool, Fool/No Nothing/My Man/I Can't Believe That You're in Love with Me/I Must Have That Man/When My Sugar Walks down the Street/I Got It Bad (and That Ain't Good)/ Melinda the Mousie/ Can't Help Lovin' Dat Man

Ella Fitzgerald: 1941–1944

840

Compilation: EF; The Ink Spots; others.

Jim/This Love of Mine/Somebody Nobody Loves/You Don't Know What Love Is/Who Are You?/I'm Thrilled/Make Love to Me/I'm Gettin' Mighty Lonesome for You/When I Come Back Crying (Will You Be Laughing at Me)/All I Need Is You/Mama Come Home/My Heart and I Decided/(I Put) A Four Leaf Clover in Your Pocket/He's My Guy/Cow Cow Boogie (Cuma-Ti-Yi-Ti-Ay)/Once Too Often/Time Alone Will Tell/Into Each Life Some Rain Must Fall/I'm Making Believe/And Her Tears Flowed Like Wine/ I'm Confessin' (That I Love You)

Ella Fitzgerald: 1945–1946

921

Compilation: EF; Louis Jordan and His Tympany Five; others.

It's Full or It Ain't No Good/How Long Must I Wait for You?/Don't Worry 'bout That Mule (1)/Salt Pork, West Virginia/Paper Boy/Don't Worry 'bout That Mule (2)/Stone Cold Dead in the Market/Petootie Pie (1)/Petootie Pie (2)/Reconversion Blues/It's So Easy/Beware!/Don't Let the Sun Catch You Crying/Choo-Choo Ch'Boogie/Ain't That Just Like a Woman/That Chick's Too Young to Fry/No Sale/If It's Love You Want Baby, That's Me/Ain't Nobody Here but Us Chickens/Let the Good Times Roll/All for the Love of Lil/Texas and Pacific/Jack, You're Dead

Ella Fitzgerald: 1945–1947

998

Compilation: EF; The Ink Spots; The Delta Rhythm Boys; Louis Jordan; Buddy Rich; Louis Armstrong.

I'm Beginning to See the Light/That's the Way It Is/(It's Only a) Paper Moon/Cry You Out of My Heart/A Kiss Goodnight/Benny's Coming Home on Saturday/Flying Home/ Stone Cold Dead in the Market/Petootie Pie (1)/That's Rich/I'll Always Be in Love with You/I'll See You in My Dreams/Petootie Pie (2)/You Won't Be Satisfied/The Frim Fram Sauce/I'm Just a Lucky So-and-So/I Didn't Mean a Word I Said/(I Love You) For Sentimental Reasons/It's a Pity to Say Goodnight/Guilty/Sentimental Journey/ Budella (Blue Skies)

Ella Fitzgerald: 1947–1948

1049

Compilation: EF; Illinois Jacquet; Hank Jones; Ray Brown; others.

A Sunday Kind of Love/That's My Desire/Oh, Lady Be Good/Don't You Think I Ought to Know?/You're Breakin' In a New Heart/I Want to Learn about Love/That Old Feeling/My Baby Likes to Be-Bop/No Sense/How High the Moon/I've Got a Feelin' I'm Fallin'/You Turned the Tables on Me/I Cried and Cried and Cried/Robbins' Nest/Tea Leaves/My Happiness/It's Too Soon to Know/I Can't Go On (Without You)/To Make a Mistake Is Human/In My Dreams

Ella Fitzgerald: 1949

1153

Compilation: EF; arrangements by Sonny Burke, Gordon Jenkins, and Sy Oliver; The Mills Brothers; Bill Doggett; Louis Jordan and His Tympany Five; others.

I Couldn't Stay Away/Old Mother Hubbard/Someone Like You/Happy Talk/I'm Gonna Wash That Man Right Outa My Hair/Black Coffee/Lover's Gold/Baby, It's Cold Out-side/Don't Cry, Cry-Baby/Crying/A New Shade of Blue/In the Evening (When the Sun Goes Down)/Talk Fast, My Heart, Talk Fast/I'm Waitin' for the Junk Man/Basin Street Blues/I Hadn't Anyone till You/Dream a Little Longer/Foolish Tears/A Man Wrote a Song/Fairy Tales/I Gotta Have My Baby Back

Ella Fitzgerald: 1950

1195

Compilation: EF; Louis Armstrong; Hank Jones; Ray Brown; The Ink Spots; Louis Jordan and His Tympany Five; others.

Baby, Won't You Say You Love Me?/Don'cha Go 'Way Mad/Solid as a Rock/I've Got the World on a String/Sugarfoot Rag/Peas and Rice/M-I-S-S-I-S-S-I-P-P-I/I Don't Want the World/Ain't Nobody's Business but My Own/I'll Never Be Free/Dream a

Little Dream of Me/Can Anyone Explain?/Looking for a Boy/My One and Only/How Long Has This Been Going On?/I've Got a Crush on You/But Not for Me/Soon/Someone to Watch over Me/Maybe/Santa Claus Got Stuck in My Chimney/Molasses, Molasses/Little Small Town Girl/I Still Feel the Same about You

Ella Fitzgerald: 1951

1261

Compilation: EF; Sy Oliver; Louis Armstrong; Bill Doggett; Hank Jones; others.

Lonesome Gal/The Beanbag Song/The Chesapeake and Ohio/Little Man in a Flying Saucer/Because of Rain/The Hot Canary/Even As You and I/Do You Really Love Me?/Love You Madly/Mixed Emotions/Smooth Sailing/Come On-a My House/I Don't Want to Take a Chance/There Never Was a Baby Like My Baby/Give a Little, Get a Little (Love)/Necessary Evil/Oops!/Would You Like to Take a Walk?/Who Walks In When I Walk Out?/Baby Doll/What Does It Take?/Lady Bug/Lazy Day

BUDDHA

Ella Fitzgerald in the Groove

(early 1940s) (Radio broadcasts) **74465 99702 2**

EF; Ella Fitzgerald and Her Famous Orchestra.

A-Tisket, A-Tasket/Oh Boy! I'm in the Groove/Day In—Day Out/(I Always Dream of) Billy/Please Tell Me the Truth/Sing Song Swing/The Starlit Hour/Yodelin' Jive/Baby, What Else Can I Do?/My Wubba Dolly/My Prayer/Betcha Nickel/To You/(Hep! Hep!) The Jumpin' Jive/Careless/Well All Right/Stairway to the Stars/That's All, Brother/The Lamp Is Low/Little White Lies/St. Louis Blues

PARROT

Ella Fitzgerald and Bing Crosby: My Happiness

(1949, 1950, 1951, 1952, 1953, 1954) **PARCD 002**

EF; *Bing Crosby, vo; John Scott Trotter Kraft Show Orchestra; The Mills Brothers, vo; Red Nichols, tpt; others.

*Way Back Home/A Dreamer's Holiday/My Happiness/*Stay with the Happy People/I Hadn't Anyone 'til You/*Basin Street Blues/Can Anyone Explain/*Silver Bells/Marshmallow World/Memphis Blues/Undecided/Medley: Trying; My Favorite Song; Between the Devil and the Deep Blue Sea/*Rudolph the Red-Nosed Reindeer/Medley: I Hadn't Anyone 'til You; If You Ever Should Leave; I Can't Give You Anything but Love/*Chicago Style/*White Christmas/Moanin' Low/Someone to Watch over Me/*Istanbul/Looking for a Boy/*That's a Plenty/Taking a Chance on Love

BALDWIN STREET MUSIC

The Enchanting Ella Fitzgerald Live at Birdland 1950–52
BJH 309

EF; Ray Brown Trio.

Old Mother Hubbard/These Foolish Things/In a Mellow Tone/Flying Home/Be in Your Own Back Yard/Jumping with Symphony Syd (1)/How High the Moon (1)/Show Me the Way to Get Out of This World/Angel Eyes/Walkin' My Baby Back Home/Goody Goody/Air Mail Special/How High the Moon (2)/It's Only a Paper Moon/Be Anything (but Be Mine)/Preview/You're Driving Me Crazy/Lemon Drop/The Frim Fram Sauce/ Imagination/How Long Has This Been Going On/Someone to Watch over Me/Jumping with Symphony Syd (2)/I Can't Get Started/Later/That Old Black Magic

TAX

Jazz at the Philharmonic 1957: Americans in Sweden
3703-2

EF; Don Abney, p; Herb Ellis, g; Ray Brown, b; Jo Jones, d; *Roy Eldridge, tpt; *Stuff Smith, vln; *Oscar Peterson, p. (Tracks with Fitzgerald listed here.)

*You Got Me Singing the Blues/Angel Eyes/Lullaby of Birdland/Tenderly/Do Nothin' till You Hear from Me/April in Paris/I Can't Give You Anything but Love/*Love for Sale/*It Don't Mean a Thing (if It Ain't Got That Swing)*

STATUS

Duke Ellington and Ella Fitzgerald: Live at the Greek Theater, Los Angeles
(1966) DSTS 1013

EF; Duke Ellington Orchestra; Jimmy Jones, p; Jim Hughart, b; Ed Thigpen, d. (There are other tracks with the Duke Ellington Orchestra only.)

Sweet Georgia Brown/Star Dust/Só Danò Samba/How Long Has This Been Going On?/St. Louis Blues/Misty/Mack the Knife/Cotton Tail/Things Ain't What They Used to Be

WARNER/REPRISE

Things Ain't What They Used to Be (and You Better Believe It)

(1969, 1970) **9 26023-2** (Ella—LP RS-6354 and Things Ain't What They Used To Be—LP RS-6432)

EF; Studio orchestras, arranged and directed by Richard Perry and Gerald Wilson.

Get Ready/The Hunter Gets Captured by the Game/Yellow Man/I'll Never Fall in Love Again/Got to Get You into My Life/I Wonder Why/Ooo Baby Baby/Savoy Truffle/Open Your Window/Knock on Wood/Sunny/Mas Que Nada/A Man and a Woman/Days of Wine and Roses/Black Coffee/Tuxedo Junction/I Heard It through the Grapevine/Don't Dream of Anybody but Me/Things Ain't What They Used to Be/Willow Weep for Me/ Manteca/Just When We're Falling in Love

LEGACY/COLUMBIA

Ella Fitzgerald: Newport Jazz Festival Live at Carnegie Hall

(2 CDs) (1973) **C2K 66809**

EF; Chick Webb Orchestra (led by Eddie Barefield); Ellis Larkins, p; Joe Pass, g; Tommy Flanagan, p; others. (Tracks with Fitzgerald listed here.)

A-Tisket, A-Tasket/Indian Summer/Smooth Sailing/You Turned the Tables on Me/Nice Work If You Can Get It/ I've Got a Crush on You/ I've Gotta Be Me/Down in the Depths/Good Morning, Heartache/What's Going On?/Miss Otis Regrets/Don't Worry 'bout Me/These Foolish Things/Any Old Blues/Taking a Chance on Love/I'm in the Mood for Love/Lemon Drop/A-Tisket, A-Tasket (excerpt)*/Some of These Days/ People/ A-Tisket, A-Tasket* (excerpt)

Ella Fitzgerald — Selected VHS/DVD Videography

TELEVISION SHOWS

The Incomparable Nat "King" Cole, vols. 1 and 2

Kultur, DVD—100 minutes. From Cole's 1957 television series. Also includes footage with the Mills Brothers, Roy Eldridge, Oscar Peterson, Harry Belafonte, Coleman Hawkins, and Sammy Davis, Jr.

Ella Fitzgerald in Concert

Video Yesteryear 763, VHS—66 minutes. Classic footage of Ella Fitzgerald on television in the 1950s and 1960s, including performances with Benny Goodman on the 1958 NBC special *Swing into Spring,* hosted by Dave Garroway, and with Duke Ellington on a special aired in 1968.

Frank Sinatra with Ella Fitzgerald and Frank Sinatra with Sammy Davis, Jr.

Passport International, VHS—approx. 100 minutes. Includes Ella Fitzgerald's appearance on a Sinatra television special on December 13, 1959. This was a Timex Spectacular called *Frank Sinatra: An Evening with Friends.* Other guests include Juliet Prowse and the Hi-Los.

Frank Sinatra: A Man and His Music + Ella + Jobim

Warner Reprise Video, VHS/DVD—50 minutes. A fantastic Frank Sinatra special on November 13, 1967. Ella Fitzgerald guests with Antonio Carlos Jobim. She sings four solo numbers and does a medley with Sinatra.

American Masters/Ella Fitzgerald: Something to Live For

WinStar TV & Video, VHS/DVD—86 minutes. Educational Broadcasting Corporation documentary of the life and artistry of Ella Fitzgerald. Hosted by Tony Bennett. Includes performance footage and interviews with several musicians.

Biography—Ella Fitzgerald: Forever Ella

A&E/New Video, VHS—100 minutes. A&E Television Network *Biography* hosted by Nancy Wilson. Chronicles the life and artistry of Ella Fitzgerald. Includes concert footage and interviews with several musicians. Exceptional excerpts from an interview of Ella in the mid-1980s.

Ella Fitzgerald: The Singer, Not the Song

Films for the Humanities & Sciences, VHS/DVD—25 minutes. Brief study of Ella Fitzgerald's life and music. Includes interviews and some performance footage.

FILMS

Ride 'Em Cowboy

Universal Studios, VHS—approx. 85 minutes. Inane comedy about peanut and hot dog vendors turned cowboys. Directed by Frank Skinner. Principle stars are the legendary Bud Abbott and Lou Costello. Ella Fitzgerald sings "A-Tisket, A-Tasket" in the film.

Pete Kelly's Blues

Warner Home Video, VHS—approx. 95 minutes. Film from 1955 about jazz musicians and mobsters in Kansas City during prohibition. Directed by Jack Webb. Stars include Webb, Edmond O'Brien, Janet Leigh, Peggy Lee, Lee Marvin, and Ella Fitzgerald.

Bibliography

BOOKS AND SELECTED ARTICLES ABOUT ELLA FITZGERALD

Bernstein, Nina. "The Gap in Ella Fitzgerald's Life." *New York Times.* June 23, 1996.

Burman, Maurice. "Ella: 'I Prefer Ballads,' She Tells Burman." *Melody Maker.* May 10, 1958.

Dunbar, Ernest. "Ella Still Sings Just This Side of the Angels." *New York Times.* November 24, 1974.

"Ella Admires Bebop but Prefers to Sing Ballads." *Ebony.* May 1949.

Feather, Leonard. "Ella." *Los Angeles Times.* January 30, 1983.

———. "Ella Meets the Duke." *Playboy.* November 1957.

———. "Ella Today." *Down Beat.* November 18, 1965.

Fidelman, Geoffrey Mark. *First Lady of Song: Ella Fitzgerald for the Record.* New York: Citadel Press, 1996.

"Fitzgerald Mementos Jazz up Smithsonian." *Newark Star-Ledger.* April 26, 1997.

Giddins, Gary. "First Lady." *Village Voice.* December 1976.

Gourse, Leslie, ed. *The Ella Fitzgerald Companion: Seven Decades of Commentary.* New York: Schirmer Books, 1998.

"Granz Contract Signed by Ella." *Down Beat.* May 19, 1954.

Hall, Lawrence. "For the Love of Ella." *Newark (N.J.) Star-Ledger.* May 4, 1994.

Haskins, Jim. *Ella Fitzgerald: A Life through Jazz.* London: New English Library, 1991.

Hentoff, Nat. "Ella Tells of Trouble in Mind Concerning Discs, Television." *Down Beat.* February 23, 1955.

Holden, Stephen. "A Voice That Always Brings a Happy Ending." *New York Times.* April 25, 1993.

"Honor Ella Fitzgerald." *Variety*. March 28, 1984.

"'I Don't Like to Sing Bop Most,' Says Ella." *Down Beat*. September 22, 1948.

Ingham, Sandy. "Everyone Gets a Kick out of Ella Rehearsal." *The Home News*. May 22, 1980.

Johnson, J. Wilfred. *Ella Fitzgerald: An Annotated Discography; Including a Complete Discography of Chick Webb*. Jefferson, N.C.: McFarland & Company, 2001.

Kliment, Bud. *Ella Fitzgerald*. New York: Chelsea House Publishers, 1988.

McDonough, John. "Ella: A Voice We'll Never Forget." *Down Beat*. September 1996.

———. "The Ella Fitzgerald Legacy." *Down Beat*. September 1996.

———. "Tales from Ella's Fellas." *Down Beat*. September 1995.

Nicholson, Stuart. *Ella Fitzgerald: A Biography of the First Lady of Jazz*. New York: Charles Scribner's Sons, 1993.

Rockwell, John. "Half a Century of Song with the Great 'Ella.'" *New York Times*. June 15, 1986.

"She Who Is Ella." *Time*. November 27, 1964.

Siegel, Joel. "Ella at 65." *Jazz Times*. November 1983.

Tynan, John. "Ella: It Took a Hit to Make Miss F. a Class Nitery Attraction." *Down Beat*. November 28, 1956.

"Will Rogers Award to Ella Fitzgerald." *Variety*. March 12, 1980.

Other Selected Articles

Bailey, Mildred. "My Life, Part I." *Swing*. June 1940.

———. "My Life, Part II." *Swing*. July 1940.

Balliett, Whitney. "Tommy Flanagan." *The New Yorker*. November 20, 1978.

Bamberger, Werner. "Connee Boswell Is Dead at 68; Long a Popular Singer and Actress." *New York Times*. October 12, 1976.

"Basie's Band Termed 'Best.'" *Down Beat*. February 10, 1954.

"Chick Webb Receives 5,000 Letters a Week." *Down Beat*. March 1937.

"'Cuts' Basie in Swing Battle." *Down Beat*. February 1938.

Dance, Stanley. "Rockin' Chair Lady, Barrelhouse Gal." *Saturday Review*. October 13, 1952.

———. "Tommy Flanagan: Out of the Background." *Down Beat*. January 13, 1966.

Davis, Francis. "The Loss of Count Basie." *The Atlantic Monthly*. August 1984.

"Devol Proves Musicians' Claim That He's Fastest and 'Great' at Same Time." *Down Beat*. November 3, 1948.

Dexter, Dave, Jr. "'Living like I Want to' Says Mildred Bailey." *Down Beat*. August 1, 1940.

Dilts, James D. "Baltimore's Gentleman of Jazz." *Baltimore City Paper*. February 15, 1995.

Egan, Jack. "Egan Finds Billy May Is a Big Man in the Biz." *Down Beat*. October 7, 1948.

Ellington, Duke. "Reminiscing in Tempo." *Down Beat*. July 2, 1964.

Ellis, Chris. "Connee Boswell: 3 Dec. 1907–11 Oct. 1976." *Storyville*. June–July 1977.

Emge, Charles. "Granz Flops in Home Town." *Down Beat*. April 1947.

———. "How Norman Granz' Flourishing Jazz Empire Started, Expanded." *Down Beat*. December 15, 1954.

Feather, Leonard. "The Blindfold Test: Anita's Chance." *Down Beat*. April 4, 1957.

———. "The James Joyce of Jazz." *Esquire*. June 1945.

———. "Mildred Bailey—A Tribute." *Down Beat*. January 25, 1952.

Fraser, C. Gerald. "Ethel Waters Is Dead at 80." *New York Times*. September 2, 1977.

Giddins, Gary. "Ethel Waters: Mother of Us All." *Village Voice*. October 10, 1977.

Goldberg, Joe. "Jimmy Rowles: Beauty on a Borrowed Piano." *Musician*. April 1988.

Gottlieb, Bill. "Sy Oliver No Personality Kid, but Big Band Has Talent." *Down Beat*. January 15, 1947.

"Granz Forms Two Labels, Dickers for Mars Masters, Cuts EP Price." *Down Beat*. February 8, 1956.

"Granz Makes Four of One." *Down Beat*. February 20, 1957.

Granz, Norman. "Granz Throws Leon's Own Words Right Back at Him." *Down Beat*. December 16, 1946.

"Hank Jones." *Down Beat*. October 30, 1958.

Hentoff, Nat. "Hank Jones: Hentoff on a Pianist Who Always Surprises." *Wall Street Journal*. November 9, 1992.

———. "Writer Underlines Granz' Top Jazz Accomplishment." *Down Beat*. December 15, 1954.

Holden, Stephen. "Joe Pass Is Surprise Guest of Fitzgerald at Carnegie." *New York Times*. June 24, 1985.

Jeske, Lee. "Tommy Flanagan on His Own." *Down Beat*. July 1982.

Korall, Burt. "Chick Webb: The Total Experience." *Modern Drummer*. January 1988.

"Leo Watson." *Metronome*. July 1950.

"Leo Watson, 52, Dies on Coast." *Down Beat*. June 16, 1950.

Levin, Mike. "All Recording Stops Today." *Down Beat*. August 1, 1942.

"Lou Levy." *Down Beat*. February 20, 1958.

Lucas, John. "Another Boswell Chronicle." *Jazz Journal*. January 1974.

———. "Cats Hepped by Connee's Chirping." *Down Beat*. October 15, 1944.

———. "Visionary Scoring Put Boswells Over." *Down Beat*. November 1, 1944.

Lyons, Len. "Jimmy Rowles: Noted New York Jazz Pianist and Accompanist." *Contemporary Keyboard*. July 1982.

Maynard, Jackie. "The Touch of Paul Smith." *Disc & That Magazine* 1, no. 5 (1978).

McDonough, John. "Norman Granz: JATP Pilot . . . Driving Pablo Home." *Down Beat*. October 1979.

———. "The Norman Granz Story, Part II: Pablo Patriarch." *Down Beat*. November 1979.

Meadow, Elliot. "The World of Tommy Flanagan." *Down Beat*. October 15, 1970.

Noonan, John P. "The Secrets of Chick Webb's Drumming Technique." *Down Beat*. September 1938.

Oakley, Helen. "Call Out Riot Squad to Handle Mob at Goodman-Webb Battle." *Down Beat*. June 1937.

Pareles, Jon. "Same 88 Keys, but 3 Piano Styles." *New York Times*. September 6, 1985.

Pease, Sharon. "Hank Jones Is Termed One of Top Modernists." *Down Beat*. January 26, 1951.

———. "Lou Levy One of Top Pianists in Bop Circles." *Down Beat*. August 26, 1949.

"Princeton Grads Get the 'Gate' as Some 1,600 Receive Degrees." *Newark Star-Ledger*. June 13, 1990.

Rowles, Jimmy. "Jimmie [*sic*] Rowles Reflects on Songs, Lyrics, Feelings . . . And Ella." *Crescendo International*. January 1982.

"Sy Oliver." *Ebony*. June 1951.

Watrous, Peter. "Sy Oliver, 77, a Jazz Composer, Arranger, and Band Leader, Dies." *New York Times*. May 28, 1988.

Wilder, Alec. "Ellis Larkins: An Appreciation." *Down Beat*. October 26, 1972.

Wilson, John S. "Count Basie, 79, Band Leader and Master of Swing, Dead." *New York Times*. April 27, 1984.

Wilson, Russ. "Marty Paich Turned Corner, Found Fame." *Oakland Tribune*. December 28, 1958.

Wolff, D. Leon. "Granz Bash a Caricature on Jazz." *Down Beat*. November 18, 1946.

Zwerin, Michael. "Key to Joe Pass: A Capo in His Head." *International Herald Tribune*. August 4, 1981.

Other Autobiographies and Biographies

Armstrong, Louis. *Louis Armstrong, in His Own Words: Selected Writings*. Edited by Thomas Brothers. New York: Oxford University Press, 1999.

Basie, Count, and Albert Murray. *Good Morning Blues: The Autobiography of Count Basie*. New York: Random House, 1985.

Bergreen, Laurence. *As Thousands Cheer: The Life of Irving Berlin*. New York: Viking, 1990.

———. *Louis Armstrong: An Extravagant Life*. New York: Broadway Books, 1997.

Clarke, Donald. *Wishing on the Moon: The Life and Times of Billie Holiday*. New York: Viking, 1994.

Collier, James Lincoln. *Benny Goodman and the Swing Era*. New York: Oxford University Press, 1989.

———. *Duke Ellington*. New York: Oxford University Press, 1987.

———. *Louis Armstrong: An American Genius*. New York: Oxford University Press, 1983.

Dance, Stanley. *The World of Count Basie*. New York: Charles Scribner's Sons, 1980.

Davis, Miles, and Quincy Troupe. *Miles: The Autobiography*. New York: Simon and Schuster, 1989.

Delannoy, Luc. *Pres: The Story of Lester Young*. Translated by Elena B. Odio. Fayetteville, Ark.: The University of Arkansas Press, 1993.

Ellington, Edward Kennedy (Duke). *Music Is My Mistress*. New York: Da Capo Press, 1993.

Firestone, Ross. *Swing, Swing, Swing: The Life and Times of Benny Goodman*. New York: W. W. Norton, 1993.

Fordin, Hugh. *Getting to Know Him: A Biography of Oscar Hammerstein II*. New York: Random House, 1977.

Giddins, Gary. *Bing Crosby: A Pocketful of Dreams—The Early Years, 1903–1940*. New York: Little, Brown and Company, 2001.

Gillespie, Dizzy, and Al Fraser. *To Be or Not to Bop*. Garden City, N.Y.: Double & Company, 1979.

Gourse, Leslie. *Every Day: The Story of Joe Williams*. New York: Da Capo, 1985.

————. *Sassy: The Life of Sarah Vaughan.* New York: Da Capo Press, 1994.

————. *Unforgettable: The Life and Mystique of Nat King Cole.* New York: St. Martin's Press, 1991.

Hajdu, David. *Lush Life: A Biography of Billy Strayhorn.* New York: Farrar Straus Giroux, 1996.

Hammond, John, and Irving Townsend. *John Hammond on Record: An Autobiography.* New York: Ridge Press/Summit Books, 1977.

Jablonski, Edward. *Alan Jay Lerner: A Biography.* New York: Henry Holt and Company, 1996.

Jewell, Derek. *Duke: A Portrait of Duke Ellington.* New York: W. W. Norton, 1977.

Jones, Max, and John Chilton. *Louis: The Louis Armstrong Story, 1900–1971.* New York: Da Capo Press, 1988.

Lees, Gene. *Oscar Peterson: The Will to Swing.* Rocklin, Calif.: Prima Publishing & Communications, 1990.

Lydon, Michael. *Ray Charles: Man and Music.* New York: Riverhead Books, 1998.

McBrien, William. *Cole Porter: A Biography.* New York: Alfred A. Knopf, 1998.

Nicholson, Stuart. *Billie Holiday.* Boston: Northeastern University Press, 1995.

O'Meally, Robert. *Lady Day: The Many Faces of Billie Holiday.* New York: Arcade Publishing, 1991.

Peyser, Joan. *The Memory of All That: The Life of George Gershwin.* New York: Simon & Schuster, 1993.

Schwartz, Charles. *Cole Porter: A Biography.* New York: Da Capo Press, 1992.

Secrest, Meryle. *Somewhere for Me: A Biography of Richard Rodgers.* New York: Alfred A. Knopf, 2001.

Shipton, Alyn. *Groovin' High: The Life of Dizzy Gillespie.* New York: Oxford University Press, 1999.

Taraborrelli, J. Randy. *Sinatra: A Complete Life.* Secaucus, N.J.: Birch Lane Press, 1997.

Tormé, Mel. *Traps—The Drum Wonder: The Life of Buddy Rich.* New York: Oxford University Press, 1991.

Tucker, Mark. *Ellington: The Early Years.* Urbana and Chicago, Ill.: University of Illinois Press, 1991.

Waters, Ethel, and Charles Samuels. *His Eye Is on the Sparrow.* Garden City, N.Y.: Doubleday & Company, 1951.

Topical and Historical Studies, Reference Works

Balliett, Whitney. *American Musicians: Fifty-Six Portraits in Jazz.* New York: Oxford University Press, 1986.

————. *American Singers: Twenty-Seven Portraits in Song.* New York: Oxford University Press, 1988.

Clarke, Donald, ed. *The Penguin Encyclopedia of Popular Music.* New York: Penguin Books, 1998.

Connor, Donald R. *BG—Off the Record: A Bio/Discography of Benny Goodman.* Fairless Hills, Pa.: Gaildonna Publishers, 1958.

Crow, Bill. *Jazz Anecdotes.* New York: Oxford University Press, 1990.

Crowther, Bruce, and Mike Pinfold. *Singing Jazz: The Singers and Their Styles.* San Francisco: Miller Freeman Books, 1997.

David, Norman. *Jazz Arranging*. New York: Ardsley House, 1998.

Erenberg, Lewis A. *Swingin' the Dream: Big Band Jazz and the Rebirth of American Culture*. Chicago: The University of Chicago Press, 1998.

Feather, Leonard. *The Passion for Jazz*. New York: Horizon Press, 1980.

Finkelstein, Sidney. "Jazz: A People's Music." In *Keeping Time: Readings in Jazz History*, edited by Robert Walser. New York: Oxford University Press, 1999.

Friedwald, Will. *Jazz Singing: America's Great Voices from Bessie Smith to Bebop and Beyond*. New York: Da Capo Press, 1992.

Giddins, Gary. *Visions of Jazz: The First Century*. New York: Oxford University Press, 1998.

Gitler, Ira. *Swing to Bop: An Oral History of the Transition in Jazz in the 1940s*. New York: Oxford University Press, 1985.

Harrison, Daphne Duval. *Black Pearls: Blues Queens of the 1920s*. New Brunswick, N.J.: Rutgers University Press, 1988.

Hennessey, Thomas J. *From Jazz to Swing: African-American Jazz Musicians and Their Music, 1890–1935*. Detroit: Wayne State University Press, 1994.

Hyland, William G. *The Song Is Ended: Songwriters and American Music, 1900–1950*. New York: Oxford University Press, 1995.

Kammen, Michael. *The Lively Arts: Gilbert Seldes and the Transformation of Cultural Criticism in the United States*. New York: Oxford University Press, 1996.

Kernfeld, Barry, ed. *The New Grove Dictionary of Jazz*. London: Macmillan Press Limited, 1988.

Korall, Burt. *Drummin' Men: The Heartbeat of Jazz—The Swing Years*. New York: Schirmer Books, 1990.

Lees, Gene. *Singers and the Song II*. New York: Oxford University Press, 1998.

Martin, Henry. *Enjoying Jazz*. New York: Schirmer Books, 1986.

Nestico, Sammy. *The Complete Arranger*. Delevan, N.Y.: Kendor Music, Inc., 1993.

O'Neill, William L. *Coming Apart: An Informal History of America in the 1960s*. New York: Times Books, 1971.

Owens, Thomas. *Bebop: The Music and Its Players*. New York: Oxford University Press, 1995.

Pearson, Nathan W., Jr. *Goin' to Kansas City*. Urbana and Chicago, Ill.: University of Illinois Press, 1987.

Pleasants, Henry. *The Great American Popular Singers*. New York: Simon and Schuster, 1974.

Porter, Lewis, Michael Ullman, and Ed Hazell. *Jazz: From Its Origins to the Present*. Englewood Cliffs, N.J.: Prentice Hall, 1993.

Raynor, Henry. *Music and Society Since 1815*. London: Barrie and Jenkins, 1976.

Riddle, Nelson. *Arranged by Nelson Riddle*. Miami, Fla.: Warner Brothers Publications, 1985.

Schuller, Gunther. *Early Jazz: Its Roots and Musical Development*. New York: Oxford University Press, 1968.

———. *The Swing Age: The Development of Jazz, 1930–1945*. New York: Oxford University Press, 1989.

Simon, George T. *The Big Bands*. New York: Macmillan, 1971.

Stuessy, Joe, and Scott Lipscomb. *Rock and Roll: Its History and Stylistic Development*. 3rd ed. Upper Saddle River, N.J.: Prentice Hall, 1999.

Tucker, Mark, ed. *The Duke Ellington Reader*. New York: Oxford University Press, 1993.

Ulanov, Barry. *A History of Jazz in America*. New York: Da Capo Press, 1972.

Walker, Leo. *The Wonderful Era of the Great Dance Bands*. New York: Da Capo Press, 1990.

Walser, Robert, ed. *Keeping Time: Readings in Jazz History*. New York: Oxford University Press, 1999.

Wilder, Alec. *American Popular Song: The Great Innovators, 1900–1950*. With an introduction by James T. Maher. New York: Oxford University Press, 1990.

Williams, Martin. *Jazz Heritage*. New York: Oxford University Press, 1985.

Index

"Abide With Me," 151
Abney, Don, 182
"Ac-cent-tchu-ate the Positive," 139
Adler and Ross, 147
"After You," 137
"After You've Gone," 150, 180
"Ain't Misbehavin,' " 171, 179
"Air Mail Special," 149
"Alexander's Ragtime Band," 123
Alexander, Van, 78, 79, 101
"All by Myself," 123
"All I Do Is Dream of You," 153
"All of You," 111
All That Jazz, 101
"All the Things You Are," 130–32
"All Too Soon," 118, 235
"Almost Like Being in Love," 148
"Alone Together," 135
"Alright, Okay, You Win," 153
American Federation of Musicians
    (AFM), 157
"Angel Eyes," 87, 105, 206, 212
"Any Old Time," 137
"Anything Goes," 111, 217
Anything Goes (TV special), 109
Apollo Theater, 10, 40, 51
"April in Paris," 24, 192

Arlen, Harold, 140. *See also specific
    songs* and *Harold Arlen Song Book,
    The*
Armstrong, Louis, 8, 18–30, 32, 33, 42,
    49, 51–54, 57, 61, 64, 70, 75, 103,
    104, 120; "Cheek to Cheek," 24,
    51–56; "A Fine Romance," 27–28,
    29; "Heebie Jeebies," 19–20; Hot
    Five and Hot Seven, 19–20;
    "Makin' Whoopee," 199–201; "The
    Nearness of You," 24, 25; *Porgy and
    Bess,* 28, 30; reaction to bebop,
    82–83; and scat singing, 19–20;
    "When Your Lover Has Gone,"
    188–90
"As Long As I Live," 146
Atlantic Records, 137
"At Last," 239
"At Long Last Love," 137
"At Sundown," 153
"A-Tisket, A-Tasket," 78–80, 86, 105
Auld, Georgie, 152
"Autumn in New York," 26, 137
"Azure," 117

"Baby, What Else Can I Do," 198
Bacharach, Burt, 5, 148, 153, 164, 225

Bailey, Mildred, 35–37, 150, 155
"Basella," 180
Basie, Count, 12, 58, 101, 105, 167–80, 240
"Basin Street Blues," 104
Bassman, George, 70, 101
Bayes, Nora, 126
Beatles, The, 14, 153, 154, 171
Bebop, 4, 11–12, 81–83
"Because of Rain," 104
"Begin the Beguine," 119, 175
"Bei Mir Bist du Schoen," 75
Bellson, Louis, 26, 152
Bennett, Max, 211
Best is Yet to Come, The, 137–38
Betts, Keter, 87, 175, 180
"Between the Devil and the Deep Blue Sea," 139
"Bewitched," 116
"Billie's Bounce," 228
"Black Coffee," 154, 206
Blakey, Art, 13
"Bli-Blip," 118
Blood, Sweat, and Tears, 225
"Blue and Sentimental," 240
"Blue Lou," 106
"Blue Moon," 116
"Blue Room," 116
"Blues in the Night," 139, 146
"Body and Soul," 87, 130, 137, 228
"Born to Be Blue," 221
"Born to Lose," 152
Boswell, Connee, 8, 18–19, 35, 37–57; arranging prowess, 38; "Cheek to Cheek," 49, 51–55; "I Can't Give You Anything but Love," 42–45; "I Could Write a Book," 46–47; "Star Dust," 45–46; "Where or When," 47–49; "With Every Breath I Take," 40–42
Boswell Sisters, 8, 37–38
"Boy from Ipanema, The." See "Girl from Ipanema, The"
Bregman, Buddy, 108–11; first recordings with Ella Fitzgerald, 109
Brighten the Corner, 151
"Broadway," 149

Brown, Ray, 22, 26, 117, 184, 185, 186, 215, 220
Bryant, Ray, 182
Bulling, Erich, 107
"But Not for Me," 127, 195
"By Strauss," 126

"Cabaret," 226
Camel Caravan (TV special), 157
"Can Anyone Explain," 104
"Can't Help Lovin' Dat Man," 132, 216
"Can't We Be Friends," 23
Capitol Records, 109, 122, 124, 138, 151–53
"Caravan," 118–20, 212, 217
"Careless," 106
Carmichael, Hoagy, 35, 45, 74, 199
Carmichael, Ralph, 151–52
Carson, Tee, 153, 182
Carter, Benny, 10, 70, 139, 152, 175, 179
"C'est Magnifique," 137
"Change Partners," 123
Charles, Ray, 150, 152, 175
"Cheek to Cheek," 24, 49, 51–56, 217
"Chelsea Bridge," 118
"C-Jam Blues." See "Duke's Place"
"Clap Hands, Here Comes Charlie," 221
Clap Hands, Here Comes Charlie (album), 220–22
Clapton, Eric, 153
Clarke, Kenny, 82
Classy Pair, A, 175–79
"Clementine," 118
"Close Your Eyes," 143
Cole, Nat King, 92, 104, 124, 150, 175
Coleman, Ornette, 14
Cole Porter Song Book, The, 13, 95, 109–14
Collier, James Lincoln, 13–15, 21, 74, 102
Coltrane, John, 19, 20, 21, 31, 118, 158
Columbia Records, 31, 32, 116, 122
"Come Rain or Come Shine," 140, 228
"Comes Love," 26, 239

Complete Ella Fitzgerald and Louis Armstrong, The, 21, 22
Complete Ella Fitzgerald Song Books, The, 127
Complete Ella in Berlin: Mack the Knife, The, 86, 203–6
Cote d'Azur Concerts, 165–66
"Cotton Tail," 117, 162, 164
"Crazy Rhythm," 225
Crosby, Bing, 20–21, 35, 36, 37, 38, 138, 144
Crosby, Bob, 124
"Cry Me a River," 220

Dance bands: advent of arranging, 100; evolution of, 99–100
"Dancing on the Ceiling," 116
"Darktown Strutters Ball," 75
"Darn That Dream," 137
David, Hal, 148, 153, 164
Davis, Eddie "Lockjaw," 175
Davis, Miles, 13, 14, 27, 83, 150
Davis, Wild Bill, 149
Day, Doris, 104
"Day By Day," 228
"Day Dream," 118
"Day In-Day Out," 133
"Days of Wine and Roses," 154
Decca Records, 75, 84, 94–95, 100–102, 103, 149, 169; arrangers for Ella Fitzgerald, 101–2; commercializing Ella Fitzgerald, 100–101, 106
"'Deed I Do," 173
"Deedle-De-Dum," 75
"Deep Purple," 137, 153
De la Rosa, Frank, 153, 224
DeVol, Frank, 142–44, 151, 153
Dexter, Dave, 151–52
"Did You Mean It," 157
"Dites-Moi," 147–48
Dixon, Charlie, 101
Dodgion, Jerry, 149
Doggett, Bill, 106, 148–50
"Don'cha Go 'Way Mad," 153
"Do Nothing till You Hear from Me," 117
"Don't Be That Way," 26, 135, 137
"Don't Fence Me In," 111

"Don't Get Around Much Anymore," 117
"Don't Let the Doorknob Hit You," 152
"Don't Touch Me," 152
"Don't Worry 'Bout Me," 179
"Down in the Depths (on the Ninetieth Floor)," 137
"Dream," 133
"Dream a Little Dream of Me," 104, 173
Dream Dancing, 137
"Dreams Are Made for Children," 146
"Drop Me Off in Harlem," 118
Duke Ellington Song Book, The, 116–22
"Duke's Place" ("C-Jam Blues"), 162, 164, 175

"Early Autumn," 105, 133
Easy Living, 234
"Easy to Love," 112
Edison, Harry "Sweets," 152, 175
Eldridge, Roy, 146, 175
Ella, 153, 154. See also *Things Ain't What They Used to Be (and You Better Believe It)*
Ella Abraca Jobim, 107
Ella and Basie, 171–75
Ella and Louis, 22–25, 56
Ella and Louis Again, 26–28, 29, 199–201
Ella and Oscar, 135, 186–92
Ella at Duke's Place, 162–64
Ella Fitzgerald's Christmas, 151
Ella in Berlin: Mack the Knife. See *Complete Ella in Berlin: Mack the Knife, The*
Ella in Budapest, 224–27
Ella in Hamburg, 87–89
Ella in Rome: The Birthday Concert, 211–15
Ella Returns to Berlin, 215–20
Ella Sings Broadway, 146–48
Ella Sings Cole. See *Dream Dancing*
Ella Sings Gershwin, 193, 194–98. See also *Pure Ella*

Ella Swings Brightly with Nelson,
133–36
Ella Swings Gently with Nelson, 136–37
Ella Swings Lightly, 145–46
Ella Wishes You a Swinging Christmas,
144, 151
Ellington, Duke, 12, 69–70, 72, 158–67;
assessment of Norman Granz, 97;
Ella Fitzgerald remembers, 161–62.
See also *Duke Ellington Song Book,
The*
Ellis, Herb, 22, 26, 117, 185, 215, 220
"Embraceable You," 127
"Everything but You," 118
"Everything Happens To Me," 144
"Everything I Have Is Yours," 153
"Evil on Your Mind," 152
"Ev'rything I've Got," 116
"Ev'ry Time We Say Goodbye," 111

"Fascinating Rhythm," 126
Feather, Leonard, 33, 37, 59, 60, 66,
67, 162, 175–76, 234
Feldman, Vic, 127
Feller, Sid, 152
Fidelman, Geoffrey Mark, 147,
150–51, 153, 203
"Fine and Mellow," 180
Finegan, Bill, 124
"Fine Romance, A," 27–28, 29, 129
First Lady of Song, 109
Fitzgerald & Pass. . .Again, 234–37
*Fitzgerald/Basie/Pass: Digital III at
Montreux,* 180
Fitzgerald, Ella: amateur contest
victory at the Apollo Theater, 10;
and arrangers at Capitol, 151–53;
and arrangers at Decca, 101–6; and
arrangers at Prestige, 153; and
arrangers at Reprise, 153–54;
and arrangers at Verve and Pablo,
106–50; and arrangers for Chick
Webb, 101; "A-Tisket, A-Tasket,"
78–80; attraction to bebop, 12,
83–85, 95; and the blues, 30–31;
Carnegie Hall debut, 84; eclectic
repertoire, 4–5, 225; hired by Chick
Webb, 71–72; impersonating Louis

Armstrong, 23–24, 206, 215, 219;
importance of her accompanists,
181; influence of Connee Boswell,
39–40; influence of Louis
Armstrong, 8, 75, 120; landmark
achievement on the *Song Books,*
107–8; legendary performance of
"How High the Moon," 86–87;
parents, 7; receives Kennedy
Center Medal, 15; scatting prowess,
84–86; touring with Dizzy
Gillespie, 83–84; troubled
childhood, 9; vocal quality in later
years, 234; with Benny Goodman,
157–58; with Chick Webb, 11, 19,
26, 58, 71–80, 100–101, 105, 216;
with Count Basie, 58, 170–80; with
Duke Ellington, 97, 116–22, 159,
162–67; with Ellis Larkins, 45, 46,
193–201; with Hank Jones, 2, 105,
150, 183–84; with Jimmy Rowles,
232; with Joe Pass, 180, 182, 233–40;
with Lou Levy, 5, 125, 145, 167,
182, 211–22; with Nelson Riddle,
124, 125–38; with Oscar Peterson,
22, 26, 91, 117, 126, 135, 185–92;
with Paul Smith, 86, 116, 117, 137,
180, 182, 202–10; with Tommy
Flanagan, 1, 3, 5, 87–88, 95–96, 153,
175, 202, 203, 223–31. *See also
specific accompanists, arrangers,
bandleaders, record companies, and
songs*
Flanagan, Tommy, 1, 3, 5, 87, 153, 175,
182, 202, 203, 222–31; assessment of
Norman Granz, 95–96; joins Ella
Fitzgerald full-time, 223; rapport
with Ella Fitzgerald, 223–24
"Flower Is a Lovesome Thing, A,"
162
"Flying Home," 83, 84, 180
"Foggy Day, A," 23, 126, 212
Foster, Frank, 170, 173
"From This Moment On," 112–14
"Frosty the Snowman," 144

Gabler, Milt, 11, 12, 84, 94, 193
Gale, Moe, 11, 73, 84, 94; signs Chick
Webb, 71

Garcia, Russell, 28, 30, 107, 139, 144
Garner, Errol, 203, 207, 217
Gaye, Marvin, 5, 175
"Gee, Baby, Ain't I Good to You," 27
"Gentleman is a Dope, The," 135
*George and Ira Gershwin Song Book,
    The,* 125–29
"Georgia on My Mind," 137, 240
Gershwin, George, 28, 102. *See also
    specific songs* and *George and Ira
    Gershwin Song Book, The*
"Get Happy," 139
"Get Out of Town," 112
"Get Ready," 153
Getz, Stan, 143, 175
Gillespie, Dizzy, 12, 13, 73, 82, 83–84,
    88, 165, 220
"Girl [Boy] from Ipanema, The," 150,
    226
"Girl Talk," 240
"Give a Little, Get a Little," 105
"Give Me the Simple Life," 216
"God Bless the Child," 137
Goldkette, Jean, 155
"Gone with the Wind," 203, 239
"Good-bye," 62, 86
Goodman, Benny, 11, 26, 39, 70,
    72–73, 75, 102, 95, 155–58; *Let's
    Dance* radio broadcast, 156;
    recordings with Ella Fitzgerald,
    157–58
"Good Morning Heartache," 220
"Goodnight, My Love," 153, 157
"Goody Goody," 105
"Gotta Be This or That," 146
"Got to Get You Into My Life," 154
Granz, Norman, 2, 5, 12, 13, 14–15,
    26, 30, 59, 74, 91–97, 106, 139;
    becomes Ella Fitzgerald's manager,
    94; establishes Jazz at the
    Philharmonic, 92–93; first hires Ella
    Fitzgerald, 94; founds Pablo
    Records, 96; founds Verve Records,
    95; on producing Ella Fitzgerald
    and Louis Armstrong, 22; on
    recording Ella Fitzgerald, 108;
    takes a break from producing Ella
    Fitzgerald, 150–51

Greatest Jazz Concert in the World, The,
    167
Green, Freddie, 26
Green, Urbie, 1
"Gulf Coast Blues," 75
"Guy Is a Guy, A," 104
"Guys and Dolls," 147

Haggart, Bob, 102
"Hallelujah!," 77–78
"Hallelujah, I Love Him [Her] So,"
    150
Hall, Jim, 4, 86, 183, 203
Hammerstein, Oscar, II, 114, 130
Hammond, John: and Mildred Bailey,
    35; and Count Basie, 169; and
    Benny Goodman, 156; assessment
    of Norman Granz, 93, 94; and Billie
    Holiday, 57; and Ellis Larkins, 193;
    and Bessie Smith, 31, 32
Hampton, Lionel, 158
"Hard Day's Night, A," 87
"Hark the Herald Angels Sing," 151
Harold Arlen Song Book, The, 138–42
Hart, Lorenz, 114–15
"Have You Met Miss Jones," 115
"Hawaiian War Chant," 153
Hawkins, Coleman, 167
Hecksher, Ernie, 153
"Heebie Jeebies," 19–20
Hefti, Neal, 110
Hello Dolly, 21
Hello Love, 144
"He Loves and She Loves," 126
Henderson, Fletcher, 10, 33, 71, 100,
    155, 156
"Here in My Arms," 116
"Here's That Rainy Day," 87
"Hernando's Hideaway," 147
"He's Funny That Way," 137
"Hey Jude," 153
Holiday, Billie, 32, 34, 36, 57–59, 173,
    205, 231; showdown with Ella
    Fitzgerald, 58
Holman, Bill, 153
"Honeysuckle Rose," 171–73, 176–79,
    180

"Hooray for Love," 139
"House Is Not A Home, A," 153
"How About Me," 123
"How Deep Is the Ocean," 123
"How High the Moon," 86–87, 206
"How Long Has This Been Going
    On," 126, 143, 187–88, 196
Hudson, Will, 101

"I Ain't Got Nothin' But the Blues,"
    228, 234
"I Can't Face the Music," 150
"I Can't Get Started," 137
"I Can't Give You Anything but
    Love," 42–45, 206–7, 208, 209,
    213–15
"I Can't Stop Loving You," 175
"I Could Have Danced All Night,"
    148
"I Could Write a Book," 46–47
"I Cried for You," 206
"I Didn't Know About You," 118, 235
"I Didn't Know What Time It Was,"
    116
"(I Don't Stand) A Ghost of a Chance
    with You", 180
"I Don't Want to Take a Chance," 104
"If I Could be With You," 150
"If I Were A Bell," 146, 147
"I Get a Kick Out of You," 26, 112
"I Got a Guy," 220
"I Got It Bad (and That Ain't Good),"
    75, 118
"I Got Rhythm," 34, 61–64, 127–28;
    musical significance of, 127
"I Hadn't Anyone Till You," 207
"I Heard It Through the Grapevine,"
    154
"I Hear Music," 135–36, 190–92
"I Let a Song Go Out of My Heart,"
    228
"I Like the Sunrise," 162
"I'll Always Be In Love With You,"
    150
"I'll Be Hard to Handle," 129
"I'll Never Be the Same," 144
"I'll Never Fall in Love Again," 225

"Ill Wind (You're Blowin' Me No
    Good)," 26
"I Love Paris," 111
"I Loves You Porgy," 212
"Imagination," 137, 198
"Imagine My Frustration," 164
"I May Be Wrong," 239
"I'm Beginning to See the Light,"
    120–21, 174–75
"I'm Getting Sentimental Over You,"
    179, 210
"I'm Glad There Is You," 198
"I'm Gonna Go Fishin'," 133
"I'm Just a Lucky So and So," 118
"I'm Old Fashioned," 129
"I'm Puttin' All My Eggs in One
    Basket," 27
"I'm Through With Love," 144
"In a Mellow Tone," 117
"In a Sentimental Mood," 117
"Indian Summer," 175
"I Never Had a Chance," 143
Ink Spots, The, 11, 148, 173
"In the Evening (When the Sun Goes
    Down)," 103
Intimate Ella, The, 206–10
"Into Each Life Some Rain Must
    Fall," 173
"I Only Have Eyes for You," 135
"I Remember You," 133
Irving Berlin Song Book, The, 49, 51, 52,
    54, 55, 123
"I Said No," 148
"Isn't It Romantic," 116
"Isn't This a Lovely Day," 23, 123
"It Came Upon a Midnight Clear,"
    151
"I Thought About You," 143
"It Never Entered My Mind," 116
"It's a Wonderful World," 153
"It's All Right with Me," 111, 175, 212
"I Used to Be Color Blind," 123
"I've Got a Crush on You," 127, 196
"I've Got My Love to Keep Me
    Warm," 27, 123
"I've Got the World on a String," 104,
    140–42, 236
"I've Got You Under My Skin," 111

"I've Got Your Number," 148
"I've Grown Accustomed To His Face," 144
"I Want to Be Happy," 76–77
"I Wished on the Moon," 137
"I Wonder Where Our Love Has Gone," 137
"I Won't Dance," 27, 134

James, Harry, 158
Jazz at the Opera House, 185
Jazz at the Philharmonic (JATP), 4, 12, 92–94, 175, 183, 184, 185; Ella Fitzgerald's first appearance with, 94
Jazz at the Santa Monica Civic '72, 175
Jenkins, Gordon, 102
Jerome Kern Song Book, The, 129–32
"Jersey Bounce," 221–22
Jewell, Derek, 167
"Jingle Bells," 144
Jobim, Antonio Carlos, 165, 237
"Joe Williams Blues," 219
Johnny Mercer Song Book, The, 129, 132–33
Johnson, Gus, 86, 87, 149, 203, 211, 215, 220, 223
Johnson, James P., 33
Johnson, J. Wilfred, 5, 126, 133, 137, 173, 199, 239
Jones, Hank, 105, 149, 150, 182, 183–84, 222–23
Jones, Jimmy, 152, 162, 182
Jones, Jo, 58, 169, 185
Jones, Quincy, 107, 170, 171, 175
Jordan, Louis, 19, 146, 149
Jordan, Taft, 19, 73, 149
"Just a Closer Walk With Thee," 151
"Just a Simple Melody," 75
"Just A Sittin' and A Rockin,' " 179
"Just One of Those Things," 110, 203, 212–13
"Just You, Just Me," 146

Kessel, Barney, 112, 116, 117, 126, 182, 185
King, Carole, 175
"Knock Me A Kiss," 146

Korall, Burt, 69, 70
Krupa, Gene, 60, 73, 156

"Lady Be Good." *See* "Oh, Lady Be Good"
"Lady Is a Tramp, The," 115, 204–5, 212
Lafayette Theater, 10
"Lamp Is Low, The," 153
Larkins, Ellis, 101, 137, 182, 192–201
Last Decca Years, 1949–1954, The, 103–6
"Laughin' On the Outside," 150
"Laura," 133
"Learnin' the Blues," 28
Lee, Peggy, 158, 211
Lerner and Loewe, 148
"Let It Snow," 144
Let No Man Write My Epitaph. See *Intimate Ella, The*
"Let's Begin," 129
"Let's Call the Whole Thing Off," 27, 126
"Let's Do It (Let's Fall in Love)," 26, 112, 164
"Let's Face the Music and Dance," 123
"Let's Fall in Love," 139
"Let's Take a Walk Around the Block," 139
"Let Yourself Go," 123
Levey, Stan, 220
Levy, Lou, 5, 125, 127, 145, 167, 182, 203, 210–22
Lewis, John, 182
"Like Someone in Love," 143
Like Someone in Love (album), 143–44
"Little Jazz," 146
"Little White Lies," 145, 175
Live at the Greek Theater, Los Angeles, 167
"Loch Lomond," 58
"Looking For a Boy," 196
"Lorelei," 205
"Lost in a Fog," 144
"Lost in Meditation," 118
"L-O-V-E," 175
"Love for Sale," 111, 203

"Love Is Here to Stay," 28
"Love Me or Leave Me," 135
"Lover," 115
"Lover Man," 148, 165
"Love Walked In," 127
"Love You Madly," 117
"Lullaby of Birdland," 106
Lunceford, Jimmie, 155
"Lush Life," 117

"Mack the Knife," 21, 86, 205–6, 219
"Madalena," 175
"Make Me Rainbows," 180
"Makin' Whoopee," 26, 199–201
"Manhattan," 115
"Man I Love, The," 127, 205
"Manteca," 154
"Mas Que Nada," 154
"Matchmaker, Matchmaker," 148
May, Billy, 138–42
"Maybe," 196
McRae, Teddy, 73
"Mean to Me," 135, 187
"Melancholy Me," 106
Mercer, Johnny, 165, 232; founds
    Capitol Records, 122. *See also*
    specific songs and *Johnny Mercer*
    Song Book, The
Middlebrooks, Wilfred, 86, 203, 215,
    216, 220
"Midnight Sun," 143, 190, 212
Mills, Irving, 106
"Miss Otis Regrets," 112
"Misty," 203–4, 207–9, 217
Misty Blue, 152
Mondragon, Joe, 112, 116, 117, 220
Monk, Thelonious, 27, 82, 219, 220
"Mood Indigo," 117
"Moonlight in Vermont," 23, 144
"Moonlight on the Ganges," 145
"More Than You Know," 143, 190
Moten, Bennie, 155
"Mr. Paganini," 75, 105, 217, 225
Murphy, Rose, 215
"Music Goes 'Round and Around,"
    221
"My Cousin in Milwaukee," 126

"My Heart Belongs to Daddy," 137,
    198
"My Heart Stood Still," 115
"My Kinda Love," 146
"My Kind of Trouble is You," 179
"My Last Affair," 173
"My Man," 58
"My Melancholy Baby," 207
"My Old Flame," 234
"My One and Only," 126, 195
"My One and Only Love," 137
"My Reverie," 220
"My Romance," 116
"My Shining Hour," 140

"Nature Boy," 236
"Nearness of You, The," 24, 25
Nestico, Sammy, 99, 170
"Nice Work if You Can Get It," 126,
    198
Nice Work if You Can Get It (album),
    102
Nicholson, Stuart, 11, 57, 71, 212
"Night and Day," 111, 175
"Night in Tunisia," 220
"No Moon At All," 150
"No Other Love," 148
Norvo, Red, 36, 158
"Now It Can Be Told," 123

"O Come All Ye Faithful," 151
O'Day, Anita, 115
"Oh, Lady Be Good," 83–84, 125, 127
"O Holy Night," 151
"Oh, What A Night For Love," 146
"Oh, Yes, Take Another Guess," 157
"Ol' Devil Moon," 153
"Old McDonald Had a Farm," 87. *See*
    also "Ol' MacDonald"
"Old Rugged Cross, The," 151
"O Little Town of Bethlehem," 144
Oliver, Joe "King," 71
Oliver, Sy, 102–6, 124, 149, 154, 173
"Ol' MacDonald," 148. *See also* "Old
    McDonald Had a Farm"
"On a Slow Boat to China," 216
"Once In a While," 153

"One for My Baby (and One More for the Road)," 139, 210
"One I Love, The," 236
"One I Love Belongs to Somebody Else, The," 221
"One Note Samba," 228, 237
"On Green Dolphin Street," 153
"On the Sunny Side of the Street," 173
"Ooo Baby Baby," 154
"Open Your Window," 154, 226
"Organ Grinder's Swing," 75, 179
"Ornithology," 86
Orsted-Pedersen, Niels-Henning, 102, 184
"Our Love Is Here to Stay," 126, 203
"Over the Rainbow," 138, 140

Pablo Records, 12, 15, 96
Paich, Marty, 144–48, 153, 175
Parker, Charlie, 18, 82, 83, 84, 86, 88
Pass, Joe, 182, 183, 185, 233–40
"Passion Flower," 162
"People Will Say We're in Love," 198, 216
"Perdido," 118
Perfect Match, A, 179–80
Perry, Richard, 153
Peterson, Oscar, 22, 26, 167; 182, 184–92, 215, 220; debut with Jazz at the Philharmonic, 184; legendary association with Ella Fitzgerald, 185–87
"Pick Yourself Up," 134
Pleasants, Henry, 33, 35, 74
"Please Be Kind" 198
"Please Don't Talk About Me When I'm Gone," 180
Pollack, Ben, 155
Porgy and Bess, 28, 30, 107
Portrait of Ella Fitzgerald (Ellington/ Strayhorn composition), 117–18
"Prelude to a Kiss," 117
Prestige Records, 153
"Preview," 105
Previn, André, 102
Pure Ella, 194. See also *Ella Sings*

Gershwin and *Songs in a Mellow Mood*
"Puttin' on the Ritz," 123

"Rain," 235
"Raindrops Keep Falling on My Head," 225
Rainey, Ma, 31, 33
"Reach for Tomorrow," 210
"Reaching for the Moon," 123
"Real American Folk Song," 126–27
Redman, Don, 70, 101
"Remind Me," 132
Reprise Records, 153–54
Rhythm is My Business, 149–50
Rich, Buddy, 22
Riddle, Nelson, 110, 123, 124–38, 175; on working with Ella Fitzgerald and Norman Granz, 96–97
"Ridin' High," 111
Roach, Max, 13
"Rockin' Chair," 35
"Rockin' in Rhythm," 118
"Rock It for Me," 216
Rock music: in the 1950s, 13; in the 1960s, 14
"Rock of Ages, Cleft for Me," 151
Rodgers and Hammerstein, 147–48
Rodgers and Hart Song Book, The, 114–16
Rodgers, Richard, 114–15, 147. *See also specific songs* and *Rodgers and Hart Song Book, The*
Roker, Mickey, 180
Rollins, Sonny, 5, 13
"Rough Ridin'," 149
"'Round Midnight," 180, 219, 220
Rowles, Jimmy, 181, 182, 194, 231–33
Royal, Ernie, 149
"Rudolph the Red-Nosed Reindeer," 144
"Runnin' Wild," 150

Sampson, Edgar, 26, 70, 101, 106, 156
Sanford and Son (TV sitcom), 175
"Santa Claus Is Coming To Town," 144
"Satin Doll," 117, 165–66, 173, 226–27

Sauter, Eddie, 124
Savoy Ballroom, 58, 71–72, 72–73
Schaap, Phil, 19, 34, 39, 58, 95, 110, 149, 183, 185, 194, 202, 212, 216, 224, 232
Schuller, Gunther, 32, 38
"Secret of Christmas, The," 144
"September Song," 209
"720 In The Books," 146, 153
Shaw, Artie, 58, 60
"She Didn't Say 'Yes,' " 130
"Shine," 75
"Shiny Stockings," 173, 175
"Show Me," 148
"Show Me the Way to Go Out of This World," 150
"Signing Off," 221
"Silent Night," 151
Silver, Horace, 13
Sinatra, Frank, 37, 124, 138, 139, 194, 204–5, 212, 216, 232
"Single-O," 133
"Sing Me a Swing Song (and Let Me Dance)," 75
"Skylark," 133
"Sleep, My Little Lord Jesus," 151
"Sleigh Ride," 144
Smith, Bessie, 30–32, 33, 38, 57
Smith, Paul, 111, 116, 117, 180, 182, 202–10
Smith, Stuff, 117
"Smooth Sailing," 87, 149
"Só Danço Samba," 165
"Solid as a Rock," 104
"Solitude," 117, 235
"Somebody Somewhere," 147
"Someone to Watch Over Me," 127, 194
"Some Other Spring," 180
"Something's Gotta Give," 133
"Something to Live For," 162, 164
"Somewhere in the Night," 137
"So Near and Yet So Far," 137
Song Books, 40; historical significance, 107–8. See also individual Song Books
"Song Is Ended, The," 123
Songs in a Mellow Mood, 137, 193–94, 198–201. See also Pure Ella

"Soon," 196–98
"Sophisticated Lady," 117, 212
Sophisticated Lady (album), 234
"So Rare," 144
Speak Love, 237–40
"Speak Low," 237–39
"Spinning Wheel," 225
"Spring Can Really Hang You Up the Most," 148, 175, 220
"Spring Is Here," 116
"Spring Will Be a Little Late This Year," 144
"Squatty Roo," 117
Stafford, Jo, 158
"Stairway to the Stars," 75, 144
"Star Dust," 45–46, 199
"Stars Fell on Alabama," 23
"Steam Heat," 147
"Stella by Starlight," 221
"St. Louis Blues," 180, 212
Stockholm Concert, 1966, The, 164–65, 166
Stoller, Alvin, 112, 116, 117
"Stompin' at the Savoy," 26–27, 215
"Stormy Weather," 139
Strayhorn, Billy, 116, 117, 118, 160–61, 162
"Street Beater," 175
"Street of Dreams," 137, 192
"Strike Up the Band," 126
Styne, Jule, 109
"Summertime," 205, 226
"Sunny," 154
Sunshine of Your Love, 153
"Sweet and Slow," 137
"Sweet Georgia Brown," 148, 180
"Sweet Lorraine," 179
Swing Era, 11–12, 81–82, 155–57
Swing Into Spring (TV special), 158
" 'S Wonderful," 126

Take Love Easy, 234
"Take the 'A' Train," 118, 130, 161, 216
"Taking a Chance On Love," 150
Tatum, Art, 187, 222–23
"Teach Me Tonight," 179
"Tea for Two," 173

"Teardrops from My Eyes," 146
"Tenderly," 23, 144
"Tennessee Waltz," 236
"Thanks for the Memory," 148
"That Certain Feeling," 126
"That Old Black Magic," 87, 139, 203, 212
"That Old Feeling," 235
"Them There Eyes," 173
"Then I'll Be Tired of You," 143
"Then You've Never Been Blue," 207
"There Never Was a Baby Like My Baby," 105
"There's a Lull in My Life," 143, 190
"There's No You," 239
"These Foolish Things," 26, 212
"They All Laughed," 26, 126
"They Can't Take That Away from Me," 23, 127
Thigpen, Ed, 153, 175, 184, 220, 224
Things Ain't What They Used to Be (and You Better Believe It), 154
"Things Are Looking Up," 126
30 by Ella, 152–53
"This Can't Be Love," 115, 220
"This Could Be the Start of Something Big," 221
"This Girl's [Guy's] In Love With You," 153
"This Gun Don't Care," 152
"This Time the Dream's on Me," 140
"This Year's Kisses," 220
"Thou Swell," 115
Three Keys, 11
"Thrill Is Gone, The," 239
"Tight and Gay" ["Night and Day"], 67–68
"Time After Time," 148
" 'Tis Autumn," 234
Tizol, Juan, 118
"To Keep My Love Alive," 116
"Too Close for Comfort," 228–29
"Too Darn Hot," 110, 205, 175
"Too Marvelous for Words," 133
"Too Young for the Blues," 109
Tormé, Mel, 70
"Turn the World Around (the Other Way)," 152
"Tuxedo Junction," 154

"Undecided," 22
"Under a Blanket of Blue," 23
"Until the Real Thing Comes Along," 199

Vaughan, Sarah, 31, 206, 211
Verve Records, 12, 14, 95, 96, 109
"Very Thought of You, The," 137

"Wait Till You See Her," 116
Waller, Fats, 168
"Way You Look Tonight, The," 132
"Walking in the Sunshine," 152
"Walk Right In," 87
"Warm All Over," 147
Waters, Ethel, 32–34
Watson, Leo, 59–68; "I Got Rhythm," 61–63; "Ja-da," 64–66; "Tight and Gay" ["Night and Day"], 67–68
Webb, Chick, 11, 69–80, 83, 105, 106, 156, 216; arrangers for, 70, 100–101; hires Ella Fitzgerald, 71–72; Savoy Ballroom and the battle of the bands, 58, 72–73; superior drumming ability of, 70
Webster, Ben, 117
"We'll Be Together Again," 143
Weston, Paul, 122–23
"We Three Kings of Orient Are," 144
"What A Friend We Have In Jesus," 151
"What Am I Here For," 133, 163–64
"What Are You Doing New Year's Eve," 144
"Whatever Lola Wants," 147
"What Is There to Say," 198
"What Is This Thing Called Love," 111
"What's Going On," 175
"What's New," 102, 143
"What's Your Story, Morning Glory," 146
"What Will I Tell My Heart," 143
"When the Sun Comes Out," 139
"When Your Lover Has Gone," 134–35, 187–90
"Where or When," 47–51, 116
"Whisper Not," 148

Whisper Not (album), 148
"White Christmas," 144
Whiteman, Paul, 35, 100, 155
"Who's Sorry Now," 210
"Why Was I Born," 132, 216
Wicks, Virginia, 2, 3, 4, 17, 22, 83, 125, 185, 186
Williams, Paul, 5
"Willow Weep for Me," 26, 144, 154
Wilson, Gerald, 154, 162, 175
Winding, Kai, 149
"Witchcraft," 216
"With a Song in My Heart," 116
"Without Love," 137
"Wives and Lovers," 148, 164
Wofford, Mike, 182
Wonder, Stevie, 5
Woodman, Britt, 149
Woods, Phil, 149

"Yellow Man," 153
"Yesterdays," 132
"You Are the Sunshine of My Life," 228

"You Brought a New Kind of Love to Me," 146
"You Can Depend On Me," 149
"You Couldn't Be Cuter," 130
"You Do Something to Me," 111
"You Go to My Head," 144
"You Hit the Spot," 145
"You Keep Coming Back Like a Song," 123
"You Leave Me Breathless," 198
Young, Lester, 57, 92
"You're an Old Smoothie," 146
"You're a Sweetheart," 153
"You're Blasé," 143
"You're Driving Me Crazy," 137, 216
"You're Laughing at Me," 123
"You're My Thrill," 220
"You Stepped Out Of a Dream," 153
"You Took Advantage of Me," 116, 235–36
"You've Changed," 148, 180
"You've Got a Friend," 175
"You Won't Be Satisfied (until You Break My Heart)," 21

About the Author

NORMAN DAVID is a musician, author, and educator, currently on the music faculties of The University of the Arts (Philadelphia) and Franklin & Marshall College. A past recipient of a Fellowship Grant in Jazz Composition from the National Endowment for the Arts, he is also the author of *Jazz Arranging*.